I warmly commend this defence, against some
contemporary alternatives, of the biblical unde
cross, of justification and of authority. What is
than historic Christianity, and without its truth:
nothing to say in our postmodern world.

C000064025

David F. Wells, Distinguished Research Professor, Gordon-Conwell Theological Seminary

It is no secret that evangelical theology is in a period of rapid transition.
Long-established and central doctrines are being re-examined, rightly and
necessarily so in the light of contemporary cultural challenges. The received
apostolic gospel always needs to be addressed to the present rather than
the past and the task of the evangelical theologian is to work through the
tension of conservation and innovation. If some merely conserve, others
rush too quickly to innovation. The fact that a position is fashionable does
not make it right. The relics of 1960s and 70s architecture should warn us
that the latest is not always the best. In this book the veteran evangelical
theologian Geoffrey Grogan examines some of evangelicalism's internal
debates with consummate skill, combining comprehensive knowledge and
long experience with admirable clarity and a wonderfully eirenic spirit.
He proves an expert guide. Though generous, he raises critical questions
about some recent developments and injects a note of wise caution into
the headlong rush to revise everything. Those who are innovators need
to engage with this book so that their innovations do not turn in the next
decade to being the theological equivalent of the 'left-over hippies' of the
Woodstock generation.

*Derek Tidball, Visiting Scholar, Spurgeon's College; formerly Principal of London School
of Theology*

The Faith
Once Entrusted
to the Saints?

[signature]

2 Cor 8:9
2 Cor. 9-8

For those students it has been my great privilege to teach over a period of nearly sixty years, mostly in Glasgow but also in London and in several overseas locations. Your questions have often forced me to think more deeply and to study the Scriptures more diligently, and the depth of your commitment to Christ and his service has often moved and challenged me.

The Faith
Once Entrusted
to the Saints?

Engaging with issues and trends
in evangelical theology

Geoffrey W. Grogan

INTER-VARSITY PRESS
Norton Street, Nottingham NG7 3HR, England
Email: ivp@ivpbooks.com
Website: www.ivpbooks.com

First published 2010

British Library Cataloguing in Publication Data
A catalogue record for this book is available from the British Library.

ISBN: 978-1-84474-478-7

Set in Monotype Garamond 11/13pt
Typeset in Great Britain by Servis Filmsetting Ltd, Stockport, Cheshire
Printed and bound in Great Britain by Ashford Colour Press Ltd, Gosport, Hampshire

Inter-Varsity Press publishes Christian books that are true to the Bible and that communicate the gospel, develop discipleship and strengthen the church for its mission in the world.

Inter-Varsity Press is closely linked with the Universities and Colleges Christian Fellowship, a student movement connecting Christian Unions in universities and colleges throughout Great Britain, and a member movement of the International Fellowship of Evangelical Students. Website: www.uccf.org.uk.

CONTENTS

PREFACE

In these days of ecological concern for the rainforests, the writing of yet another book may seem to require some justification. The better it sells, the more trees will be turned into paper. Of course this is true even of books on ecology!

Nothing can be more important than the gospel. If you doubt this, read the epistle to the Galatians. If the gospel is important, it is vital that it be rightly conceived. In Galatians, and again in 2 Corinthians, especially 11:1–5, Paul inveighs against those who promote another gospel. His concern in these two epistles is with ideas that were regarded by their promoters not as alternatives to the Christian gospel but as versions of it, in fact as the true version of it, but as Paul says of one of these, it is 'a different gospel – which is really no gospel at all' (Gal. 1:6–7). This means that time taken to discern what is and what is not a true gospel is time well invested.

A perusal of the chapter headings in this book may lead the prospective reader to think all these new approaches have been identified in advance by the author as other gospels, and that the book is simply an exercise in heresy-hunting. This is certainly not true. It is rather an attempt to subject some new approaches to a biblical critique. In the course of this, we may find that they have positive lessons to teach us as well as revealing inadequacies.

I have been greatly helped in this project by a panel of scholarly friends who have read the chapters as I have produced them and who have made constructive criticisms of them. The work would have been much poorer without their help. All of them have commented on at least one of the main chapters, and some on all of them. I want therefore to express my thanks to them all. I want to give pride of place to Ted Herbert and David Wright, two dear friends whom the Lord took into his immediate presence during the writing of the book, and who gave me very helpful comments on the earlier chapters. Others who have been very helpful are James Anderson, Oliver Barclay, Roy Kearsley, Stephen Levinsohn, Fergus Macdonald, Scot McKnight, Alec Motyer, Derek Newton, Tony Sargent, Richard Schultz, Ian Shaw, David Smith and Derek Tidball. I am also grateful to Hugh Trevor, who provided some useful information. Please note, however, that responsibility for any remaining mistakes of fact or errors of theological judgment is mine alone.

I want also to thank my niece and her husband, Joy and Derek Guest, and a former student of mine, Stuart Wadsworth, for reading the chapters through pastoral eyes to ensure that they are pastorally relevant.

Philip Duce, senior commissioning editor at IVP, has given considerable help, answering my many questions with courtesy and helpfulness and replying to my emails with amazing promptness.

My wife Eva, as ever, has been a great support in prayer and encouragement.

I am thankful to God for giving me the health and strength to complete this book, as I am no longer a young man.

Geoffrey W. Grogan

1. WHAT IS EVANGELICALISM?

Sometime in the late 1960s, on a bus journey, I sat next to a man who turned out to be a Roman Catholic priest. Learning that I was a minister, he opened his heart to me, telling me that he was just recovering from a nervous break-down. What was the cause of this? It was the Second Vatican Council. He said that he was a Roman Catholic by conviction and that he had always attached great importance to the fact that the church never changed, particu-larly in its theology, and that this had given him a sense of security. Now this had gone.

It may, of course, be open to question whether the Roman Catholic Church really has changed in its theology, but some observers of evan-gelicalism may wonder whether this too has been changing in recent years, as there are writers within the evangelical fold who appear to be question-ing some of its central tenets. Of course, evangelicalism does not have a central ecclesiastical structure in the way that Roman Catholicism does, but it has been for many years a recognizable and relatively stable theological position. The nature of God, the meaning of the cross, the significance of justification – these are some recent subjects of debate, and they are not side issues. Some influential writers are revisiting these doctrines and arguing that traditional interpretations of them within evangelicalism have been in error.

It is this situation that has occasioned the writing of this book.

The nature of evangelicalism

So then, this book is about Christian theology. This does not mean it is concerned with ideas for their own sake, nor that Christianity is to be viewed exclusively as a theological system. It is true that there is more to it than theology, for it is about a Bible that is to be read, understood and applied, a church to be extended and strengthened, a Christian life to be lived, a world to be impacted and (most important of all) a Christ to be trusted, worshipped and served. But a moment's reflection shows us that in all this we cannot avoid theology. If we ask what the Bible is, or what the church or the Christian life are, or even (in fact especially) who Jesus is, we are asking theological questions, and authentic practice is heavily dependent on good theology. So theology must concern us.

Moreover, not only is this book about Christian theology, it is about evangelical theology. It is written in the conviction that evangelical theology is authentic Christian theology. In fact, the conviction underlying it is what some would regard as the audacious claim that evangelical theology is *the* authentic Christian theology.

What, then, is this evangelical theology? At the present time its nature is widely misunderstood, so that we need to establish a definition. Now definitions of movements are not easy to give, especially if they lack a central organization as is the case here, and even more so when some of the terms used of them are somewhat fluid in meaning. So, without descending to pedantry, we will need to seek a clear understanding of evangelicalism.

It is essentially a theological position. It treats the evangel, the gospel, the good news of Jesus crucified for our sins and risen again, as the centre from which the whole Christian faith is to be viewed. It should be distinguished from 'evangelism', which is an activity, the proclamation of that gospel. To say that is not by any means to downgrade evangelism, rather it is to emphasize its importance, for it is a major implication, in fact a major imperative, of the embracing of evangelical theology.

A distinction is sometimes made between conservative and liberal evangelicalism, but when used on its own 'evangelicalism' has most often stood for conservative evangelicalism, which involves a consistently high view of the authority of holy Scripture. A 'liberal evangelicalism' which seeks to conserve the doctrines of the gospel while moving in some significant ways away from a high view of Scripture is bound to be somewhat unstable. It is conservative evangelicalism that is in view in this book.

It should also be distinguished from fundamentalism. This was a perfectly respectable term at one time, used to describe Christians holding to the central doctrines of the gospel as expounded and defended in a series of small books published in 1909, entitled *The Fundamentals*.[1] Many of the articles in these books were well written by good scholars, but the term has gradually come to be used (often pejoratively) of evangelical Christians who are suspicious of academic scholarship. It is now being applied also to fanatical movements associated with other faiths, sometimes even to positions with no religious content at all.

'Conservative evangelical' is also being used in some circles in a sense which brings it close to 'fundamentalist'. R. E. Olson says,

> 'Conservative' in theology . . . has come to mean adherence to a particular tradition such that it becomes inseparably united with the word of God itself . . . A 'conservative evangelical', then, is not just someone who is *not liberal*; it is someone who emphatically rejects reform of evangelical belief and practice *even when such reform is consistent with scripture*.[2]

So we find some writers describing themselves as 'progressive evangelicals' or 'post-conservative evangelicals'. For some, the implication is that biblical scholarship has moved on, discovering new truth in the Bible, but that conservative evangelical theology has not moved with it.[3]

The use of the term in the way referred to by Olson is regrettable, as it opens the door to confusion. 'Conservative evangelical' is a perfectly good term for a definable theological position and this use of it could lead readers of works professedly conservative evangelical to make unfavourable prior assumptions about them from the mere use of the term. To resist reform required by Scripture is totally inconsistent with conservative evangelicalism as understood in this book.

Some writers are using the term 'radical evangelical'. This has its merits and

---

1. D. W. Bebbington, *Evangelicalism in Modern Britain: A History from the 1730s to the 1980s* (Grand Rapids: Baker, 1992).

2. R. E. Olson, 'Postconservative Evangelical Theology and the Theological Pilgrimage of Clark Pinnock', in S. E. Porter and A. R. Cross (eds.), *Semper Reformandum: Essays in Honour of Clark H. Pinnock* (Carlisle: Paternoster, 2003), pp. 17–18 (italics his).

3. Others, however, especially in North America, are using these terms to make it clear that they are not conservative or right-wing Republicans politically. It is unfortunate that the use of some of these terms differs somewhat between Britain and North America.

in some ways I like it very much, for nothing can be more radical than a commitment to the authority of Scripture that is so strong and so comprehensive that it is allowed to expose and challenge everything unbiblical, no matter how hallowed it is by tradition. If it is thus used, conservative and radical evangelicalism should be identical, and the more consistently conservative a theology is, the more profoundly, even disturbingly, radical it will be. This term may, however, degenerate into something of a party slogan and so induce a destructively negative approach, not always properly thought through, to certain aspects of evangelicalism as historically understood. Nevertheless, the term should always be a reminder to us that the biblical status of our theological ideas should never be simply assumed or taken for granted.

In a personal communication, Oliver Barclay helpfully suggested 'classic evangelicalism' as a useful and appropriate term which avoids the ambiguity that for some now adheres to 'conservative evangelicalism'. This is good, although the term 'conservative' is still useful in laying emphasis on our commitment to a high view of Scripture.

One further point needs to be made: in general terms there is some difference between British and North American perceptions of evangelicalism in that the latter is often viewed (rightly or wrongly) as having a political dimension. Does this mean, then, that this book has no relevance to North American evangelicalism? No, for the theological dimension is common to both varieties and it is this dimension that is in view in this book.

So then, that we may be quite clear on the matter, let me say that, reduced to its basics, the conservatism of the movement to which this book relates is not essentially political, nor social, nor cultural, nor even historical, but theological, relating to its commitment to the authority of the Bible. The term 'evangelical' is likewise to be viewed as theological, relating to the gospel, the evangel. Conservative evangelicals accept the authority of the Bible and interpret it in terms of the gospel. In this book I will use 'evangelical' when a theological position is being discussed and 'conservative' when it is more a matter of biblical research and exegesis by those committed to a high doctrine of Scripture.

The evangelical principle of interpretation is not arbitrary, for the very nature of the gospel is to be determined by its presentation and exposition in the Bible. We need not only to teach what the Bible teaches, but to emphasize what the Bible emphasizes, and without doubt it emphasizes the gospel. Paul, for instance, writing of 'the gospel I preached to you', says to the Corinthian Church, 'What I received I passed on to you *as of first importance*: that Christ died for our sins according to the Scriptures, that he was buried, that he was raised on the third day according to the Scriptures' (1 Cor. 15:1, 3, italics mine).

Although 'conservative' is an adjective while 'evangelical' functions in this phrase as a noun, the two are of equal importance. Not only should the Bible be interpreted in terms of the gospel, but the authenticity of the gospel needs to be tested by its conformity to Scripture. There are, for instance, sects that profess to accept the authority of the Bible, but their interpretation of it in terms of the gospel is seriously open to doubt.

Later on in this same chapter in 1 Corinthians, Paul links preaching and faith when, in relation to this gospel, he says, 'This is what we preach, and this is what you believed' (1 Cor. 15:11). A survey of the New Testament makes it clear that the gospel centres in Christ, especially in his death and resurrection, and that it promises salvation from divine judgment by grace through faith.

So then, conservative evangelicalism is a theological position. A succinct summary of the main doctrines on which conservative evangelicals have normally agreed is given in the UCCF (Universities and Colleges Christian Fellowship) basis of faith, as follows:

The basis of the Fellowship shall be the fundamental truths of Christianity, as revealed in Holy Scripture, including:

1. There is one God in three persons, the Father, the Son and the Holy Spirit.
2. God is sovereign in creation, revelation, redemption and final judgement.
3. The Bible, as originally given, is the inspired and infallible Word of God. It is the supreme authority in all matters of belief and behaviour.
4. Since the fall, the whole of humankind is sinful and guilty, so that everyone is subject to God's wrath and condemnation.
5. The Lord Jesus Christ, God's incarnate Son, is fully God; he was born of a virgin; his humanity is real and sinless; he died on the cross, was raised bodily from death and is now reigning over heaven and earth.
6. Sinful human beings are redeemed from the guilt, penalty and power of sin only through the sacrificial death once and for all time of their representative and substitute, Jesus Christ, the only mediator between them and God.
7. Those who believe in Christ are pardoned all their sins and accepted in God's sight only because of the righteousness of Christ credited to them; this justification is God's act of undeserved mercy, received solely by trust in him and not by their own efforts.
8. The Holy Spirit alone makes the work of Christ effective to individual sinners, enabling them to turn to God from their sin and to trust in Jesus Christ.
9. The Holy Spirit lives in all those he has regenerated. He makes them increasingly Christlike in character and behaviour and gives them power for their witness in the world.

10. The one holy universal church is the Body of Christ, to which all true believers belong.
11. The Lord Jesus Christ will return in person, to judge everyone, to execute God's just condemnation on those who have not repented and to receive the redeemed to eternal glory.[4]

There are obviously many different varieties of evangelicalism, some related to denominational differences reflecting, especially but not exclusively, different conceptions of church government. This may be seen in longer historical statements like the Westminster Confession of Faith and the Thirty-nine Articles, which promote a Presbyterian and an Episcopalian form respectively. There are other variations that tend to run across denominational divisions, even though some of them are also characteristic of particular denominations, so that we may distinguish Calvinists, Arminians, dispensationalists, charismatics, etc. All of these, however, unite around the theological position briefly outlined already.[5]

Finding a place to stand

Conservative evangelicals see their commitment to this theological stance as an important implication of their commitment to Christ. Perhaps it may be useful to indicate at this point how I came to this position myself, as it may be of help to some readers.

I was converted to Christ at the age of twenty. Before this God had used a Bible class teacher with a somewhat liberal outlook who nevertheless presented the life and teaching of Jesus in such a way that I found myself immensely attracted to him. He then used a preacher who might be classed as a liberal evangelical to show me the importance of a definite commitment to Christ. Largely because of my background in a liberal church, I had many theological difficulties, but one day God used a book by a Christian apologist who was a self-styled 'mere Christian' (C. S. Lewis) to deal with my major theological difficulties. That evening I was enabled to make a decisive personal faith-commitment and received an assurance that I was accepted in Christ.

---

4. B. Horn, *Ultimate Realities: Finding the Heart of Evangelical Belief*, 2nd ed. (Leicester: Inter-Varsity Press, 1999).
5. Further exploration of the characteristics of evangelicalism may be found in Bebbington, *Evangelicalism in Modern Britain*.

Then he used a group of evangelical friends to show me the importance of Bible study and an expository sermon on Ephesians 1 by a scholarly evangelical (Alan Stibbs) to bring me to a high doctrine of biblical inspiration and authority after a period of wavering. This then became an even deeper conviction through a personal study of the attitude of Christ to the Scriptures.

Early on in my Christian experience I think I assumed that evangelical theology was a fixture. Perhaps it was the use of creeds and the Reformation confessions that made me think this. Certainly the Nicene Creed is longer than the Apostles' Creed, and the Westminster Confession and the Thirty-nine Articles longer than both, but I tended to think these were just so many shorter or longer expositions of the basic doctrines of the faith. The idea that there could be substantial change never even occurred to me in those days. I knew, of course, that Christians differed somewhat on issues like baptism and church order, but it seemed to me then (I know better now!) that these were more about practice than theology. Many years of teaching both biblical and systematic theology, plus much teaching time spent on exegesis of the biblical text and a personal interest in and some teaching of philosophy followed. At every stage and increasingly I discovered how immensely strong this theological position is.

The tension between conviction and openness in theology

With regard to long-term education, life is about learning and forming convictions. A child is born into a family and in the early years is (hopefully) given a structure within which to live her or his life. This structure comes to be taken for granted as a kind of 'given', a fixed point not much questioned. Then in the adolescent years he or she may question this structure or parts of it, so that orientation is succeeded by some measure of disorientation. As adolescence passes into young adulthood, there is movement towards a reorientation, which often includes some elements of the old structure plus new ones.

This can sometimes happen in a person's theology. Perhaps she or he is converted in a particular church and given early Christian training there. This becomes part of the person concerned, but then comes a period of change. Perhaps a charismatic experience, or a new interest in prophetic interpretation, or something else that has doctrinal implications, comes into life and even perhaps virtually takes over for a while. Later there comes a synthesis in which some of the new and old elements come together in a new combination, which is then passed on to the next generation.

As Christians we need a firm theology, a structure for life and thought, and maturing as a Christian involves securing such. It is important to get beyond opinions to convictions. What matters is that by whatever path or means (and these will vary), we should come to biblically induced and biblically based convictions so that we are not tossed about theologically but are mature in the faith.[6]

Sadly today many Christians never get to this point. Much of our church life is experience-based rather than truth-based. Now Christian experience is very important and truth and life must never be separated. Healthy Christian living can only, however, be properly grounded when it is based on biblical truth.

Christians are often more conditioned by their cultural environment than they realize. We live increasingly in an age when flexibility is more popular than structure. Throughout the twentieth century there was an increasing revolt against classical forms in the arts and there were some important paradigm shifts in science. History, too, once viewed as a science, is no longer seen as such. All this prepared the way for the advent of postmodernism with its reaction against the scientific mentality and with its interest in flexibility, in change, in the importance of the subjective factor in all our thinking, knowing and experiencing. In this matter of biblical truth, however, evangelical Christians need to swim against the postmodern tide. We are committed to the fact that there is such a thing as objective truth and to the special importance of biblical truth. Doctrinal vagueness is not conducive to sound spiritual growth.

Oliver Barclay, who probably knows the British evangelical scene as well as anybody, once wrote,

> There are two main streams emerging in the evangelical community, and this division may prove more fundamental in its long-term effects than any other. It runs right across denominational divisions and any special-interest and party groupings. It is between those who make the Bible effectively, and not only theoretically, the mainstay of their ministry, and those who do not.

He said that the former will produce strong realistic Christians, while the latter 'are almost certain to produce vulnerable Christians or painfully dependent people, who dare not move out from the particular congregation where they have been supported unless they can go somewhere else where they will be equally propped up'.[7]

---

6. See Eph. 4:11–16, the whole of which is relevant to this topic.

7. O. Barclay, *Evangelicalism in Britain 1935–1995: A Personal Sketch* (Leicester: Inter-Varsity Press, 1997), pp. 139–140.

But the views we have, especially on more minor matters, should never be so inflexible that new truth from the Word of God cannot get through. We must be willing to learn more and adjust if necessary. Original research in any field of study which has a literary dimension always needs to engage with primary documents. For the Christian these are primary not only in the historical sense, but because they are holy Scripture and therefore are of supreme authority for us.

Our theological system needs to be checked, amplified and constantly refreshed from the Bible. We will not change our fundamental beliefs easily if these are grounded in study of Scripture, but we will always be open to receive new truth. This will sometimes come from personal study of Scripture, but we must also be open to what others have found in the Word of God.

For this reason I have tried in this book to be both firm and eirenical. Three convictions lie behind its writing. The first is that the Bible is an inexhaustible book and that we can never assume we have already learned all the truth it has to convey to us. When the Word of God is expounded in ways unfamiliar to us, we should listen and ask God to enable us to assess what is being said or written. The second is that we are called to 'contend for the faith that was once for all entrusted to the saints' (Jude 3). This is not always easy, but it must be done. The third is that when we are in debate with other Christians this must always be in a spirit of love and without acrimony. The reader must judge whether these three convictions are reflected in what I have written.

Theologians and biblical scholars

These are sometimes wrongly identified. A theologian is concerned with ideas about God and their relationships, a biblical scholar with the biblical text and issues arising from a study of it. In evangelicalism the two are obviously closely linked because of its strong commitment to Scripture. The subject known as Biblical Theology is a discipline which bridges the two concerns, and the biblical theologian seeks to set forth the theological content of Scripture in its historical development within the Bible by using terms derived from the Bible itself.

Biblical and systematic theology are not identical. The greatest concern of evangelical systematic theologians is to be true to Scripture, but they are concerned too with theological debates that have taken place in the history of the church or that are current today. So, for instance, issues that arise in interpreting the biblical data and which have long divided Roman Catholics and Protestants may well be given fuller treatment in a systematic theology than in a biblical one.

This book is concerned with issues in systematic theology because the themes of all its chapters are currently being debated. We will be looking at the theological teaching of the Bible on these issues, because we recognize Scripture as the touchstone of authentic Christian theology.

When it comes to contentious issues of theology, biblical scholars can make important contributions by insisting that particular biblical passages be taken fully into account, and they should also scrutinize and, if necessary, challenge the exegesis on which theological statements are based. In this respect, James Barr, an Old Testament scholar highly critical of conservative evangelicalism, nevertheless performed a real service to theology in his book *The Semantics of Biblical Language* when he criticized systematic theologians for their tendency sometimes to focus on particular biblical words rather than more broadly on biblical ideas. He pointed out that the ideas may be present in passages where the theme's main terms do not occur. So, for instance, the idea of God's love for human beings certainly runs through the Synoptic Gospels, even though the word 'love' in this connection is rare.[8] Really he was saying that such theology was not biblical enough.

Biblical scholars may sometimes show more openness to new ideas than theologians and may seem less concerned about theological niceties. Their researches are important for theologians, and the latter should not criticize them too harshly when they try out ideas that appear to cause theological problems, provided this is done in a tentative way. It is here that dialogue between the two groups could be most profitable, as each needs to learn from the other. In this book our concern is with theology and theologians, but inevitably this will involve us in engaging with some biblical scholars as well.

Theology and philosophy

Thinking about God is not confined to theologians, but concerns many philosophers also. How do their disciplines relate?

Theologians do not work in an intellectual vacuum. A theological movement often displays divergent tendencies, the one more biblical and the other more philosophical, with some writers influenced more by the former and others by

---

8. J. Barr, *The Semantics of Biblical Language* (Oxford: Oxford University Press, 1961), especially pp. 288–296.

the latter. This was evident, for instance, in the nineteenth century, when the main successive influences were Romanticism,[9] Hegelianism, Kantianism[10] and evolutionary philosophy.

Diverse views as to their relationship

Some theologians have considered philosophy and theology *incompatible*. The early Christian writer Tertullian asked, 'What has Athens to do with Jerusalem?' Yet, as we have already indicated, a theologian may be unconsciously affected by current philosophies.

Some say we should settle if necessary for *double truth*. Some medieval Aristotelians reckoned a statement could be true in philosophy but false in theology, or vice versa. Yet if truth is characterized by coherence,[11] this is unsatisfactory. Of course, we may be convinced of truth's oneness even though we encounter mysteries preventing its full demonstration.

Some think *philosophy may supply theology with a comprehensive world view* as a context for biblical truth. The major thirteenth-century theologian Thomas Aquinas used Aristotelianism in this way, while many nineteenth-century theologians were influenced by Hegel's philosophical idealism. In the twentieth century two very different theologians, Bultmann and Tillich, both used Heidegger's existentialism with what many theologians consider major distortion of biblical truth.

The distinction between theology and philosophy should not be blurred. The Dutch evangelical philosopher Herman Dooyeweerd saw Scripture as the indispensable basis for true knowledge of God, but he also devised an interesting philosophy of modal laws.[12] Such philosophies must never, however, be given a status comparable to Scripture and should always be regarded as tentative.[13]

In God's infinite mind all truth coheres, and we may suggest ways in which apparent antinomies in Scripture may be held together, but we should not employ forced biblical exegesis. The Roman Catholic writer Thomas

---

9. This was hardly a coherent philosophy, but in some ways it functioned like one in the way it influenced theology.

10. Kant's dates precede Hegel's, but his main theological influence was later.

11. Whether intellectual coherence may be regarded as *defining* truth is more debatable.

12. He expounds this in *A New Critique of Theoretical Thought*, 4 vols. (Lampeter: Edwin Mellen, 1997).

13. See the critique of Dooyeweerd's philosophy in O. Barclay, *Developing a Christian Mind* (Leicester: Inter-Varsity Press, 1984), pp. 202–207.

Weinandy, among others, rightly advocates calling major gaps in our theological understanding mysteries rather than problems. James Anderson, from an evangelical perspective, takes the same view.[14] Problems take us to the study for research, but mysteries into the sanctuary to worship.[15]

Finally, there is the view that *philosophy can aid theology* by providing questions for theology to answer. Sometimes Scripture provides its own theological questions, especially in the Psalms and wisdom literature, fairly calmly in Ecclesiastes, agonizingly in Job. We will see later how some Old Testament theologians have approached these questions,[16] but it is important too for us to listen to questions raised by others.

Philosophers may also challenge theologians to clarity of expression. The theologian Paul Tillich once spent some days debating with a group of philosophers keen to understand his theology, but failed to make himself clear to them.[17] This may take much work, but it will benefit the theologian as well as his or her readers, for ideas that are obscurely presented may not even be clear to their author.

Issues raised by the use of philosophical terms in theology's engagement with contemporary thought are of special importance. Such use of philosophy has both value and dangers, and we need to consider what guidance Scripture gives us here.

Guidance from Scripture

Paul made contact with the Athenians at a religious level and quoted two Greek philosophers, Epimenedes and Aratus, in this way using truth his hearers knew through general revelation to argue against their idolatry. He also declared that God does not live in temples, that he is no needy receiver but a bounteous giver, and, over against the Athenian belief that their ancestors sprang fully grown from the soil of Attica, that he made all humanity from one man (Acts 17:22–29). So he used contact points, but also confronted error with truth.

God's general revelation imparts some truth about him, but natural theology (what people make of general revelation) often combines truth and

---

14. J. Anderson, *Paradox in Christian Theology: An Analysis of its Presence, Character and Epistemic Status* (Carlisle: Paternoster, 2007).

15. See T. G. Weinandy, *Does God Suffer?* (Edinburgh: T. & T. Clark, 2000), pp. 30–39.

16. See pp. 236–237.

17. See S. Hook (ed.), *Religious Experience and Truth* (New York: New York University Press, 1961).

error. We can see this in the fact that in this address Paul seemed at some points to side with the Epicureans against the Stoics, at others the opposite. He then proclaimed God's special revelation in Christ. Bertil Gärtner has demonstrated that, although in this address Paul makes no explicit reference to the Old Testament, he is consistently true to it. The God he proclaims is the God of special revelation even for those without previous contact with that revelation.[18]

The prologue to John's Gospel is profound in its simplicity. Its *Logos* ('word') theme would make immediate contact with Jewish readers, for whom the Word of God was all-important, but also with Gentile readers of a philosophical bent, for *logos* was a familiar philosophical term meaning 'reason' as well as 'word'. John's references to the Logos as the source both of light and of life, two perennial concerns of philosophers, would interest them and they would then read his amazing claim that the Logos became incarnate in a man, Jesus Christ, implying for them that if philosophers would find truth this will be at the feet of Jesus.

The epistle to the Colossians teaches the same lesson. The heresy Paul combats in it fused biblical and non-biblical ideas. He appears to use its terminology in opposing it, words like 'wisdom', 'mystery' and 'fullness'. He indicated that the fullness of God's revelation in Jesus provides all that the heretics professed to offer through secret knowledge received in mystical experiences, but provides it actually and truly.

The 'unknown god', 'logos', 'mystery', 'wisdom' and 'fullness' – all these were contact points to introduce vital realities vainly sought by non-Christian philosophy and religion, but now made known and available in Jesus. This shows we need to listen to others to find such contact points if we are to speak relevantly and effectively. A Christian I knew could start a discussion on the Christian faith from any page of a newspaper except the racing page, and could use language well understood by non-Christians, but it was always the authentic biblical gospel that he commended to them. So then, we need to contextualize the gospel, but never with loss of its biblical content.[19]

We should therefore be constantly self-critical. Are any of us fully biblical in our thinking? Not even the use of biblical words guarantees that we are

---

18. B. Gärtner, *The Areopagus Speech and Natural Revelation*, tr. C. H. King (Lund: Gleerup, 1955).

19. A starting point and common ground are not necessarily identical, and the very fact of a different outlook can be a starting point. See the discussion of presuppositionalism on pp. 180–187.

theologically biblical, for we may fail to understand them biblically. In the second century various forms of Gnosticism, which taught the need for esoteric spiritual knowledge communicated mystically to the initiated, mounted a major assault on the gospel, often using biblical words in an unbiblical way. Irenaeus, in his great work *Against Heresies*,[20] reveals that he saw clearly what was happening precisely because he was himself a diligent student of Scripture. Regular, deeply committed, reflective and prayerful Bible study is so important as God's means of creating and developing a godly wisdom to counter this world's wisdom which is all around us and traces, sometimes large traces, of which still linger in our minds.[21]

Philosophical ideas may penetrate people's minds very deeply, especially if they give emotional as well as intellectual satisfaction. Many have seen that truth is often approached through beauty, with theories often attracting first of all by their form. I once asked a man why he was attracted to a particular philosophy. 'Because it is so beautiful,' he replied.

When an idea has engaged with us deeply, it often influences us long after we think we have set it aside.[22] In 1 Corinthians Paul wrote to a church enamoured by an arrogant pseudo-intellectualism, the language of which was derived from the Greek intellectual world which was all around them and which undoubtedly would have influenced them, often in a major way, before they became Christians. He says, 'In the wisdom of God the world through its wisdom did not know him' (1 Cor. 1:21), and in this connection he mentions the philosopher (v. 20). Instead of worldly wisdom, he advocated a Christianity centring in Christ and his cross and finding its wisdom there, producing humble joy in what Christians have received through Christ's atoning work and in union with him.

To be wise we need to sit humbly before God's Word both to unlearn and to learn from him. Nothing is more attractive than godly wisdom (Jas 3:17–18) based on a supremely winsome gospel coming through the cross from the God of all grace.

All the New Testament passages we have been considering contain important lessons. Our use of terms should not only be understandable but faithful to the

---

20. Irenaeus, *Against Heresies*, in *The Ante-Nicene Fathers*, vol. 1 (Grand Rapids: Eerdmans, 1973), pp. 309–567.

21. See chapter 6.

22. Dialecticism, for instance, which focuses on the clash and subsequent reconciliation of opposites, continued to influence the early Marxists long after they had given up Hegelianism, in which this idea is of great importance.

biblical gospel. So, for instance, we may engage with philosophers but without taking our bearings from philosophy. To do the latter would be particularly serious as far as the foundational doctrine of God is concerned and it probably happens more often in relation to this doctrine than any other, because the existence, nature and knowableness of God are recognized topics of philosophy. If we are wrong here, is it any wonder if we are wrong elsewhere?[23]

So, in summary, Christianity is based on God's self-revelation in Scripture culminating in Christ, giving a wisdom inaccessible to philosophers as such. Philosophical language has value in engaging with non-Christians of a philosophical cast of mind, but treating the gospel as a kind of religious philosophy or using its language uncritically has great dangers. We must be faithful to the gospel and its Old Testament background and walk humbly with God.

One more question: are philosophy's language and concepts of any value in *setting forth Christian truth for the benefit of Christians*? Yes, in certain circumstances and for certain purposes. Terms like 'transcendence' and 'immanence', for instance, abstract terms not reflecting any particular philosophy, are useful and they often appear in theological works, but we should never imagine such language superior to that of Scripture.

Every subject's academic practitioners seek language that combines clarity and conciseness, qualities often difficult to achieve together, for concise terminology often requires explanation. To be told that the Bible teaches, for instance, God's simplicity, immutability or transcendence can raise a host of questions in Christian minds. Moreover, language can have emotional as well as intellectual impact. This is true of words like 'impassibility' and 'predestination'. It applies negatively to 'wrath' and positively to 'love', but we should remember that both are biblical words.

Stated and unstated presuppositions

In order to understand people we need often to consider what is behind what they say. We are not always conscious of the presuppositions we have ourselves and moreover others may not be, so that in dialogue there is the danger that we may never get beyond the surface to the deeper issues. There have occasionally been major disputes between theologians which have arisen largely because they were using important terms differently.

---

23. See A. McGrath, *A Passion for Truth: The Intellectual Coherence of Evangelicalism* (Leicester: Apollos, 1996), p. 34.

Particularly relevant to issues of theology and biblical scholarship is the question of supernaturalism. A critic with rationalistic assumptions may discuss the biblical account of a miracle and suggest explanations of it without ever taking into account the possibility that something supernatural, something beyond the normal web of cause and effect, actually happened. Presuppositions are frequently of very great importance, arising as they often do from deeply held beliefs.

Of course, there are times when a presupposition may be intentionally hidden. We assume that Christian theologians and biblical scholars will be people of integrity, but occasionally, just occasionally, we may be mistaken in this. In this book, however, we will assume consistently that those expressing the views we are considering are uniformly persons of honesty and integrity.

The present situation

Evangelicalism in the Western world has arrived at a most challenging stage in its history. Early in the nineteenth century it seemed to be in the ascendant, and a high percentage of Protestant churches were evangelical in theology. In Britain, for instance, the Methodist revival had brought great blessing to the church scene and church attendance was high. In the world of biblical scholarship, however, there were disturbing developments. During the latter part of the previous century the rationalism of the Enlightenment had begun to affect biblical studies, and this approach became increasingly dominant throughout the nineteenth century. Alongside this a sequence of theological movements arose, each affected by the changing cultural and philosophical scene in such a way that both biblical and theological studies often sat more lightly to the supreme authority of Scripture.

Some of the philosophical influences that were affecting biblical studies and theology, such as evolutionary philosophy, continued into the twentieth century, but with their eventual waning[24] others took their place, including existentialism, Marxism,[25] process philosophy and the philosophy of language. We are all now aware of the advent of postmodernism, which although

---

24. Biological evolution is still very much alive, but Herbert Spencer's all-embracing evolutionary philosophy has now been largely replaced by the process philosophy which developed out of it.

25. This arose in the nineteenth century, but its major influence was in the twentieth.

not expressed in a widely agreed philosophy,[26] is nevertheless a cultural phenomenon with wide influence, and this too is affecting both biblical studies and theology.

What, then, about evangelicalism? In the late nineteenth and early twentieth centuries it found itself increasingly under attack or sidelined as both obscurantist and irrelevant. Many who had accepted the Bible as the authoritative Word of God, but whose commitment to it had been undermined, moved towards a more liberal outlook, although others stood firm. Without doubt evangelicals felt their backs were to the wall. We owe a debt of gratitude to those who under God stood firm at this time. There was a tendency then for evangelical scholarship to be somewhat defensive and in the circumstances this is fully understandable. If there was dialogue with liberal scholars and theologians, this was usually at a distance.

Today the situation is quite different, chiefly for two reasons. First of all, after the Second World War there was a major rebirth of conservative scholarship, and this has grown more and more over the years. Then, happily, some of the more arid approaches of liberal scholarship have either disappeared or at least are no longer in the forefront of discussion. I. H. Marshall identifies three ways in which biblical scholarship in general is concentrating on areas more congenial to evangelicals: the recognition that all the biblical books are theological documents with a theological message, that they are all literary entities to be studied in their final form rather than in terms of sources, and that they should be studied canonically, that is in their place in the Bible as a whole.[27]

Evangelical theologians and conservative scholars have their own learned societies, but they now freely mix in societies which embrace those of many different outlooks. In this way they may make many valuable contributions while at the same time they may be influenced by the views of others. Many budding theologians and scholars now do doctoral research on the thought of Christian writers who are not conservative evangelicals in the sense outlined earlier in this chapter. To do such research at such a venue as Tyndale House in Cambridge, which is committed to in-depth research but which is also evangelical, is of obvious value, although of course it is not possible for many.

---

26. Fergus Macdonald has pointed out to me that this is hardly possible when it is so individualistic in its outlook.

27. I. H. Marshall, *Beyond the Bible: Moving from Scripture to Theology* (Grand Rapids: Baker, 2004), pp. 19–20.

A new theological movement may include some important biblical insights, even if they are to be found alongside elements that must be regarded as unbiblical and consequently as spiritually unhelpful. So, for instance, theologies affected by existentialism focus attention on the importance of decision, and the Bible is full of imperatives. The theologies of Moltmann and the first generation of liberation theologians, who were influenced by Marxism, have emphasized the importance of the social element in the Bible, especially God's concern for the poor and the oppressed. Process theology, emerging from evolutionism, underlines the dynamic nature of the biblical revelation. In the philosophy of language, speech-act theory has stressed the differing effects varied forms of language, and therefore of the Word of God, may have on the reader or hearer. It may, of course, be said that a balanced evangelicalism has always recognized each of these truths.

As we have already noted, study of theological movements shows how often they are influenced by particular philosophies, and in engaging with a theology we have to engage often with the philosophy as well. In the process there may be an imbibing, consciously or unconsciously, of ways of thinking which are actually inimical to the faith we hold. We may be so aware of the positives in a point of view that we miss the fact that they often appear in theological contexts which present serious theological error. The very presence of the positives may add to the danger of deception. They alert us to the importance of discerning between the theological wheat and the chaff.

In some evangelical circles there has been a measure of theological reorientation so that not all old beliefs have been retained and some new ones have been taken on board. This has accelerated somewhat over the past quarter of a century, and proposals have been made for the revision and recasting of a number of traditional evangelical beliefs.[28]

What really matters, however, is not whether a theological position is old or new, but whether it is biblical. The main purpose of this book is to attempt a biblical appraisal of some of these developments.

---

28. D. F. Wells, in *The Courage to be Protestant: Truth, Marketers and Emergents in the Postmodern World* (Nottingham: Inter-Varsity Press, 2008), pp. 1–21, shows how the renewal of classical evangelicalism that developed after the Second World War became a cohesive movement by focusing agreement only on the authority of Scripture and penal substitution, so that many gradually ceased to give deep thought to theological issues while at the same time becoming too affected by contemporary culture.

The contents of this volume

Appropriately, we begin with *the doctrine of God*. A group of evangelical theologians has developed and promoted the concept of open theism. Put briefly, this challenges the classic doctrine of God and in particular its concepts of God's changelessness, sovereignty and foreknowledge. In their view, God is subject to change. His power, although great, is limited, because he relates to other personal beings and their decisions, and his knowledge of the future, although considerable, is limited. These limitations are not imposed on him from without but are self-imposed. The open theists regard themselves as consistent Arminians,[29] although many Arminians reject their revision of the doctrine of God.

Next comes *the atonement*. Traditionally, evangelicals have held that penal substitution (Christ at Calvary bearing in our place the penalty of our sins) is central to the atonement, but without affirming that this is the whole meaning of the cross. Today some are challenging the whole idea of penal substitution and the cross is being viewed increasingly as finding its central meaning elsewhere, for instance as Christ's victory over the powers of evil, or in terms of his identification with the oppressed.

Some have called for and are promoting a new perspective on Paul, especially in relation to his *doctrine of justification*. There are some variations in their outlook, but in general they argue that Paul has been read too much through the lens of the tortured conscience of Luther, that New Testament Judaism was not so much legalistic as nationalistic, and that Paul's doctrine of justification is not so much about how we get into God's covenant as about the recognition that in Christ both Jews and Gentiles are authentic and equal members of God's covenant people.

The doctrine of biblical authority is obviously very important. Some scholars generally reckoned conservative are embracing critical positions once regarded as unacceptable, and it is clear that the theological implications of these must be carefully thought through. Most conservative evangelicals have stood for biblical inerrancy, but more reservations about this are now being voiced.

Biblical hermeneutics is concerned with how the Bible and its eternal truths are to be interpreted and applied today, and therefore its importance needs

---

29. Arminians follow the teaching of the sixteenth- and early seventeenth-century Dutch theologian Arminius, who saw divine election not as unconditional but as contingent on foreseen faith.

no arguing. Our hermeneutics cannot be wrong in important ways and our theology right. This is why a chapter is being devoted to hermeneutics.

Many readers of this book will be aware of other theological issues within evangelicalism that raise serious questions, in addition to those already mentioned. An obvious example is prosperity theology, which is much more widespread than is often realized, and which often occurs in a milder form in churches which would reject its more extreme expressions.[30]

What is common to all theological aberrations, of course, is a mishandling of Scripture and it seems best, instead of making this book unduly long by dealing at length with other issues, to explore the main principles of biblical interpretation. My hope is that this will provide readers with general guidance which can then be particularly applied. In doing this we must, of course, consider the postmodern attitude to truth and what philosophers, and theologians affected by them, are saying about the nature of verbal communication, but we must also look at the way in which contemporary culture so often affects the way the Bible is handled in the pulpit and in popular evangelical literature.

In the final chapter, in looking at the evangelical scene as a whole, we ask the question, '*Whither evangelicalism?*'

It is not the purpose of this volume to teach the doctrines of God, the atonement, justification and Scripture in all their aspects, but only those features of them about which questions have been raised by some evangelicals in recent years. In the course of this, it will be necessary to consider the biblical teaching on some of these features fairly fully. I hope such sections of the book will be of positive theological value to its readers.

Special note: chapter 2 is undoubtedly the most difficult in the book for readers unused to serious theological reading. It has been put where it is to fit the logical structure of the book, but I would advise such readers to leave it until they have read the other chapters.

---

30. To deal with this fully would require a different sort of book as there is a lack of scholarly literature which supports it and which we could engage with here.

2. THE CHALLENGE OF OPEN THEISM TO THE CLASSIC CHRISTIAN DOCTRINE OF GOD

The Christian doctrine of God

Its fundamental importance

This needs no arguing. The most important relationship of any person or thing is to God. The Bible's exalted teaching challenges and enables us to think deeply about him. Unsurprisingly, Christian systematic theologies usually start with God.

Studying biblical teaching about him expands the heart as well as the mind. I suspect I am not alone in finding that books of good biblical theology are often more stimulating devotionally than specifically devotional books. Where theological exposition and devotional application are wedded, here is a feast indeed! Many Bible books too provide exactly that.

Read Psalm 103 prayerfully, letting your mind and heartfelt praise move out from 'my soul' to 'all his works everywhere in his dominion', then back to 'my soul'. The great doctrinal statement in Ephesians 1:3–14 is set in a framework of praise (vv. 3, 14), itself in turn punctuated with praise (vv. 6, 12). The expansion of godly thinking and worship that must have taken place in both the psalmist and the apostle before they expressed this deepened thought and worship in their words should find an echo in you and me. 'Theology' means 'thinking about God', and I like the suggestion that we should view it as 'thinking about God in his presence'.

The Puritans loved this union of theology and devotion. When *Knowing God* by James Packer, a lover of the Puritans, was first published in 1973, it was widely read.[1] It still sells well, but I suspect many Christians today favour instead other books, books focusing on 'me' (yes, me as a Christian, but still me!) rather than on God. Certainly my spiritual growth is important, but basic to it is my recognition that God, not I, should be central. In fact that could even serve as a definition of what Christian sanctification means.

The whole scope of Christian doctrine is known as 'theology', for all its aspects are extensions of the doctrine of God, often called 'theology proper'. As everything in Christian theology rests on this doctrine,[2] challenges to it are serious, and the contemporary theological movement usually known as 'open theism', which had its origins in North America, challenges at several important points the doctrine as it has been traditionally understood. Russell Fuller is right when he says that the open theism debate is not about some second-order doctrine.[3]

The classic model for this doctrine

Before we can consider open theism we must first ask what the traditional or classic doctrine of God teaches. No summary, no matter how full, can do anything like justice to what the Bible teaches about God, so I will focus on aspects of the doctrine which are most relevant to our theme in this chapter. Christian theology in its major traditional forms[4] teaches that God is both one and triune. He is the self-existent, unchanging Creator of the universe, who relates to it as omnipotent, omniscient and omnipresent, who revealed

---

1. J. I. Packer, *Knowing God*, 2nd ed. (London: Hodder and Stoughton, 1993).

2. The doctrine of Scripture too is of fundamental importance, but Scripture is our authority because it is *God's* Word, which assumes God's priority and an awareness of him given through general revelation. Of course, the God of the Word tells us much not disclosed in general revelation, and corrects misunderstanding of this revelation due to the effects of sin on our minds, so that Scripture teaching should affect the content of the primary article(s) about God in our statements of faith.

3. R. Fuller, 'The Rabbis and the Claims of Openness Advocates', in J. Piper, J. Taylor and P. K. Helsketh (eds.), *Beyond the Bounds: Open Theism and the Undermining of Biblical Christianity* (Wheaton: Crossway, 2003), p. 13; cf. B. A. Ware, *God's Lesser Glory: A Critique of Open Theism* (Leicester: Apollos, 2000), p. 9, who challenges Gregory Boyd's view that it is peripheral.

4. Orthodox, Roman Catholic, Calvinist, Arminian, etc.

himself in Israel's history and supremely and uniquely in Christ, and who acts always in his character of holiness, love and wisdom.

Open theism and its criticism of the classic model
In *The Openness of God*,[5] a symposium presenting the open theist point of view, the preface, presumably written by its editor, Clark Pinnock, says,

> This book presents an understanding of God's nature and relationships with his creatures, which we call the openness of God. In broad strokes, it takes the following form. God, in grace, grants humans significant freedom to co-operate with or work against God's will for their lives, and he enters into dynamic, give-and-take relationships with us. The Christian life involves a genuine interaction between God and human beings. We respond to God's gracious initiatives and God responds to our responses. God takes risks in this give-and-take relationship, yet he is endlessly resourceful and competent in working toward his ultimate goals. Sometimes God alone decides how to accomplish these goals. On other occasions, God works with human decisions, adapting his own plans to fit the changing situation. God does not control everything that happens. Rather, he is open to receive input from his creatures. In loving dialogue, God invites us to participate with him to bring the future into being.

Also for open theists God has unlimited knowledge of past and present, but limited knowledge of the future. They maintain too that classical theism is deeply indebted to philosophy, especially Greek philosophy, and that the result of this is serious distortion in the interpretation of the biblical data. They tend to view biblical anthropopathisms (passages where feelings we normally associate with human beings are attributed to God) more literally than do classical theists.

There are obviously important issues here. This is because we are called to faith, and what is most significant about faith is not its depth or its purity, important as these undoubtedly are, but its Object, the God who is trusted. Christian faith gains its distinctiveness from its Object, the God of the Bible, and it is the traditional understanding of God that is under threat.

The challenge of open theism requires us to address a number of distinct but interrelated issues.

---

5. C. H. Pinnock, R. Rice, J. Sanders, W. Hasker and D. Basinger, *The Openness of God: A Biblical Challenge to the Traditional Understanding of God* (Downers Grove: InterVarsity Press, 1994), p. 8.

The influence of philosophy

Both classical and open theists rightly hold that it is the teaching of Scripture which must decide all theological issues, and most of this chapter will discuss biblical teaching. There have, however, been allegations on both sides that there has been a muddying of the theological waters by the influence of non-Christian philosophy, so we must briefly consider this.

Philosophy and classical theism

The claim that classical theism has been significantly corrupted by philosophy was made over a hundred years ago, and therefore many years before the advent of open theism, by Edwin Hatch[6] and Adolph Harnack.[7] Harnack directed criticism particularly at the patristic doctrines of the Trinity and of Christ's Person, holding that in the early Christian creeds the influence of Greek philosophy can be clearly seen.

When open theism arrived on the theological scene, its advocates maintained that the Greek philosophical corruption of theology found its ultimate patristic expression in the theology of Augustine of Hippo, who had been a Neoplatonist before his conversion, that it gained an Aristotelian slant in the Middle Ages through philosopher-theologians like Thomas Aquinas, Duns Scotus and William of Occam, that the Reformers were influenced by all these, and that through the writings of the Reformers this influence has continued to the present day.

This is no small claim, and it has to be taken very seriously. If true, it would call into question what most theologians have taught about God. What can we say in answer to it?

Long before the advent of open theism, Leonard Hodgson and others had argued persuasively that in the patristic period, the years when the doctrine of God was being given its classical formulation, Christian thought, which was seeking to spell out the theological implications of the biblical facts, was moving against rather than with the general trend of philosophy. The most prominent philosophy during this period was Neoplatonism, which was a monistic system. Philosophical monists (not to be confused with mono-theists) hold that no distinctions are ultimate, so that anything like the

---

6. E. Hatch, *The Influence of Greek Ideas and Usages on the Christian Church*, Hibbert Lectures, 1988 (London: Williams and Norgate, 1991).

7. A. Harnack, *History of Dogma*, 7 vols. (1894–9), tr. N. Buchanan (Whitefish: Kessinger, 2008).

trinitarian distinction of persons or even the Christological distinction of the two natures in Christ was quite unacceptable to the Neoplatonists.[8]

Certainly some expressions of classical Christian theism, especially in the patristic and medieval periods, have a somewhat philosophical flavour. Augustine's *De Trinitate* (*On the Trinity*), for instance, has some Platonic presuppositions, as any reader of it familiar with Platonism would quickly realize. Aquinas was clearly affected by Aristotle and made no secret of it.

The reader who turns to the Reformers, however, becomes immediately aware that what really mattered to them was that their theology should be biblical. They often quoted Augustine with approval, but not without discrimination, while their references to the leading medievalists were as often critical as they were approving. These authors, as theological resources, were for them always subsidiary to the Bible, and, more importantly, Scripture was always their theological authority and was employed to test all that had come down to them from the past.

This does not, of course, rule out the possibility of unconscious influence, and this means that no writings from the past, no matter how eminent or worthy their authors, can be treated as immune from critical scrutiny. For this reason, we should never resent a call for a new appraisal of our theological heritage, so long as the criterion of appraisal is holy Scripture.

In the current debate the immutability of God is the main issue. Other questions such as the possibility that his power and his knowledge of the future are limited are related to this.

The open theist William Hasker says,

> In the philosophical lineage stretching from Parmenides to Plato to Plotinus,[9] there is a strong metaphysical and valuational preference for permanence over change ... And this bias against change has been powerfully influential in classical theology, leading to the insistence on an excessively strong doctrine of divine immutability – which, in turn, provides key support for divine timelessness, since timelessness is the most effective way (and perhaps the only way) to rule out, once and for all, the possibility of any change in God.[10]

---

8. L. Hodgson, *The Doctrine of the Trinity*, Croall Lectures, 1942–3 (New York: Charles Scribner and Sons, 1944).

9. i.e. from the fifth century BC to the third century AD.

10. W. Hasker, 'A Philosophical Perspective', in Pinnock et al., *The Openness of God*, p. 129. He mentions Plotinus because he was Neoplatonism's great creative thinker.

Open theists allege too that the emphasis on God's will by the Reformers, which was certainly strong, shows the influence of the Aristotelian schoolmen, a group of scholars who wrote on theological and philosophical themes in the late Middle Ages.

Without doubt, classical theists have not been averse to using the tools of philosophy in expounding and defending their doctrine of God. What matters, however, is whether the actual grounds of these doctrines are philosophical or biblical. Much of this chapter will be given to considering this.

Philosophy and open theism

If open theists ask whether classical theism has been affected by philosophy, they also need to face the same question.

As Hasker notes, permanence and stability were emphasized by Greek philosophy and by much subsequent thought. Since Kant in the early nineteenth century, however, the philosophical focus has altered considerably. He taught that, with the sole exception of moral experience, nothing certain can be known about the noumenal world, by which term he meant the world as it really is beyond the phenomenal world that is accessible to sense-perception. So then, there can be no certain route from the physical to the metaphysical; we cannot get 'behind the scenes' so that we can know things as they really are. A little later Hegel taught that God is subject to change and that because, as he thought, all human minds reflect something of the mind of God, God comes gradually to a deeper understanding of himself in the human history of ideas. These two motifs, uncertainty and change, became features of much philosophy from then on and their influence is still with us.

This kind of outlook can be seen in process theology, based on process philosophy, which emerged from evolutionary philosophy[11] and which has promoted the idea of God as 'an ever-changing being evolving toward the perfection that is potentially his'.[12] That this is quite different from the classical theistic position is patently obvious.

While some open theists may have been influenced by process thought, others try to distance themselves from it, not wanting to be accused of holding to a finite God and to process theology's quasi-pantheism. In fact the open theist Hasker agrees that process theology with its link with process

---

11. Evolutionary philosophy, the brainchild of Herbert Spencer, starts from biological evolution, but sees 'the survival of the fittest' as operating in every sphere, including history, science, art, social theory, politics, ethics, religion, and so on.

12. Hasker's summary of it, in 'A Philosophical Perspective', p. 93.

philosophy is even more damaging to the biblical conception of God than the link he reckons classical theology had with Neoplatonism in early church history.[13]

Pinnock says his aim in his chapter in *The Openness of God* is to 'seek a way to revise classical theism in a dynamic direction without falling into process theology'.[14] He says,

> Anticipating the criticism that the open view of God is a form of process theology, let me reiterate two chief ways in which it differs. First, God is ontologically other than the world, which is not necessary to God – the world exists only because God wills it. Therefore, God is not dependent on the world out of necessity but willingly, because he chose to create a world in which there would be mutuality and relational interdependence. Second, God not only sustains the world as the ground of its being but also acts in history to bring about salvation. God was particularly active in that stream of human history which culminated in the life, death and resurrection of Jesus, and involved himself in marvellous actions that go beyond his undergirding of the world process. God is also active in the entire history of the world by the Spirit, which sustains and directs all things.[15]

This statement may seem reassuring, but the points of comparison between the two movements of thought constitute an ever-present danger. Open theism is congenial to the philosophical world which gave birth to process thought. It is also congenial to the postmodern world and this is undoubtedly part of its appeal, but this does not prove its truth, and the somewhat positive outlook of some open theists towards process thought could yet prove to be the movement's Achilles heel.

The main problem

For many attracted to open theism, the main problem may be not so much the meaning as the emotional tone of many of the words used in classical theism. Abstractions lack the warmth that personal language about God has, and a theological work that overuses them, no matter how orthodox it is, may seem more like a philosophical treatise than an exposition of biblical truth.

With the important exception of 'impassibility',[16] however, the main words

---

13. ibid., p. 141.
14. Pinnock, 'Systematic Theology', in Pinnock et al., *The Openness of God*, p. 107.
15. ibid., p. 125, n. 49.
16. See pp. 70–75.

employed in classical theism have clear dictionary definitions, but as either negatives (like immutability) or at least abstractions (like omniscience) they can give an impression of remoteness and even of irrelevance in terms of God's personal relations with human beings. Omnipresence, which might seem rather better than most of these terms, is so misunderstood that many people, sometimes even preachers, speak of 'parts' of God being everywhere, when in fact he is fully present everywhere. Even an overuse of the indispensable adjective 'divine', instead of the noun 'God', can be unhelpful.

Open theism, on the other hand, needs to avoid the error, not of making God seem remote by abstract language, but rather of moving towards pantheism, which itself tends to depersonalize him. This would in fact undermine one of its major concerns. It must be said in fairness, however, that most open theists have not only retained but have placed considerable emphasis on the biblical revelation of a personal and living God.

It would be as well for both classical and open theists with a philosophical interest to avoid the excessive use of abstract language.

The anthropomorphic language of the Bible

Open theists are interested in anthropomorphisms and without doubt the interpretation of these is of considerable importance.

In disputes, it is important to have an agreed starting point. Classical and open theists agree that theology should not start from general views of God shaped somewhat by philosophy, but from Scripture. They both show concern for good exegesis and good biblical theology. So Richard Rice, an open theist, says, 'The Scriptures contain such vast and varied material that it is not difficult to surround an idea with biblical quotations. The crucial question is whether the idea is faithful to the overall biblical portrait of God – the picture that emerges from the full range of biblical evidence.'[17] Horton, a classical theist, says, 'An analogical approach . . . in order to work properly, must listen to the symphony of biblical analogies, knowing that none of the analogies by itself can be reduced to the whole (univocal) score.'[18] This raises the whole question of anthropomorphism in the Bible.

---

17. R. Rice, 'Biblical Support for a New Perspective', in Pinnock et al., *The Openness of God*, p. 15.

18. M. S. Horton, 'Hellenistic or Hebrew? Open Theism and Reformed Theological Method', in Piper et al. (eds.), *Beyond the Bounds*, p. 212.

The nature of anthropomorphism

It is a language form

It is analogy employing language about God which is normally used of human beings, describing him, his thoughts and feelings and words, his decisions and actions, as if he were human. When used of feelings it is called anthropopathism.[19]

In Scripture it is the language of divine revelation

It is given by God's gracious initiative, and in it he accommodates his revelation to human understanding.

God reveals himself, conveying his word in identifiable human languages, in Hebrew and Greek, not in some 'heavenly' speech. He uses everyday speech forms and analogies from what is familiar to human beings. In this way he accommodates his whole revelation to our creaturely understanding. Missionaries need to employ the language and cultural forms of the people to whom they are sent, and God is the supreme cross-cultural Missionary. So to dispense with anthropomorphism is to dispense with Scripture.

Although we *understand* these terms because of our human experience, that experience should not be employed to make judgments about God. So, for instance, 'Father' is only meaningful because there are human fathers, but we must not judge God's fatherhood by human, but vice versa. The imperfect copy is judged by the perfect archetype.[20] So Scripture's presentation of God as King, Father, Shepherd, is meaningful from our human experience, but then God's perfect exemplification of these roles serves to critique human kings, fathers and shepherds.[21] He uses our language to bring us into his way of thinking, which then establishes norms for ours. In general terms this is not contested by open theists.

It presupposes the doctrines of creation and of the divine image

God has revealed something of himself in his creation, so it is not surprising that his special revelation recorded in Scripture employs features of that same

---

19. This chapter will use 'anthropomorphisms' to cover anthropopathisms as well.

20. See C. Van Til, *An Introduction to Systematic Theology* (Nutley: Presbyterian and Reformed, 1976), p. 212.

21. See A. B. Caneday, 'Veiled Glory: God's Self-Revelation in Human Likeness – A Biblical Theology of God's Anthropomorphic Self-Disclosure', in Piper et al., (eds.), *Beyond the Bounds*, p. 163. The whole of Ezek. 34 illustrates this principle.

creation, likening him, for instance, to an eagle, a lion, a rock. These too are anthropomorphic in that they are personified, so that in them anthropomorphism takes up further analogies into itself.

The image of God means that by God's own creative act human beings have a special likeness to him not shared by other creatures.[22] We are personal, moral and articulate beings. This is why Scripture employs human analogies much more than non-human. A. B. Caneday says, 'The image of God is his revelatory nexus infused into our very being . . . To this first analogical disclosure of himself, God associates all other revelation.' He also says, 'God makes himself known to his creatures in their likeness, as if he wears their form and qualities, when in fact they wear his likeness.'[23] This last important point will be taken up again later.

It is comprehensive, embracing the whole Bible

It takes the form of a general, extended metaphor that runs right through the Bible.

It is often wrongly thought to occur only in certain passages, where God is spoken of in terms normally applied to finite human beings, while, it is thought, elsewhere he is presented in a way that excludes such human finitude.[24] On this basis we would take the former figuratively and the latter literally, but this is wrong. Caneday pertinently asks what in this case we do when the Old Testament says that God is different from human beings both because he does not change his mind (Num. 23:19; 1 Sam. 15:29) and because he does (Hos. 11:8–9).[25]

Aquinas, Luther and Calvin were surely right to maintain that anthropomorphism characterizes the whole biblical revelation, not just special parts of it.[26] Even activities like thought and speech, or qualities like love and

22. For full discussion of the meaning of the image of God and of the exegesis of Gen. 1:26–27, see D. J. A. Clines, 'Humanity as the Image of God', *On the Way to the Postmodern, Old Testament Essays 1967–1998*, vol. 2, *JSOT* Supp. 292 (Sheffield: Sheffield Academic, 1998), pp. 447–497. Whatever it means it is clearly unique to human beings.

23. Caneday, 'Veiled Glory', pp. 170, 161.

24. As, e.g., in Bruce Ware's description of anthropomorphism in 'An Evangelical Reformulation of the Doctrine of the Immutability of God', in *Journal of the Evangelical Theological Society* 29 (1986), p. 442.

25. Caneday, 'Veiled Glory', p. 154; cf. Horton, 'Hellenistic or Hebrew?', p. 216.

26. This makes them remarkably close to those postmodern philosophers of language who argue that all language is metaphorical, although they differ over the truth-claims of traditional theology, which postmoderns so often reject.

anger, are meaningful only from our experience of them. We are so used to such language that we overlook its pervasive character, only identifying it when it causes theological difficulty, for example in appearing to attribute to God physical qualities, or change, or emotions thought unacceptable. Horton says, 'Scripture is no less analogical when it says that God does not repent than when it represents him as doing just that.'[27] This is because repentance is something we would know nothing about apart from human experience.

Both classical and open theists can be inconsistent in this connection. So Caneday says, 'Sanders may legitimately fault evangelicals for inadequate consideration of biblical anthropomorphisms,' although he goes on to say, 'Sanders does not seem to understand that all God's revelation truly is analogical, including his negative assertions.'[28] Pinnock too seems inconsistent when he says of certain Bible stories, 'We must take seriously how God is depicted in these stories and resist reducing important metaphors to mere anthropomorphic or accommodated language. God's revelation is anthropomorphic through and through. We could not grasp any other kind. We must take it all seriously, if not all literally.'[29] This is confusing, as if he is being pulled in two directions. If all God's revelation is anthropomorphic, then surely to treat it as such cannot be properly described as reduction!

We cannot pick and choose. We must recognize the radical nature of anthropomorphism, that the Bible is anthropomorphic, for example, in speaking not only about God's wrath but also about his love, an important point which constantly passes unnoticed. Such recognition must precede any serious attempt to interpret the biblical revelation. This is true, of course, even when the Bible attributes physical characteristics to God.

It includes many particular metaphors normally used of human beings
We take from language used about God what we would if it were used of a human being, unless the Bible elsewhere forbids this. Particular metaphors are contained within the comprehensive human-life metaphor. These include those taken from inanimate things, plants, animals and human life, so that if God is said to be a lion, this is because a man can be so described metaphorically. It is therefore a metaphor within a metaphor.

---

27. Horton, 'Hellenistic or Hebrew?', p. 216.
28. Caneday, 'Veiled Glory', p. 191.
29. C. H. Pinnock, *Most Moved Mover: A Theology of God's Openness* (Carlisle: Paternoster, 2001), p. 20.

We still have to ask in what sense both a human being and God are like a lion, just as in the overarching metaphor we have to ask in what ways God is like (and, of course, unlike) a human being. Sanders points out that some metaphors indicate greater similarity than others. He says, 'The Bible variously refers to God as a rock (Ps. 31:2–3), a shepherd (Ps. 23:1) and a human parent (Hos. 11:1). But most Christians would agree that God is more like a shepherd than a rock, and more like a parent than a shepherd. So within the broad spectrum of biblical metaphor, some are more important than others.'[30]

Each particular metaphor tells us something about God. In fact, the use of so many metaphors reminds us that we can never know all that God is.

Sallie McFague seeks to replace models of God as lord, king and patriarch by those of mother, lover and friend. She considers these better portraits of God for our own day, especially in projecting a different view of power.[31] But if we are to balance biblical metaphors, as we must, we cannot jettison any we find in Scripture.

Metaphor's sister figure, simile, is also employed in Scripture. It is very fully used in Ezekiel 1, climaxing in verse 28 when Ezekiel says, not that he saw God, but rather, 'This was the appearance of the likeness of the glory of the LORD.' The terms 'appearance', 'likeness' and 'glory', each building on its predecessor, suggest a revelation needing description but actually never fully describable. Even the final term, 'glory', is itself described by a simile, that of fire, in Exodus 24:17.[32]

The likeness and unlikeness of God and human beings

We understand the perfect archetype from the imperfect copy
In many passages God and humans are said to be unlike.[33] As we have seen already, anthropomorphism is the conceptual starting point even when God is viewed as different from human beings, for each negative, either stated or implied, starts from a positive known to us. So, for instance, to say that God is immutable is meaningful to us from our own experience of change.

---

30. J. Sanders, 'Historical Considerations', in Pinnock et al., *The Openness of God*, p. 17.

31. S. McFague, *Models of God: Theology for an Ecological, Nuclear Age* (Philadelphia: Fortress, 1987).

32. This in turn reminds the reader of the fire theophany in Exod. 3:1–4.

33. e.g. Num. 23:19; 1 Sam. 15:29; Isa. 46:5, 55:8–9; Hos. 11:9; Acts 17:29; Rom. 1:22; 1 Tim. 6:16.

Likeness does not necessarily rule out some unlikeness[34] and metaphor implies contrast as well as comparison, because metaphor is never identity. So in the nature of the case God must be both like and unlike human beings. Walter Brueggemann says, 'The metaphor will be misunderstood and misused if it is not recognized that the One named by the metaphor is not contained or comprehended by the noun.'[35] We know, for instance, from the parable of the dishonest steward (Luke 16:1–9), that God approves of wisdom; we learn from other parts of the Bible that he does not approve of dishonesty.

This is confirmed by the way God is often described. The Bible writers employ many negatives to contrast him with human beings, for although he has made us in his image he has not made us gods (Joel 2:27). Only Psalm 82:6 (quoted by Jesus in John 10:34–35) uses language suggestive of this and this too must have its basis in analogy. Those referred to in this verse have, by his gift, one of his functions, that of acting as judges.

In fact, some passages imply that the difference is greater than the likeness, especially when idolatry is in view, as in Isaiah 46:5 where God says, 'To whom will you compare me or count me equal? To whom will you liken me that we may be compared?' As creatures we are finite and in our fallen state sinful, so that we are unlike God both in our creaturehood and our moral state. His unchangeable nature surely applies in both realms (Jas 1:17; Mal. 4:6), for he is the holy Creator.

Another way Scripture underscores his uniqueness is by using the language of eminence, indicating that God is pre-eminent in some quality, often one he has bestowed on human beings, like power or knowledge. In a particular situation both God and a human being may be present, powerful and knowledgeable, but God is also omnipresent, omnipotent and omniscient. Some passages not stating his pre-eminence nevertheless clearly imply it.[36] This is true of Ephesians 1:11 ('the plan of him who works out everything in conformity with the purpose of his will'), for what is asserted here of God is clearly not

---

34. So, in the Arian debate, the Nicene Christians saw the *homoian* ('alike') and even the *homoiousian* ('alike in nature') formulae used about Father and Son by various groups to be inadequate as not excluding possible dissimilarity of nature.

35. W. Brueggemann, *Theology of the Old Testament: Testimony, Dispute, Advocacy* (Minneapolis: Fortress, 1997), pp. 230–231.

36. e.g. Ps. 103:11–12; v. 13 uses a simple comparison, although of course God's fatherly love is greater than that of humans. Isa. 55:8–9 combines negation and implied pre-eminence.

true of humans, as we see also in Romans 11:33–36, a great passage celebrating his pre-eminence and in which Paul worships him as utterly unique.

In terms of eminence God differs from us in degree, the ultimate degree, while in terms of negation he differs in kind. There can, however, be only one ultimate, so that in both respects he is without peer.

Even when there is no contrast either explicit or implicit between God and ourselves, it is important to remember that any human qualities ascribed to him are found in their perfection only in him. Isaiah says that a woman may forget her child, but God will not forget Israel; his love is perfect (Isa. 49:15–16). J. K. Mozley points out that love, joy, anger, jealousy and repentance are 'all ascribed to God, differing from their application to humans only by their conformity with God's perfect righteousness'.[37]

Negation, eminence, perfection – in all these ways the Bible writers show the awesome uniqueness of the one true and living God.

Some passages refer both to his likeness and his unlikeness. Psalm 103:13–15 identifies two points of dissimilarity and one of similarity. It is particularly striking that in Isaiah 40:18 and 25 the affirmations of Yahweh's incomparability over against the products of the idol-makers occur in a chapter where anthropomorphism is a most evident feature.

The perfect archetype judges the imperfect copy

Because God and human beings are not only alike but also unlike, we cannot argue that what is true of humans must necessarily be true of God.

Is it better for us to say that God is like us or that we are like him?[38] Unquestionably the latter, because there is much more to God than there is to us even apart from sin, which obviously distinguishes us. It has been truly said that we cannot say 'God' by saying 'man' with a loud voice. Fallibility and sinfulness cannot adequately represent the infallible and all-holy God.[39]

In Psalm 50, God rebukes his people for imagining he needs burnt offerings for sustenance. He says, 'You thought I was altogether like you' (Ps. 50:21). Such thinking can lead to idolatry. If he is like humans, the idolater reasons, then he must have human form. Caneday says, 'Idolatry begins in the imagination by conceiving of God in one's own likeness. Therefore, the Lord

---

37. J. K. Mozley, *The Impassibility of God* (Cambridge: Cambridge University Press, 1926), p. 3.

38. For many centuries analogy and metaphor have been important topics of research and discussion both within philosophy and theology.

39. See Caneday, 'Veiled Glory', pp. 152–153.

guides proper imagination of his anthropomorphic self-disclosure by emphasizing dissimilarity.'[40] Even the most beautiful idol insults the true and living
God. Idolatry is largely based on a faulty understanding of the significance of
anthropomorphism, and may even be viewed as the ultimate conclusion of
the principles of open theism.

John Sanders says that writers such as Geisler, Ware and Nash (all classical theists) reckon open theism reduces God to human proportions, but he
says that the biblical writers themselves do this. Pointing to Deuteronomy
10:17–18 and Joel 2:13, he says, 'A God who cares about orphans, widows
and aliens? A God who is slow to anger? How anthropomorphic can you get?
According to the authors cited above, the biblical writers are guilty of reducing God to human proportions.'[41] But this criticism is only valid if the likeness
is total. In fact, God's care and his slowness to anger go far beyond what we
see in human beings.

This aspect of anthropomorphism may be well illustrated from Isaiah
40 – 48, where the nature and qualities of the God of Israel are frequently
contrasted, either explicitly or implicitly, with both the gods of Babylon and
human beings. This was clearly intended to encourage the exiles in Babylon,
who may well have been overawed by its grandiose idols.

God through his prophet may use anthropomorphic language to describe
himself and his actions, but human beings are not at liberty to portray him
in human or some other idolatrous physical form. Chapter 40 emphasizes
that Yahweh is the Creator of the universe and chapter 41 that he is the Lord
of history, and these themes are never far out of sight in the chapters that
follow.

In these chapters there is quite special emphasis on his power to predict
the future, so that the present situation of the people was foreknown, as
also were God's actions for them in days to come (Isa. 41:21–29; 42:9; 43:9;
44:7–8; 48:3–8). The total impression of these chapters on the reader is quite
overwhelming, yet at the same time the loving concern of God for his people
comes through clearly (e.g. Isa. 40:1, 9–11; 41:8–20, etc.). The prophet exalts
Yahweh in order to encourage the people to trust in him.[42]

---

40. ibid., p. 178.

41. J. Sanders in S. E. Porter and A. R. Cross (eds.), *Semper Reformandum: Essays in
    Honour of Clark H. Pinnock* (Carlisle: Paternoster, 2003), p. 116.

42. The fourth book of Psalms was probably organized around the same time, and
    with the same general purpose. See G. W. Grogan, *Praise, Prayer and Prophecy: A
    Theology of the Book of Psalms* (Fearn: Christian Focus, 2001), pp. 225–235.

These chapters bring out the significance of the great name, I AM, which features so importantly in Exodus 3, showing more of the significance of that name, which is clearly alluded to in Isaiah 43:13, 46:4 and 48:12. The first person singular is often employed in relation to God in the section of the prophecy which begins at chapter 40, which would remind the people of the great Exodus revelation.

Here then God is revealed as both comparable and incomparable. Is there a more obviously anthropomorphic chapter in Scripture than Isaiah 40? Yet here God asks, "'To whom will you compare me? Or who is my equal?' says the Holy One' (Isa. 40:25; cf. v. 18 and 46:5), and the chapters which follow often criticize and even lampoon idolaters for their folly in misusing anthropomorphism by creating images for worship. When the Bible uses negatives about God, we know from experience what is being negated, but not what God's existence is like in terms of his negative attributes, except in so far as he tells us.

The interpretation of anthropomorphism

Anthropomorphism needs to be interpreted both exegetically and theologically (i.e. through biblical theology), so that its significance both in particular Bible books and in the whole context of the biblical revelation may be seen.

In Psalm 121:3–4, for instance, the psalmist says that God neither slumbers nor sleeps, while in Jeremiah, God frequently speaks of rising up early to send the prophets to his people (see e.g. Jer. 7:13; 25:3–4; 29:19, all KJV).[43] Both these apparently contradictory images in their differing contexts reveal the abiding concern of God for his people, in the first case to protect them and in the second to instruct them. In another case, also in Jeremiah, Caneday sees the words 'which I did not command, nor did it come into my mind' (Jer. 7:31; 19:5; 32:35) as a rebuke, 'an intensive idiom to express what is unthinkable', in other words, 'I thought better of you.'[44]

We now need to consider how this general principle relates to issues raised by open theism.

The basic question: is God immutable or mutable?

This question is very important. Classical theism teaches the immutability of God, but this is challenged by open theists. They say change is an essential aspect of interpersonal relations and that intercessory prayer in particular may

---

43. Most modern versions reduce this vivid language to a dull paraphrase. This may express the thought faithfully, but all its power to engage with the imagination is lost.

44. Caneday, 'Veiled Glory', p. 194.

effect alteration in the plans of God, in detail although not necessarily overall. They take literally passages where he is said to change his mind.

In Psalm 102:26–27 and James 1:17, God is said to be unchangeable in relation to the created universe. Other passages state the unchangeable nature of his purposes (e.g. Isa. 14:24–27; Eph. 3:11; Heb. 7:17), and as we have already seen Ephesians 1:11 teaches that his purposes are all-encompassing. Purpose reflects character and God is utterly faithful.

There are passages where in contrast to human beings it is said that God does not change his mind, but is true to his promise of blessing (e.g. Num. 23:19) or his threat of judgment (e.g. 1 Sam. 15:29). In each case the context shows that what is at issue is God's character as revealed in his declared word. The people of Israel shared their father Jacob's unreliability, but Jacob's God was unchanging in his attitude to them (Mal. 3:6). The frequency of the Hebrew word *ḥesed* [45] underlines this. Imagery such as the rock suggests both strength and stability. In view of this, it is not easy to accept the idea of a God whose outlook and plans may be subject to change, especially if his knowledge of the future is complete.

Yet it must be admitted that in numerous passages God is said to or is seen to change his mind in his dealings with people (e.g. Gen. 6:5; Amos 7:1–6; Jon. 4:1–2). Rice says, 'So important is the notion of divine repentance in biblical thought that it deserves to be regarded as one of the central themes of Scripture. It represents "an important uninterpreted vehicle for understanding the divine activity throughout the canon".'[46] He here quotes Fretheim.

What are we to say to this? Taken literally, these two sets of passages are irreconcilable, but when God is said to change this is normally because those with whom he is dealing have changed, either for good or ill – mostly the latter, although in Jonah 4:1–2 it is the former. Far from suggesting ontological change, an actual change of nature, this actually implies immutability, for it means that unlike humans God remains consistent in his approval of godliness and his disapproval of sin. This is surely the hermeneutical key to the matter. We need to use ordinary canons of exegesis and take full account of each context.

Hosea 11:8–9 may seem strange, with its portrayal of God as deeply, passionately and irrevocably committed to Israel, for wayward Israel had not changed, but this passage shows that God will preserve her despite her sin because of his abiding loving purpose for her, which is foundational to the

---

45. Normally rendered 'unfailing love' in the NIV.
46. Rice, 'Biblical Support for a New Perspective', p. 34.

whole prophecy of Hosea. She is in covenant with him by his grace and although he will judge he will not destroy her as he destroyed Admah and Zeboiim (Gen. 14:8). The prophetic books contain not only many warnings of judgment, but many promises of salvation, showing that God's long-term purpose of blessing was not negated by such judgments as the exile. Hence God's wrath *against Israel* is his 'strange work' (Isa. 28:21).

Why is God represented as regretting that he made Saul king? Surely to remind the hearers of his moral nature and the standards he requires of people in general and kings in particular.

Although immutability is the main issue, the need for careful interpretation relates to other matters too. Caneday asks, 'If all God's revelation comes to us analogically, as creatures made in his image, how should we understand God's self-disclosure as one who asks questions, who uses common human idioms, who regrets, who uses suppositional language?'[47]

The answer is that it is because these are normal human conversational forms and as such are means of conveying truth to us. But we must understand them in the context of the Bible as a whole. John Frame says of this kind of language, 'Exegesis of these texts must take into account both their surface meaning and what the rest of Scripture teaches about God.'[48] Always there is positive revelatory content in such passages as in the rest of Scripture.

Fretheim sees a need for this kind of interpretation, seeing one purpose of the conversations between God and prophets like Jeremiah and Hosea to be to elicit repentance. He says,

> The announcements of judgment are 'interrupted' with such divine questions in order to move Israel to repentance . . . When God shares such questions with Israel about its own future, God's questions then become questions for Israel, and they are drawn into the process of moving toward an answer. The people now have a role to play in determining what the answer to the question will be, not unlike that given by a rebellious child when asked by the parent 'What am I going to do with you?'[49]

Some open theists appear to be dealing largely with a misunderstanding, for God's immutability is really to do with his nature and character, not his

---

47. Caneday, 'Veiled Glory', p. 193.

48. J. W. Frame, *No Other God: A Response to Open Theism* (Phillipsburg: Presbyterian and Reformed, 2001), p. 48.

49. T. E. Fretheim, *The Suffering of God: An Old Testament Perspective* (Philadelphia: Fortress, 1984), p. 55.

actions. Rice appears to recognize this, yet still writes of God changing when it is his actions that are in view.[50] The real issue is whether God changes his original intention(s). Open theists say 'Yes!' but classical theists say 'No!' Just as we must distinguish the person and work of Christ, who he is and what he does,[51] so we must distinguish immutability and immobility.

In our personal dealings with others we normally look for two things. The first is the reliability of confirmed character. If we feel the need of this at the human level, how much more in our relations with God! 'Change and decay in all around I see, O Thou who changest not, abide with me.'[52] When Luther and his friend Melanchthon were finding life difficult in the strenuous days of the Reformation, they used to sing Psalm 46 together as an assurance that the unchanging God would protect them. David Livingstone took great encouragement from the words, 'I am with you always, even to the end of the age' (Matt. 28:20). The various forms of the grace of our unchanging God (1 Pet. 4:10) are more than equal to our ever-changing circumstances. Rice, in fact, seems close to classical theism when he says that God is 'unchangeable in essence but ever changing in the relationships of love he values'.[53]

Also, in our dealings with others, we look for a degree of flexible sensitivity. Do we find this in God in the realm of petitionary and intercessory prayer, and does this actually change God's mind? Certainly many passages suggest it. Bruce Ware and John Frame in their helpful books on open theism both take them seriously, but are surely right to view them in the context of the eternal purposes of God. Ware says, 'God does not change in his essential nature, purposes, will, knowledge or wisdom, but he does interact with his people in the experience of their lives as these unfold in time. God actually enters into relationship with his people, while knowing from eternity all that they will face.'[54] We should never regard the eternal counsels of God as ruling out

---

50. Rice, 'Biblical Support for a New Perspective', pp. 47–48.

51. Much modern theology avoids ontological questions by merging Christ's person in his work, so that Christ is what he does and this must suffice us. But it cannot suffice us, for it does not suffice Scripture, which presents him as both God and man, yet as one Person.

52. H. F. Lyte, 'Abide With Me', in *Methodist Hymn Book* (London: Methodist Conference, 1933), no. 948, p. 362.

53. In Pinnock, *Most Moved Mover*, p. 86.

54. Ware, *God's Lesser Glory*, pp. 73–74. Frame deals with the whole issue, including conditional prophecies, very helpfully, in *No Other God*, pp. 161–178.

any of the activities he has commanded us to engage in, such as prayer and evangelism.

It is important to see the whole issue of prayer in the light of Romans 8:26–27,[55] where Paul highlights the role of the Holy Spirit in guiding us to pray in accordance with God's will. This means that prayer that finds an answer does not only end at the throne of God, for it also starts there. So then, effective Christian prayer is God's gracious way of giving us a share in accomplishing his eternal purposes. If this is true under the new covenant, it must surely also have been true under the old. The initiative in such availing prayer is always with God. Perhaps, then, we should always begin our prayer times by saying, 'Lord, teach us to pray' (Luke 11:1).

Other interpretative issues

We need to consider further both the omnipotence and the omniscience of God and also his impassibility. Before we can adequately consider them, however, we must give thought to the nature of human freedom and the implications of the incarnation, the cross and the Trinity.

The Bible writers do not constantly introduce caveats or reminders of God's uniqueness, and if they had done so the Bible would be an almost unreadable book. But we are left to interpret each passage in the light of the whole revelation.

The character of God

The study of God's character as revealed in Scripture is of immense importance.

The essential nature of God

Although there may be some differences of emphasis, open theists all regard love as God's dominant character quality[56] and see emphasis on it as the chief feature of their outlook. In introducing their symposium, *The Openness of God*, Pinnock says, 'Love and not freedom was our central concern because it was God's desire for loving relationships which required freedom.'[57] Sanders too

---

55. cf. perhaps Eph. 6:18.

56. This issue is important for the theme of the next chapter, but is considered briefly here in order to integrate these chapters theologically.

57. Pinnock et al., *The Openness of God*, p. 3.

maintains that his concern is much more to show that God is love than to deal with the problems of evil and freedom.[58]

In fact they often treat God's love as his essence. So Rice says,

> From a Christian perspective, *love* is the first and last word in the biblical portrait of God . . . The statement *God is love* is as close as the Bible comes to giving us a definition of the divine reality . . . and . . . indicates that love is central, not incidental, to the nature of God. Love is not something God happens to do, it is the one divine activity that most fully and vividly discloses God's inner reality. Love, therefore, is the essence of the divine nature. Love is what it means to be God.[59]

He also affirms that 'love is . . . the basic source from which *all* of God's attributes arise. This means that the assertion *God is love* incorporates all there is to say about God'.[60] Rather than demonstrating this (and how vitally important for his viewpoint such a demonstration is!) he simply goes on to expound it.

But is any attribute so definitive of God's essence as to control our understanding of all the others? Only if Scripture makes an unambiguous statement to this effect, for otherwise we have no authority for such an identification – but does it?

Without doubt the brief repeated statement 'God is love' is extremely impressive (1 John 4:8, 16). The context shows it to be based on the revelation of God's love in the person and work of Jesus. But the very epistle in which it occurs presents us with another statement in the same form, 'God is light' (1 John 1:5). Which is the more important and can either be regarded as *the* definitive statement?

It might seem that a case could be made out for either. Certainly 'God is love' is repeated, but John seems to regard 'God is light' as summing up the Christian message about God ('This is the message we have heard from him and declare to you: God is light. . .'), placing it right at the start of his letter, preceded only by a clear reference to the incarnation, the event which revealed it so powerfully. In terms of emphasis, therefore, there is little to choose between the two and therefore we should not make such a choice. Our tendency to choose love rather than light as the essence of God may well say

---

58. J. Sanders, *God who Risks: A Theology of Providence* (Downers Grove: InterVarsity Press, 1998), p. 14.

59. Rice, 'Biblical Support for a New Perspective', pp. 18–19.

60. ibid., p. 21 (italics his).

more about us than about him. Often unbiblical inferences have been made from it, such as denials of the severity of God's judgment. We should note too that in addition to these two statements there is another in the same form: 'God is spirit' (John 4:24).

Love, light, spirit – all these are enormously important aspects of God's being, but no two of them can be resolved into the third. And what about kingship or lordship, which John Bright identified as the central feature of the Old Testament revelation of God and which J. L. Mays sees as the great theme of the theology of the Psalter, in many ways a microcosm of Old Testament theology? This implies supreme power.[61] It may be argued perhaps that power is only significant when there are objects of power, but the act of creation shows that immense power was latent in God's being before its exercise in creation and so must belong to his essence. We must not forget that the New Testament never denies the Old Testament doctrine of God, but rather builds on it.

Pinnock seems more balanced than Rice when he says, 'Love is the mode in which God's power is exercised. God neither surrenders power in order to love nor denies love in the need to rule, but combines love and power perfectly.'[62] Nevertheless, he goes on to say, 'Love is God's essence and power only an attribute.'[63]

Both in English and Greek, sentences like 'God is love' which are of the type *subject–copula–noun complement* do not necessarily imply identity and inter-changeability between the subject and the complement. In the sentence 'lamb is meat', for instance, the two are not identified.

Then all words need definition through other words, for no word exists in a verbal vacuum, but is defined by its context and so by other words. The use of 'love' in contemporary culture clearly shows how important definition of it is and for Christian thought this must be in biblical terms. P. T. Forsyth popular-ized 'holy love' to describe God's character, and this is acceptable except that it makes love substantival and holiness adjectival, and as we shall see holiness needs a higher status than this.

It is best for us to give thorough recognition to the many-sidedness of God's nature. Writing of God's attributes, Frame says, 'Each of them describes everything that God is, from a different perspective.'[64] He also says,

---

61. J. L. Mays, *The Lord Reigns: A Theological Handbook of the Psalms* (Louisville: Westminster John Knox, 1994).

62. Pinnock, *Most Moved Mover*, p. 144.

63. ibid.

64. Frame, *No Other God*, p. 52.

> Rather than making any single attribute central, classical theology teaches that all
> of God's defining attributes are ways of describing his simple essence. So God's
> attributes are not parts or divisions within his nature, but each attribute is necessary
> to his being. Each is essential to him, and therefore his essence includes all of them
> . . . Each is qualified by the others. God's wisdom is an eternal wisdom; his goodness
> is a wise goodness and a just goodness.[65]

The acts of God reveal the union of his attributes, so that when we encounter
God we encounter his fullness.

The special importance of God's moral attributes

All the attributes of God to which Scripture testifies are essential to his being,
but it is right to see his moral qualities as particularly important when we are
considering his dealings with us.[66] Nothing is more basic to any person than
his or her character, and this is true of God. Moral character is the motivat-
ing force in a person, determining his or her purposes, intentions, plans and
consequent actions. God's power as known to us is a channelled power and its
channels are determined by his character.

The Old Testament in particular contains many moving passages in which
God, presented as great in power, shows an equally great gentleness in his
dealings. We see this in Job where God, revealing himself out of the powerful
storm, speaks of his tender care of the animals and deals with Job with gentle
irony, even ironically suggesting he tries sitting on the throne of the universe
(Job 40:6–14)! Isaiah 40 presents him as a God of immense power and yet it
is that God who carries the lambs in his bosom (Isa. 40:11). Such examples
could be multiplied.

To put the moral attributes of God in the first place is not to downgrade
others, nor to see them as somehow not essential to God's being. The open
theists are right when they insist that God exercises his power only as a function of his character, but we have already had cause to doubt whether they
conceive of that character in a way that does justice to his total revelation in
Scripture. We must now explore this more fully.

God's love and his holiness

Many older works on theology tend to regard holiness as God's main moral
attribute and to see some of his other qualities and activities like righteousness,

---

65. ibid., p. 51.
66. ibid., pp. 50–56.

justice and wrath as its manifestations, while many more recent works instead emphasize love and its manifestations in mercy, grace, compassion and so forth. In fact, as we learn from broad-based study of the whole Bible, from the revelation of God's character in Christ and particularly from the cross, both qualities are ultimate and are perfectly united in his profoundly integrated character.

We have already noted the importance of John's statement, 'This is the message we have heard from him and declare to you: God is light and in him is no darkness at all' (1 John 1:5). The context shows that God's light reveals and judges the darkness of sin.

Also we must ask what 'God' would mean to this letter's readers. For the whole New Testament it is a word filled with Old Testament content and the Old Testament presents God as not only loving and gracious to his people, but also as awesomely holy and with a deep passion for justice.[67]

But could John's statement 'God is love' mean 'This word "God" used to suggest power and holiness, but now it should mean love'? No, for the whole epistle is strongly moral, and between the two occurrences of 'God is love', John says, 'This is love: not that we loved God, but that he loved us, and sent his Son as an atoning sacrifice for our sins' (1 John 4:10). Love deals with sin because love is concerned with holiness.

Certainly 'holiness', signifying separateness or distinctness,[68] concerns not only God's character but other qualities such as his transcendence, but it is so clear in Scripture that there is in God a total commitment to moral purity and rejection of all that is evil. The affirmations 'I am holy' and 'I am Yahweh' come with great frequency in Leviticus, for all its legislation is related to who and what God is. In Isaiah, the expression 'the holy one of Israel' binds the whole book together.

The term 'open theism' implies that in love God is open to the world and to persons. It raises the question as to whether the Bible views him as self-contained, with no need outside himself. This has to be asked, because if 'holiness' is indeed 'separateness', this implies he is self-sufficient, and this is suggested too by Romans 11:35–36:

> Who has ever given to God,
>   that God should repay him?
> For from him and through him and to him are all things.
>   To him be the glory for ever! Amen.

---

67. See Packer, *Knowing God*, p. 132.

68. This is widely held by biblical scholars to be its basic meaning.

We should remember that a person may be self-sufficient and yet self-giving, not to meet some internal personal need but for the sake of others. In his work on the Trinity, Augustine maintained that there is a sense in which God is both self-contained and yet open even within his triune life, for he saw love as what binds the three holy Persons together in their triunity.[69] God does not need to express love beyond his triune life, but he chooses to do so. Pinnock is right when he says, 'God did not need to create in order to love. He chose to create in order to share love.'[70] This is, of course, supremely true of God's redemptive grace in Christ.

Does this aspect of Augustine's trinitarian doctrine mean that love is more fundamental to God than any other attribute and therefore that the open theists are right? No, for if the three were not holy, there could be no perfect expression of love, because love that is not holy is not God's love. There can be no love revealed in a universe in which holiness also is not ultimate. If evil were to be allowed to remain among God's people in his eternal community, this would not manifest love, for it would make a hell out of heaven. As we shall see in the next chapter, these two great attributes were expressed in perfect unity at the cross.

We may perhaps with due reverence think of God as like a city surrounded by impregnable walls but with a broad gate.[71] The walls save its integrity from violation while the gate enables blessing to be outpoured to all around. God's holy perfection secures that he has so much to give for the loving and holy enrichment of his people.

God's love and his wrath

How does God's wrath relate to his love? Pinnock says,

> God becomes wrathful because he loves us. God would not become angry if he was not loving. If he did not care about the creature, there would be neither love nor wrath . . . Wrath does not belong to God's nature in the way that love does. It arises out of the pathos of love. God becomes angry because he is love. He does not become wrathful spontaneously out of his nature.[72]

This is misleading. Certainly the acts of God are motivated by love but also by holiness (which often manifests itself in wrath against sin) and never by one

---

69. Augustine, 'On the Holy Trinity', in *The Nicene and Post-Nicene Fathers*, vol. 3 (Grand Rapids: Eerdmans, 1974), pp. 125–133.

70. Pinnock, *Most Moved Mover*, p. 28.

71. Pinnock accepts this, *The Openness of God*, p. 108.

72. ibid., p. 83.

without the other. For instance, when God opened the Red Sea, this was an act both of holy love and of holy wrath, with Israel experiencing the former and the Egyptians the latter.

Rice refers to Psalm 30:5, 'His anger lasts only a moment, but his favour lasts a lifetime', and he compares Exodus 34:6 and Isaiah 54:8 with this. We should note, though, that these passages all refer to God's dealings with his covenant people and have his ultimate purpose for them in view. How different, for instance, is what Paul says about the manifestation of God's wrath against sin in Romans 1:18–32! Rice also says of God's wrath that it is always described 'as a moment, something that happens rather than something that abides',[73] but this is to ignore John 3:36, which says, 'Whoever rejects the Son will not see life, but God's wrath remains on him.'

The God who shows wrath is at the same time the God of love. To leave sin unjudged is unloving, for it means that God has surrendered the perfection of his universe, and this must be to the detriment of the creatures he made in love to inhabit it and those he has redeemed in love as part of his new creation. The final judgment could be viewed also as the final redemption, for through it everything will be judged which hinders the perfect expression of God's loving purpose for his people. Psalm 96 shows God's people rejoicing when he comes to judge the earth. Why? Surely because it shows his holy and loving concern to put all things right!

God's character and Christian character

This has important implications for us as Christians, for it is God's character revealed supremely in Christ which furnishes the standard to which the Holy Spirit works in our sanctification. To play down either holiness or love in our thinking and living of the Christian life is to be in danger either of sentimentality or harshness, both alien to Christ's perfect character. Obeying God and loving him and others are not alternatives for the Christian, but rather each is bound up with the other.

Understanding human freedom

Frame says, 'In my judgment, the concept of human freedom in the libertarian sense is the engine that drives open theism, often called freewill theism. For the open theists, libertarian free will serves as a kind of grid, through which

---

73. Rice, 'Biblical Support for a New Perspective', pp. 20–21.

all other theological assertions must pass – a general criterion for testing the truth of all other doctrines.'[74] The open theists are concerned to preserve human freedom because they tie human responsibility to it.

The power and knowledge of God

Classical and open theists agree that God is all-powerful, although open theists say he deliberately limited his power to accommodate decisions made by free persons. Classical theism certainly teaches that God is by no means doing all the time all that he can do; he has decided courses of action according to his purposes, which determine the channelling of his power. The question is whether these decisions are still being made because of contingent factors due to the decisions of others. This raises sharply the issue of human freedom.

God's knowledge is a subject of sharp disagreement between the two parties. There is much discussion of what is called Middle Knowledge (or Molinism),[75] of counter-factuals, the view that God knows what would or could happen in any given circumstance. Such questions seem speculative and it is easy to get tied up in logical knots, but if God is truly omniscient then his knowledge in all these realms must surely be complete. Clearly knowledge of what has happened, is happening and will happen is knowledge of facts, but so also is knowledge of counter-factuals, for if a fact is defined as something that exists, then ideas too are facts.

Sometimes it is asked whether, if God knew what was going to happen, he could alter it, thus pitting God's knowledge and his power against each other, but this is to contemplate an absurdity.

Varieties of determinism

It should be evident by now that freedom badly needs definition, and definition in relation to determinism, which has several forms.

There is *philosophical* determinism. H. D. Lewis calls the problem of freewill 'one of the most persistent and perplexing of all philosophical problems'.[76] The question of freedom and determinism is especially important for philosophies of development, like Aristotelianism and a number that arose in the nineteenth and twentieth centuries, notably Hegelianism, Marxism, evolutionism

---

74. Frame, *No Other God*, p. 119.

75. Named after Luis de Molina, a sixteenth-century Jesuit.

76. H. D. Lewis, *Philosophy of Religion* (London: English Universities Press, 1965), p. 268.

and process philosophy.[77] In all these, diverse as they are, the universe is seen to be so constituted that all things move towards a predetermined end, predictable if we had perfect knowledge. So no beings, divine, superhuman or human, have a freedom which can influence the result. *Historical* determinism, the philosophy of Marxism, is a particular application of this.

Then there is *psychological* determinism, which is consistent with philosophical determinism but focuses on human action. On this view freedom is an illusion because our personal actions are all determined by our psychological constitution. The behaviourist school of Watson, Skinner and Pavlov held to this and some other psychological schools lean in this direction, so that Freud and Adler, for instance, identified one aspect of the human psyche (sex for Freud and power for Adler) which is particularly determinative of conduct.

Finally there is *self-determinism*, sometimes called 'soft determinism'. The term 'self-determinism' is sometimes used as a virtual synonym for libertarianism, but it is better to reserve it for the view that focuses on the determinative role of character. The most important issue in the debate about freedom concerns moral action and moral responsibility, which involve purpose, motive and intention, all connected to character. In fact it would seem difficult if not impossible to distinguish between personal moral freedom and self-determinism. We are free in that we are able to express what we are. Of course, character is not static, but is moulded by various influences, such as heredity and education.

As H. D. Lewis says, 'There is an obvious continuity between character and conduct,'[78] and of course character refers to what we are and conduct to what we do because of what we are. This does not mean our awareness of freedom and moral struggle is an illusion, but it does mean that I, and so my character, will determine what choice I eventually make. The choice is determined from within my character, not apart from it. A. A. Hodge is surely right in saying, 'A man freely chooses what he wants to choose. He would not choose freely if he chose in any other way. But his desire . . . is determined by his whole intellectual and emotional state at the time.'[79] This certainly appears to be in line with the teaching of Jesus in Matthew 7:15–20 and Luke 6:43–45, where he speaks of the heart as the source of our moral conduct.

---

77. The fact that evolutionism is so congenial to Marxism is largely because they are both deterministic philosophies.
78. Lewis, *Philosophy of Religion*, p. 269.
79. A. A. Hodge, *The Confession of Faith: A Handbook on Christian Doctrine Expounding the Westminster Confession* (Edinburgh: Banner of Truth, 1958), p. 160.

If all personal beings are self-determined, it is a great source of assurance to us that this is true even of God, so that we can rely on his total consistency.

Libertarianism or *indeterminism*, the view espoused by open theism, holds that the only free choices are those where we have genuine options and are not determined by any forces, either within or without. Frame says, 'This position assumes that there is a part of human nature that we might call the will, which is independent of every other aspect of our being, and which can, therefore, make a decision contrary to every motivation.'[80]

A weakness in libertarianism and a consequent strength in self-determinism is the difficulty of isolating the will from other aspects of the inner life. A person is sometimes said to act out of character, but this may simply mean there are aspects of that person's character normally out of sight that are occasionally expressed. An important exception to this, and a wonderful one too, is when God changes a person's character by the internal working of his grace.

Freedom in Scripture and in the current theological debate

In his critique of open theism, Frame summarizes its libertarianism by saying that 'if our decisions are caused by anything or anyone (including our own desires), they are not properly our decisions, and we cannot be held responsible for them'.[81] If this were true we could not be held responsible for breaches of the Tenth Commandment, which is all about wrong desires, and it appears to have been this very commandment that most clearly showed Paul he was a sinner (Romans 7:7–8). James too declares that sin is due to 'our own evil desire' (Jas 1:14).

Not all open theists hold consistently to the libertarian view of freedom, for, as Frame points out, Boyd and Pinnock both concede that sometimes God overrides the human will, as for instance when a person has consistently refused God's way and so he hardens them or when their action is absolutely necessary for some special purpose.[82] These cases are, however, significantly different. The former does not completely negate open theist principles, for open theists believe, as all evangelicals do, that God eventually calls a halt to every human life and that this is followed by judgment. In such a case the end of opportunity simply comes at some point before death. The latter, however,

---

80. Frame, *No Other God*, p. 121.

81. ibid., p. 121.

82. G. A. Boyd, *God of the Possible* (Grand Rapids: Baker, 2000), p. 38; Pinnock, 'Systematic Theology', p. 116.

is wholly different, for in it God's sovereignty overrides human moral choice as this is understood in open theism.

Scripture teaches that in human beings self-expression is corrupted by sin, so that in an important sense they are not free. Jonathan Edwards, the great eighteenth-century American preacher, theologian and philosopher, who wrote a classic work on the issue, distinguished between natural and moral ability. We have natural ability, for we are endowed with all that is needed for choosing in terms of mental and volitional abilities, but because we are sinful our desires and therefore our choices are directed not towards God's will, but rebelliously away from it. Morally we are unable to do God's will, while it is the possession of the natural abilities that renders us responsible.[83] We are helpless, yet responsible.

The wonder of the gospel is that the grace of God in Christ meets us in our enslavement to sin and sets us free (John 6:44; Eph. 2:1–10; Col. 2:13), and this freedom in Christ is the truest freedom, for there is no bondage worse than sin. When the grace of God works within us, this radically alters our choices and our actions and sets us free to do what now we most want to do: trust and love, serve and worship the Christ who has thus given us freedom. To know this personally is a marvellous experience of God's grace.

The main views on the relationship between divine sovereignty and human responsibility

Theologically, there have been four main views on this issue.

1. *Hyper-Calvinism* places all the emphasis on divine sovereignty and therefore plays down or even denies the significance of human decision.
2. *Classical Arminianism*, while holding in general terms that without God's grace there would be no salvation and that there can be no salvation by works, emphasizes the crucial importance of the individual human will in salvation.
3. *Wesleyan Arminianism* takes the depraving effects of sin on human nature seriously and holds that, left to himself or herself, no human being could be saved, but that God in his 'prevenient grace' has restored to all the ability to believe,[84] so that when the gospel is presented, saving grace may be embraced or rejected in freedom.

---

83. J. Edwards, *Freedom of the Will* (New York: Cosimo Classics, 2007).

84. So that faith is a gift of God, as Charles Wesley wrote, '*Give* me the faith which can remove and sink the mountain to a plain' (italics mine), *Methodist Hymn Book*, no. 390, p. 150.

4. *Classical or compatibilist*[85] *Calvinism* accepts both God's full sovereignty over all that exists and all that happens, but also the full responsibility of human beings to repent and believe.

Because there are many passages emphasizing the importance of repentance and faith, but also others affirming God's sovereignty in salvation, it is difficult, it seems to me, in the full light of Scripture to hold to either Hyper-Calvinism or Classical Arminianism.

Numerous Old Testament passages stress the importance of human choice (e.g. Deut. 30:19; Josh. 24:15 and 1 Kgs 18:21), while all the preaching recorded in the Acts of the Apostles includes an appeal to the hearers to repent or to believe or to be baptized or a combination of these. Paul said we are all commanded to repent (Acts 17:30) and he used persuasion in preaching the gospel (2 Cor. 5:11). We must not play down the call of God to humans to act responsibly and to repent and believe. On the other hand, when any unclear passages have been eliminated, there is a hard core of passages difficult to interpret along Arminian lines. These include Psalm 33:13–15; Mark 4:11–12; John 6:40–52; Acts 13:48; Romans 9:1–29; Ephesians 1:11 and 2 Thessalonians 2:10–12.

What about Wesleyan Arminianism? The doctrine of prevenient grace moved Wesleyan Arminianism somewhat nearer to Calvinism and without doubt many find it attractive. Pinnock is right, however, in saying that its biblical basis is thin. The passages quoted for it include Genesis 6:3; Jeremiah 1:5; 31:3; John 1:9; 6:44; 12:32; 16:8–11; Acts 2:37; 16:14; 17:4; Romans 2:4–5 and Titus 2:11. In fact all these passages may be interpreted in other ways and none seems unambiguously to assert prevenient grace in Wesley's sense of the term. We cannot here give the Wesleyan Arminian position the attention its wide influence deserves, because open theists have in fact abandoned it and it is open theism that is the subject of this chapter.

For many of its adherents, open theism has involved movement from Wesleyan Arminianism into Classical Arminianism, which is then taken to its logical conclusion. In commenting on his theological pilgrimage Pinnock says, 'The Bible has no developed doctrine of prevenient grace, however convenient it would be for us if it did.'[86] He therefore opts for open theism.

---

85. The significance of this word in this connection will be explored later. See pp. 65–66.

86. C. H. Pinnock (ed.), *The Grace of God and the Will of Man* (Minneapolis: Bethany House, 1995), p. 22.

A number of considerations must be borne in mind as we address this issue.

The relationship between God's sovereignty and human responsibility

Scripture clearly teaches both, and in many passages they are set side by side. Mark Talbot refers to Genesis 50:20 as evidence of God ordaining something evil for a good purpose. Joseph explains the one event in two ways. The difference is in the intent of God and that of the brothers (Gen. 45:5–8 and 50:20; cf. Ps. 105:16–22 and Acts 7:9–11.). He points out that Joseph twice says God sent him to Egypt (Gen. 45:5, 7) and that he stresses the point by saying, 'So it was not you who sent me here, but God' (v. 8). Moreover, 'In Genesis 45:4–8, what Joseph attributes to God is *not* the evil inherent in his brothers' act of selling him into Egypt but only the good involved in God's sending him there before his brothers "to preserve life" (45:5).'[87] He then says, 'It was Joseph's brothers' free and unfettered and wicked intention to do him harm; it was God's free and unfettered and good intention that Joseph's brothers would freely intend to do him harm, but that their free act would actually bring good to him and many others.'[88]

In Exodus God is said to harden Pharaoh's heart (e.g. in Exod. 4:21; 9:12; 10:1), but Pharaoh is also said to harden his own heart (Exod. 8:15, 32; 9:34). In Isaiah 10:5–7 God sends Assyria as the instrument of his judgment, but Assyria is very differently motivated (cf. Judg. 14:3–4). In the book of Job, what Job and his friends say and do on earth they say and do freely, but behind the scenes we see God and Satan, with God firmly in control but allowing Satan certain circumscribed actions which in fact serve God's purpose of testing Job (Job 1 and 2).

The crucifixion was both a predestined act of amazing grace on God's part and an expression of great human wickedness (Luke 22:22; Acts 2:23; 3:14–15; 4:28; cf. Acts 13:29). Earlier the wilderness temptations of Jesus had shown the malignity of Satan, but he was led to the wilderness by the Spirit, for what Satan had intended as temptations God meant as testing (Matt. 4:1). In 2 Corinthians 12:7–8 a thorn in the flesh is given to Paul, and God's intention was to keep him from pride while Satan's was to harass him. So many passages show us that God sometimes uses the evil acts of personal beings for a larger good, as he did also in the story of Joseph.

---

87. M. R. Talbot, 'True Freedom: The Liberty that Scripture Portrays as Worth Having', in Piper et al., *Beyond the Bounds*, p. 92.

88. ibid., p. 99.

The most sustained example of this principle is to be found in the epistle to the Romans. We may well suspect that Paul had himself been wrestling with this issue on a large, national scale, because of the way so many Jews had rejected the message of the gospel as he had preached it to them. Here he writes first at length about God's sovereign choice (Rom. 9:1–29), and then at almost equal length about human responsibility (Rom. 9:30 – 10:21). He then indicates that God's gracious acceptance of the Gentiles may, indeed will, lead to Israel's repentance (Rom. 11:23–34). Here again God is seen to use acts of human sin to further his good purposes.

John Bright sees both the Mosaic and Davidic covenants to be covenants of God's grace, but the Mosaic emphasizes more the obligations of Israel and the Davidic more God's immutable purpose. He says that the church too lives under both patterns: 'It is the tension between grace and obligation.'[89]

It seems therefore that the Bible is compatibilist. By this is meant that its writers do not play down either God's sovereignty or human responsibility, clearly regarding them as both true and therefore as compatible, *whether this can be proved or not*. We can be sure, not only that they are compatible with each other in God's mind, but also that they will be seen ultimately to be fully compatible with his perfect holiness, love and wisdom.

Talbot, in a fine chapter, has well said,

> We cannot understand how divine and human agency are compatible in such a way that allows the exercise of each kind of agency to be fully explanatory of some event's coming about. Yet – and this is the absolutely crucial point – we *can* understand why we cannot understand it. It is because attempts on our part to understand it involve our trying to understand the unique relationship between the Creator and his creatures in terms of our understanding of some creature-to-creature relationship. But this attempt, it should be clear, involves us in a kind of 'category mistake' that dooms our attempt from the start. A *category mistake* involves attempting to think about something under the wrong category.[90]

Once again, then, as in our study of anthropomorphism, we see that God and human beings are not only comparable but incomparable, and that God's ways are not our ways.

Don Carson has well said,

---

89. J. Bright, *Covenant and Promise: The Future in the Preaching of the Pre-Exilic Prophets* (London: SCM, 1977), p. 198.

90. Talbot, 'True Freedom', p. 99 (italics his).

From God's knowledge and sovereignty we must not justify prayerlessness; from the exhortations to pray and not give up, we must not suppose God is coerced by our much speaking (compare Matt. 6:7–8 and Luke 18:1). Precisely because God is so gloriously rich and complex a being, we must draw out the lessons the biblical writers draw out, and no others.[91]

The relationship between foreordination and foreknowledge

Both Calvinists and open theists see clearly that foreordination and fore-knowledge belong together, but they draw different conclusions from this fact. Calvinists argue that God knows the future because he has foreordained it, while open theists deny comprehensive foreknowledge because they deny comprehensive foreordination. They do accept, however, that God has determined to act in certain specific ways in the future, and therefore that he has foreknowledge of these things. They argue that if God has *detailed* knowledge of the future including the decisions and actions of human beings, this means it is fixed and unalterable so that no place can then be found for human freedom even within a compatibilist theology, for such freedom must be totally illusory.

Arminians often approach the interpretation of such passages by appeal-ing to God's foreknowledge, so that it is those foreknown by God to believe who are also described as predestined. They point to the verb 'to foreknow' in Romans 8:28–30,[92] which reappears in Romans 11:2.

If these verses stood on their own, this interpretation would present no problems, but they have to be taken along with other biblical evidence.[93] The verb 'to know', in both the Old and New Testaments, is employed at times to mean 'to enter into a personal relationship with', sometimes there-fore rendered 'choose' in the NIV (Josh. 4:1; Jer. 31:34; Dan. 11:32; Amos 3:2; Matt. 7:23; John 8:19), so that 'to foreknow' in Romans *could* signify 'to determine beforehand to enter into a relationship with'.[94] This would give a different slant to a passage seeming otherwise to be a bar to the Calvinistic interpretation.

---

91. D. A. Carson, *The Gagging of God: Christianity Confronts Pluralism* (Leicester: Apollos, 1996), p. 286.

92. Of course, this is not an approach taken by the open theists, for they reject the idea of God's comprehensive foreknowledge.

93. See the list of passages difficult to reconcile with Arminianism, referred to on p. 63.

94. The same verb is translated 'chosen' in 1 Pet. 1:20 (NIV).

Open theists restrict God's foreknowledge to major features of his future purpose, but Sanders comes close to denying it altogether. He holds that if God foreknew what would happen, he would be quite helpless to alter it and therefore could not answer prayer.[95] Not only so, but, as the God who risks, God can make mistakes. So, for example, he thought Saul would be a good king, but found he had to reject him for David.[96]

It is very difficult to restrict God's foreknowledge in the way the open theists do. It involves taking events out of their historical contexts. In the Bible there are predictions involving named persons as yet unborn: Josiah in 1 Kings 13:2 and Cyrus in Isaiah 44:28 and 45:1 (on the assumption of Isaianic authorship of this part of the book that bears his name) are examples of this. Such predictions of named individuals surely imply knowledge of their historical circumstances and antecedents, involving the actions (presumably self-motivated) of many other persons and even nations.

At what limit, then, can God's future knowledge be set? Surely there can be no limit at all! The interpretation of the book of Revelation bristles with problems for open theism if we accept that it is in any way predictive. To accept any future events as coming within God's knowledge must involve his knowledge of human actions. The most obvious examples concern the drama of the crucifixion, in which the actions of so many human beings were involved.

If God exists simply within a time frame, foreknowledge is a difficult concept, but if he is eternal, the case is different. If he has even the amount of foreknowledge most open theists allow for, this must mean that although acting within history he also stands outside it and views it from an eternal perspective, knowing the end from the beginning.

Malcolm Maclean, in a personal communication, wrote, 'It seems to me that open theism puts the future on the throne and takes God off it, and always has the future as greater than God since he does not know what it is.'

Further aspects of the compatibility principle

Compatibility is not restricted to the issues we have been discussing, as we would expect if it is a factor of major importance. The unity of the three Persons of the Trinity in the one Godhead, the unity of the divine and human natures in the one Person of Christ, the Bible as fully the Word of God and fully the word of man, these are all examples of truths that are not easy to

---

95. Sanders, *God who Risks*, p. 201.

96. ibid., p. 119.

reconcile, but which must be compatible if truth is one. Here are deep mysteries which may be explored but not fully resolved. This does not mean they are ultimately irreconcilable, but only that they meet not in the theological mind, not even in the biblical revelation, but in the mind of God, for 'the secret things belong to the LORD our God' (Deut. 29:29).

Moreover, the truth of them is not just for a season, nor for the duration of the mediatorial reign of Christ. A distinction is often made between an economic view of God (which is about God as he has revealed himself to us) and an ontological one (which is about God as he really is). This distinction may be useful in some ways, but it is most important to recognize that the threefoldness of God is not a kind of 'front', nor is the humanity of Jesus, but that they are utterly real. If it were not so, then revelation would be a lie and we would have no authentic knowledge of God. The same principle is surely true in this matter of divine grace and human responsibility. They must both be for ever true.

The mystery of evil

Evil is present in a world ruled by a perfectly good and holy God and yet is utterly opposed by him, for his commitment to righteousness and his loathing of evil are both total. How, then, did it originate? We know how sin came into human life and with it many evils and that this came through Satanic temptation, but we cannot trace its remote origin. The Bible neither raises nor answers this question, so that it lies beyond the scope of the revelation God has given us.

D. Basinger and R. Basinger, both open theists, discuss the approaches of process theism, open theism and theological determinism and conclude that none of the three is able to deal fully with unjustified evil and that therefore there is no winner, so that all groups are at the same disadvantage.[97] Whether or not these writers have made out their case, it is important to remember that the Bible is very clear both that God is in overall control of the universe and that he is implacably opposed to evil.

This may be the best setting in which to mention passages which refer to God's desire for all to be saved. It is, of course, important to exegete such passages with integrity and yet also in a way that is consistent with biblical teaching as a whole. Arminians often treat them as decisive for their viewpoint, while they are not easy for Calvinists to interpret. The latter often say that

---

97. D. Basinger and R. Basinger, 'Theodicy: A Comparative Analysis', in Porter and Cross (eds.), *Semper Reformandum*, pp. 144–159.

1 Timothy 2:3–4, where Paul refers to 'God our Saviour, who wants all men to be saved', should be understood in the light of the reference to 'kings' (plural) in verse 2, and, following as it does an exhortation to pray for all, as meaning people of every nation. Also 2 Peter 3:9, which says that 'he is patient *with you*' (italics mine), could mean all Christians. Contextually these interpretations, although not certain, are possible.

We may certainly take from these passages that if individuals are not saved this should not be attributed to any reluctance to save on God's part, but rather to the sinner's stubborn refusal to repent and believe which God does not override. The New Testament emphasizes that salvation is always due to God's grace while condemnation takes place because we refuse his way.

Without doubt evil is the ultimate mystery. I have been helped by thinking about the fact that there is an irrational element in our experience of sin. As sinners we know in our hearts that we cannot sin and get away with it; it is in fact the ultimate stupidity, but this does not stop people from indulging in it.[98] Perhaps, then, we are simply too close to it to understand it rationally. As with other mysteries, we need trustfully to leave this in God's hands as something he has not chosen to reveal.

The wisdom of God and the faith of the Christian believer

Holiness and love are often regarded as God's two primary character qualities, but I believe wisdom should be placed alongside them. Both Job and Jeremiah needed to trust the wisdom of God and so did the psalmists when they so often asked, 'Why?' Jesus too on his cross asked 'Why?' but also commended himself trustfully into his Father's hands.

In Romans 9 – 11 Paul attempts no reconciliation of God's sovereignty and human responsibility, and he eventually concludes with Romans 11:33–36 in praise to the God of all wisdom whose paths are beyond tracing out. So he recognizes the limitations of his own mind (even under divine inspiration), and turns to praise as the only appropriate reaction to God's marvellous grace and his unsearchable wisdom.

We should remember the pastoral nature of the New Testament and of the passages which deal with the sovereignty of God, for pastoral concern expresses itself in a deep desire for believers to increase in faith. The doctrine is not intended to torment the introspective but to be encouraging, teaching us that God has everything in hand, that we need fear nothing, and that he

---

98. See the comments of G. C. Berkouwer, *Sin* (Grand Rapids: Eerdmans, 1971), pp. 130–148; and D. Macleod, *Behold your God* (Fearn: Christian Focus, 1990), p. 209.

can be utterly trusted. Because mysteries challenge faith, when that faith is exercised in the face of them they actually promote its growth.

The self-revelation of God in Christ

The incarnation and the cross raise a number of serious issues for our subject. Open theists argue that because God is revealed in Christ, in his human life and death, we can see that God suffers. The cross shows the intensity of that suffering. This has been held in various forms by others besides open theists, but the latter go on to argue that suffering necessarily involves change, so that if God suffers he changes. They also seek support for this contention from God's self-revelation in the Old Testament.

There are obviously two distinct but related issues here. Does God suffer, and, if he does, then does this imply change in him? This involves discussion of God's impassibility.

The impassibility of God

This term or idea occurs in various church confessions. Both the Thirty-nine Articles and the Westminster Confession, for instance, say that God is 'without body, parts or passions'.[99] Impassibility has been much discussed in recent years,[100] and many writers beside open theists have concluded that the term is inappropriate when applied to God. It has not, however, been without defenders and a particularly able defence of it ('brilliant', says Pinnock, who rejects impassibility) has been mounted by the Thomist, Thomas Weinandy.[101]

Much depends on how the word is understood. Does it mean God is never passionate or rather that he is never passive? The two are almost exact

---

99. 'Thirty-nine Articles', in *The Book of Common Prayer* (Oxford: Oxford University Press, n.d.), Article 1, p. 564; R. Shaw, *An Exposition of the Westminster Confession of Faith* (Fearn: Christian Focus, 1973), II.1, p. 23.

100. As long ago as J. K. Mozley in *The Impassibility of God*, published in 1926. Also he mentions that A. M. Fairbairn said, 'Theology has no falser idea than that of the impassibility of God' (*The Place of Christ in Christian Theology*, 2nd ed., London: Hodder and Stoughton, 1893, p. 484), quoted in Mozley, pp. 146–147.

101. T. G. Weinandy, *Does God Suffer?* (Edinburgh: T. & T. Clark, 2000). A Thomist follows the teaching of the thirteenth-century theologian and philosopher Thomas Aquinas.

opposites. Also does 'without passions' mean 'without emotion' or 'without the lower emotions'? In fact, the words 'passible', 'passion' and 'passive' in English all come ultimately from the Latin verb *pati*, 'to suffer'. As words do, they have gone their separate ways somewhat. Moreover, 'impassible' has acquired an emotional tone which certainly suggests unfeeling aloofness.

In fact the impassibility and the passibility of God are both defensible, so such a contradiction reveals a semantic problem. Those promoting these two positions understand the words somewhat differently. There is a striking historical example of this within the writings of one man, for Luther held that Christ's sufferings affected his divine and not simply his human nature, while at the same time he maintained the impassibility of God.

If impassibility is defined as indicating that God is never passive but always active, never simply the reactor but rather the initiator, which is the understanding of the term that Weinandy defends, then this unites two facts that are clearly evident in Scripture: that God is sovereign and that he is the living God. Jürgen Moltmann too denies that God is subject to unwilling suffering, but affirms that he suffers actively, embracing suffering in love.[102] As Pascal said, he is not the God of the philosophers, an object chiefly to be intellectually contemplated, but Abraham's God of the covenant, taking action to accomplish his purposes, including his marvellous purpose of grace.

I propose to set this particular semantic discussion aside meantime and ask what we can learn from the Bible.

The revelation of God in the Old Testament

Fretheim has surveyed the Old Testament material in which emotional language is used of God. He has demonstrated its extensiveness, especially but not only in the prophetic literature.[103]

With reference to Calvary, Nigel Wright says,

> At this horrific place, who and what we consider God to be was reconstructed from the bottom up. God is *most of all* to be found in the cross of Christ . . . This God associates with the lowly, the rejected, the outcast and the godforsaken, and reverses our assumption about how gods, or fathers, or kings and rulers ought to be. He defines himself as the humble God who, whatever his undoubted powers to rule over

---

102. J. Moltmann, *The Crucified God: The Cross of Christ as the Foundation and Criticism of Christian Theology*, tr. J. Bowden (London: SCM, 1974), p. 230; see also Packer, *Knowing God*, p. 133.

103. Fretheim, *The Suffering of God*.

and dispose of his creation, is most truly himself as he has shown himself to be in Christ and his cross.[104]

'Our assumption', referred to by Wright, may be influenced by our culture. It is most important to note, however, that the 'reconstruction' began in the Old Testament, when the true and living God clearly distinguished himself from the gods of the pagans. The situation of a people with a special revelation existing within a larger society did not begin in the New Testament, and not only the life of Jesus but the book of Psalms provides ample evidence that God is concerned for 'the lowly, the rejected, the outcast and the godforsaken'.

In fact this reconstruction started even within 'the Old Testament of the Old Testament' (Moberly),[105] the book of Genesis. Abraham's God showed his great difference from the pagan gods, for example, not at first by expressing his abhorrence of child sacrifice, but rather by calling Abraham to offer his son and then, by his dramatic intervention, showing clearly and once for all that this was not his will but rather that divinely provided substitutionary sacrifice was. We do not have to wait until the New Testament to encounter the God of Calvary, for he is here in Genesis, even though the crucifixion had not yet taken place.

In Genesis 1, God's pleasure at his creation is evident, for the word *ṭôb*, 'good' or 'beautiful', used repeatedly there, seems in such a context to convey the emotion of pleasure. This contrasts greatly with his later grief at human sin, for whatever may be said of God's words 'Where are you?' in Genesis 3, the emotional tone of Genesis 6:6–7, where God's grief and pain at heart are expressed, is unmistakable.[106]

Fretheim says, 'It can reasonably be claimed that the idea of a God who suffered with his people had its roots in the exodus and in the subsequent reflections on the significance of that event.'[107] He refers to Exodus 2:23–25 and 3:7–8, where a Hebrew verb is well translated 'was concerned about' (NIV), and also to Judges 2:18 and 10:16, 'he could bear their misery no longer'.

---

104. N. Wright, *The Radical Evangelical: Seeking a Place to Stand* (London: SPCK, 1996), p. 14 (italics his).

105. R. W. Moberly, *The Old Testament of the Old Testament: Patriarchal Narratives and Moses Yahwism*, Overtures to Biblical Theology (Minneapolis: Fortress, 1992).

106. J. H. Sailhamer points to a word-play between this and Josh. 5:29 and also to the use of 'God saw' in both Josh. 1:31 and 6:6 ('Genesis', in F. E. Gaebelein [ed.], *Expositor's Bible Commentary*, vol. 2, Grand Rapids: Zondervan, 1990, pp. 80–81).

107. Fretheim, *The Suffering of God*, pp. 127–128.

God's main concern in the prophets is with Israel's unfaithfulness to the covenant. In Deuteronomy 5:28–29, he says of Israel's response to the Ten Commandments, 'Everything they said was good. Oh, that their hearts would be inclined to fear me and keep all my commands always, so that it might go well with them and their children for ever!' This seems to be a cry from the very heart of God (cf. Pss 78:40–41; 81:8–14).

Many attitudinal words are applied to God's dealings with Israel, words like love, grace, mercy, compassion and pity, on the one hand, and wrath, indignation and jealousy on the other. In human experience these attitudes are accompanied by emotions. Some other words are necessarily emotional. In Isaiah 63:9, for instance, 'grief' is applied to God's attitude to the people's sin in the wilderness and is the probable background to Ephesians 4:30, where Paul says, 'Do not grieve the Holy Spirit of God.'

The prophets were so identified with God in his concerns for Israel that we often cannot make a clear distinction between them and God. So, for instance, is it God or the prophet who laments over Moab in Isaiah 15 – 16? There can, however, be no mistaking the use of the language of birth-pangs specifically of God in Isaiah 42:14:

> For a long time I have kept silent,
>> I have been quiet and held myself back.
> But now, like a woman in childbirth,
>> I cry out, I gasp and pant.

This emotional language reaches its most poignant expression in Hosea 11:8–9:

> How can I give you up, Ephraim?
>> How can I hand you over, Israel?
> How can I treat you like Admah?
>> How can I make you like Zeboiim?[108]
> My heart is changed within me,
>> all my compassion is aroused.
> I will not carry out my fierce anger,
>> nor will I turn and devastate Ephraim.
> For I am God and not man –
>> the Holy One among you.
>> I will not come in wrath.

---

108. Admah and Zeboiim were judged and destroyed by God (Josh. 14:8).

How should we understand this? The words are deeply moving and no doubt this is their intention. Moreover they were not a response to Israel's repentance because she was not repentant. They were surely intended rather to lead to repentance. Here modern language-theory has positive value, for philosophers of language recognize the many and varied functions of language, noting for instance its emotive power as well as its informative function. The Old Testament writers, especially the prophets, clearly mean us to understand that God is not only angry but also deeply grieved at human sin.

Is it possible, however, that the emotion is really the prophet's and not God's? No, for divine inspiration means that the language here is both human and divine. This is God's word in human language and if emotive power is a feature of it, this will express God's own concern. Also we see, especially in Hosea and Jeremiah, how close was the bond between God and his prophets. This is particularly poignant in Hosea, because the prophet's grief over his wayward wife Gomer became a parable and reflection of God's grief over Israel. Amos is sometimes contrasted with Hosea in this respect because he was from Judah, not from Israel (the Northern Kingdom, to which he was called to preach), and so it is suggested had less sense of solidarity with those he was addressing. That he too was deeply concerned for the people, however, is clearly seen in Amos 7:1–6, where he shows prayerful identification with them in the repeated words, 'I cried out, "Sovereign LORD, forgive! How can Jacob survive? He is so small!"'

While there are biblical passages that deny change and lying to God, there is none denying emotion. Lacking these, we should assert it, although view it as perfect and sinless. God does not have fits of anger or a love that wavers. His love is *ḥesed* ('abiding love') and he will not give up his people even though their love is like the morning mist or early dew (Hos. 6:4). 'God's jealousy is not a compound of frustration, envy and spite, as human jealousy so often is, but appears instead as a (literally) praiseworthy zeal to preserve something supremely precious.'[109]

In us emotion does normally involve change and our feelings are often stimulated or provoked by something outside us. As God's emotions are both real and perfect, they must be unvarying, always angry against sin, always gracious towards the repentant sinner. It is also true that their historical expression is related to what God sees to be appropriate in each situation, so that we must see his wisdom as an important character quality in his actions.

Yet, of course, the repentant sinner is still a sinner. How, then, can God be

---

109. Packer, *Knowing God*, p. 89.

both angry and gracious at the same time? This question is never asked and therefore never answered in the Old Testament, but, as we shall see in the next chapter, their union is most amazingly, clearly, decisively and uniquely revealed at the cross, where Christ took our place and experienced the wrath of God against sin while securing the justification of sinners.[110]

So, then, the Old Testament supports the claim that God is a deeply, indeed perfectly, emotional being, but we must reject the open theist contention that this involves change in him.

The incarnation, the Trinity and the cross

The open theists are, of course, committed to the fact that the whole Bible is a revelation of the one true God, but before looking specifically at their concerns, it will be helpful to address briefly two questions that have been raised by others and that bear on the question as to whether there is change in God as he presents himself in Scripture.

First of all, is there a God beyond God, such as the second-century heretic Marcion and some others have thought? No, for to contemplate such a possibility is virtually to reject the biblical revelation. The God of redemption is not superior to the God of creation, as Marcion taught, for the true God is both Creator and Redeemer. It is significant that Marcion could only support his theology by eliminating much of Scripture from his canon.

Moreover, while recognizing the distinctiveness of the incarnation, we should not drive a wedge between the God of the Old Testament and the God of the New. These are not two different Gods (or 'gods' in this case). Jesus said, 'Anyone who has seen me has seen the Father,' and, 'I am in the Father and the Father is in me' (John 14:9–11). In worshipping and serving Christ we are worshipping and serving the only God there is. In the poetry of Charles Wesley, he is 'our God contracted to a span, incomprehensibly made Man'.[111]

Second, is there then a God *against* God? Writers like Jürgen Moltmann and Walter Brueggemann, the first a systematic and the second a biblical theologian and both influenced by the unorthodox Marxist Ernst Bloch, have made use of this paradoxical idea. It probably originated for Bloch in his fascination with the book of Job.[112] Moltmann, in particular, forces his readers

---

110. See ch. 3.

111. *Methodist Hymn Book*, no. 142, p. 55.

112. E. Bloch, *Atheism in Christianity: The Religion of the Exodus and the Kingdom* (New York: Herder and Herder, 1972).

to confront the great cry of dereliction, 'My God, my God, why have you forsaken me?' which, as we shall see in the next chapter, has profound implications that are so central to the New Testament doctrine of the atonement. We need, though, to remember that in Job the view of God the comforters had was a caricature, a misapplication of the doctrine of God's providence, and not a valid alternative to the true God, for, we are told, it was Job, not the comforters, who had spoken what was right of him (Job 42:7).

It has sometimes been suggested that there was a *kenōsis* of God prior to the incarnation,[113] so that the very existence of a created universe and created persons, and the fact that God relates to both, must imply self-limitation. But is 'limitation' really the right word? Do we say that *The Last Supper* reveals the limitations of Leonardo da Vinci, or the *Ninth Symphony* those of Beethoven? We may say that God expressed *himself* in the act of creation and then in the context of his relations with a created world, but surely not his limitations! The most we can say is that God decided to channel his power in one particular way because he created our universe and not some other.

It is clear that Christ's likeness to the Father cannot be exhaustive, for the Father is the Father, while he is not the Son. Moreover, the Father did not become incarnate, nor did he suffer and die physically on the cross. There is total oneness in nature, but diversity in the way the three Persons relate to each other.

It is deeply reassuring to know that Christ is one with the Father in character, but in his divine nature he is also one with him in power and knowledge and in his omnipresence. Along with the Holy Spirit, the Father and the Son have distinctive roles in relation to the universe and to created beings, but their mutual indwelling means that each is involved in the work of the others. Moreover, they have distinctive modes of relationship to each other.

The revelation of the Son's oneness with the Father was made in the context of his incarnate life. Now what most evidently unite the two natures of Christ are his character qualities. Here in a human life all the holiness, the wisdom and the love of God were perfectly revealed. Of course his power and knowledge were too, but these were somewhat muted *in their actual exercise* by the conditions of his earthly life of obedience to the Father and guidance by the Spirit.

---

113. *Kenōsis* (Phil. 2:7) is better rendered 'made himself nothing' (NIV) or 'made himself of no reputation' (KJV) than 'emptied himself'; its sense is defined by the phrase that follows, 'taking the very nature of a servant' (NIV). It is not about surrender of power but of prestige.

So, then, we cannot infer from the fact that Jesus asked questions that there are limits to God's knowledge, nor from the fact that, on one recorded occasion, it is said that because of unbelief 'he could not do many mighty works there' (Mark 6:5; cf. Matt. 13:58),[114] that God's power is limited. This 'could not' was undoubtedly a moral and vocational impossibility because it was against the Father's purpose that such unbelief should witness his power.

Of course, in the Old Testament God sometimes asks questions. In the light of our earlier discussion of anthropomorphism,[115] we must ask what their function is. Because they occur within God's revelation of himself to his people, it is surely most likely that they are intended to make them face the implications of these questions for themselves. God's question to Adam, 'Where are you?' would make Adam realize that through his sin he had become lost and removed from fellowship with God. God knew this already, but now Adam needed to know it.

What, then, about God's presence? The deity of Jesus means that during his earthly life God was incarnately present in his world. We note, though, that the concept of God's presence is a very flexible one in Scripture, for we read, for instance, of his presence in the universe, in the tabernacle, in Christian people and uniquely in Christ. These are different modes of his presence and without doubt they were often simultaneous. If they were not, the question raised by William Temple about the *kenōsis* doctrine would certainly apply, 'What was happening to the rest of the universe during the period of our Lord's earthly life?'[116]

What about emotion? Jesus had a profound emotional life. Probably we should say that God possesses in himself a full and perfect range of emotions, but that he possesses them simultaneously and not in succession, whereas Jesus as human experienced them in sequence.

Is Jesus to be viewed as consistently acting or as often reacting? Without doubt our first impression is that both are true, but we must look deeper. In John's Gospel, he often referred to 'my hour', with a sense of a predestined

---

114. See Carson's note in 'The Gospel of Matthew', in F. E. Gaebelein (ed.), *Expositor's Bible Commentary*, vol. 8 (Grand Rapids: Zondervan, 1984), p. 336, where he mentions, for instance, other miracles recorded in Mark where the recipients showed no faith. He says, 'The "could not" refers to Jesus' mission: just as Jesus could not turn stones into bread without violating his mission . . . so he could not do miracles indiscriminately without turning his mission into a sideshow.'

115. See pp. 40–52.

116. W. Temple, *Christus Veritas: An Essay* (London: Macmillan, 1924), p. 142.

course of action (e.g. John 7:6), and he referred to the importance of the Scriptures being fulfilled (e.g. Matt. 26:56). It is surely significant too that we are told not simply that he was tempted by the devil, but that 'he was led by the Spirit into the desert to be tempted by the devil' (Matt. 4:1). The devil, wicked as his thoughts, words and deeds were, was accomplishing God's purpose of the testing of his Son so that his perfect fitness for his work should be evident to all. In Gethsemane he walked forward to meet his captors, thus in effect seizing the initiative (John 18:4). This does not mean that his reactions were play-acting, for this they were certainly not, but it does mean that the total sequence of events in his life was a fulfilment of God's plan. Here is compatibility again.

What, then, of the Trinity? Here we must consider the views of Jürgen Moltmann. Not since Barth has any theologian outside their own circle influenced English-speaking evangelical theologians so much. This is not surprising, for in his 'post-Auschwitz' theology he is always stimulating and often writes very movingly. Although he has many helpful things to say, we must suggest some cautions. His influence can certainly be seen in the open theists (that is why we need to look at his views), although open theism is not an inevitable development from his outlook.

Moltmann is strongly committed to the deity of Jesus, and in *The Crucified God*[117] and *The Trinity and the Kingdom of God*[118] he underlines the fact that God is like Christ. So, if we are to construct a doctrine of God, we must go to the New Testament and do so on the basis of Christ's revelation of him.

An implication of this for Moltmann is a 'social' doctrine of the Trinity, with the unity of God approached from the standpoint of his triunity, and not vice versa. His trinitarianism combines certain concepts from the past. From the Cappadocians[119] there is what was later called *perichoresis*, the idea of the mutual interpenetration of the three Persons, which means that what one does all three do, because, although distinct, the three are never separate. This means that their relations with each other come more into view than their one nature; in fact in Moltmann's thought there can be no divine nature that is independent of or abstracted from the relations of the three Persons. The unity of the Persons, for him, is therefore more of relations than of essence.[120]

---

117. J. Moltmann, *The Crucified God: The Cross of Christ as the Foundation and Criticism of Christian Theology*, tr. J. Bowden (London: SCM, 1974).

118. J. Moltmann, *The Trinity and the Kingdom of God*, tr. M. Kohl (London: SCM, 1981).

119. Basil of Caesarea, Gregory of Nyssa and Gregory of Nazianzus, three important theologians of the fourth century.

120. See especially Moltmann, *The Trinity and the Kingdom of God*, pp. 148–150.

Moltmann is also influenced by Augustine. Augustine's approach to the doctrine of the Trinity is often criticized today as being too much influenced by Neoplatonic philosophy, to which he subscribed before his conversion, but Moltmann makes positive use of his view that it is love which binds the three Persons together, which shows that Augustine used ideas of relation as well as substance in his doctrine.[121] This element in Augustine's doctrine is important also for the open theists even though they are critical of other aspects of his doctrine of God.

We must agree with Moltmann that the question of the relationship between the three Persons is very important, yet any relationship must tell us something about those who are thus related, about what they are in themselves. Can we really talk about a relationship unless we think, *first of all*, about those who will enter into it? Its quality is derived from what they are, rather than vice versa. So, then, questions of the nature of God must not have a lower status for us than those concerning his internal relationships.

In fact Moltmann's view seems to move somewhat away from a *homoousian* doctrine of the Trinity in the direction of a *homoiousian* one (from the oneness of substance of the three Persons to their likeness of substance), although he does not put it in these terms, preferring rather to speak in terms of their relations. A *homoiousian* doctrine was being promoted by some in the fourth century during the Arian debate, but it came to be regarded as inadequate to secure the deity of Jesus beyond all doubt.

It seems to me that the social Trinity does not give us a sufficient hedge against heresy, not Arianism this time but tritheism, and that this has special dangers at a time when we live in a society which, in religious terms, is increasingly pluralistic.

To suggest that we should start from the triunity rather than the unity of God is to imply that we should opt for the diachronic approach of biblical theology,[122] rather than the synchronic approach which is general in systematic theology.[123] To teach both disciplines is to recognize the great value of cross-fertilization. Here is a kind of hermeneutical circle, in which two approaches can be constantly employed so that each may critique the other and so guard against possible imbalance or excess. So, God is one but he is also three; God is three, but he is also one.

---

121. The use of the word 'substance' in discussions of the Trinity does not have material connotations, but is equivalent to 'essence', which in this case is spiritual.

122. i.e. one that focuses on the historical nature of God's revelation.

123. i.e. one that focuses on the revelation in its ultimate form, the revelation in Christ.

Moltmann goes further than this, however, and says that the doctrine of God must start at the cross. He is interested in Luther's doctrine that there Christ suffered in his divine as well as in his human nature.[124] To discuss this adequately would take us too far from the main theme of this chapter. What we can and surely must say is that the God of Christ is a suffering God, otherwise what does it mean that God is revealed at the cross? Of course the cross shows the simultaneous manifestation of the holiness and love of God, and this is a profound and central truth, but we should also recall the evidence of divine grief shown in the Old Testament and the fact that there is a continuity between the Testaments. If the suffering of grief was a real element in the earlier revelation, surely it must have been also in the final revelation in Christ! Moltmann sees this as a real counter to the protest atheism of Albert Camus and others, for the God of the cross is anything but apathetic in the face of evil and suffering.[125]

This does not require us to say that the Father suffered physically,[126] but it does mean accepting that there is a depth of spiritual suffering in God while at the same time insisting that divine suffering only became truly redemptive when the cross was erected on Golgotha. We must not detract from the historicity and finality of redemption in that amazing act of grace.

Moltmann applies this theology to ethical and particularly to political issues. Before we leave his view of the cross, however, we should note that although he has highlighted truth that emerges from the *story* of the cross as recorded in the New Testament, this should not be allowed to overshadow the main *interpretation* of the cross there, which, as we shall see, is particularly in terms of penal substitution.

Summary and an attempt at assessment

As in every movement in theology its adherents are not completely uniform in their thought, but a measure of generalization in our assessment is unavoidable.

When open theists insist that the Christian faith must be Bible-centred,

---

124. See especially Moltmann, *The Crucified God*, pp. 70–75, 211–214.

125. ibid., pp. 212–227.

126. Pinnock agrees that we must distinguish ways in which God does and does not suffer as we do (*Most Moved Mover*, p. 91). Moltmann sees that the impassibility doctrine contained an important truth 'that God is not *subjected* to suffering against his will *as creatures are*' (Moltmann, *The Crucified God*, pp. 229–230, italics his).

Christ-centred, cross-centred and trinitarian we can wholeheartedly agree. They rightly remind us that the biblical God is a living God, that prayer is a living encounter with him, and that it matters very much whether we pray.

We have considered open theism's criticism of classical Christian theism's relations with philosophy. In the patristic period, when this Christian theism was doctrinally formulated, at the Reformation when everything was under scrutiny but this doctrine was reaffirmed, and then under the threat of negative biblical criticism, important issues of biblical truth were at stake. The cut and thrust of debate was helpful in sharpening thought when its main reference point was the holy Scriptures. Understandably theologians used the philosophical tools available in their day and certainly some did not (and some still do not) altogether escape a kind of theological/philosophical syncretism, but the main concern in these important periods was to set forth biblical truth, and much work of lasting value was done. This must still be the main concern of classical theists today.

If classical theists should always take this kind of criticism seriously, so also should the proponents of open theism, for they need to take great care if they make any use of the language of process philosophy. The personal nature of God, which they rightly view as very important, could be under serious threat.

Their dislike of theological jargon reminds us that theology and preaching should not only be biblical but be seen (or heard) to be so. Abstractions cannot be completely avoided but should be used sparingly in the pulpit, or the preacher will not only lose contact with the Christian in the pew but be in danger of making listening to preaching a purely intellectual exercise and not a call to action. Theologians and preachers should subject themselves to a kind of Socratic self-criticism of the terms they use. Open theists challenge us also to a clearer understanding of impassibility, so that if we use the term at all we conceive of it in terms of activity, not passivity, and without denying emotion to God.

Misinterpreting the Bible's anthropomorphic language plus a libertarian view of human freedom have produced for many open theists a seriously defective view of God. This dishonours him and can affect many other beliefs, and in consequence our worship, our prayer, our daily life. There can be no surrender of any aspect of the biblical revelation of God. We must take his holy wrath as seriously as his holy love, and recognize our utter helplessness and complete dependence on his grace. All open theists need to recognize the immutability not only of his character but also of his positive commitments and also that in grace he is always and at every point the Initiator.

Their libertarianism is difficult to justify from Scripture and has led them into all kinds of unacceptable positions from a biblical standpoint. We must insist that God is not only present everywhere but is in control of everything and knows everything. None of this is negotiable. He is the Rock of Ages, not only of ages past and present but also future. Open theism's defects on these matters raise serious questions about its evangelical standing.

Prayer as petition and intercession does not need open theism as its theological foundation if we accept the principle of compatibility. The challenge is to take prayer with great seriousness as both a privilege and a responsibility. We should regard the Christian life as a daily faith-adventure with God but at the same time find deep security in him. Without doubt he will surprise us, but all his surprises will turn out to be consistent with his self-disclosure in Scripture and in Christ.

We have a God who is both consistently active and actively consistent. No wonder the Christian faith is so satisfying both theologically and emotionally! He is God, Elohim, the Rock of Ages, and also the LORD, Yahweh, ever redeeming, delivering, seeking his people and answering their prayers. He is always the glowing ember, always the living flame. Here is a God for the head, a God for the heart, not two different gods but the one unchanging, living and true God.

3. THE RETREAT FROM PENAL SUBSTITUTION

It is Sunday and I am at church for worship. At the Lord's Table the focus is on Calvary. It is Holy Week and the notices remind me that there will be services every day. I recall a radio discussion programme when three of the four panel members expressed their opinion that Bach's passion music was the greatest music ever written. I remember too that at home my books on art history often feature crucifixion scenes. Can I doubt the central importance of the cross for the Christian faith and also its deep cultural influence? So often it serves as a powerfully moving reminder not only of the greatness but also of the costliness of God's love. What a shameful contradiction of this, then, that as a symbol it was so often misused in Christendom as the rallying standard of an aggressive army!

Although this focus on the cross characterizes Christian churches everywhere, David Bebbington sees it as a special emphasis of evangelicalism.[1] An important event in evangelicalism's modern history was the decision of the Cambridge Inter-Collegiate Christian Union in 1918 to confirm its pre-war decision to leave the Student Christian Movement and, as John Stott

---

1. D. Bebbington, *Evangelicalism in Modern Britain: A History from the 1730s to the 1980s* (London: Unwin Hyman, 1989), pp. 14–17.

notes, the deciding issue was the centrality of the cross for the Christian faith.[2]

Not only so, but historically evangelicals have interpreted the cross chiefly in terms of penal substitution, holding that by the gracious initiative of the triune God, Jesus Christ the Son of God, personally innocent of all sin, took the place of sinners and died sacrificially[3] to pay the penalty of their sins. Helpful volumes expounding this doctrine which may be especially recommended are those by Leon Morris, John Stott, Robert Letham, Derek Tidball, a joint publication by Steve Jeffery, Michael Ovey and Andrew Sach, and a good briefer treatment by Ian Shaw and Brian Edwards.[4]

This doctrine has, however, come under criticism in recent years by some writers from within evangelicalism. This criticism, already voiced by some others, came to public notice in Britain in 2003 in a book by Steve Chalke and Alan Mann.[5] Discerning readers saw the influence in it of a book by two North American authors, Joel Green and Mark Baker, published three years earlier.[6] The main purpose of this chapter is to address these criticisms.

Penal substitution in Christian history

This emphasis is not new. It was a leading characteristic of the theology of the Reformers. Their main concern was with justification, but they were very clear that justification rests on atonement. It is no legal fiction, but a real

---

2. J. R. W. Stott, *The Cross of Christ* (Leicester: Inter-Varsity Press, 1986), pp. 8–9, quoting Norman Grubb.

3. Please note that throughout this book, 'sacrifice' and 'sacrificial', when used in a biblical or theological context, relate specifically to divinely ordained blood-offerings made to God, and are not employed as general words for costly abnegation of some sort.

4. L. Morris, *The Cross in the New Testament*; J. R. W. Stott, *The Cross of Christ*; R. Letham, *The Work of Christ*; D. Tidball, *The Message of the Cross*; S. Jeffery, M. Ovey and A. Sach, *Pierced for our Transgressions*; I. J. Shaw and B. H. Edwards, *The Divine Substitute*. Somewhat earlier works include J. Denney, *The Death of Christ*; and H. E. Guillebaud, *Why the Cross?* It is no accident that so many of these works became available through the publishing arm of the IVF/UCCF. See Bibliography for full details.

5. S. Chalke and A. Mann, *The Lost Message of Jesus* (Grand Rapids: Zondervan, 2003).

6. J. B. Green and M. D. Baker, *Recovering the Scandal of the Cross* (Downers Grove: InterVarsity Press, 2000).

acquittal of sinners on the basis of the work of Another, the Son of God. Calvin, for instance, wrote, 'Our acquittal is in this, that the guilt which made us liable to punishment was transferred to the head of the Son of God.'[7] Luther expressed the same theology, saying, for example, in commenting on Galatians 3:13, 'God hath laid our sins, not upon us, but upon his Son, Christ, that he bearing the punishment thereof might be our peace, and that by his stripes we might be healed.'[8]

This kind of atonement theology was not held only by predestinarians like Calvin and Luther. In the preaching and hymns of the Wesley brothers it was associated with moderate Arminianism. For instance, John Wesley says, 'There was a real infliction of punishment on our Saviour.'[9] Philip Bliss, in a popular hymn of the cross, expressed both its truth and the Christian's deep sense of indebtedness to the Saviour in writing, 'Bearing shame and scoffing rude, in my place condemned He stood, sealed my pardon with His blood. Hallelujah! What a Saviour!'[10]

This theology is found also in the patristic writers. Chrysostom uses the illustration of a king who, 'beholding a robber and malefactor under punishment, gave his well-beloved son, his only-begotten and true, to be slain and transferred the death and the guilt as well, from him to his son'.[11] Augustine said that 'as He died in the flesh which He took in bearing our punishment, so also, while ever blessed in His own righteousness, He was cursed for our offences, in the death which He suffered in bearing our punishment'.[12] It is true, of course, that at this period the cross was given other interpretations, some quite grotesque, like ransom to the devil or even God's deceiving of him, often by the same writers who express penal substitution.[13]

Anselm, Archbishop of Canterbury (1033–1109), wrote a small but

7. J. Calvin, *Institutes of the Christian Religion*, tr. F. L. Battles, 2 vols. (Philadelphia: Westminster, 1960), II, xvi, 5.

8. M. Luther, *St Paul's Epistle to the Galatians* (London: James Clarke, 1953), p. 271.

9. J. Wesley, *Explanatory Notes upon the New Testament* II (London: Epworth, 1976), on Romans 3:25–26.

10. *Methodist Hymn Book* (London: Methodist Conference, 1933), no. 176, p. 69.

11. John Chrysostom, *Homilies on Second Corinthians*, in *Nicene and Post-Nicene Fathers*, sect. I, vol. 12 (Grand Rapids: Eerdmans, 1969), Homily XI, sect. 6, p. 335.

12. Augustine, 'Against Faustus', in *Nicene and Post-Nicene Fathers*, vol. 14 (Grand Rapids: Eerdmans, 1974), p. 207.

13. There is a survey of patristic teaching on this theme in Jeffery, Ovey and Sach, *Pierced for our Transgressions*, pp. 164–184.

important book on the atonement called *Cur Deus Homo?* ('Why Did God Become Man?'),[14] often viewed as a precursor of the Reformation doctrine. There are important differences, but a major virtue is his concern with the Godward aspect of the atonement, whereas many of the Fathers were preoccupied with Satan as our oppressor. He took sin seriously and saw the cross as dealing decisively with it.

The biblical witness to penal substitution

I fully recognize that this doctrine has other aspects, as will appear later, but Jeffery, Ovey and Sach are right in saying of penal substitution, 'It is not a tangential inference drawn from a few obscure texts, but a central emphasis of some foundational passages.'[15]

The importance of sacrificial concepts in this respect is generally recognized. Green and Baker, for instance, refer to more than two dozen New Testament passages.[16] This is a big subject and the reader is referred to fuller treatments.[17] Some important points must be made here, however.

The Old Testament

The Mosaic sacrificial system
The sacrifices within the Mosaic system are consistently viewed as God-ordained, occurring within the context of divinely given law. In Leviticus 17:11, God says of sacrificial blood, 'I have given it to you to make atonement for yourselves on the altar; it is the blood that makes atonement for one's life.'

Sacrifices and offerings were of various kinds and had different purposes,[18] but a common factor of many was their association with blood and so with death. There were exceptions, such as the cereal offerings, but these were placed on the altar where blood-offerings were regularly made and this could

---

14. Anselm of Canterbury, *Cur Deus Homo?* (London: David Nutt, 1903).

15. Jeffery, Ovey and Sach, *Pierced for our Transgressions*, p. 33.

16. Green and Baker, *Recovering the Scandal of the Cross*, p. 103.

17. See, for instance, R. T. Beckwith and M. J. Selman (eds.), *Sacrifice in the Bible* (Exeter: Paternoster, 1995).

18. Green and Baker rightly say sacrifice had no monolithic meaning in ancient Israel (*Recovering the Scandal of the Cross*, p. 103). Yet there are several shared features which must be significant.

be significant. Atonement for sin was particularly prominent in the sin and guilt offerings, but burnt-offerings too are said to 'make atonement' (Lev. 1:4; 14:20; 16:24).[19] Both Testaments connect sin and death, as in Joshua 7; Ezekiel 18:13; Romans 5:12–21 and James 1:15, making it natural to see significance in the animal's death when reconciliation with God was to be effected.

What in the Old Testament does 'to make atonement' mean? Clearly it does not relate simply to an attitudinal change in the offerer, but effects something objective and yet related to the individual offerer. Does it mean expiation (i.e. satisfaction for sin) or propitiation (i.e. the removal of God's wrath)? The latter would, of course, include or at least presuppose the former. We must investigate this.

The Hebrew verb rendered 'to make atonement' (*kipper*) is from the root *kpr*, frequent in Leviticus,[20] which also occurs in other Old Testament contexts. Its meaning has been much debated. It is discussed by Peterson and by Morris, both connecting it with *kōper* ('ransom price'), although Peterson also refers to the view that it sometimes means 'to purge'.[21]

Milgrom, quoted with approval by Peterson, points out that the latter sense is always related to the sanctuary and its objects, never to persons, and he says of both senses, 'The common denominator . . . is their avowed goal: to siphon off the wrath of God from the entire community.'[22] This 'siphoning off' is tantamount to propitiation, not simply expiation. Stott says of *kipper*, 'Even in passages where the natural translation is to "make atonement for sin", the context often contains explicit mention of God's wrath, which implies that the human sin can be atoned for only by the divine anger being turned away.'[23]

---

19. G. J. Wenham sees burnt-offerings appeasing God's anger in passages such as Num. 15:24; 2 Sam. 24:25; Job 1:5; 42:8; 2 Chr. 29:7–8 (*The Book of Leviticus*, NICOT, Grand Rapids: Eerdmans, 1979, p. 57).

20. D. Peterson gives the statistics in 'Atonement in the Old Testament', in D. Peterson (ed.), *Where Wrath and Mercy Meet: Proclaiming the Atonement Today* (Carlisle: Paternoster, 2001), p. 6, n. 10.

21. ibid., pp. 9–12; L. Morris, *The Atonement: Its Meaning and Significance* (Leicester: Inter-Varsity Press, 1983), pp. 116–117, 158–163; and *The Apostolic Preaching of the Cross* (London: Tyndale, 1953), pp. 160–174.

22. J. Milgrom, 'Atonement in the OT', *Interpreter's Dictionary of the Bible*, supp. vol. 3A (Nashville: Abingdon, 1976), p. 80.

23. Stott, *The Cross of Christ*, p. 171. He gives examples from Exod. 32:30 (cf. v. 10), Deut. 21: 1–9; 1 Sam. 3:14; 26:19.

The Day of Atonement

God gave Israel the annual Day of Atonement (Lev. 16) when the high priest officiated for the whole nation,[24] surely showing its special significance and importance. Its central rituals featured two goats.[25] One was sacrificed, its blood sprinkled on the altar and throughout the tabernacle, while the high priest placed both hands on the other's head, confessing the people's sins over it (he 'put them on the goat's head', v. 21), and banished it to a solitary place.

Besides this unique element in the ritual, it is important to note that the term 'sin-offering' was in this passage uniquely used of the two goats together (Lev. 16:5). Perhaps this ritual was to dramatize annually that the removal of sin by a substitutionary death was involved in every sin-offering. This occasion clearly and eloquently witnessed to sin's consequences both as death and exclusion and to the Lord's gracious provision of an answer to both.

This second goat is called 'the scapegoat' in the NIV and KJV (Lev. 16:8, 10, 26). The Hebrew word is transliterated and capitalized as Azazel in the NRSV and some other versions. In the second-century BC *Book of Enoch*, Azazel is the leader of a band of evil angels, leading some writers to view the word here as designating a desert demon. A little reflection indicates, however, that this does not fit the ethos of Israel's God-given religion at all well.[26] *Enoch* incorporates several Jewish legends and this identification of Azazel could have arisen from the word's obscurity. Another interpretation links it to the Arabic *azala*, meaning 'for removal', on the assumption that Hebrew also had some such root.[27] This is, of course, exactly what happened to this goat.

The scapegoat bore the sins of the people (Lev. 16:22). In the Old Testament 'to bear sin' normally means to bear its consequences. Exodus 28:43, for instance, says the priests should observe God's requirements 'so that they will not incur guilt and die', where 'incur guilt' is literally 'bear sin'. Bearing sin has serious consequences, either excommunication ('cut off from his people')[28] or death, in Leviticus 22:9 and many other places.[29]

---

24. For a fuller treatment of this, see L. Morris, *The Atonement*, pp. 88–105.

25. A bullock and two rams also featured in the ritual.

26. Also it seems to be ruled out by Lev. 17:7.

27. Hebrew and Arabic, for all their differences, both belong to the Semitic language group. This theory involves reduplication of the first syllable, a not uncommon feature of Hebrew.

28. cf. 'to a solitary place' (Lev. 16:22).

29. Stott lists some of these (*The Cross of Christ*, p. 143, n. 15).

John Stott has well said,

> It is clear from Old Testament usage that to 'bear sin' means neither to sympathize
> with sinners, nor to identify with their pain, nor to express their penitence, nor to
> be persecuted on account of human sinfulness (as others have argued), nor even to
> suffer the consequences of sin in personal or social terms, but specifically to endure
> its penal consequences, to undergo its penalty.[30]

His negatives are almost a roll-call of interpretations of atonement that deny
penal substitution.

The Fourth Servant Song (Isa. 52:13 – 53:12)

The Day of Atonement was the Mosaic system's supreme sacrificial ritual.
It may all seem remote from Jesus and the New Testament, but it is not, for
the Fourth Servant Song in Isaiah takes up its significance but goes beyond it,
applying the language of sacrifice, especially although not exclusively Day of
Atonement language, uniquely to a person, the Lord's Servant, and the New
Testament applies this to Jesus.[31] In this Song we find him carrying the sins of
others, who are referred to by the first person plural. In fact verbs stating or
implying carrying are a major feature of two sections of this chapter, 53:4–6
and 11–12, reminding us of the scapegoat's fate. If the iniquity of others
was laid on him, this clearly means that he was bearing their sins and the
consequences of those sins.

Although specifically called 'righteous' (Isa. 53:11), the astonishing fact is
that in this passage the Lord's Servant endures the punishment of death (Isa.
53:7–9) for others. The affirmations 'the punishment that brought us peace
was upon him' and 'the LORD has laid on him the iniquity of us all' (vv. 5, 6; cf.
v. 10) could hardly be clearer as statements of penal substitution.[32] When he

---

30. ibid., p. 143.

31. The only other such passage is Jer. 11:19, but the point there is the lamb's
    unawareness of its impending death.

32. Perhaps the most important verse in this passage theologically is Isa. 53:6.
    Strangely, Goldingay comments on every verse in the Fourth Song apart from
    this, although in his translation of the passage (on pp. 158–159) he renders it, 'All
    of us have strayed like sheep, we have each of us taken his own way, but Yahweh
    has brought down on him the guilt that belonged to all of us' (God's Prophet, God's
    Servant: A Study of Jeremiah and Isaiah 40 – 55, rev. ed., Toronto: Clements, 2002, pp.
    139–159).

is said to have been crushed and wounded for us (Isa. 53:5), we are reminded, perhaps intentionally, of Isaiah 1:4–6, where the punishment of the people, loaded like him but with their own sins, is somewhat similarly described.

The one offering this passage explicitly mentions is the guilt-offering (Isa. 53:10), which involved restitution as well as sacrifice (Lev. 5:14 – 6:7). This striking fact perhaps suggests that because of his sufferings nothing else whatever needed to be done.

The New Testament

The Gospels

We need to recognize what a place the cross had in the mind of Jesus. The Synoptic Gospels record his recurrent warnings of his impending death and its necessity as an important feature of his disciple-teaching on the way to Jerusalem (Matt. 16:21; 17:22–23; 20:17–19; Mark 8:31–32; 9:31; 10:34, 45; Luke 9.22; 17:24–25; 18:31–33).

His death was going to fulfil Scripture (Mark 9:12; Luke 18:31). The one Old Testament passage clearly in his mind was the Fourth Servant Song, for Isaiah 53:12, 'And he was numbered with the transgressors', is quoted in Luke 22:37. He follows this quotation with an assertion, repeated as if for special emphasis,[33] that this was to be the fulfilment of what was written. It is therefore no surprise to find him saying, 'The Son of Man comes . . . to give his life a ransom for many' (Mark 10:45; cf. 1 Tim. 2:6; Heb. 9:28). This appears to be reminiscent of Isaiah 53:11–12, which as we have seen presents a figure experiencing punishment for others. Here, then, he declared the substitutionary meaning of this dread event.

He pictured his destiny as undergoing a baptism and drinking a cup. Although both figures have a varied Old Testament background, it is evident that for Jesus they symbolized a most painful experience (Mark 10:38–40; Luke 12:50). The wording of the Markan saying exhibits the influence of Hebrew parallelism, in which consecutive clauses express the same basic thought in two or more ways. This suggests that we should interpret each figure in terms of the other. What, then, do they have in common? The one concept uniting them in the Old Testament background is divine judgment (cf. Pss 75:8; 106:11; 124:4–5; Isa. 8:7–8; 51:17; Zech. 12:2). This makes Christ's words in Gethsemane, 'If it be possible, let this cup pass from me',

---

33. This is the only example in the Gospels of this kind of repetition in connection with the quotation of Scripture.

fully understandable. After taking all this in, the reader is surely meant to ponder the awful cry of dereliction, which two evangelists allow to stand as their one recorded cry from the cross (Matt. 27:46; Mark 15:34). Here he was bearing the awful judgment of God on sin.

In John's Gospel, chapter 1 is prefatory, introducing, like some operatic overture, many of the great themes, in this case Christological ones, developed later. It records John the Baptist's saying, 'Look, the Lamb of God, who takes away the sin of the world' (John 1:29), where 'takes away' (Greek *airein*, as in 1 John 3:5) probably echoes the Hebrew *nāśāʾ*, rendered 'took up' in Isaiah 53:4 and 'bore' in Isaiah 53:12. 'Lamb of God' is reminiscent of so much Old Testament sacrificial teaching. In the context there is a sense of prophetic anticipation, so that not only Isaiah 53, but perhaps even more markedly the anticipated lamb from God in the story of Abraham and Isaac in Genesis 22:13–14, could be in view.

The feast of the Passover was given by God as a reminder, not simply of the exodus from Egypt, but of the event which preceded it, the slaying of the Egyptian firstborn, an event of judgment from which Israel was exempt (Exod. 12). We have seen enough so far not to be surprised that this feast was associated with the slaying of lambs. John notes each Passover in the ministry of Jesus as it occurs (John 2:13, 23; 6:4; 12:1), which suggests that he saw a theological connection between the Passover and that ministry.

In John 6:4, just before the feeding of the five thousand and the bread of life discourse, we learn that the Passover was imminent, which seems like a typical Johannine interpretative hint.[34] His people were to depend not simply on his person ('the bread of God . . . who comes down from heaven', John 6:29, 33) but on his atoning work ('my flesh . . . my blood', John 6:53–57). In this Gospel too he speaks of his 'hour' several times, eventually with clear reference to the cross (John 12:20–28; cf. 13:1; 17:1). We can see in this his constant awareness that his death was the time of destiny for him.

The Acts of the Apostles
After the resurrection and Pentecost the apostles proclaimed the gospel. The cross was not only a gracious act of God but a wicked human deed, made particularly vile because of the hypocritical courtroom procedures which led to it, and so they often stressed the resurrection as God's reversal of the human

---

34. The Passover's penal substitutionary significance is well explored in Jeffrey, Ovey and Sach, *Pierced for our Transgressions*, pp. 34–41.

verdict on Jesus. Does this mean that in these sermons the resurrection was everything and little significance was given to the cross? By no means!

Three aspects of the preaching both feature and interpret the cross. The first is the reference to God's purpose in the crucifixion (Acts 2:23). The second is the word 'tree', used both by Peter (Acts 5:30; 10:39) and by Paul (13:29), recalling Deuteronomy 21:23, 'Anyone who is hung on a tree is under God's curse.' This would cry out for and probably receive interpretation along the lines of Galatians 3:13, where Paul says that 'Christ redeemed us from the curse of the law by becoming a curse for us', after which he quoted Deuteronomy 21:23.[35] The third is the Greek word *pais* (Acts 3:13, 26; 4:27, 30),[36] which means 'servant' here (and, significantly, in the quotation from the first Isaianic Servant Song in Matt. 12:18). This word clearly alludes to Isaiah 53, which as we have seen interprets the Servant's sufferings in terms of penal substitution. So there is continuity between the apostolic preaching and the teaching of Jesus which preceded it.

The epistles

The main theme of Romans 1:18 – 3:20 is not simply sin, as is sometimes carelessly said, but it is God's wrath against and judgment of human sin (Rom. 1:18, 32; 2:1–9, 12, 16; 3:3–8, 19). The length of this passage surely reflects Paul's awareness of the importance and seriousness of this. Judgment in this passage is both a future event (Rom. 2:5) and a principle at work by God's action in human history (Rom. 1:24, 26, 28).[37] This is to be expected, for New Testament eschatology has both a realized and an unrealized dimension (reflecting the two comings of Christ), with the two intimately related.[38]

This is the background to Paul's exposition of the gospel in Romans 3:21–31. As in the sacrificial system and the Fourth Servant Song, God's initiative is affirmed (v. 25). 'A sacrifice of atonement' translates *hilastērion*, used in the Septuagint to render the Hebrew *kipper*, from the root *kpr*, which is discussed

---

35. See also Peter's interpreted reference to the tree in 1 Pet. 2:24.

36. Most scholars now take this to mean 'servant' and not 'child' (KJV) here.

37. Note the present tense in Rom. 1:18 and the future in 2:5. Jeffery, Ovey and Sach (*Pierced for our Transgressions*, p. 297) shrewdly observe the similarity of the list of sins referred to in Col. 3:5–6, to which future judgment applies, to those referred to in Rom. 1.

38. So, e.g., eternal life is both future gift and present experience, the latter being the earnest of the former.

at length and with great thoroughness by Leon Morris.[39] He concludes that it should be rendered 'propitiation', rather than 'expiation', for this term, unobjectionable in itself, does not convey all *hilastērion* implies. It is possible it refers to the lid of the ark of the covenant, where the blood was sprinkled on the Day of Atonement, because that was the place of propitiation. If so, this would be yet another link of our theme with the ritual of that day.

Verses 25b and 26, with their emphasis on the justice of God, expound verses 24 and 25a, and it is difficult to understand verse 26 unless it means that the sins left unpunished (presumably those of the Old Testament saints, cf. Heb. 9:15) were dealt with in the propitiatory death of Jesus.

In 2 Corinthians 5:14–21, the apostle interprets the cross in terms of reconciliation. In verse 19 he says, 'God was reconciling the world to himself in Christ, not counting men's sins against them' (cf. Rom. 3:25), and then in verse 21 we find the remarkable affirmation, 'God made him who had no sin to be sin for us, so that in him we might become the righteousness of God.' Here is a graphic statement of mutual imputation which only makes sense in terms of substitution. It can hardly mean anything else than that Christ bore the punishment of our sins so that we might come to share his righteousness.

The epistle to the Hebrews presents the cross in terms of priestly sacrifice, a theme treated very fully in chapters 7 – 10 but anticipated in several earlier passages. Christ is here not simply priest but High Priest, leading us once again to expect a Day of Atonement background, and this is an important feature of it.[40] The gracious divine initiative is made clear in Hebrews 2:9, where Christ is said to have tasted death for everyone 'by the grace of God'.

This epistle stresses the decisiveness and finality of Christ's sacrifice so that there is always a contrast, stated or implied, between the Old Testament sacrifices and his when they are referred to. The Day of Atonement itself had a special role because it related to the sins of the whole people and Jesus is said to have 'made atonement [*hilaskesthai*] for the sins of the people' (Heb. 2:17). The annual repetition, however, showed it was not finally effective. Having effected purification for sins our great High Priest sat down (Heb. 1:3; 10:12), suggesting finality, for no priest sat while executing his duties. His sacrifice, unlike those under the Old Covenant, was once for all (Heb. 7:27; 9:12, 26,

---

39. Morris, *Apostolic Preaching of the Cross*, pp. 160–174.

40. The second most important background feature is the covenant sacrifice (Exod. 24; cf. Heb. 9:14–22). That Christ's sacrifice secured a new covenant shows its decisive significance.

28; 10:10), never requiring repetition,[41] so that he has done away with sin (Heb. 9:26), and when he comes again this is therefore not to deal with sin (Heb. 9:28).

If the Day of Atonement ritual influenced Isaiah 53, we would expect this Servant Song's language to be echoed here. This happens only once but at an important point, in Hebrews 9:28, where 'many' recalls Isaiah 53:11–12. Nothing in the context leads us to expect this word, so it has all the appearance of a literary allusion, and such allusions in the New Testament are almost always to Old Testament Scripture. We can hardly doubt that its first readers would recall its use in Isaiah 53. If the Day of Atonement and the Isaianic Servant of the Lord were in the mind of this author, his atonement theology would surely focus on penal substitution!

Another feature of the epistle is the purging of the conscience by Christ's sacrifice (Heb. 9:9, 14; 10:2, 22). The Old Testament sacrifices, because constantly repeated, did not give final relief to guilty consciences, but Christ's once-for-all sacrifice did, for it cleared up the issue of sin permanently.

In 1 Peter 2:24, Christ is said to have borne our sins in his own body on the tree. This makes a link not only with the scapegoat but with Deuteronomy 21:23. The main background, however, is the Fourth Servant Song (Isa. 52:13 – 53:12), as a study of the context in the epistle clearly shows. So, then, the Isaianic Servant of God, seen by Christ and the New Testament writers as Jesus himself, fulfilled the roles of both Day of Atonement goats by bearing the guilt of sinners and by taking their punishment in death.

In 1 John *hilasmos* occurs twice, in 1 John 2:2 and 4:10,[42] and means 'propitiation', coming as it does from the same root as *hilastērion*. Significantly, it appears here in contexts where two great moral attributes of God are featured, his holiness (1:5) and his love (4:7–21). The former required the *hilasmos*, and the latter wonderfully provided it. The New Testament doctrine of the atonement is firmly grounded in the Bible's teaching about God.

The Apocalypse

The Apocalypse specially features a Lamb. The word is *arnion*, originally a diminutive, not *amnos* as elsewhere in the New Testament, and it occurs over

---

41. This surely implies too that his sacrifice requires no supplementing.

42. Rather strangely, Green and Baker refer to 1 John 4:10 as showing the *subjective* aspect of Christ's work (*Recovering the Scandal of the Cross*, p. 139, n. 35) and they do not mention 2:2.

thirty times in the book in reference to the crucified and risen Christ.[43] If it possessed even a suggestion of a diminutive nuance still, it was probably chosen to intensify the striking paradox in the key passage, chapter 5, where Christ is described as a Lion but actually appears to view as an *arnion* (Rev. 5:5–6). Paradoxically too, he has been slain and yet is now alive. It is the fact that he has been slain that causes praise in heaven (Rev. 5:9, 12). There is no exposition of atonement doctrine here, but the sacrificial bearing of this image is clear.

Criticisms of penal substitution considered in the light of Scripture

Penal substitutionary theology has long been criticized by writers outside evangelicalism, especially by those embracing some form of liberal Christianity. Now, however, criticism is coming from some regarding themselves as evangelicals, probably largely due to the pressure of changes in culture affecting not only those the churches wish to win for Christ, but also those who seek to win them, although many of the latter have a genuine concern also to re-examine traditional understandings of Scripture. In Britain this first emerged clearly in 1995 in the volume *Atonement Today*,[44] a symposium containing some essays consistent with or in support of penal substitution, while a few, particularly those by Goldingay and Travis, move in the opposite direction.

The issue did not, however, become a matter of widespread public concern among evangelicals until the publication of *The Lost Message of Jesus*, by Steve Chalke and Alan Mann, in 2003.[45] This concern was largely because Steve Chalke was well known in Britain as a Christian broadcaster and as the founder-director of Oasis, a Christian service enterprise for young people, and because the book was written in a popular style. It was strongly influenced by an American publication by Joel Green and Mark Baker, *Recovering the Scandal of the Cross*.[46]

A scholarly refutation of any view should in all fairness present that view at its strongest. Major systematic theologies by great theologians like Calvin

---

43. The exception is 13:11, where the beast from the earth clearly suggests a satanic counterfeit.

44. J. Goldingay (ed.), *Atonement Today* (London: SPCK, 1995).

45. S. Chalke and A. Mann, *The Lost Message of Jesus* (Grand Rapids: Zondervan, 2003).

46. J. B. Green and M. D. Baker, *Recovering the Scandal of the Cross* (Downers Grove: InterVarsity Press, 2000).

and Hodge always give good coverage to the atonement and Green and Baker comment on these, especially on Hodge. It is, however, a reasonable expectation that for a major, well-balanced exposition of a doctrine, carefully nuanced, a substantial volume devoted specifically to it should be considered, preferably a recent one, to see whether the author deals satisfactorily with difficulties felt by the modern reader. A number have been published in fairly recent times.[47] Probably the most widely read is *The Cross of Christ* by John Stott, a superb, well-balanced treatment far removed from the somewhat stereotypical caricatures so often criticized.[48] It is a pity that instead of reviewing a substantial volume of this sort, Green and Baker direct their criticisms at a very brief article by David Clark published in a little-known periodical.[49] Stott's book and three volumes by Leon Morris are included in their bibliography, but only warrant a footnote each.[50]

Without doubt penal substitution should be carefully preached, and clumsy presentation of it can be offensive, but this is not to deny its essential truth. Green and Baker say their concern is 'that popularly interpreted and characterized, this brand of atonement theology has been understood in ways that have proven detrimental to the witness of the church'.[51] Yet they do criticize the doctrine itself, sometimes blurring the distinction between the doctrine and faulty presentations of it, giving the impression that the latter are almost inevitable once the former has been embraced. It is not helpful, for instance, to say that Paul does not use the metaphor of penal substitution 'at least as popularly defined' in a chapter on the New Testament teaching,[52] for it is that teaching which there needs to be expounded, not contemporary presentations of it.

Although many of these criticisms have also been made by other writers more theologically remote from evangelicalism, I am concentrating chiefly on writers generally considered or considering themselves to be evangelical.

The main criticisms are as follows.

---

47. See p. 84 n. 2, n. 4.

48. J. R. W. Stott, *The Cross of Christ* (Leicester: Inter-Varsity Press, 1986).

49. Green and Baker, *Recovering the Scandal of the Cross*, pp. 145–146, commenting on David Clark, 'Why Did Christ Have to Die?', *New England Reformed Journal* 1 (1996), pp. 35–36.

50. Green and Baker, ibid., p. 202, n. 2, p. 36, n. 2.

51. ibid., p. 32.

52. ibid., p. 95. In fact, an important task for theologians consists in balancing biblical metaphors.

Its use of Scripture imagery is at best selective and at worst mistaken

It is rightly pointed out that the New Testament writers use a number of metaphors in their treatment of the atonement, and that no interpretation should be based on just one metaphor or image.[53] It is said that this is just what advocates of the penal substitution 'theory' do when they focus on the image of the law-court. What can be said in answer?

First we must take issue with the idea that penal substitution is just one of many theories of the atonement. Occasionally even those who write positively about it call it a theory.[54] This is particularly unfortunate, for it implies that the theologian is left to construct one from biblical material lacking a clearly articulated rationale, and, of course, the theories of theologians necessarily lack the authority that biblical doctrine has. The impression is thus given that commitment to penal substitution is optional for a Christian wishing to be true to Scripture.

Do the New Testament writers teach a coherent doctrine, does it focus on penal substitution, and if so is it based on the teaching of Jesus? In their opening chapter, Green and Baker refer to the Emmaus Road story in Luke 24 and the perplexity of the two disciples who met the risen Jesus there. They say, 'For these two disciples, the death of Jesus on a Roman cross was an event that lacked within itself a self-evident, unambiguous interpretation . . . These disciples have no interpretive tools for making sense of his execution at the hands of the Romans. Their dilemma is ours, though we rarely experience it at such depth.'[55] They then say that after chiding them 'Jesus does not articulate any doctrine of the atonement at all'.[56]

But is this our dilemma? Surely not, for the Gospels show us that on his last journey to Jerusalem Jesus taught his disciples not only the fact but the meaning of the cross, most notably in Mark 10:45 (cf. Matt. 20:28), 'The Son of Man did not come to be served, but to serve, and to give his life as a ransom for many.' We cannot, of course, be sure these two disciples received this teaching, but it seems likely, for *edei pathein* ('have to suffer', Luke 24:26), which reminds us of the phrase of identical meaning (*dei . . . pathein*) in Luke 9:22, certainly implies an interpretation and it will presumably have gained meaning at the Last Supper when Jesus spoke of 'the new covenant in my

---

53. ibid., pp. 97–108; also A. Mann, *Atonement for a 'Sinless' Society: Engaging with an Emerging Culture* (Milton Keynes: Paternoster, 2005), p. 98.

54. e.g. C. Baxter, in Goldingay, *Atonement Today*, pp. 54, 70–71.

55. Green and Baker, *Recovering the Scandal of the Cross*, pp. 11–12.

56. ibid., p. 13.

blood, which is poured out for you' (Luke 22:20). We are heirs to this teaching and to the New Testament epistles, which present us with very helpful 'interpretive tools'.

Green and Baker say atonement references only occur in parts of three verses in Luke/Acts, i.e. in Luke 22:19–20 and Acts 20:28.[57] But Luke 9:31 and 12:50 both imply a theology, the first one of deliverance, for 'departure' is the Greek word *exodos*, and the second of a baptism of blood and a cup of suffering, both suggesting divine judgment. Also in Acts 13:38 and 39 justification is said to be through Christ in a sermon where the cross is called a tree, a symbol of God's curse (Deut. 21:23). Are we not meant to put two and two together?

It is much better to think in terms of images or models or metaphors than of theories. If through his death Jesus cleansed us (Heb. 9:22–23; 1 John 1:7, 9), ransomed, redeemed or freed us (Mark 10:45; Eph. 1:7, Rev. 1:5), paid our debt and turned his cross into a victory chariot, triumphing over his foes (Col. 2:13),[58] we are clearly encountering metaphors. Stott says, 'Theories are usually abstract and speculative concepts, whereas the biblical images of the atoning achievement of Christ are concrete pictures and belong to the data of revelation.'[59]

Green and Baker also make much of the variety of atonement metaphors in the New Testament,[60] and they say, 'To affirm biblical books as Scripture is itself to embrace the ongoing relevance of their message, including their metaphors.'[61] They are right, and Christian thought about the meaning of the cross has certainly been greatly enriched by these metaphors.

They also say, however, that 'although Paul uses an almost inexhaustible series of metaphors to represent the significance of Jesus' death, penal substitution (at least as popularly defined) is not one of them.'[62] Again they are right, although in this case not in the sense they intend, for I hope to show not only that Paul does teach penal substitution, but also that it is not a metaphor but should be understood literally.

---

57. ibid., p. 70.

58. Col. 2:13–15 brings together several metaphors; cf. Stott, *The Cross of Christ*, pp. 233–235.

59. Stott, ibid., p. 168.

60. Green and Baker, *Recovering the Scandal of the Cross*, particularly in ch. 4.

61. ibid., p. 99. See also Pinnock, in C. Pinnock and D. Brown, *Theological Crossfire: An Evangelical/Liberal Dialogue* (Grand Rapids: Zondervan, 1990), p. 148..

62. Green and Baker, ibid., p. 95.

Colin Gunton notes that the main ways of interpreting the significance of Christ's work 'contain a considerable metaphorical and imaginative content, drawing . . . from a number of human institutions: notably the legal system, the altar of sacrifice, the battlefield and the slave-market'.[63] But is it right to call the legal system and the altar of sacrifice 'human institutions', in relation to biblical doctrine? Certainly they exist in many human cultures, but in Scripture they are divinely given institutions and therefore must have special status when employed there to interpret the cross. In addition, they are directly related to sin.

Is the idea that we are under God's law purely an exercise in analogy? No, not in Scripture, for Israel was a theocracy whose human laws were divinely given. This gives special status to the Bible's legal language in relation to the atonement and it should not be deemed metaphorical. Of course, legal categories are by no means the only ones used in connection with the atonement, for the personal concept of reconciliation is also important as we see, for instance, in Paul's writings.[64] We should not, however, set aside one set of biblical terms for another, and it is in the legal and sacrificial realms that penal substitution is most clearly set forth.

Views of atonement are related to views of sin. John Goldingay helpfully summarizes different ways sin is viewed in Scripture.[65] He gives these as a series of comparisons, using simile constructions. In some cases, however, this is misleading. Certainly sin is like getting dirty or like wandering out of the way, but it is not just *like* transgression of law, it *is* transgression of law. Divine and human law, however they may differ, both prescribe acceptable and unacceptable conduct by an authority, the one divine and the other human.

Sacrifice too has a special place in New Testament atonement theology.[66] In the Old Testament it occurs within the context of law and, while clearly revealing God's grace, shares law's divinely given status. Certainly sacrifice was practised throughout the Near East, but Old Testament thought starts not

---

63. C. E. Gunton, *The Actuality of Atonement: A Study of Metaphor, Rationality and the Christian Tradition* (Edinburgh: T. & T. Clark, 1988), pp. 17–18.

64. e.g. in 2 Cor. 5:18–21; Col. 1:20–21.

65. Goldingay, 'Your Iniquities Have Made Separation between You and Your God', in Goldingay (ed.), *Atonement Today*, pp. 39–45.

66. Vincent Taylor wrote three major books demonstrating this, *Jesus and His Sacrifice: A Study of the Passion Sayings in the Gospels* (London: Macmillan, 1929); *The Atonement in New Testament Teaching*, 2nd ed. (London: Epworth, 1946); and *Forgiveness and Reconciliation*, 2nd ed. (London: Macmillan, 1946), although his denial of a substitutionary meaning to sacrifice must be questioned.

from the practices of others but from the cult the God of Israel gave to his people.

The New Testament inherited Old Testament sacrificial language and the elements of comparison are so extensive that we can hardly call this metaphor. Christ's death was not simply *like* a sacrifice, it *was* a sacrifice. So, for instance, in the epistle to the Hebrews (e.g. in Heb. 10:11–12), a straightforward contrast is made between the Old Testament sacrifices and that of Christ in terms of their effectiveness. This is not the language of analogy; rather it implies that both were viewed literally.[67]

Metaphor, although valuable, is the language of illustration and raises the question as to what literal truth it illustrates. If it is objected that every language is so shot through with metaphor that purely literal statement is difficult to find, we note that much that originated in metaphor is now 'dead metaphor', its power to evoke images now over, and its originally metaphorical sense has become its primary or literal sense. Gunton mentions, for instance, that the English 'muscle' appears to have originated from the Latin *musculus*, 'little mouse', but that it does not now evoke the image of a mouse.[68]

So, then, legal and cultic language applied in the New Testament to the cross has a special status not shared, for instance, by a metaphor like debt cancellation. The qualifying phrase 'in the New Testament' is important, for the history of theology shows that sometimes such language has been abstracted from its biblical context and interpreted in terms of a theologian's own culture, as in Anselm's *Cur Deus Homo?* with its feudal system background.

Do either law or sacrifice or both imply penal substitution in the New Testament? Paul relates the cross to God's law both in Romans (especially Rom. 2:12 – 3:31) and Galatians. The translation of *hilastērion* in Romans 3:25 is important and Morris has argued cogently for 'propitiation'.[69] Romans 1:18 – 3:31 stresses God's wrath and judgment so that when Paul writes of Christ's work we expect something relating not only to sin but to God's concern about it. This we find in *hilastērion*. In Galatians 3:10–14 Paul says that Christ has borne the curse of the law (i.e. as traditionally understood, this is the curse the law pronounces against the sinner),[70] by becoming a curse for us. Here both penalty and substitution are related to Christ.

---

67. See the discussion of metaphor on pp. 44–46.

68. Gunton, *The Actuality of Atonement*, p. 34.

69. See especially the detailed linguistic arguments in Morris, *Apostolic Preaching of the Cross*, pp. 155–174.

70. See ch. 4.

Without doubt the New Testament employs metaphors in connection with the atonement. Preachers should ensure their congregations understand their meaning and this will sometimes entail an excursion into biblical culture. In due course new Christians usually realize that greater understanding of Christian truth requires inhabiting two worlds, the Bible's and their own.[71]

Occasionally metaphors in the New Testament are taken from the Greco-Roman world where the gospel was preached. Debt cancellation and a Roman triumph, both referred to in Colossians 2:14–15, well illustrated the effects of the cross for those who knew their background, and the modern preacher can still employ them with explanation. Legal and sacrificial language, however, has special theological weight, originating in divinely given institutions deeply embedded in the Old Testament. They were a major part of the God-given religious culture of God's ancient people and so of the theological preparation for the gospel.

Illustrative language normally needs a resting place in the literal. Doctrine should not be based on illustrations, for their function is not to establish truth but to illuminate it. Even Paul Tillich, who treated the language of the New Testament as almost exclusively symbolic, asserted that the symbols rest on the literal fact that God is being.[72] Bultmann too, although viewing much New Testament language as mythological, sought a resting place for his thought in the kerygma, the basic message of the gospel, which he found (controversially) in the participationist language of Romans 6.

Is there something literal on which the New Testament's atonement metaphors and images rest? Yes, if penal substitution is not a metaphor but a literal fact. We are subject to God's authority as law-giver. In dying Christ took the punishment for our sins so that we need not bear it ourselves. In other words, he endured our penalty in our place. The laws and the sins are literal and Scripture warns us that punishment is also.

As Green and Baker recognize, penal substitution is so clear a concept that even a child can understand it.[73] This does not mean we should not

---

71. A. C. Thiselton explores this issue in its philosophical and theological implications, especially in *The Two Horizons: New Testament Hermeneutics and Philosophical Description* (Grand Rapids: Eerdmans; Exeter: Paternoster, 1980), and *New Horizons in Hermeneutics: The Theory and Practice of Transforming Biblical Reading* (Grand Rapids: Zondervan; Carlisle: Paternoster, 1992).

72. P. Tillich, *Systematic Theology*, vol. I (Chicago: University of Chicago Press, 1951), pp. 238–239.

73. Green and Baker, *Recovering the Scandal of the Cross*, p. 140.

seek illuminating contemporary illustrations, but we must exercise great care, for it is in terms of illustrations that the atonement has so often been misunderstood.

Those who object to making penal substitution foundational or deny it altogether sometimes employ metaphors of their own which are not always found in Scripture. This is not only permissible but hermeneutically positive if they are employed appropriately to illuminate biblical thought. As Green and Baker say, 'Metaphors work within cultures where a shared encyclopaedia can be assumed. Crossing cultures requires the creation of new metaphors, new ways of conceptualizing and communicating.'[74]

New metaphors must, of course, be meaningful. For instance, in commenting on Galatians 3:13 and 2 Corinthians 5:21, Stephen Travis says, 'Christ has experienced the sinner's estrangement from God, he has absorbed and thereby taken away sin, so that we might be brought into a right relationship with God.'[75] But what does 'absorbed' mean?[76] What is the significance of the estrangement? It is not clear. This applies too to a similar metaphor, one used by Chalke and Mann, when they say, 'Just as a lightning-conductor soaks up powerful and destructive bolts of electricity, so Jesus, as he hung on that cross, soaked up all the forces of hate, rejection, pain and alienation all around him.'[77] But how did this happen? The metaphor does not tell us.

Other ways of interpreting the cross have much to offer
It has been said that theologians are frequently right in what they affirm but wrong in what they deny. This is often true of the critics of penal substitution. There is much variety in the New Testament presentation of the cross and it is important for preachers to employ the full range of its teaching.[78] If this is

---

74. ibid., pp. 20–21.

75. S. H. Travis, 'Christ as Bearer of Divine Judgement in Paul's Thought about the Atonement', in Goldingay (ed.), *Atonement Today*, p. 26.

76. S. Westerholm too writes of Christ's 'absorption of our condemnation' (*Perspectives Old and New on Paul: The 'Lutheran' Paul and his Critics*, Grand Rapids: Eerdmans, 2004, p. 284).

77. Chalke and Mann, *The Lost Message of Jesus*, p. 179.

78. Peterson points out that a number of dimensions of the cross are highlighted in 2 Cor. 5:14 – 6:2 and Rom. 5:1–11, but that penal substitution is foundational to both passages. ('Atonement in the New Testament', in D. Peterson (ed.), *Where Wrath and Mercy Meet: Proclaiming the Atonement Today*, Carlisle: Paternoster, 2001, p. 36).

not done, in the worst scenario some congregations may conclude that despite his many texts their minister has only one sermon.

How, then, should we present the cross? As revelation of God's love, as victory over Satan, as willing suffering because of faithfulness to God, as identification with the sufferings of the marginalized, the shamed, the excluded, and so on? Yes, in all these ways, for all are true. I am convinced, however, that penal substitution is most basic and that so many other views relate to its consequences.[79] As Stott says, '"Substitution" is not a further "theory" or "image" to be set alongside the others, but rather the foundation of them all, without which each lacks cogency.'[80] It is, for instance, because Christ as God incarnate took the punishment for our sins that we see how much God loves us.

In the heyday of theological liberalism the main view of the atonement was subjective. The cross, revealing the greatness of God's love, was calculated to cause sinners to repent and trust themselves to the Saviour. But how God's love was revealed was often unclear. Evangelical preaching, however, can present the cross as the supreme revelation of God's love for the very reason that it involved substitutionary sin-bearing.

This moral influence view in a somewhat postmodern form is expressed by Alan Mann when he says, 'To try and account for *how* the death of Jesus reconciles the isolated, alienated self to the "Other" – for that is what atonement is – can only ever be a personal interpretation that may or may not be recognizable as a narrative of atonement to others. After all, no two encounters with the storied-Jesus are the same.'[81] In this context, 'for that is what atonement is' clearly shows he is thinking in subjective terms.

The New Testament makes clear that the atonement reveals God's love, but Chalke and Mann go too far in saying, 'The Bible never defines God as anger, power and judgment – in fact it never defines him as anything but love. But more than that, it never makes assertions about his anger, power or judgement independently of his love.'[82] This is misleading, for as we have already seen, the statement 'God is love', made twice in 1 John 4:8 and 16, is exactly parallel

---

79. We could use more space very profitably on these varied images of the atonement, but this chapter is an apologia for penal substitution, not an exposition of the many-sidedness of the cross.

80. Stott, *The Cross of Christ*, p. 168.

81. Mann, *Atonement for a 'Sinless' Society*, p. 133. His exposition of atonement in this book is almost entirely subjective.

82. Chalke and Mann, *The Lost Message of Jesus*, p. 63.

grammatically to 'God is light' (1 John 1:5),[83] which certainly refers to God's character, for the verse goes on to say, 'in him is no darkness at all'. Moreover, Scripture says much about God's anger, power and judgment, although not in terms of definitions of him. Probably they mean that these statements should only be considered in relation to his love, but this is a theological and not an exegetical comment and it raises important and contentious issues.

The word *hilasmos* occurs in the context of each of these two great statements (1 John 2:2; 4:10), and is from the same root as *hilastērion*, so that it concerns the turning aside of God's wrath against sin. Thus 1 John 4:10 asserts, 'This is love, not that we loved God, but that he loved us and sent his Son as a *hilasmos* for our sins.' So, then, at the heart of the supreme revelation of God's love in the cross we discover it dealing with his wrath against sin.

Today there is renewed interest in the view designated by Gustav Aulèn as *Christus Victor*,[84] in which the chief significance of the cross is that there Christ fought with the powers of evil and overcame them. He argued that Luther's main understanding of the cross was in such terms. Certainly Luther writes ecstatically about the defeat of Satan and his hosts at Calvary. If, however, we ask *how* this was accomplished we cannot find an answer within this frame of reference. It would seem that the answer must be in terms of penal substitution, which also Luther frequently expounded. The devil, who constantly endeavours to promote sin and who accuses God's people of sin,[85] was defeated when Christ bore sin's penalty. Satan's defeat is certainly an important New Testament theme, but abstracted from its other teaching about the cross it lacks proper rationale. Penal substitution provides this.

In his ministry's closing days Jesus was much aware of Satan (John 14:30; 16:11). Approaching his death he said, 'Now is the time for judgment on this world; now the prince of this world will be driven out' (John 12:31). The programmatic position of John 1:29 in John's Gospel, however, suggests we should not abstract this conquest of Satan from the role of Jesus as the atoning Lamb. In this case, the later passage gains illumination from the earlier.

Penal substitution, or at least satisfaction for sin, and victory over Satan

---

83. Also by 'God is spirit' (John 4:24).

84. G. Aulèn, *Christus Victor: An Historical Study of the Three Main Types of the Idea of the Atonement*, tr. A. G. Hebert (London: Macmillan, 1931).

85. See especially Zech. 3:1, and H. Blocher, 'Agnus Victor: The Atonement as Victory and Vicarious Punishment', in J. G. Stackhouse (ed.), *What Does It Mean To Be Saved?* (Grand Rapids: Baker Academic, 2002), pp. 67–91.

come together in Colossians 2:14–15 where Christ's work is both debt-cancellation and military triumph. The order of treatment may suggest that forgiveness through Christ's death was the cause of the disarming of the evil powers, for sin is the sphere of Satan's operations and it was sin Christ dealt with in his death, so thwarting the designs of the evil powers. Hebrews 2:14–17 also refers both to Christ's victory over the devil through his death and to his propitiatory sacrifice, although without explicitly relating them.

Gregory Boyd, however, points out that in both Ephesians and Colossians, exposition of the cosmic dimension of the cross precedes its application to human beings (Eph. 1:22 – 2:8; Col. 1:15–23), and he then says, 'This passage clearly presents our reconciliation to God as one aspect of the cosmic recon-ciliation to God accomplished through the cross. The cosmic conquest, one might say, logically precedes the anthropological application.'[86] We should not forget, however, the occasional nature of Paul's correspondence with the churches. These two epistles were written when some of the churches in the province of Asia were encountering teaching which exalted other spiritual beings at the expense of Christ, so that it is understandable that Paul should put special stress on the defeat and subjugation of these by Christ in his death and exaltation. This need not in any way demote to a secondary position the relevance of the cross to human sin.

No Christian would want to diminish the cosmic significance of the cross, but to say that Christ defeated Satan or to say that he has made universal rec-onciliation or peace does not tell us how all this was done. The rationale of the cosmic view must surely be penal substitution. God overcame Satan through his act of reconciliation, of peace-making, of redemption, all of which are interpreted elsewhere in penal substitutionary terms. Sometimes Paul paints a large scene with a large brush, but what is it that is happening at its heart? It is Christ bearing sin in substitutionary fashion.

That the cross reveals God's love and that there Christ defeated Satan are really effects of the atonement on us and Satan respectively, rather than the atonement itself, for 'at-one-ment' is a term better kept for Christ's work in objectively bridging the gulf between God and sinful humanity. These effects meet aspects of our spiritual need, assuring us that God loves us and that we need not fear the evil powers.

A view of the cross increasingly promoted and expounded today and which owes much to Moltmann and the liberation theologians stresses that through

---

86. G. A. Boyd, *God at War: The Bible and Spiritual Conflict* (Downers Grove: InterVarsity Press, 1997), p. 250.

Christ's sufferings at Calvary God identified with and so can empathize with the oppressed and the unjustly accused. This means that the cross, which was a stumbling block to people in New Testament times, can in fact be viewed as a major argument for Christianity.

What can be said for this view? At the human level Christ died because he disturbed the *status quo*, and of the seven sayings from the cross three are from Old Testament psalms. In each the writer is aware of the malignity of his enemies (Ps. 22:1/Matt. 27:46; Ps. 69:21/John 19:28; Ps. 31:5/Luke 23:46).[87] Stott says, 'Although of course they were written to express the distress of the psalmist himself, yet Jesus had evidently come to see himself and his own sufferings as their ultimate fulfilment.'[88] Perhaps on the cross he was meditating on these psalms just as he may have focused in devotion on Deuteronomy 6 – 8 during his wilderness temptations (Matt. 4:4, 7, 10). Without doubt, to ponder his experience of suffering can greatly help those facing apparently undeserved suffering. The epistle to the Hebrews says he came to share the conditions of our human life (Heb. 2:17–18; 4:15–16).[89]

The New Testament does not, however, relate these psalms theologically to the identification of Jesus with the oppressed, whereas we may discern the influence of the cry of dereliction in a verse like 2 Corinthians 5:21, where the cross is interpreted in a way that implies penal substitution. This means, then, that although we should certainly take Moltmann's point this must not displace for us the New Testament's strong emphasis on Christ's cross as a death for our sins.

I was disturbed recently in reading the quite detailed Easter weekend service sheet of a local church to see that the focus was entirely on the relevance of Christ's sufferings for our sufferings, with no reference to their relevance for our sins. T. Smail rightly says,

> Much contemporary preaching of the cross, whatever the formal theology of
> the preacher, simply abandons all thought of Christ's having done once for all
> for us on the cross that which reconciles us to God, and presents the cross as the

---

87. Moltmann tells how, as a prisoner of war, the cry of dereliction enabled him to see that Christ understood his sense of God-forsakenness. J. Moltmann (ed.), *How I Have Changed: Reflections on Thirty Years of Theology* (London: SCM, 1997), p. 13.

88. Stott, *The Cross of Christ*, p. 31.

89. See M. Ovey, 'The Son Incarnate in a Hostile World', in D. Peterson (ed.), *The Word Became Flesh: Evangelicals and the Incarnation. Papers from the Sixth Oak Hill College Annual School of Theology* (Paternoster: Carlisle, 2003), p. 53.

demonstration in time of God's eternal love for and identification with humanity in its misery and failure. We speak much more with Moltmann of Christ justifying God to us by sharing on the cross our suffering and God-forsakenness than of Christ justifying us to God by bearing our sins . . . The former approach is to be welcomed but not if it replaces or excludes the latter.[90]

All our thinking should start with God. The theologies of Bultmann and Tillich, so widely influential in the third quarter of the twentieth century, abandoned the time-honoured and moreover biblical way of starting with God. Instead they began with humanity, with its *Angst* (Bultmann) or its ultimate concern (Tillich). In this they followed the existentialist Martin Heidegger, who was a major influence on them both and who, although not an atheist, did not take God into account in his philosophy.[91] Of course our theology must engage with human need, but we see this best in the light of God's revelation of himself. So often the Godward dimenson of Christ's work is played down, sidelined or even denied, and this must rob the Christian of full assurance. What will happen when I, a sinner, face the judgment of God if Christ did not bear the penalty of my sins?

It misconceives the significance of sacrificial atonement
Pinnock says,

> There is . . . work to be done on the evangelical doctrine of atonement, which has focused on penal substitution in altogether too crude and exclusive a manner. I am not surprised that liberals have turned away from it sometimes in disgust. For example, when people suggested that Jesus appeased the Father to make him be merciful to sinners, they are on very shaky ground. They make it sound as if God really hates sinners and has to be persuaded/placated to them through an innocent victim.[92]

What Pinnock describes as 'the evangelical doctrine of atonement' is actually a serious misunderstanding or faulty presentation of it only a hair's breadth from pagan views of sacrifice in which a worshipper seeks to placate a god's

---

90. T. Smail, 'Can One Man Die for the People?', in J. Goldingay (ed.), *Atonement Today: A Symposium at St John's College, Nottingham* (London: SPCK, 1995), pp. 75–76.

91. See W. Barrett, 'Heidegger and Modern Existentialism', in B. Magee (ed.), *Men of Ideas: Some Creators of Contemporary Philosophy* (London: BBC, 1978), pp. 92–95.

92. Pinnock, in Pinnock and Brown, *Theological Crossfire*, p. 148.

anger. Abstract the idea from its biblical setting and this conclusion seems appropriate, but this we must not do.

May we interpret the cross in terms of sacrifice? At one time the Old Testament prophets were often viewed as opposed to sacrifice *per se*. This view faces major difficulties and is much less held today. Not only would it completely polarize the prophets and the Mosaic law, but it misses the fact that in the prophetic view of the future sacrifice plays an important part, so that Ezekiel visualizes a great future temple (Ezek. 40 – 48) and Jeremiah, often reckoned one of the strongest critics of sacrifice, envisages priests and sacrifices in the people's future under God's blessing (Jer. 31:14; 33:18, 21).[93] The prophetic passages critical of sacrifice as practised in their day all highlight either sincerity or obedience, both largely lacking in Israel's ritualism at the time.[94] In fact, obedience, if it is obedience to the Word of God, would have embraced the sacrifices, for in the law the people were commanded to bring them.

God's gift of the Old Testament sacrifices and his supreme gift of Christ's one final sacrifice reveal the marvel of his grace to sinners. It is hardly possible to exaggerate the importance of this, so well expressed in the Old Testament by Leviticus 17:11 where God says of the blood of sacrifice, 'I have given it to you to make atonement for yourselves on the altar,' and in the New by Romans 3:25 and 2 Corinthians 5:21, in both of which the cross is seen as God's act. The way back to God was provided by God himself.

But why was sacrifice needed? Because of God's wrath against sinners. Propitiation cannot be adequately discussed without consideration of this, its correlative. In his commentary on the epistle to the Romans, however, C. H. Dodd argued that Paul uses the term 'not to describe the attitude of God to human beings, but to describe an inevitable process of cause and effect in a moral universe', in effect depersonalizing it.[95] Inevitably this affected his view

---

93. These passages in Jeremiah are strangely absent from the index of J. Skinner, *Prophecy and Religion*, an important volume on Jeremiah which promoted the idea that he and other prophets completely repudiated sacrifice (London: Cambridge University Press, 1936).

94. See Isa. 1:11–17; Jer 7:22–23; Hos. 6:6; Amos 5:21–27; Mic. 6:6–8; cf. 1 Sam. 15:22–23; Ps. 50:7–15), and the treatment of these passages by E. C. Lucas, 'Sacrifice in the Prophets', in Beckwith and Selman (eds.), *Sacrifice in the Bible*, pp. 59–74.

95. C. H. Dodd, *The Epistle of Paul to the Romans* (London: Hodder and Stoughton, 1932), p. 23. But 'from heaven' (v. 18) and the threefold phrase 'God gave them over' (vv. 24, 26, 28) all imply definite divine action, not simply an impersonal law.

of Romans 3:25 where he rejected 'propitiation' as misleading and rendered *hilastērion* as 'means by which guilt is annulled'.[96]

Green and Baker show Dodd's influence.[97] They dwell mostly on the historical operation of divine wrath[98] and say of Paul's references to coming wrath that 'even in this context, divine anger or retributive justice are alien concepts', and that Paul is referring to 'the climactic, end-time scene of judgment when those who prefer to worship idols rather than the living God receive the fruits of their own misplaced hopes and commitments'. But what is this if it is not 'retributive justice'? Obviously Paul does not contemplate here a reformative or dissuasive purpose for this judgment.[99]

Moreover, Dodd's depersonalizing of God's wrath seems anachronistic, for the biblical writers do not deal with impersonal principles (more the province of philosophers) but with personal attitudes and actions. This means that a destiny of judgment for idol-worshippers must originate in the mind and heart of God and so express his wrath against sin. Paul says to stubborn sinners that 'you are storing up wrath against yourself for the day of God's wrath, when his righteous judgment will be revealed' (Rom. 2:5). The double use of 'wrath' and the full phrase 'the wrath of God' here seem anything but impersonal, and this verse is soon followed by the comment that 'for those who are self-seeking and who reject the truth and follow evil, there will be wrath and anger' (v. 8).

Of course we must be careful how we express this. Green and Baker say that penal substitution is easy to caricature,[100] but they tend to do that themselves! Modern linguistic philosophy recognizes, as we all do in conversation, that words, phrases and sentences have not only dictionary definitions but emotional tones. Green and Baker refer to terms such as 'rancor', 'vengeful', 'vindictive', 'enraged or infuriated . . . bent on retribution',[101] all suggestive of a bad-tempered man. They do not necessarily identify with such language, but

---

96. ibid., p. 55. Against this view, see e.g. Morris, *The Cross in the New Testament*, pp. 190–191.

97. So also does Travis, 'Christ as Bearer of Divine Judgement', pp. 21–38.

98. Green and Baker, *Recovering the Scandal of the Cross*, pp. 53–55.

99. Stott recommends C. S. Lewis's essay, 'The Humanitarian Theory of Punishment', in P. E. Hughes (ed.), *Churchmen Speak* (Marcham Manor Press, 1966), pp. 39–44. See also L. Hodgson, *The Doctrine of the Atonement*, Hale Lectures 1950 (London: Nisbet, 1951), pp. 52–67; and Letham, *The Work of Christ*, pp. 125–126.

100. Green and Baker, *Recovering the Scandal of the Cross*, pp. 30, 32.

101. ibid., pp. 63, 98, 147, 195, 202.

is penal substitution really preached so very badly? Nor does even Anselm's view merit the criticism, paraphrased from other writers without adverse comment, 'God plays the role of the sadist who willfully inflicts punishment, and Jesus embraces the character of the masochist who willingly suffers it.'[102] Such language is inappropriate, for its normal use is in contexts of personal animosity or of abnormal psychology rather than regulative justice. The writers of this book do not appear to employ this distinction.

Their comment on the Day of Atonement is most misleading. They refer only to the scapegoat and they say, 'Note that in this rite the scapegoat is not butchered and presented as a sacrificial offering, and there is no attempt (or necessity) to appease God.'[103] Yet the complete ritual involves *two* goats, together constituting a sin-offering (Lev. 16:5), which as we have noted makes the implications of the whole ceremony clear.[104] Moreover, the use of the same type of animal for both purposes underlines this fact, for a number of different animals were involved in the sacrificial system, some on the Day of Atonement itself.

At one point, Green and Baker do deal with Christ's death as a sacrifice,[105] and not only do they embrace substitution but their own treatment cries out for the word 'penal'. Writing of Old Testament sacrifice, they emphasize (the italics are theirs) that 'the beast represented the sinner *in his or her sin* (i.e. *qua* sinner)', and they then say, 'the sinner's sin was identified with the beast, and its life became forfeit',[106] but they do not say why this was. If by God's decree death is sin's penalty as Scripture indicates,[107] then surely all the elements of penal substitution are in those two sentences.[108]

After examining Galatians 3:13; 2 Corinthians 5:21; Romans 3:24–26 and 5:9–10, Travis says that Christ experienced divine judgment on our behalf, but that to say he underwent punishment for our sins is to go further than Paul himself goes.[109] But are not judgment and punishment so closely linked that the one must imply the other?

---

102. ibid., pp. 91–92, paraphrasing B. W. Harrison and C. Heyward.

103. ibid., p. 80.

104. See p. 88.

105. Green and Baker, *Recovering the Scandal of the Cross*, pp. 63–65.

106. ibid., p. 64.

107. e.g. in Rom. 5:12; 6:23; 1 Cor. 15:21.

108. cf. the well-known admission by Vincent Taylor that Paul's teaching is 'within a hair's breadth of substitution'. The whole passage in *The Atonement in New Testament Teaching*, pp. 288–289, is worth reading.

109. Travis, 'Christ as Bearer of Divine Judgement', p. 33.

Did the cross of Christ, an act in history, actually effect a change in God?[110] Pinnock says,

> Evangelicals seem to think that, until the Cross, the divide had not been bridged, as if the Cross actually changed God in AD 32. Do we mean that there was no salvific will of God before that moment? Do we actually think that the Cross changed God's wrath into rather than its being the gift of his love? . . . Surely it would be better to say that God is everywhere and always love, and that what we needed from Christ was a decisive presentation of it in history. What we needed once and for all was a representative act on the part of the Messiah that would deal with something in the holiness of God's nature that would open up the perfect satisfactory basis of reconciliation.[111]

Strangely, this last sentence sounds almost like a statement of penal substitution.

Stott says, 'If it is God's wrath which needed to be propitiated, it is God's love which did the propitiating. If it may be said that the propitiation "changed" God, or that by it he changed himself, let us be clear he did not change from wrath to love, or from enmity to grace, since his character is unchanging. What the propitiation changed was his dealings with us.'[112]

Because God is eternal, this act was efficacious also for those who were objects of his grace before it ever took place (Rom. 3:25–27; Heb. 9:15). This is in line with Calvin's words, 'It is because he first loves us that he afterwards reconciles us to himself.'[113] In fact, as the cross reveals God's eternal purpose (1 Pet. 1:19–20), it is best for us to say that his wrath and grace, his holiness and love, were *simultaneously* revealed there.

The idea that one may bear the penalty of another is of doubtful morality

Does penal substitution serve the ends of justice? Smail says guilt and punishment are not like fines which can be incurred by one person and settled by another.[114] There would perhaps be some weight to this objection if we were to think simply of an analogy from human law, but the gospel makes it clear

---

110. This could not be, as God is unchanging in his nature. See ch. 2.

111. In Pinnock and Brown, *Theological Crossfire*, p. 149.

112. Stott, *The Cross of Christ*, p. 174.

113. Calvin, *Institutes*, II, xvi, 3.

114. Smail, 'Can One Man Die for the People?', p. 78; cf. also Smail, *Once and for All: A Confession of the Cross* (London: Darton, Longman and Todd, 1998), pp. 97–99.

that God's way is both like and unlike the way things happen in human society. If it were not so, we would have no gospel, for God's grace is unique. As God says, in one of the Old Testament's most moving revelations of his love, 'For I am God, and not man' (Hos. 11:9).

We noted in chapter 2 that we should recognize the importance of each of God's attributes.[115] The gospel reveals not only God's love and justice but also his wisdom. A major purpose of retributive punishment is to show the offender the seriousness of his or her offences. If this can only be by the sinner's punishment our situation is beyond hope, but the gospel shows that God does forgive sinners, although in a way indicating with crystal clarity his serious view of their sin. If our penalty is borne by Christ and if the cry of dereliction gives us some insight into what this penalty is, we see how heinous our sins are and how God loathes them while at the very same time he shows us his marvellous love and grace.

If I am a sinner and if in the gospel my sins are forgiven (as all the main views of the atonement recognize), how immoral this would be if it happened without any change in my attitude to my sins, which must surely involve my recognition of the punishment-worthiness of my offences! The moral influence view abstracted from penal substitution is inadequate for this purpose and lacks an adequate rationale. It is when we see God taking our sins seriously that we begin to take them seriously ourselves. When we see that Christ has borne the awful penalty of our sins, we begin to realize how great is God's love and are moved to turn from our sins to Christ.

Green and Baker are concerned that proponents of penal substitution 'often leave little room for ethical comportment . . . Apart from allowing my name to be moved to the correct side of God's legal ledger, what significance has the cross of Christ for faith and life, according to this view?'[116] It is, of course, possible so to compartmentalize biblical teaching that we do not allow two great doctrines to interact, but the same New Testament that teaches us that Christ bore the penalty for our sins also teaches that the Holy Spirit works in our sinful hearts to bring us to a new attitude to our sins.[117] When Peter preached the gospel in the power of the Holy Spirit at Pentecost, he called the hearers to repent and to be baptized and he promised them the gift of the Holy Spirit (Acts 2:37–39). In such a situation the purpose of punishment is achieved, because I, the sinner, now realize how awful my sins are. In the

---

115. See pp. 54–55.

116. Green and Baker, *Recovering the Scandal of the Cross*, p. 31.

117. See Gal. 5:16–25; Eph. 4:29–31.

highly paradoxical and thought-provoking words of an old hymn, 'A sinner is a sacred thing; the Holy Ghost hath made him so.'[118]

Writing about justification Stott says,

> There are those who have a strong antipathy to legal categories in all talk about salvation on the ground that they represent God as Judge and King, not as Father, and therefore cannot adequately portray either his personal dealings with us or our personal relationship with him. This objection would be sustained if justification were the only image of salvation. But its juridical flavour is balanced by the more personal imagery of 'reconciliation' and 'adoption'.[119]

It is through the Spirit that adoption, secured by Christ, becomes an inward reality (Gal. 4:4–7).

Luke placed the story of Zacchaeus (Luke 19:1–10) close to the parable of the Pharisee and the taxman (Luke 18:9–14). What would the taxman do when he went home after his expression of deep penitence and God's amazing verdict that he was 'righteous'? He would act like Zacchaeus and show evidence of a changed life. John 3:7 and 14 give the two imperatives of the gospel, for our justification through the cross is always inwardly sealed by our new birth by the Spirit. As the Puritans saw so clearly, justification and regeneration are distinguishable but can never be separated.

Penal substitution misconceives the role of Christ in the atonement

What is the appropriate term for Christ's role in his saving work? This has been much discussed. The two chief terms employed are 'representative' and 'substitute'. Many prefer the former while others, as Paul Wells notes, are prepared to use 'substitute', but object to 'penal'. He points out that some of the terms used are not very precise, and 'like credit cards [they] can be used in different theological banks. By adding the word *penal* to *substitute* things are more precise.'[120] 'Representative' is a legitimate and even necessary term, but there is a vital truth it does not convey clearly and for which the appropriate word is 'substitute'.

A representative acts on behalf of others and what he or she does they in

118. Quoted by C. H. Spurgeon, *All of Grace* (Fort Worth: R. D. McCormack, 2001), p. 15.

119. Stott, *The Cross of Christ*, p. 183; cf. also his comment on Rom. 6 (p. 188).

120. P. Wells, 'A Free Lunch at the End of the Universe?', *Themelios* 29:1 (Autumn, 2003), pp. 41–42.

fact do through him or her. The representative may pledge subsequent action by those represented, in some cases acting as a prototype providing a pattern for their later action. Sometimes those represented need to ratify the actions of their representative. The precise nature of the representation can be made plain by the context, but 'substitute' is more specific in its normal use, with the substitute exhausting the responsibility of the person substituted.

A substitute or representative may be appointed by the person acted for or in some circumstances by somebody else. Christ our Substitute was appointed by God and he endured the penalty for our sins to exempt us from bearing it. As our Representative too, he is divinely appointed and the prototypical pattern of death (to sin) and resurrection (to new life) he established is meant to be reproduced in our experience. We are to reckon ourselves to have died with Christ and risen again with him.

Three Greek prepositions occur in such a statement as 'Christ died for us' or 'Christ died for our sins'. *Hyper* and *peri* are less specific than *anti*, and indicate that something is done in relation to or concerning something or someone. This can involve substitution, but not necessarily,[121] whereas *anti* normally does. It is found in Mark 10:45 (cf. Matt. 20:28) and 1 Timothy 2:6. The Gospel saying is particularly significant as it climaxes a course of teaching about the cross that our Lord gave his disciples (Mark 8:31; 9:12, 30–32; 10:32–34). Having reiterated that he 'must' suffer, he now indicates why.

A careful examination of Paul's epistle to the Romans gives us a correct perspective. In Romans 6, Paul writes about our participation, our involvement, in what Christ did for us, implying that he acted representatively. Some writers regard this as the central feature of Paul's thinking about the cross,[122] and for Bultmann it represented the whole gospel. If, however, he teaches penal substitution in chapter 3, as we have seen, we need to explore the relationship between these two perceptions of Calvary's meaning.

In these chapters Paul pursues a consecutive argument in which

---

121. But see Morris (*Apostolic Preaching of the Cross*, pp. 62ff.), who argues that *hyper* very often has clear substitutionary significance in the New Testament; cf. Jeffery, Ovey and Sach, *Pierced for our Transgressions*, pp. 75–77 on the use of *hyper* in John's Gospel.

122. Travis says, 'It is notable how often Paul refers to Christ's death with a brief sacrificial allusion and then goes on to elaborate its purpose in terms of participation in Christ' ('Christ as Bearer of Divine Judgement', p. 36). He instances 1 Thess. 5:9–10; Rom. 8:3–4; 14:9; 2 Cor. 5:14–15, 21. He is right, but the reason surely is because Paul writes as a teacher concerned to show the moral implications of the message his readers have already embraced.

substitution, and penal substitution at that (3:21–26), is the basis of representation (5:12–21) and representation the basis of participation (ch. 6). Because Jesus bore our penalty on the cross as our Substitute and Representative, both our ultimate destiny and our life in this world are bound up with him and shaped by what he has done. How unthinkable, then, that we should continue in sin![123]

It is not simply that the penal idea occurs first, but also that chapter 5 links them theologically. As we have now been justified by Christ's blood (i.e. Christ's blood is already efficacious for us), so it is certain we shall be saved from God's wrath through him (Rom. 5:9). This is virtually a summary of Romans 3:21–26 and shows that what Paul expressed there is still in his mind. Then comes his great comparison and contrast between the two representative men, Adam and Christ, and he again says that Christ dealt with our judgment and condemnation (5:16), surely meaning, as in 3:25, that this was effected through his death. So this passage about Adam and Christ provides the basis for the participatory language of chapter 6.

These two chapters are linked by 'grace' (5:20–21; 6:1), and in chapter 6 Paul sets a true inference from God's grace to us in Christ over against a false one. This certainly indicates that our participation in Christ's death was very important for him, but also that it was based on his substitutionary work. We should note too that Romans 5:12 is linked by *dia touto*, 'therefore', to the earlier verses in chapter 5 and that Paul uses a conjunction with the same force (*oun*) at the start of chapter 6.

It does not place sufficient emphasis on the life and resurrection of Christ

This is strongly stressed by Chalke and Mann.[124] Without doubt not only should the cross not be separated from the life preceding it and the resurrection which followed it, but these should be given full theological value. The cross is central to the Christian faith, but the significance of what Christ effected there depends on his nature and character revealed during the course of his life and on the fact that his atoning work was vindicated by his resurrection from the dead. Calvin, for instance, held that the chief circumstance of Christ's death was his obedience, and J. K. Mozley is right in saying, 'Something less than justice has at times been done to the Reformers . . . Their

---

123. As Smail says, 'On the cross we are excluded only that we might be included, substitution for the sake of participation' ('Can One Man Die for the People?', p. 91).

124. Chalke and Mann, *The Lost Message of Jesus*, pp. 171–193.

soteriology is not concentrated to such an extent upon Christ's death that His life ceases to have any redemptive value.'[125]

To say this, however, is not altogether to deal with the concerns of Chalke and Mann, for they appear to be insisting that Christ's life and his resurrection have value in their own right. Now it is true, as we have noted earlier, that Christians in their thinking and devotions and preachers in their preaching should not only believe and preach what the Bible teaches but emphasize what the Bible emphasizes. An outstanding statement of this occurs in 1 Corinthians 15:3–4, where Paul refers to the death, burial and resurrection of Christ as of 'first importance'. This does not mean, though, that other aspects of Christian truth and other features of the life and ministry of Christ are unimportant, but simply that these facts need special emphasis.

It might seem at first sight that Paul's chief concern in these verses is with the resurrection. Without doubt he had an apologetic motive in this, but we should note that although he adduced the witness of Old Testament Scripture for both Christ's death and his resurrection, only his death is assigned a particular meaning here. This may suggest that his burial and particularly his resurrection take their main significance from his death for our sins. Theologically, special importance attaches to his death, while apologetically, it attaches to his resurrection.

Study of each Gospel, however, shows each writer's particular concern to emphasize the cross, to do precisely what Paul does in 1 Corinthians 15. Certainly the amount of explicit atonement theology in the Synoptic Gospels is not large, but this is to be expected. The disciples were so possessed by triumphalist concepts of messiahship that they needed first to be told repeatedly and emphatically that Jesus was going to suffer and die.[126] Once this was patently clear, he could then start teaching the meaning of the cross, as he does in Mark 10:45 and 14:24. It is worth noting that the ransom saying in Mark 10:45 is preceded by references to his death as a cup and a baptism (Mark 10:38), both of which probably indicate experiencing punishment.

Green and Baker say the resurrection is not needed for the penal substitution model,[127] but it is. It is often referred to in Acts, frequently in passages

---

125. J. K. Mozley, *The Doctrine of the Atonement* (London: Duckworth, 1937), p. 143.

126. That this repetition was not only to clarify the nature of his messiahship but also to stress the importance of the cross is confirmed by Paul's words, 'For what I received I passed on to you as of first importance: that Christ died for our sins according to the Scriptures. . .' (1 Cor. 15:3).

127. Green and Baker, *Recovering the Scandal of the Cross*, p. 108.

which call the cross a tree (Acts 5:30; 10:39, 13:29), suggesting the bearing of God's curse against sins worthy of death. In such passages the resurrection signifies God's reversal of the crucifixion viewed as an act of sinful men. Moreover, Romans 4:25 ('He was delivered over to death for our sins and was raised to life for our justification'), in the light of Romans 3:24–26, strongly suggests that the demonstration of God's gracious and just deed in giving Christ to be our Substitute required his resurrection to seal it as evidence of the efficacy of his sacrifice.

This by no means exhausts the significance of his resurrection. For one thing, faith cannot be a reality unless it is placed in a living Person. We may so present atonement through the cross as to give the impression that salvation comes by accepting a formula rather than by trusting a Person. This would make becoming a Christian similar in principle to becoming a Muslim, which simply requires acknowledgment that there is no God but God and that Mohammed is his prophet. 'Putting my faith in it' (the gospel) must mean 'putting my faith in him' (the crucified and living Christ as presented in the gospel).

It is through uniting us to Christ in practical terms that the Holy Spirit provides the dynamic for living the Christian life, which is itself viewed as a resurrection life.[128] Romans 6 gives equal weight to the death and the resurrection of Jesus. In his epistle to the Ephesians, Paul also stresses that the Christ to whom Christians are united is now exalted at God's right hand, showing us that for our new life in Christ all the resources of heaven are available.

What place do the life and ministry of Jesus have in the gospel? Each Gospel informs us about his ministry as a whole, so that writers complaining at the playing down of the life of Jesus are right to protest and we should listen to them. If in the gospel we call people to trust themselves to Jesus, the Gospels are indispensable in their witness to his utter trustworthiness. Here is Somebody quite unique in his combination of saving power and deep compassion and the former is manifestly an expression of the latter. This means that the reader is powerfully drawn to Christ as a person before it becomes clear that he is going to die, and the cross may therefore be seen as the place where that saving power and deep compassion find fullest expression.

It divides the Trinity

Penal substitution is sometimes presented, at least by its critics, in such a way as to suggest that the Father forced his innocent Son to take the punishment

---

128. Jeffery, Ovey and Sach emphasize the importance of union with Christ (*Pierced for our Transgressions*, pp. 242–249) in relation to the morality of penal substitution.

of guilty sinners. Chalke and Mann describe this as 'cosmic child abuse',[129] a shocking description which would have a measure of truth if this presentation were to be accurate. If the atonement has ever been so presented in preaching (a good question!), its rejection is no surprise. In fact it must be rejected, for it is not the gospel and it grossly misrepresents the relationship of the Father and the Son.

Christ's experience in Gethsemane clearly shows that the passion meant he had to drink an awful cup of suffering, but also that he accepted this because he loved his Father and was committed to his will. His willingness is tested but is never in doubt. Indeed, this willingness is essential to his character and that character, too, is important for the atonement, for only the supremely Obedient could take the place of disobedient sinners.[130] It might be objected that this could simply have been submissive complicity in abuse,[131] but this would be to overlook Christ's own emphasis on the love of the Father for the Son (John 3:35; 5:20; 17:23–24) and the fact that this is referred to in the context of his teaching that the Father is concerned to honour him (John 5:16–30) and, in line with this, the Son's prayer that the Father would glorify him (John 17:1, 24).

A most helpful feature of Stott's book is his presentation of the atonement as the self-substitution of God for our sins.[132] Paul says that 'God was in Christ, reconciling the world unto himself' (2 Cor. 5:19 KJV). It matters little whether or not 'in' here designates Christ as the 'location' of God the Reconciler, so affirming the incarnation, or as the Agent of the reconciliation, if we believe in his deity on other biblical grounds. Green and Baker hardly mention his deity, which is of course the indispensable basis of John Stott's emphasis. These authors show concern to relate the atonement to other aspects of Christian truth and so it is reasonable to expect them to handle this theme.

The cry of dereliction, 'My God, my God, why have you forsaken me?', is

---

129. Chalke and Mann, *The Lost Message of Jesus*, p. 182. Green and Baker refer to 'divine child abuse' (*Recovering the Scandal of the Cross*, p. 31). See also B. D. McLaren, *The Story We Find Ourselves In* (San Francisco: Wiley, 2003), p. 102; contra D. A. Carson, *Becoming Conversant with the Emerging Church* (Grand Rapids: Zondervan, 2005), p. 166, n. 26.

130. Guillebaud, *Why the Cross?*, pp. 146–154, is helpful on moral objections to penal substitution.

131. It was Roy Kearsley who warned me of this possible objection.

132. This is the title of his sixth chapter (Stott, *The Cross of Christ*, pp. 133–163).

not only beyond plumbing emotionally but is also as theologically profound as anything in Scripture. It must be the deepest question ever asked, taking up into itself the greatest questions of human concern such as the nature of God, the existence of evil, the meaning of suffering. It is so disappointing and disturbing to find no reference to it in Green and Baker's book. This is surprising not simply because of its importance in Moltmann's very influential work, *The Crucified God*, but particularly because of its presence at the climax of the passion story in both Matthew and Mark.

It stands in these two Gospels as the one saying from the cross they record and it is uninterpreted except for the crowd's misunderstanding of it (Matt. 27:45–47; Mark 15:33–35).[133] Both these facts make us wonder if the writers meant to compel readers to ponder its meaning and perhaps to read the Gospels again for interpretative clues. Probably this is so. Clues are there in Mark 10:45 and 14:24 (and the Matthaean parallels) and in the repeated 'must' of Mark 8:31 and 9:12. No wonder these Gospels also record the darkening of the sky, the rending of the temple veil and in Matthew's case the geological repercussions and the emergence of the Old Testament saints from their tombs. How amazing, too, that the centurion who had heard this man ask why God had forsaken him should *then* affirm, 'Surely he was the Son of God!' (Matt. 27:54; Mark 15:39)

Oral reading of Scripture giving careful attention to emphasis, pausing, tones of irony, delight, sadness and so on is really a form of exegesis, helping the hearers' understanding. But where should we place the emphasis in this awful cry: on 'why' or 'you' or 'me' or 'forsaken'? Given the perfect fellowship of Jesus with his Father not only throughout his life but in all eternity, each word is amazing, each giving its own dimension to an utterance unique in human history and human literature. Hosea 11:1–11 is one of the Old Testament's most moving passages, especially verses 8 and 9 and particularly the remarkable words 'For I am God and not man', but how much more moving still is the revelation of God's love in Christ and the great costliness of its supreme expression!

We cannot empty the atonement of its awesome mystery. Employ logic as we may, seek adequate illustrations as we may try, we will never find a complete analogy in human relationships. This is to be expected. Every great Christian doctrine has at its heart some unique fact, for there is only one Trinity, only one God-Man, and so on. It is therefore no surprise to find Christ's atoning

---

133. As Smail points out, it is inconceivable it could have been invented by Christians (*Once and for All*, p. 22).

work to be unique. That God should act in love to effect his own propitiation can have no real parallel on the human scene and should fill us with wonder and praise.[134] Some things can, however, be said and some aspects of the doctrine illustrated, always with care, from human life, for otherwise we could hardly preach in a way that relates to human experience.

The nearest we have to an interpretation of the cry of dereliction is Paul's profound statement, 'God made him who had no sin to be sin for us, so that in him we might be made the righteousness of God' (2 Cor. 5:21). We should, however, set alongside these verses his affirmation, 'God was in Christ, reconciling the world unto himself.' The Father and the Son were acting together in the atonement if, as we know, the cross expressed God's will.

If it be objected that taking the cry of dereliction as pointing to an actual forsaking means dividing the Trinity, what is meant? Is it division of being or purpose or function? The ontological oneness of the three holy Persons is itself a profound mystery and the relationship of the atonement to it simply deepens that mystery. There was a difference of function between the Father and Son in the work of atonement, but in any case theologians accept this as a feature of the trinitarian life both in creation and redemption. Gethsemane reveals that despite the dreadful cost of the cross, there was no division of purpose between Father and Son.

The purpose of doing the Father's will, which had characterized Christ's whole ministry, was sustained to the end. Indeed, nothing could be more endearing to the Father than such costly obedience from his Son. Here, then, is a most moving paradox: he loved him for himself, but punished him for us. Even Calvin, convinced as he was of penal substitution, nevertheless wrote, 'How could he be angry with the beloved Son, with whom his soul was well pleased?'[135]

In the nature of the case, we must resist pressure to find an explanation for everything. If revelation is essential to true worship, so also is mystery and in true Christian worship the two find combination. How can we presume to tell the full truth about the atonement when it was no mere man but the very Son of God who asked, 'Why?'

---

134. Smail asks, 'What does it mean to say "God propitiated himself"'? Can the verb really have the same person for its subject and object and still retain its meaning?' (ibid., p. 87). But it is inevitable that language should be strained almost to breaking point to express a unique truth.

135. Calvin, *Institutes*, II, xvi, 11.

It is more an exercise in theological logic than a doctrine drawn from Scripture

Green and Baker seem somewhat preoccupied with Anselm.[136] It is true that *Cur Deus Homo?* is in part an exercise in theological logic, that consequently it somewhat lacks warmth and that the logic rests on feudal concepts of law, crime and punishment. I have long been uneasy, however, when the Reformation atonement doctrine is viewed as a modification and improvement of Anselm's, for the differences are important and the idea that the Reformation doctrine is itself largely an exercise in theological logic goes back to its supposed connection with him.

Unlike the Reformers, Anselm did not view Christ as bearing sin's penalty, but rather as offering God the one thing he had no need to offer, his death (for, as a sinless person, he was immortal), so that God as Governor of the universe could justly forgive human beings. So he saw the atonement as satisfaction (by Christ) *instead of* punishment (of us). His book has the merit, however, that it views the atonement in objective terms and in relationship to God, and that it takes sin very seriously. As Anselm said to Bozo, the 'man of straw' student with whom he dialogues in the book, 'You have not yet considered the exceeding weight of sin.' This applies to more than Bozo.

The Reformers held that in dying for our sins satisfaction for them came *through* punishment, with Christ taking our place. This is not to deny that there is a logic in penal substitution, for logic is clarity and the teaching of Scripture on this is clear, but it is a logic internal to Scripture, binding its statements and themes together, rather than one brought to it.

This chapter will not discuss the extent of the atonement,[137] as this would divert us from our main concern. Whatever view we take, however, it would be wrong to focus on quantitative considerations. In Romans 5:12–21 Paul sets Christ's obedience over against Adam's sin, but clearly the measure of the former far outweighs that of the latter. Kevin Vanhoozer, following Ricoeur, points out that there is here a logic not of equivalence but of superabundance.[138]

---

136. Green and Baker, *Recovering the Scandal of the Cross*, p. 47.

137. i.e. whether Christ died efficaciously for all, or only for the elect.

138. K. J. Vanhoozer, *Biblical Narrative in the Philosophy of Paul Ricoeur: A Study in Hermeneutics and Theology* (Cambridge: Cambridge University Press, 1990), p. 142, n. 28.

It is meaningless to many people today

Barriers against understanding

These often reflect cultural changes.

There is the *ignorance* barrier. There is profound ignorance in 'Christendom' not only of atonement theology but also of the great biblical truths providing its theological context. Television quiz programmes reveal that people well informed on many subjects are often totally ignorant of basic Christian truth. Even many church people show great ignorance. In Western society there has, of course, been a massive retreat from belief in God and especially in the biblical God, although there is some evidence that the tide may be starting to turn.[139]

Then there is the *caricature* barrier. God is often viewed either as harsh or indulgent. This is reflected in the way Christians and particularly ministers are depicted on television, for they are seen either as harsh, unfeeling, doctrinaire and censorious or as indulgent, sentimental, easily swayed and socially irrelevant.

The first of these pictures is particularly unattractive when, as now, the concept of authority is increasingly unpopular. Authority figures are viewed as interfering and as seeking to impose norms of behaviour infringing individual liberty. God is the ultimate authority Figure, and people project on him their general distaste for such. When this authority concept is dubbed 'Victorian' this makes matters worse, for such figures in the Victorian age are often viewed as self-serving and uncaring.

It is said that to a significant degree the penal substitutionary doctrine is a cultural product of the West.[140] Certainly concepts of satisfaction and punishment in relation to the atonement were largely developed at first by Latin theologians, in whose minds such ideas were more firmly embedded than in the more philosophical and speculative minds of Greek theologians. Actually this gave them important points of contact with much biblical atonement teaching.[141] Notions of authority may be under attack today, but law still exists and nobody can properly escape its strictures. So, unpalatable as being under law may be, it is inescapable and is not outside most people's understanding.

The second and opposite picture of God is one of ultimate indulgence. On his deathbed, the writer Heinrich Heine is reputed to have said, 'Of course God will forgive me; that's what he's for!' The idea that love can be strict,

---

139. See D. MacLaren, *Mission Implausible* (Carlisle: Paternoster, 2004), p. 1.

140. ibid., p. 29.

141. cf. Jeffery, Ovey and Sach, *Pierced for our Transgressions*, p. 220.

that it may hurt in order to heal, and that ultimately those who have spurned its advances must give account and face an awful destiny, is no part of many people's view of God. He is even seen as a means to an end, a last resort for people in desperate need.

How different is the biblical understanding of God! At the cross he showed both his love and his holiness in perfect unity. There by his loving provision human sin was judged in Christ as the willing Substitute for sinners. God's love can never be trivialized or sentimentalized if we always relate it to his holiness, nor will his holiness appear harsh if at Calvary holiness and love are together manifested in atonement. Here, too, his wisdom was strikingly revealed, for such simultaneous disclosure of his moral qualities in a deeply costly deed was beyond human devising.

Then there is the *philosophical* barrier. Many philosophical ideas have a way of influencing general culture, ultimately influencing the outlook of the man or woman in the street. Church people can be affected too, for philosophy so often influences theology, with successive theological movements reflecting philosophical changes.

Kant's erosion of certainty in what lies beyond sense-perception has had an abiding influence. Postmodernism, which prefers the feelings to the intellect and the arts to the sciences, is evidence of this. There is an extreme form of postmodernism in Derrida's philosophy of language, for in his 'deconstruction' a verbal communication has no fixed objective meaning. Words are let loose like the contents of Pandora's box and their meanings constantly change not only for those who listen to or read them, but even for those who speak or write them.

Then there is the '*sin-free*' barrier. Not surprisingly, the sense of sin has reached an all-time low. Actions may affect our relations with others and may clash with society's norms and laws, but there is little sense that they are offences against God. Writing about the message of the cross Smail says, 'Contemporary society is not interested in the solution because it is not even aware of the problem . . . People nowadays are more worried about their sufferings than about their sins, and modern evangelicals are often more interested in their charismatic experiences than in the death of Christ for us.'[142]

---

142. Smail, 'Can One Man Die for the People?', p. 76. In *Once and for All* (p. 45) he quotes P. T. Forsyth as saying, 'The supreme theodicy is atonement.' Smail shows much sympathy with Moltmann but stresses that atonement rather than theodicy is emphasized in the New Testament and that we should not make secondary what in the New Testament is clearly primary (ibid., pp. 48–50).

What about guilt? This term is often used simply for a *sense* of guilt and so is subjectivized, while in reality guilt is an objective fact, a demerit due to wrong action which exists whether the culprit feels it or is even aware of it. In fact insensitivity to personal wrongdoing can itself be evidence of guilt when the conscience is dulled. To regard it simply as an inward feeling is particularly serious in relation to infringement of God's law.

For many today forces are at work to minimize even the *sense* of guilt. Alan Mann says, 'Geneticists, sociologists and psychologists increasingly legitimize our narrative and allow us to live in the confidence that we do no wrong,'[143] and again he says,

> Influenced by psychological and sociological theory, academics offer to us their
> theories about the effects on behaviour of poverty, parental abuse and environmental
> factors. These external forces are to be held responsible, not the 'innocent' individual
> . . . It would seem that we move ever closer to a society free from personal guilt, free
> from the traditional religious language of sin. In their person-centred narratives, post-
> moderns become victims of the world.[144]

Of course we cannot be indifferent to 'the effects on behaviour of poverty, parental abuse and environmental factors', but neither can we think this accounts for all wrongdoing, for this is patently untrue.

The preaching of the cross today

How can we preach the gospel of divine atonement in such a situation? Twice we find Paul speaking to people with no knowledge of the biblical revelation. In Acts 14:8–20 people at Lystra attempt to worship Barnabas and Paul. Paul rejects their paganism, but says God has given testimony to himself by his gifts of food. In Acts 17:16–34 he finds a point of contact with his Athenian listeners in the altar to an unknown God and quotes a Greek poet with approval, but he also takes issue with Athenian idolatry. On both occasions he recognized general revelation but also the effects of sin on religion.[145] Natural theology may be subject to sinful distortion, but despite this people still have a sense of moral responsibility.

The quotation marks in Alan Mann's book title ('Sinless') remind us that refusing to recognize sin as a fact is refusing the truth. To feel we are simply

---

143. Mann, *Atonement for a 'Sinless' Society*, p. 5.
144. ibid., p. 29.
145. This is confirmed too in Rom. 1:18–32.

victims and never wrongdoers is to be self-deceived. Moreover, as Mann discerns, 'If "sin" exists at all, we encounter it only when we fail to devote ourselves to the project of self-realization . . . The pursuit of self-awareness, self-esteem, wholeness and well-being is paramount. To be *self-centred* is a twenty-first-century virtue'.[146] He says, 'This is the "sin" that pervades our "sinless" society . . . The result is an inevitable dysfunction in all our relationships'.[147]

If self-centredness is regarded as virtue, this reminds us of Isaiah's words,

> Woe to those who call evil good
>   and good evil,
> who put darkness for light
>   and light for darkness,
> who put bitter for sweet
>   and sweet for bitter.
> (Isa. 5:20)

Here is a possible way into contemporary minds for the message of the cross, because self-centredness is both unattractive and sinful and the passion story in the Gospels illustrates this. The Pharisees, for instance, reacted with self-centred religious pride when Jesus questioned their interpretations of religion, while Pilate probably agreed to the crucifixion to curry favour with the Jews for fear of losing his job.[148] In contrast Jesus was so evidently concerned for others. His death for us is the ultimate proof of this as well as of his single-minded devotion to God. Self-centredness is deeply sinful, for it robs God of his central place in human life.

Today there is much interest in story, in narrative theology and so in the Gospels. Many hymns feature the message of the cross as a story: 'Tell me the old, old story of Jesus and his love'.[149] Significantly the film *The Passion of the Christ* focuses on the story and another film about Jesus has been effectively used in worldwide evangelism. Perhaps in considering, for instance, the cry of dereliction and 2 Corinthians 5:21 we should normally start with the first, embedded as it is in the passion narrative, and then move on to the second. In

---

146. Mann, *Atonement for a 'Sinless' Society*, p. 21.

147. ibid., p. 166.

148. Their words, 'If you let this man go, you are no friend of Caesar' (John 19:12), probably implied a threat to report him to Rome.

149. *Methodist Hymn Book*, no. 161, p. 63.

fact, it might be wise to begin with the life of Jesus. Stephen Williams says of the Synoptic Gospels, 'The order of exposition is clear and deliberate. First we must be arrested by the person; then we are introduced to the work.'[150] In a self-centred world the character of Jesus is compellingly attractive and his crucifixion by such a world must provoke thought.

Biblical references to final punishment are largely in terms of death, pain, shame and exclusion, which significantly occur also in Genesis 3 and are all present in the crucifixion story. A way into the gospel for Eastern people, with their concern about 'losing face', but increasingly also for Westerners, may be through the cross as an experience of shame for Jesus. Their emphasis on this is a more positive feature of Chalke and Mann's book.[151]

The physical act of crucifixion is referred to very briefly in each Gospel with no spelling out of the details. Even the scourging is stated simply, with no description remotely like that vividly presented in *The Passion of the Christ*. This is not to minimize the extent of the pain, which even at the physical level must have been horrendous, but simply to recognize that the Gospels do not make as much of it as we might have expected. I am not suggesting that this element in the Saviour's sufferings should be omitted from our preaching, but rather that there are other elements that should be highlighted.

Robert Letham says, 'What made the presentation of the atoning death of Jesus so novel and, frequently, so repulsive to its hearers, was that Jesus did not die as a hero to deliver his community or his friends but as a condemned criminal sentenced to the repugnant fate of crucifixion.'[152] Doubtless hearing that such a death was indispensable for their salvation would attack the pride of the early listeners to the gospel, but this is in fact a positive factor, for the humbling of pride is always a feature of true conversion.

Green and Baker seem so set against penal substitution that they do not appear to discern that shaming is itself punishment. There is a reaction against corporal punishment in Western society and it is being largely replaced

---

150. S. Williams, *Revelation and Reconciliation: A Window on Modernity* (Cambridge: Cambridge University Press, 1995), p. 152.

151. See especially *The Lost Message*, ch. 6, which, however, also repeats their rejection of penal substitution. Shame is a major theme in Alan Mann's book also, although he tends to view it in terms of self-punishment rather than shaming from without.

152. Letham, *The Work of Christ*, p. 135. Martin Hengel points out how different this was from the admiration felt by people of the day at self-sacrifice voluntarily suffered in the place of others in the community (*The Atonement: The Origins of the Doctrine in the New Testament*, tr. J. Bowden, London: SCM, 1981, pp. 1–32).

by shaming the erring child. But is this not also punishment? The psalmist often asks for his enemies to be shamed.[153] The affirmation of resurrection in Daniel 12:2 makes 'everlasting life' and 'shame and everlasting contempt' opposite destinies.

The cross is often described in hymns as a place of shame, and many were written by people who would certainly have believed in penal substitution. For instance, Charles Wesley's hymn 'Would Jesus Have the Sinner Die?' refers not only to 'thy painful agony' but also to 'thy grief and shame, thy cross and passion on the tree'.[154]

Exclusion as punishment is also prominent in Scripture. Jesus spoke of the exclusion of the wicked (Matt. 7:23; 25:41), and Paul says, 'They will be punished with everlasting destruction and shut out from the presence of the Lord' (2 Thess. 1:9).[155] Jesus warned of a destiny of 'outer darkness' (Matt. 8:12; 22:13; 25:30, 41, 46; cf. 25:10), so how significant is his cry at the close of a time of preternatural darkness, 'My God, my God, why have you forsaken me' (Matt. 27:45–46)![156]

In our society punishment is often imprisonment, exclusion from society. Moreover, many people today long for a deeply satisfying personal relationship which, whether they realize it or not, is really a cry for an intimate relationship with God. How moving, then, to be told that to secure this for us, Jesus, who had known fellowship with his Father throughout all eternity, was prepared to endure outer darkness in our place!

If it is true that realization of personal sin prepares us for the message of God's grace in the cross of Christ, it is also true that the preaching of the cross may make us smartingly aware of our sin. So preaching needs to emphasize Christ's bearing of our sin's penalty. What our society needs more than anything is a God-given revival in which a new, deep awareness of God and of sin will come into the church and into society and for this we should earnestly pray. But gospel proclamation is urgent and cannot wait until that day comes.

How, then, can we contextualize the gospel of the cross, especially for unchurched people, in our society today? Every aspect of the biblical gospel is relevant to the needs of sinners and in faithfulness to God's Word

---

153. e.g. in Pss 35:4, 26; 40:14–15.

154. *Methodist Hymn Book*, no. 173, p. 68.

155. Although this verse may mean that the judgment is from God's presence, i.e. this is where it takes place.

156. See Smail's comment, in *Once and for All*, p. 23.

none should be denied or overlooked, but in particular generations and for particular societies some may be more quickly *seen* to be relevant.

I believe we should emphasize that our self-centredness is not only the enemy of good human relationships but is deeply offensive to God. This attitude, persisted in, will result in a dreadful destiny of shame and eternal exclusion from God the source of all good, of all love, joy and peace. This is to be seen not as the operation of an impersonal law but as divine punishment. This is the background for the disclosure of God's marvellous grace in the coming of Christ as the supremely selfless one, willingly enduring shame and the horror of exclusion from his Father in our place to bring us at such cost a salvation wonderful beyond description.

May God give us grace to be faithful as we proclaim this gospel!

4. JUSTIFICATION AND THE NEW PERSPECTIVE ON PAUL

Some theological issues do not belong to the essence of the Christian faith, while others are crucial to its proper understanding and proclamation. Most Christians would reckon justification by faith one of the latter. As most of the core New Testament passages on this doctrine are in his epistles, many will feel concerned to hear that a 'New Perspective on Paul' involves a new interpretation of his teaching on justification.

What is this New Perspective?

Some of its ideas are not new, but it has developed as a common approach to the interpretation of certain features of Pauline thought since the early 1980s. It is not so much a theological school of thought as an exercise in New Testament scholarship,[1] although it has important implications for systematic theology.[2] It does not take quite the same form in its main proponents, so that

---

1. I am grateful to Scot McKnight for pointing this out to me.
2. See especially H. Blocher, 'Justification of the Ungodly (*Sola Fide*): Theological Reflections', in D. A. Carson, P. T. O'Brien and M. A. Seifrid, *Justification and Variegated Nomism: Vol. 2. The Paradoxes of Paul* (Grand Rapids: Baker Academic, 2004),

a generalized exposition and evaluation are difficult and misrepresentation all too easy. We must therefore proceed with particular care and courtesy.

Perhaps the one general statement we can make is that its advocates view justification more in terms of the doctrine of the church than that of salvation; its significance is more horizontal than vertical. They see it as God's declaration that a person is a member of the covenant community, the church. The three most influential writers of this school are E. P. Sanders, J. D. G. Dunn and N. T. Wright,[3] although there are many others. We will look at the views of these three later.

This viewpoint has become widely accepted, and for this reason it is very important for it to be appraised and, as I hope we will see, challenged.

The limits of our discussion

We must set some limits, as the writings of some New Perspective advocates touch many issues, discussion of which would take us far from our central theme here.

Our concern is quite specifically with Paul's doctrine of justification and whether the Reformers' interpretation of it is valid in the light of subsequent research. We will not deal with justification elsewhere in the New Testament (for instance in the epistle of James), unless it bears on the interpretation of Paul's teaching, nor will we discuss the debate between Protestants and Roman Catholics.

This book is addressed to evangelicals, who have a high doctrine of Scripture, so I feel free to include references in Acts to Paul's teaching and in any epistles naming him as their author. The controversial issue of the date of Galatians will not much concern us, as most scholars see it as the first of Paul's writings to use justification language. Paul often writes of faith in Christ but occasionally of 'the faith of Christ'. Are these synonyms, or does the latter mean 'the faithfulness of Christ'? These are interesting and not unimportant matters, but they do not seriously affect the main issue.[4]

This chapter will require patience in the reader and willingness to consider

---

Footnote no. 2 (*continued*)

 pp. 465–500. He says, 'The stakes for the doctrinal elaboration of Christian faith are so high that no systematic theologian can afford to remain indifferent' (p. 465).

3. He also publishes under the name Tom Wright.

4. See the further comment on 'the faith of Christ' on p. 153.

the teaching of Scripture in some detail. We will need to give close attention to some important passages in Paul's writings, and you, the reader, are
strongly advised to follow the argument with the Bible text open. The issue is
important, so I would encourage you to persevere.

The Reformation doctrine of justification

Martin Luther famously said, 'Justification is the article[5] of a standing or
falling church.' Concern about it may not have been the immediate cause
of the Reformation,[6] but it was its deeper issue. The Reformers were called
'evangelicals' in the 1520s and not 'Protestants' until the 1530s, which identifies the gospel not only as their own main focus but as seen to be by others.

Luther's words can be paralleled from other Reformers. Certainly the overarching theme of Calvin's *Institutes* is God's sovereignty, but justification needs
the doctrine of God for its proper understanding. Even more importantly, the
justification of sinners is for the glory of God.

What, then, is justification? In the Reformation doctrine *it is essentially a
declaration by God*, seemingly incredible, but in fact the most wonderful good
news, *that by his grace a sinner is reckoned righteous and so is accepted in his sight*. It is
not the imparting of righteousness, changing our characters, but the imput-
ing of it, changing our status with God.[7] It has an eschatological character,
decisively anticipating God's verdict at the last judgment, but as an anticipation it is a present as well as a future reality. As a declaration, it is an important
example of the fact that God so often acts by speaking, a principle established
at the very beginning, in Genesis 1.[8] This declaration actually effects what in it
God declares: that a sinner is now accounted righteous in his sight.

How can this be? Because *God has himself provided an objective basis for that
verdict* so that the imputation is no 'legal fiction'. As we saw in the previous
chapter, Christ's death, effecting penal substitutionary atonement, is God's
own provision for sinners. This is why Paul links justification to the cross so

---

5. i.e. the credal article.
6. This was the sale of indulgences to finance the building of St Peter's in Rome.
7. Stephen Chester has pointed out to me that Luther did not employ forensic
   terminology as much as many later Protestant writers, but preferred concepts like
   exchange and also death and life in writing about justification. The latter, of course,
   links up with the doctrine of union with Christ.
8. See the comments on speech-act theory on pp. 226–227.

intimately in such places as Romans 3:21–26, 2 Corinthians 5:21 and Galatians 3:11–14.

The Reformers taught that *justification is by faith, and by faith alone*. The function of the word 'alone' here is clarification, and at the Reformation it was the major point at issue in relation to the doctrine. Faith's exclusive role is well expressed by A. M. Toplady:

> Nothing in my hand I bring; simply to Thy cross I cling;
> Naked come to Thee for dress, helpless look to Thee for grace,
> Foul, I to the fountain fly; wash me Saviour, or I die.[9]

Justification is by the grace of God. This important link between justification and the doctrine of God is immediately apparent when Paul says of justification, 'The promise comes by faith, so that it may be by grace' (Rom. 4:16), showing that faith is not something meritorious we bring but in fact implies recognition that we can bring nothing. Grace and merit are opposites while grace and faith are correlatives. Grace is in the heart of God the great Giver and faith rests on the provision he has made. To offer allegedly meritorious works, either instead of or in addition to faith, is to reject the whole principle of the gospel and is an insult to the Saviour whose work was all-sufficient.

Not only so, but works will never at any stage, not even when Christians are glorified in the presence of Christ, become the basis of our acceptance by God, and true Christian assurance is always dependent on faith. It was a theme that moved Horatius Bonar in several of his hymns. He wrote,

> Thy work *alone*, O Christ, can ease this weight of sin;
> Thy blood *alone*, O Lamb of God, can give me peace within.
> Thy love to me, O God, not mine, O Lord, to Thee,
> Can rid me of this dark unrest, and set my spirit free.[10]

And,

> Not what I am, O Lord, but what Thou art,
> that, that *alone*, shall be my soul's true rest.[11]

---

9. *Methodist Hymn Book* (London: Methodist Conference, 1933), no. 498, p. 191.

10. P. E. G. Cook and G. Harrison (eds.), *Christian Hymns* (Bridgend: Evangelical Movement of Wales, 1977), no. 557 (italics mine).

11. ibid., no. 651 (italics mine).

Here is faith's totally sufficient Object and in consequence its exclusive trust.[12]

The Reformers did not deny that God works in the characters of true believers. In fact they affirmed that by God's grace there is always a character change in the justified, but this is practical sanctification, not justification, and it is not the basis of God's 'Not guilty!' verdict.

What, then, is the function of works in the Christian life? They are not meritorious but evidential, showing that a truly divine work of grace has taken place within the believing heart. Justification and regeneration (the new birth), which is the first moment in practical sanctification, although clearly distinguishable, are inseparable. The God who pronounces the verdict that we are righteous through Christ is also the God whose Spirit imparts new life to our hearts and he does not do the one without the other.

This sometimes troubles true believers, for grace makes us aware of personal sin and this can militate against assurance. We should see the evidential status of works as a hedge against false profession, not as a call for excessive introspection. The first epistle of John, which emphasizes it, was written when some were professing faith in Christ while showing unconcern about holiness of life. John stresses that this cannot be the case where there is true faith. True believers troubled about assurance do not show such moral unconcern. Our main focus must always be on Christ, never on ourselves. That is how faith grows and as faith grows assurance grows. We will, I hope, see the importance of this in this chapter.

Justification is not the only way the New Testament views personal salvation. It is seen, for instance, as adoption, which is God in grace bringing us into his family and giving us the blessings of that relationship. James Packer's book *Knowing God* makes his readers aware of both the marvel and the neglect of this great fact.[13] Yet it must be said that the principles of the gospel stand out with special clarity when salvation is viewed as justification, and if clarity is needed anywhere, it is here. That is why Protestant theology has largely followed Luther in emphasizing justification.

What, then, was the biblical basis of the Reformation doctrine? The Reformers went mainly to the Pauline epistles for this. Certainly Luther was an Augustinian monk and Augustine was the clearest of all patristic writers

---

12. See L Morris, *The Atonement: Its Meaning and Significance* (Leicester: Inter-Varsity Press, 1983), ch. 8 on justification.

13. J. I. Packer, *Knowing God*, 2nd ed. (London: Hodder and Stoughton, 1993), pp. 223–257. For a fuller treatment of this theme, see T. J. Burke, *Adopted into God's Family: Exploring a Pauline Metaphor* (Leicester: Apollos, 2006).

on the fact that God accepts us by an act of his sovereign and completely unmerited grace.[14] When deeply troubled about his spiritual position, Luther was influenced by long talks with Von Staupitz, his monastic superior, and many early Protestants were fellow Augustinians. But Von Staupitz, although teaching the importance of faith in relation to justification, never maintained its exclusive role. It was Luther's study of Galatians and Romans for teaching purposes that was most influential in bringing him to clear understanding of justification and so to personal peace with God.[15]

It was this question of faith's exclusive role that distinguished Luther's outlook both from the influential teaching of Thomas Aquinas who preceded him[16] and from the decrees of the Council of Trent, the theological charter of the Catholic Counter-Reformation, that followed him.

As we have already noted, faith's exclusiveness and all-sufficiency are related to the exclusiveness and all-sufficiency of Christ's sacrifice. In exalting faith, the Reformers were exalting Christ, because the whole efficacy of faith is to be found, not in faith itself, but in its Object. Interestingly, as Cottret has pointed out, as far as France was concerned the great issue in the Protestant breach from Rome was not so much the teaching of Romans on justification as that of Hebrews on Christ's sacrifice.[17] There it was the mass that the Reformers so strongly objected to, viewing the efficacy attributed to the mass as an insult to Christ. But so also is the attempt to justify oneself by meritorious works.

Antecedents of the New Perspective

Seyoon Kim asserts that 'no school of thought, not even the Bultmannian School,[18] has exerted a greater influence upon Pauline scholarship than the

---

14. This is true, even though he may not have had a clearly forensic understanding of the righteousness and justification terminology. See D. F. Wright, 'Justification in Augustine', in B. L. McCormick (ed.), *Justification in Perspective* (Grand Rapids: Baker Academic, 2006), pp. 55–72.

15. Interestingly, it was a passage in a Pauline epistle (Rom. 13:13–14) that brought Augustine himself to faith in Christ.

16. See F. Thielman, *Paul and the Law: A Contextual Approach* (Downers Grove: InterVarsity Press, 1994), pp. 14–18.

17. B. Cottret, *Calvin: A Biography* (Edinburgh: T. & T. Clark, 2000), pp. 72, 83.

18. Incidentally, Bultmann, whose theology differed radically from Paul's, nevertheless understood Paul's salvation and justification theology much in the way the

school of the New Perspective. The New Perspective School is in many ways overturning the Reformation interpretation of Paul's gospel.'[19] Even if this latter comment is exaggerated (and you, the reader, must be left to judge this), it well justifies the inclusion of the present chapter in this book.

A major concern of the New Perspective is with Luther's understanding of Paul and its influence on Protestant theology generally. Its advocates seek to define Paul's justification theology carefully, to identify the significance of his conflict with the Judaizers, who were opposed to his justification doctrine, and to clarify what first-century Judaism taught about justification before God. They hold that the classic Protestant doctrine of justification is in serious need of correction.

This outlook did not spring up overnight. A number of strands of thought which gradually emerged over a hundred years or so came together in the New Perspective. We will briefly survey its antecedents, concentrating on particularly significant writers.[20]

The most influential Protestant theologian in the late nineteenth century was the Lutheran Albrecht Ritschl. He taught that although it is the individual who is justified, he or she has this status only within the Christian church, not apart from it.[21] This anticipated the ecclesiological emphasis of the New Perspective.

Albert Schweitzer, whose major interest was New Testament eschatology, said that Jesus eventually saw that his mission to bring in God's kingdom was a failure,[22] and that Paul saw the hope of the second coming to be forlorn. The apostle now placed emphasis on faith-union with Christ as the essence of Christianity.

Increasingly scholars said union with Christ was the heart of Paul's teaching. This might have seemed in line with Calvin, who had emphasized that all the benefits of Christ, including justification, come to us only through union

---

Reformers understood it; see R. Bultmann, *Theology of the New Testament: Historical Developments and Contemporary Challenges*, tr. K. Grobel, vol. 1 (New York: Charles Scribner and Sons, 1951), pp. 185–355.

19. S. Kim, *Paul and the New Perspective: Second Thoughts on the Origin of Paul's Gospel* (Grand Rapids: Eerdmans, 2002), p. xiv.

20. See also P. M. Sprinkle, 'The Old Perspective on the New Perspective: A Review of some "Pre-Sanders" Thinkers', *Themelios* 30:2 (Winter 2005), pp. 21–31.

21. Expounded in his book *The Christian Doctrine of Justification and Reconciliation*, H. R. Mackintosh and A. B. Macaulay (eds.) (Edinburgh: T. & T. Clark, 1900).

22. To Schweitzer, this was the meaning of the cry of dereliction (Matt. 27:46).

with him. Both Ritschl and Schweitzer, however, played down the doctrine of justification, which Calvin never did.

In assessing first-century Judaism, the Judaism of Paul before he became a Christian, most scholars depended on Ferdinand Weber's source-book, first published in 1880.[23] Claude Montefiore, a Jewish scholar, showed this over-systematized study to be highly selective and largely based on Jewish literature written well after the first century. He showed too that Weber assumed that first-century Judaism was essentially legalistic,[24] whereas its attitude to the Mosaic law, Montefiore maintained, was one of joyful gratitude.[25] So, then, Weber had produced a caricature. George Moore noted that Weber got much of his material from secondary sources, largely Christian, some of them extremely biased. Reflecting on Romans 7, Montefiore also maintained that Paul was influenced not by Palestinian but by Dispersion Judaism, which may have shared some of the self-doubting introspectiveness so common in the Greco-Roman world at that time when traditional religions were suffering 'a failure of nerve'.[26]

W. G. Kümmel[27] and Krister Stendahl[28] criticized the main line of Pauline interpretation from Augustine through Luther into the twentieth century, which even Montefiore seems to have accepted as accurate. In particular, they said, interpreters had given a highly subjective view of Romans 7, which had originated in the tortured consciences of Augustine and Luther. Why had post-Luther and modern scholars not seriously challenged this? Because, said

---

23. F. Weber, *Jüdaische Theologie auf Grand des Talmud und verwandter Schriften* (Leipzig: Dörffling und Franke, 1897).

24. Imposing a system on diverse material can easily result in distortion. See S. J. Gathercole, *Where Is Boasting? Early Jewish Soteriology and Paul's Response in Romans 1–5* (Grand Rapids: Eerdmans, 2002), pp. 12–13.

25. Montefiore also noted that first-century Judaism's admitted particularism was somewhat qualified in that it provided for the inclusion of Gentiles in God's people through proselytization.

26. A phrase coined by Gilbert Murray, *Five Stages of Greek Religion* (London: Watts, 1935), p. 123.

27. W. G. Kummel, *Römer 7 und das Bild des Menschen in Neuen Testament* (Munich: C. Kaiser, 1974).

28. K. Stendahl, 'The Apostle Paul and the Introspective Conscience of the West', reprinted in *Paul among Jews and Gentiles and Other Essays* (Philadelphia: Fortress, 1976). Gathercole calls Stendahl 'in many ways a father to the New Perspective' (*Where Is Boasting?*, p. 18).

Stendahl, they were too much influenced, first of all by pietism, a movement emphasizing personal devotion which originated within the Lutheran church in the late seventeenth century,[29] and then by existentialism,[30] both of which tended to be inward-looking.

Kümmel and Stendahl pointed to evidence that Paul was not over-preoccupied with his personal sin and that except for his past persecution of the church his conscience seemed clear. They argued from the context of Romans 7 that Paul's main concern was to defend the law, and they maintained that the 'I' of Romans 7 was not Paul but simply referred in a vivid, personalized way to what it felt like to be under the law of God.

In 1960 Johannes Munck argued that Paul saw great significance in his own role in God's purposes. His mission was to bring many Gentiles to salvation in Christ, so provoking the Jews to jealousy that they too would come to Christ, after which Christ's second coming would take place. Munck's thesis did not altogether convince most scholars, but it focused attention on the importance of the Jew/Gentile relationship for Paul's theology.[31]

So, then, various writers had attacked the common view of New Testament Judaism as legalistic, had seen special significance in Paul's Gentile mission, had viewed justification in communal terms, especially in the uniting of Jew and Gentile rather than in individual guilt-ridden terms, and had treated union with Christ rather than justification as the centre of Paul's gospel. The New Perspective united all these elements in a new integrated view of Paul's justification doctrine.

The development of the New Perspective

During the 1960s and 70s, groups of scholars with widely different outlooks began to interact much more. This applied to relations between Protestant and Roman Catholic scholars and also to the relations of Christian scholars with both Marxists and Jews. E. P. Sanders wrote his epoch-making 1977 book *Paul and Palestinian Judaism* out of this kind of dialogue.

---

29. As in the case of Schleiermacher, 'the father of modern theology'.

30. As in the case of the very influential mid-twentieth-century writer Rudolf Bultmann.

31. J. Munck, *Paul and the Salvation of Mankind* (Atlanta: John Knox, 1959). He died just a few years later, otherwise he may have contested the views of his critics more fully.

His stated aim was 'to compare Judaism, understood in its own terms, with Paul, understood in his'.[32] He criticized the view of first-century Judaism generally held by Christians. After studying the Rabbinic literature, the Dead Sea Scrolls and other early Jewish literature, he concluded that it did not teach salvation by works but what he called 'covenantal nomism'. Salvation was by God's covenanted grace to his elect people Israel, so that the covenant became a gracious framework for the life and destiny of every Jew, although individuals could forfeit this covenanted salvation by disobedience, which is what gives the law its importance. They could, however, be reinstated by repentance and forgiveness, and such restoration was what 'righteousness' meant.[33]

He then gave a somewhat brief and not very satisfactory discussion of Paul, but he wrote more fully on him later in *Paul, the Law, and the Jewish People*,[34] amplifying and somewhat modifying what he had written earlier. For him Paul's deepest conviction and theological starting point was that Jesus is God's only Saviour for all, and he held that Paul saw the essence of Christianity to be participatory union with Christ. Paul had then argued 'from solution to plight', the plight of the Gentiles who were excluded from God's people. The law which excluded them was no alternative to Christ, through whom covenant membership is open to all, not Jews alone. 'Righteousness' is about belonging to the covenant community,[35] but for Judaism, it was about staying in, or being restored to, the covenant, while for Paul it was about getting into it. Paul and his Jewish contemporaries were, however, in agreement that continuance in the covenant is on the basis of works.

In 1982, J. D. G. Dunn began to use the phrase 'the New Perspective on Paul', already coined by Wright. He built on the work of Sanders on Palestinian Judaism,[36] but maintained that he had not adequately explained

---

32. E. P. Sanders, *Paul and Palestinian Judaism: A Comparison of Patterns of Religion* (London: SCM, 1977), p. xi.

33. There is a clear eight-point summary of this in ibid., p. 422. See also T. Chester, 'Justification, Ecclesiology and the New Perspective', *Themelios* 30:2 (Winter 2005), p. 6.

34. E. P. Sanders, *Paul, the Law, and the Jewish People* (Philadelphia: Fortress, 1983).

35. The terms for 'righteousness' and 'justification' come from the same Greek root.

36. e.g. in saying that Paul derived his emphasis on the initiative of divine grace not 'as a reaction against Paul's Pharisaic past or as response to his "judaizing" opponents. In its essence it was simply a restatement of the first principles of his own ancestral faith' (J. D. G. Dunn, *The Theology of Paul the Apostle*, Grand Rapids: Eerdmans, 1998, p. 345).

Paul's attitude to the law. Dunn argued that the Jews were proud of the law as it marked them out as God's people, and this induced in them both rigid nationalism and spiritual complacency.

He placed much emphasis on Galatians 2:16, saying that Paul used the term 'the works of the law' there and elsewhere in a technical sense,[37] not so much of law-keeping as a way of getting right with God but rather to identify features of the law which had become a barrier between Jews and Gentiles, like circumcision, food laws and sabbath-keeping. It was such things that both Jews and Gentiles saw as distinguishing and separating them in Gentile lands, and it was these too that the Judaizers[38] Paul encountered insisted on for Gentile converts to Christ.

Dunn clarified, or, it seems to some readers, modified his position later, indicating that '"works of the law" refer not exclusively but particularly to those requirements which bring to sharp focus the distinctiveness of Israel's identity'.[39] He says, 'The phrase "the works of the law" does, of course, refer to all or whatever the law requires, covenantal nomism as a whole. But in a context where the relationship of Israel with other nations is at issue, certain laws would naturally come more into focus than others.'[40]

Is this a major change of view? Not really, for to him works of the law are still related to the Jew/Gentile issue. What keeps the Gentile from the Jew and both of them from God, in the New Perspective, is not self-righteousness but ethnocentricism. It is not simply that the religious exclusivism of the Jew excludes the Gentile from the people of God, it excludes the Jew as well, for justification, recognition of covenant membership, comes only through Christ.

He said that the incident at Antioch described in Galatians 2:11–18 convinced Paul that 'justification through faith and covenantal nomism were not complementary, but were in direct antithesis . . . Justification through faith must determine the *whole* of life and not only the starting-point of discovering (or being discovered by) God's grace.'[41]

---

37. The NIV rendering ('observing the law') obscures this.

38. This term designates Jewish Christians who taught that Gentiles must be circumcised and agree to keep the Mosaic law to become and to be recognized as being Christians.

39. J. D. G. Dunn, *Jesus, Paul and the Law: Studies in Mark and Galatians* (London: SPCK, 1990), p. 233.

40. Dunn, *The Theology of Paul the Apostle*, p. 358.

41. Dunn, *Jesus, Paul and the Law*, p. 162.

N. T. Wright too accepts Sanders's general view of first-century Judaism. He says, 'The tradition of Pauline interpretation has manufactured a false Paul by manufacturing a false Judaism for him to oppose.'[42] He holds that the traditional Protestant preoccupation with justification, emphasizing the situation of the individual sinner, took the focus away both from the ongoing purpose of God expressed in his covenant with Abraham and also from the great objective facts of Christ's death and resurrection which to Paul were of primary importance (1 Cor. 15:3–4). He takes the witness of the Gospels to the teaching of Jesus very much more seriously than Sanders.

The gospel, for Wright, is the good news that Jesus is now, through his death and resurrection, Lord of all, and thus God's covenant promises to Israel have been fulfilled. These highly significant events, however, are relevant to the whole human race, not just the Jews. As Dunn says, the old barriers between Jew and Gentile no longer have meaning, and by faith in Jesus Gentiles are justified, meaning that they are now reckoned equal partners with the Jews in God's covenant people.

Another important feature of Wright's view is that Christ's work has effectively brought to an end the exile of the Jewish people which was due to their disobedience to God's law, for, he argued, this exile was not essentially from their land, although this had been a consequence and symbol of it, but from God himself. Mark 1:1–3 was meant to alert Mark's readers to this, and this Gospel's account of Christ's passion culminates in the cry of dereliction in which, in Wright's view, Christ experienced the full horror of exile from God. It was this that Jesus took on himself at the cross,[43] and his resurrection signified that God had now terminated the exile. Now through Israel, personally embodied in Jesus its Messiah, the promises of God's blessing to Abraham are available to the Gentiles also (Gal. 3:7–9), and because reconciliation with God has been effected through Christ, the law no longer has power to divide Jews and Gentiles.

So, then, we may characterize the distinctive contributions to the New Perspective of its three major proponents thus: Sanders in his pioneer work

---

42. N. T. Wright, 'The Paul of History and the Apostle of Faith', *Tyndale Bulletin* 29 (1978), p. 78.

43. Wright says, 'Because the Messiah represents Israel, he is able to take on himself Israel's curse and exhaust it . . . The crucifixion of the Messiah is, one might say, the *quintessence* of the curse of exile, and its climactic act' (*The Climax of the Covenant: Christ and the Law in Pauline Theology*, Edinburgh: T. & T. Clark, 1991, p. 151.

argued that first-century Judaism must be understood to be a religion of grace, not of salvation by merit as Augustine and Luther had thought, Dunn argued that Paul's concern was to show that the Jews and the Judaizers were wrong to boast in circumcision and other 'covenant markers' and to maintain that Gentiles must accept these to be recognized as members of God's people, while Wright maintained that in Christ's death and resurrection God's covenant promises to Abraham have been fulfilled, Israel's exile has been ended and Jew and Gentile can now be united in Christ. The overall effect of all this is to view Paul's theology of justification as largely, although not of course exclusively, an ecclesiological doctrine.

Gathercole has well said, 'Although all theological exposition requires attention to clarity of expression and careful choice of words, this seems even more pressing than usual with justification. There is a constant sense of the danger of miscommunication, or of "watering down", or exaggeration.'[44] He also says our discussion of the relationship of Paul's thought to Judaism should not be 'short-circuited' by 'asserting (for example) that both Judaism and Christianity are religions of grace without asking what "grace" means in the two different patterns of religion'.[45] This too is an important point. Several scholars rightly emphasize the importance of a contextual approach to both the Jewish and the Pauline material.[46] Clarity and care must be our main concerns.

There is no doubt that the popularity of the New Perspective is at least partly due to the embarrassment some Christian scholars feel, in these post-Holocaust days, about the anti-Semitism of Luther and the fact that first-century Judaism appears in a better light in the New than in the Old Perspective.[47] This is understandable, but we must look at the evidence for both views objectively.

The chief features of the New Perspective can be well argued and all three main advocates of it write with admirable clarity and Wright in particular usually most engagingly. It has been highly infuential, so much so that it has come to be viewed in many quarters as fully established.

---

44. S. J. Gathercole, 'The Doctrine of Justification in Paul and Beyond: Some Proposals', in B. L. McCormack (ed.), *Justification in Perspective: Historical Developments and Contemporary Challenges* (Grand Rapids: Baker, 2006), p. 219.

45. Gathercole, *Where Is Boasting?*, p. 21.

46. e.g. C. G. Kruse, *Paul, the Law and Justification* (Leicester: Apollos, 1996), p. 25; Gathercole, ibid., pp. 21–23. Note also the subtitle of Thielman's book *Paul and the Law: A Contextual Approach*.

47. Marion Carson made this point to me.

Without doubt, the work of this school of thought has given new insights into the New Testament and its message. There are, however, important criticisms that must be advanced, even though many scholars advancing them have acknowledged some positive gains from the New Perspective. Of special value are two volumes edited by D. A. Carson, P. T. O'Brien and M. A. Seifrid.[48] Here a substantial group of major scholars engage with all aspects of the New Perspective with a fullness of detail quite impossible in a chapter like the present one.

We will now examine the two main issues, which relate to justification in first-century Judaism and justification in the teaching of Paul.

Was first-century Judaism a legalistic religion of salvation by works?

The Reformers answered, 'Yes!' Sanders says, 'No!' A correct answer depends on what we mean by 'first-century Judaism' and even, as we shall see, on what we mean by legalism. The question is important because it was Sanders's view of first-century Judaism which laid the basis for the New Perspective.

Both Luther and Calvin viewed the Pharisaic Judaism of New Testament times as a legalistic system of self-salvation. This was also largely the way they viewed medieval Catholicism and they tended to read each in the light of the other. This estimate of Judaism prevailed among Protestant scholars and theologians until comparatively recently, but their consensus has been challenged by Sanders.[49]

It is by focusing on the covenant and God's election of Israel which lay behind it that Sanders has been able to argue that Judaism taught that salvation is by grace, for the covenant gave a framework of grace to Jewish thinking about relationship with God. According to him, this means that official Judaism did not teach justification by works. This view, diametrically opposed to that of the Reformers, has been well documented by Sanders and he is widely thought to have made his case, at least in general terms.[50] His view does, however, need significant modification for several important reasons.

---

48. *Justification and Variegated Nomism, Vol. 1: The Complexities of Second Temple Judaism;* and *Vol. 2: The Paradoxes of Paul* (Grand Rapids: Baker Academic, 2001, 2004).

49. I am focusing here on the biblical evidence for the doctrine, rather than on the Reformers.

50. A. A. Das, for example, considers Sanders's case to have been conclusively demonstrated (*Paul, the Law and the Covenant,* Peabody: Hendrickson, 1993, p. 2.

First of all, *he was somewhat selective in the material that formed the basis of his study.*

He relied quite heavily on written evidence as late as the third century, assuming that there had been little change since New Testament times, and he shared Weber's tendency to systematize rather than to give full weight to the material's literary and historical contexts.[51]

A study of the works of Josephus and of various books of the Apocrypha and the apocalyptic writings would raise serious questions about his thesis. Gathercole is particularly thorough in making this kind of criticism. He examines a wide range of pre-AD 70 apocryphal and pseudepigraphic literature,[52] and concludes, 'God is portrayed as saving his people at the *eschaton* on the basis of their obedience, as well as on the basis of his election of them.' He sees this also in the Qumran texts,[53] and in Jewish soteriology as portrayed in the New Testament.[54] It is the phrase 'as well as' which sharply distinguishes the theology of this literature from that of Luther.[55]

Second, *he did not treat the witness of the Gospels anything like seriously enough.*

There Pharisaic Judaism is portrayed as strongly legalistic. Sanders denied that Jesus held radically different views from the Pharisees over such issues as food laws and the sabbath. He could only assert this, however, by maintaining that the Gospels, particularly Matthew and John, misrepresented the views of the Pharisees, and that these documents reflect the attitude of the church to the Jews after the fall of Jerusalem and also later debates in the church.[56]

Serious documents written only a few decades after the events do not deserve such radically deconstructive treatment. The standard and long-accepted view of the Pharisees of New Testament times is that they were

---

See also S. Westerholm, *Perspectives Old and New on Paul* (Grand Rapids: Eerdmans, 2004), pp. 350–351.

51. See J. Neusner, *Rabbinic Judaism: Structure and System* (Minneapolis: Fortress, 1995), pp. 7–23.

52. Gathercole, *Where Is Boasting?*, pp. 37–90.

53. ibid., pp. 91–111.

54. ibid., pp. 112–135. This is refreshing, for some writers, including Sanders himself, do not take the New Testament evidence sufficiently seriously.

55. A very full and helpful exposition and discussion of the relevant Jewish literature can be found in Carson, O'Brien and Seifrid, *Justification and Variegated Nomism*, vol. 1, pp. 39–74.

56. He also held that there were few Pharisees in Galilee at the time, but this has been well refuted by Dunn (*Jesus, Paul and the Law*, pp. 77–81).

dedicated legalists and much New Testament evidence, especially from the Gospels, can be quoted in support of this. In fact the controversies Jesus had with the Jewish leaders almost all seem to have been concerned with legalism and its associated attitudes, except for those related to his special claims.

Frank Thielman says,

> Paul's own pre-Christian convictions about the law appear to have allowed human effort at least some role in justification (Phi 3:4–6). It is also true that such convictions led some Jews to trust in themselves (Lk 18:9), take an odious pride in their conformity with at least part of the law (Mt 6:1–6, 16–18; 23;5; Mk 12:40; Lk 18:12; 20:47), fail to see their need of repentance (Mt 9:13; Mk 2:17; Lk 5:32; 7:47; 15:7) and reject Jesus because of his willingness to associate with those who did repent (Mt 9:11; Mk 2:16; Lk 5:30; 7:39; 15:2).[57]

This is an impressive and formidable body of evidence, especially as Thielman espouses the view that such attitudes were not general among the Jews of our Lord's day.

We also note the greater emphasis of the Pharisees on tithing trivia than on heart-attitudes (Matt. 23:23–24), their stress on sabbath and food law observance (Mark 2 – 3) and their casuistry (Matt. 23:16–22). On their own, such features of their attitude would not be decisive, but they are all of a piece with the evidence put together by Thielman.

All the passages referred to above are from the Synoptic Gospels. In the fourth Gospel, which appears to record encounters of Jesus with them only in Jerusalem, the focus is rather on the special claims of Jesus, and this is true even in the Synoptics once he arrived in Jerusalem for the last time. During those final days, he continued to warn his disciples about Pharisaic legalism,[58] but his actual conflict with them was rather over his own status. Without doubt some of the more important Pharisees will have been at Jerusalem, so here he would be dealing with major authorities.

Like Jesus himself the authors of the Gospels, apart from Luke, were Jews and this type of internal criticism is common within the Old Testament itself, especially in the way the prophets criticized the prevailing religious outlook of the people of their day. Jesus was not attacking a contemporary expression of Judaism from outside but rather from within.

Third, *in the literature of Judaism the covenant is overshadowed by the Law.*

---

57. Thielman, *Paul and the Law*, p. 179.

58. See e.g. Matt. 23.

Westerholm says he cannot find in the Rabbinic literature the idea that the election of Israel was gratuitous.[59] Very often it is attributed to the merits of the fathers.[60] This may well reflect a particular mentality, a prior assumption that meritorious works must have played some part in the election of Israel.

Westerholm, among other critics of Sanders, accepts that for the Jews of this period salvation is initially by grace through the covenant, but notes how few are the references to the covenant and grace and how many are to the great importance of legal obedience, for example in the Mishnah.[61] We tend to emphasize most what we reckon most important.

Fourth, *the literature indicates that salvation is initially through the gracious covenant but ultimately through human effort.*

Paul wrote to the Galatian Christians, 'Are you so foolish? After beginning with the Spirit, are you now trying to attain your goal by human effort?' (Gal. 3:3) Something comparable to this was characteristic of first-century Judaism. As Douglas Moo says,

> Even in Sanders' proposal, works play such a prominent role that it is fair to speak of a 'synergism' of faith and works that elevates works to a crucial salvific role. For while works, according to Sanders, are not the means of 'getting in', they are essential to 'staying in'. When, then, we consider the matter from the perspective of the final judgment . . . it is clear that 'works', even in Sanders' view, play a necessary and instrumental role in 'salvation'.[62]

The word 'instrumental' here is important. To say that works are necessary as evidence of salvation and to say that they are instrumental in it is to embrace two quite different theologies, as we shall see in considering the role of works in Paul's writings.

---

59. Westerholm, *Perspectives Old and New on Paul*, pp. 348–351.

60. cf. T. Schreiner, *The Law and its Fulfilment: A Pauline Theology of Law* (Grand Rapids: Baker, 1993), p. 117. Of course, in a sense, the New Testament teaches the transfer of merits, but these are the merits of Christ and his work, not those of sinful humans.

61. The Mishnah is the written deposit of Rabbinic Judaism's oral law. Of course Leviticus also consists largely of legal material, but it emphasizes the grace of God in his provision of the sacrifices, summed up in the comment on sacrificial blood in Lev. 17:11, 'I have given it to you [*not* 'you have given it to me'] to make atonement for yourselves on the altar.'

62. D. Moo, *The Epistle to the Romans*, NICNT (Grand Rapids: Eerdmans, 1996), p. 215; cf. Gathercole, *Where Is Boasting?*, pp. 21–23.

Westerholm points out that Judaism and the opponents of Lutheranism each acknowledged human need of divine grace. 'What the opponents of "Lutheranism" emphatically did *not* do, however – what they indeed regarded as morally disastrous to do – was to suggest that humans can contribute *nothing* to their salvation. That insistence is . . . the very essence of "Lutheranism". It is fair to say that it is not depicted in Judaism as portrayed by Sanders.'[63]

Fifth, *we should distinguish between legalism as a theological system and as an attitude of heart.*

After a thorough study of Paul's theology of law, Schreiner argues that Judaism, although not uniformly or even characteristically legalistic, nevertheless contains the seeds of practical legalism. He says, 'I believe that the Reformers were profoundly correct in insisting that Paul's gospel is supremely a gospel of grace that was framed in the context of a legalistic Soteriology with roots in Judaism.'[64] It seems likely that many of the Galilean Pharisees were more legalistic than the leaders of their sect, those whose outlook found its way into its literature.[65]

Reflection on the process of hearing may help us here and modern philosophers of language are interested in this, maintaining that the import of what is spoken and what any individual hearer understands by it may differ considerably. It is even more important to note that Paul recognized the presence of the sin-factor in faulty hearing of the divine message (2 Cor. 3:7 – 4:6). The preacher may say in my hearing that salvation is by grace, and yet I may be so conditioned by years of trying by my own efforts to please God that what he says gets distorted in my mind, and I fail to take in the glorious implications of this for my personal life. A legalistic spirit is so endemic in religious people (including many members of Protestant churches) that it would be very surprising if it did not affect many Jews of that period, especially in view of the importance attached to the law in first-century Judaism.

Moo says,

> We must . . . reckon with the possibility that many 'lay' Jews were more legalistic than the surviving literary remains of Judaism would suggest. Certainly the undeniable importance of the law in Judaism would naturally open the way to viewing doing

---

63. Westerholm, *Perspectives Old and New on Paul*, p. 351.

64. Schreiner, *The Law and Its Fulfilment*, p. 243.

65. In Acts 5:33–40, Luke pictures Gamaliel, a major Pharisaic leader, as much more sensitive and conciliatory than the hardline Pharisees he depicts in recording the ministry of Jesus.

the law as itself salvific. The gap between the average believer's theological views and the informed views of religious leaders is often a wide one. If Christianity has been far from immune to legalism, is it likely to think that Judaism, at any stage of its development, was?[66]

We should recognize too that this kind of outlook can influence and distort even what professes to be official teaching when it is proclaimed from pulpits, whether Jewish or Christian. It may even be done unwittingly if the preacher does not take sufficient care. I recall once hearing a minister preaching on the importance of believers' baptism in such a way that it would suggest to the hearers that he believed in baptismal regeneration, although I knew for certain that he did not.

As we have said, it is the work of Sanders on the Judaism of the New Testament period that the New Perspective rests on, so that a balanced judgment of his thesis is of vital importance.

Our conclusion, then, is that *although Sanders is partly right, he is wrong on matters of vital importance for understanding the background to Paul's doctrine of justification.*

How are 'works of the law' related to justification in Paul's writings?

Are they boundary markers or attempts to gain merit? The importance of this question can hardly be overestimated, as our understanding of the meaning of justification depends on the answer.

Paul's pre-Christian background was in 'Judaism' (Gal. 1:13–14), a term employed first in 2 Maccabees[67] to designate Judea's national religion over against the religious Hellenism their Syrian overlords were seeking to impose on the Jews. Compromise had been unthinkable, and this gave the term something of a polemic edge. This was the religious outlook the Pharisees of the New Testament period and therefore Paul himself inherited.

Paul told the Philippians that in Judaism his desired status had been 'a righteousness of my own that comes from the law', but that after his conversion it was 'a righteousness that comes from God and is by faith' (Phil. 3:9). In Romans 10:1–4 he says that this righteousness from the law was what the Jews were vainly seeking.

---

66. Moo, *The Epistle to the Romans*, p. 217.

67. Noted by Dunn, *The Theology of Paul the Apostle*, p. 347.

As we have already noted, in both Galatians and Romans he uses the term 'works of the law'[68] to characterize the outlook of the Jews of his day.[69] There can be little doubt that 'a righteousness of my own that comes from the law' (Phil. 3:9) has the same meaning, and that it was this assumed status of his which constituted his grounds for 'boasting' prior to his conversion. He clearly saw works of the law as related in some important way to justification.[70]

What precisely do these two expressions mean? The Old Perspective understands them in terms of legalism, and the New in terms of religious ethnocentrism. This, then, is the main issue confronting us. If we can ascertain their meaning, we will be well on the way to deciding between the two perspectives.

In the literature of early Judaism, close equivalents of this term have been found only at Qumran. They refer to deeds required of the Qumran sectaries, marks of their right to be members of the community. These marks were not special to Qumran, however, for they were requirements of the law of Moses and so were mandatory for all Jews. Moreover, the terms are not used extensively enough for us to determine for certain whether they were understood to apply only to special marks of the Qumran community or to those of Judaism as a whole or to any works done in obedience to the law.

Dunn, who is particularly interested in this issue, is only able to say that the term 'works of the law' was '*probably* used initially in a polemical context . . . to denote particularly those obligations of the law which were reckoned to be especially crucial in the maintenance of covenant righteousness, in the maintenance of the individual Jew's status within the covenant'.[71] We would be wise therefore to consider the term simply in its New Testament contexts, that is in Paul's letters to the Galatians and Romans.[72]

In exegesis, context is of crucial importance, and we will therefore need first of all to survey the overall teaching of these epistles. Readers familiar with them could move straight to p. 152.

---

68. Rendered 'by observing the law' in the NIV.

69. In Gal. 2:15–16 (twice); 3:2, 5; and Rom. 3:20, 28.

70. That 'justification' is regularly recognized as a forensic term is because it is used as the opposite of the clearly forensic 'condemnation' (e.g. in Rom. 5:16–18).

71. J. D. G. Dunn, *The Epistle to the Galatians* (Peabody: Hendrickson Publishers, 1993), p. 136 (italics mine).

72. It was, of course, largely through these two books that Luther came to his understanding of justification.

The epistle to the Galatians

In this epistle, Paul writes with intense concern. Heretical teachers are influencing the Galatians, who have almost succumbed to their teaching. God made promises to Abraham and his seed, but the Galatians were Gentiles and so, they were told, they must become official members of the Jewish faith by circumcision (which implied commitment to all the prescriptions of the Mosaic law) to inherit these promises and their fulfilment in Christ.[73]

Paul knew this teaching undermined the one true gospel of grace, and so he wrote this epistle to meet its challenge. The gospel he had preached at Galatia was given to him by Christ and the other apostles had recognized it as authentic and in no way deficient (Gal. 1:1 – 2:14).

It is in Galatians 2:15 – 3:5 that he uses the phrase 'works of the law'. God's verdict of justification was not secured by such works but through faith in Christ crucified; neither did the Galatians receive the Spirit through such works.

Paul addresses the case of Abraham (not chosen arbitrarily but because the covenant promises were given to him). Abraham was justified by faith. To rely on 'works of the law' is to come under the divine curse because the law requires total conformity to its precepts, but Christ died to bear that curse in our place and to make the blessing God promised to Abraham and the gift of the Spirit available to Gentiles. Christ is himself Abraham's promised Seed, and faith, expressed in baptism, incorporates us in him so that we too are Abraham's seed (Gal. 3:6–29).

What about the law? This came 430 years after God's covenant promise to Abraham and in no way invalidated it. Before Christ came, Jews and Gentiles were both in subservience, Jews to the law (like children awaiting their majority, which came with Christ) and Gentiles to paganism, but now both can be free, with the full rights of sons, redeemed by Christ and indwelled by the Spirit. Abraham had two sons. It was Isaac, not Ishmael the son of the slave-woman, who inherited the promise, and to seek sonship to Abraham the way the heretics were teaching was to find slavery, not freedom (Gal. 4:1–31).

---

73. We gather from the epistle that the heretics were perverting the gospel (1:7), confusing the Galatians (1:7; 5:10), diverting them from the truth (5:7), seeking to enslave them (2:4; 4:8–11) and focusing on circumcision (2:3; 5:2, 11; 6:13–14) and the law (2:16, 19, 21, et al.). God's covenant was with Israel, to whom he gave the law, and circumcision was its seal. So they apparently maintained that if Gentiles were going to inherit the promises God gave Abraham, which found their fulfilment in Christ, they must be circumcised and keep the law's requirements.

Paul told the Galatians that circumcision would commit them to total legal obedience, but God's gift of the Spirit would enable them to walk in freedom. They should walk thus, living by the Spirit, so as to bear his moral fruit and not produce the ungodly works of the flesh. The false teachers want to boast that they have secured the circumcision of the Galatians, but circumcision is valueless and our boasting should be only in Christ and his cross (Gal. 5:1 – 6:18).

The epistle to the Romans

To try to summarize this letter in a few paragraphs is like trying to put an ocean into a bottle, and it risks serious omissions (some of which some readers may regard as of special importance) and too-broad generalizations, but I will need to attempt it.

It is a much calmer letter than Galatians. Its purpose has been much disputed. After outlining four proposals concerning this, Douglas Moo says, 'But what is important in these proposals for understanding the theology of Romans is their common feature: the issue of Jewish-Gentile relationships, along with its theological backdrop, the issue of continuity and discontinuity in God's plan of redemption'[74] – in other words, God's 'Big Story'.

After an introduction, which includes a Christ-centred summary of the gospel, Paul says he is not ashamed of the gospel because it saves believers, first of all Jews but also Greeks, and because it reveals God's righteousness. He then immediately declares that God's wrath is revealed against all human ungodliness and unrighteousness, which are against God's revelation in his creation and produce idolatry, licentiousness, a multiplicity of sins and approval of such practices (Rom. 1).

A disapproving bystander is self-condemned, for he too is a sinner. God will judge everybody, through Christ, by their works, on the basis of the Mosaic law for the Jew and the law of conscience for the Gentile. Paul now specifically addresses the Jew, who boasts in the law and in his relationship with God, and he asks him searching questions about his keeping of the law. What matters is not the circumcision that pledges commitment to it but actually keeping it. In a passage reminiscent of Deuteronomy 30:6, Paul says that the true circumcision is inward (Rom. 2).

He now asks some rhetorical questions which show his conviction that the failure of the Jews, who were entrusted with God's message, does not negate God's faithfulness or righteousness, which will be vindicated at the judgment

---

74. Moo, *The Epistle to the Romans*, p. 292.

to come. He goes on to show from the Old Testament the universality of sin, which clearly includes both Jews and Gentiles.

He goes on to declare the gospel, showing that it reveals God's righteousness, that its source is his grace, its basis Christ's atoning death, and that in it justification is received here and now by faith, not by works of the law (Rom. 3:20, 28). The one God is God of both Jews and Gentiles and he justifies both through faith (Rom. 3). Not only so, but he shows himself both to be righteous and to declare believing sinners to be righteous in so doing.

Then, as in Galatians, he addresses the crucial case of Abraham, crucial because God's covenant promises (perhaps he already had these in mind in 3:2) were made to him. From Genesis 15:6 he shows that he too was justified by faith, which necessarily excludes reliance on works. He became the father of all believers, for he was not even circumcised at the time, nor was he justified by the law (which, as the first readers would remember, was not even given then). Faith is the way to be credited with righteousness (righteous standing with God), and for us Christ, crucified and risen, is faith's Object (Rom. 4).

Multiple blessings come to us when we are justified by faith for, unworthy as we are, Christ died for us. His obedience to death undid the results of Adam's disobedience, which had involved the whole human race in sin. In fact God's grace, expressed in Christ's death and resulting in our justification, was even more all-embracing than Adam's sin (Rom. 5).

The implication of our baptism into Christ is that we are united to him and, because the Christ to whom we are united died and rose again, this has important moral consequences, for we should now live a crucified and risen life, serving him who is now both our new Master and Husband, Christ. Then, in an ostensibly autobiographical passage, he shows how the law reveals sin and then that through Christ we are released from the law. Knowing the law and failure to keep it induces conflict, which is resolved through Christ (Rom. 6:1 – 7:6; 7:7–25).

Through Christ's atoning work, the Holy Spirit comes to be the divine inner spring of our new life. He enables us to conquer sin, assures us of our sonship, enabling us to pray as we await our salvation's consummation, which will herald the dawn of a renewed creation, in the redemption of our bodies. Paul then utters grateful praise, punctuated by rhetorical questions, joyfully affirming the assurance of our justification by God through Christ's death (Rom. 8).

He expresses deep concern for the Jews, who were the recipients of God's covenant and its symbols and from whom Christ came, and yet who were so unresponsive to the gospel. He deals with the mystery of God's sovereign purpose of election as seen in their history. God has called Gentiles as well as Jews, and through faith they have received righteousness, whereas Jews who sought it by the law did not. The Old Testament reveals that God offers salvation to all, Jew and Gentile alike, who call on him in faith, and it also shows the hardness of Israel towards God's Word (Rom. 9 – 10).

This hardness, however, was incomplete, for in the past and present there has been an elect remnant. Neither will it be permanent, for God will accept the Jews when they repent. In fact God plans a great ingathering of both Gentiles and Jews, so great is his mercy. Paul again breaks into praise, this time because of God's great wisdom (Rom. 11).

He then deals with the ethical implications of the gospel, featuring at one point (13:8–10) the fact that love is the fulfilment of the law. He counsels the weak and strong parties (who may have been predominantly Jews and Gentiles respectively) to accept one another and respect each other's scruples, before writing about his ministry to the Gentiles, outlining his plans and sending greetings (Rom. 12 – 16).

Paul's theological perspective: the relevance of the 'Big Story'[75]

A Bible passage should always be viewed not only in its exegetical but also in its theological context, which, both in Galatians and Romans, is actually to hand here in the exegetical context itself. Tom Wright stresses the importance of the biblical metanarrative (the 'Big Story' which is really the 'Big Context') in interpreting Scripture, and we see its theological function in Galatians 3 and 4 and even more fully in Romans 4 and 5, passages with important bearing on our topic.[76] Here its most significant moments are associated with Moses (through whom the law came), Abraham (to whom the covenant promise was given) and Adam (through whom humanity fell into sin), all significant in their relationship to Christ.[77]

At this time, Judaism's adherence to the Mosaic law and its nationalism were intertwined. A Jew was defined by his nation but also by his commit-

---

75. It is, of course, important to affirm that the Big Story is a true story, that it is in fact salvation-history, the story of actual divinely initiated events with saving significance. See R. W. Yarbrough, 'Paul and Salvation History', in Carson, O'Brien and Seifrid, *Justification and Variegated Nomism: Vol. 2*, pp. 297–342. For more on the Big Story or metanarrative, see pp. 273–242.

76. Both passages contain many words indicating or suggesting the passage of time.

77. Certainly Moses is mentioned only once (Rom. 5:14), but he is there by implication in Paul's many references to the (Mosaic) law.

ment to the law. The two met in the notion of the covenant, for this was with the nation, but in its Mosaic form it was also intimately related to the law. It is different understandings of this fact that led to the conflict between Paul and the Judaizers at Galatia and which also differentiates the two perspectives on Paul.

In Galatians 3 and 4, Paul draws attention to the time-relationship of the law to the covenant with Abraham. The coming of the law could not invalidate the promise God made to Abraham and his seed centuries earlier. It was the Abrahamic form of the covenant which held out hope to the Gentiles, for, as Paul shows, Abraham was the father of all believers, both Jews and Gentiles. Wright, commenting on Galatians 3, says, 'The chapter is soaked in Abraham, and every section depends on a *historical sequence* in which Abraham comes first, the law comes next, and the Messiah – and/or "faith" – comes to complete the sequence.'[78]

Wright, among others, holds that the phrase *pisteōs Christou* (literally 'the faith of Christ') and its cognates in Paul's writings (Rom. 3:22, 26; Gal. 2:16, 20; Eph. 3:12; Phil. 3:9) refers to Christ's faithfulness to the covenant promises of God and that it should not be rendered 'faith in Christ' as in most English translations.[79] This would not mean we would have to revise our view of Paul's theology, but it would tend to increase the emphasis on the cross as a work of God in the context of his promises. It seems to me, therefore, that it is not a crucial issue in discussion of the two perspectives on Paul.

Faith may be exercised both by Jews who have the Mosaic law and by Gentiles who do not. Romans 4, another metanarrative passage, teaches essentially the same theology.

So, then, acceptance with God was on the basis of a covenant, which in Genesis 12:1–3 had promised blessing for 'all families of the earth' as well as Abraham's physical family. On its human side it was through faith, not by the law (for the Abrahamic covenant preceded the law), nor even by circumcision, a big issue at Galatia (for God made it with Abraham prior to his circumcision).

It is vital to note that in Romans Paul goes beyond the Mosaic law and focuses on Adam and Christ and therefore on the issue of universal sin. As he

---

78. N. T. Wright, *Justification: God's Plan and Paul's Vision* (London: SPCK, 2009), p. 102 (italics his).

79. ibid., pp. 96–98, 178. See also S. S. Taylor, 'Faith, Faithfulness', in T. D. Alexander and B. S. Rosner (eds.), *New Dictionary of Biblical Theology* (Leicester: Inter-Varsity Press, 2000), pp. 487–493.

clearly shows in Romans 1:18 – 3:20 and as he relates to Adam's sin and the Big Story in 5:12–21, all are sinners. So, then, there is an issue that precedes the giving of the Mosaic law and the division between those who have it and those who do not, and this is the act of Adam's disobedience which involved us all in sin. Christ's act of righteousness leads to justification for sinners, and this without (in 5:12–21) any reference to the division of Jew and Gentile at all. Fundamentally, then, this is what justification is: it is God's gift of righteousness to condemned sinners.

Here the function of the law is related to sin, and only to sin. It is highly significant that Paul uses the righteousness, condemnation, justification terminology, in other words forensic language, so extensively in this passage. It is about justification, not simply salvation conceived in some other way. The main point, from our perspective, is that here justification is about the removal of condemnation because of sin, not the removal of racial nationalism.[80] The importance of this for the current debate ought to be obvious.

It was an act of universal significance that brought condemnation, and it was also such an act which brought righteousness. Christ the justifying Sin-Bearer is not only the Seed of Abraham but the Last Adam, as Paul calls him in 1 Corinthians 15:45.[81] So, then, justification is fundamentally between God and the human race. Of course, because the lesser is included in the greater, a major consequence of Christ's act for all humanity is the breaking down of the barrier between Jew and Gentile.

Now the importance of Paul's discussion of the relationship between Adam and Christ is that it takes the focus away from the narrower issue of the relationship between Jews and Gentiles, and that it does so in terms of condemnation and justification. When we see this we see that Romans 1:18 – 3:20 should be viewed fundamentally as a condemnation of universal sin, and that the division between Jews and Gentiles, although very important in this epistle, should be viewed as subsidiary to that. Paul does refer to the law at one point in the Adam/Christ passage (Rom. 5:12–14), but entirely in connection with sin and its consequence in death. Here he makes no reference whatever to it as a barrier between Jews and Gentiles.

This is surely why in Romans 3:21–26 Paul does not simply commend faith in Christ but faith in Christ's death for our redemption. What is it about faith in Christ which is so determinate for salvation? He is to be trusted, not just because

---

80. This passage has been strangely neglected in many treatments of this subject.

81. Where a feature of the context (1 Cor. 15:22, 'as in Adam all die, so in Christ all will be made alive'), reminds us of Rom. 5:12–21.

of his status as God's Son, important as that is,[82] but because of his saving work on the cross for our redemption. And this work is a propitiatory bearing of our sins in our place. It is sin-related, not status-related. It is the nature of Christ's atoning work as penal substitution which settled the issue of sin.

We should note too that in Romans 5 the whole Jew/Gentile issue has disappeared and does not reappear until chapter 9. Particularly it is absent from Romans 8:33–34, where Paul again uses the forensic language of condemnation and justification about believers as such.

So, then, we can see that in writing of justification, Paul is not concerned only with relations between Jews and Gentiles within the covenant community, but with the much wider and even more important issue of relations between sinful human beings and God. Certainly, as N. T. Wright has emphasized in book after book and never more so than in his latest work on justification,[83] the covenant of God with Abraham is of great importance but the 'Big Story' did not begin with Abraham, but with the creation and Adam's fall.

How does the covenant with Abraham fit into all this? Paul saw what the Judaizers at Galatia had clearly failed to see, that God's covenant with Abraham not only gave hope to the Gentiles (they had at least recognized this), but that it did so quite apart from the law and circumcision.

What was needed to enable sinners, whether Jews or Gentiles, to participate together in the blessings of the Abrahamic covenant? It was sin that was the big problem. What was required was not wholesale submission to circumcision and the law on the part of repentant Gentiles, but some way of securing the fulfilment of the covenant promise by dealing with the sins of both Jews and Gentiles, whether these were against the light of nature and conscience (Rom. 1:18–32; 2:12–16) or against the Mosaic law (Rom. 2:1 – 3:20),[84] because in fact all had become involved in sin through Adam. This God graciously provided in the fullness of his time in Christ's death which turned aside his wrath against sinners (Rom. 3:21–26; Gal. 4:1–6).

Hence Christ and his cross are indispensable for salvation to come to both Jew and Gentile. If penal substitution is the heart of the atonement, as I tried to show in chapter 3, this means that the barrier between God and humans (all humans, whether Jewish or Gentile) is sin, for when used in a religious context 'penal' clearly implies sin.

---

82. See Rom. 1:1–5.

83. Wright, *Justification: God's Plan and Paul's Vision*, pp. 39, 48–49, 73–76, et al.

84. Or at least Rom. 2:17 – 3:20, where the reference to the Jews becomes quite specific.

Christ's death therefore vindicated God's justice, at the same time graciously justifying those trusting in Jesus (Rom. 3:24–26). Verse 24 is most emphatic, for Paul not only attributes justification to God's grace but says it is a gift ('freely' NIV), underlining its graciousness and, by clear implication, its independence of human merit. He underscores this again, at the Big Story level, by his repeated use of the word 'gift' in Romans 5:15–17.[85]

So far, so good. But legalism and nationalism were both features of Judaism,[86] so which did Paul have mostly in mind? Crucial for an answer is the meaning of 'the works of the law'.

Paul's use of the term 'works of the law' in these contexts

We move here from the Big Story to focus on the meaning of this small but important phrase, but in considering the phrase we must not forget the Story.

We will be considering and questioning the exegetical and so the theological soundness of the New Perspective's interpretation of 'works of the law'. We will begin with the use of the phrase in the epistle to the Romans.

Romans 2:1–16 is about an observer who passes judgment on the sinner portrayed in Romans 1:18–32. Even if this passage relates to moralists in general, as some have thought, it will include the Jews in their attitude to Gentile sin. Paul says that this observer does the same things as the sinners condemned in chapter 1.[87]

The attitude criticized is remarkably like that of the Pharisee in our Lord's parable of the Pharisee and the tax-collector (Luke 18:9–14). There the Pharisee was boasting in his works, not simply in his standing as a Jew.[88] This is, of course, a parable by Jesus, but its recording by Luke indicates his acceptance of its theology and he was also a close colleague of Paul.

In Romans 2:17 – 3:20 Paul demonstrates that Gentiles and Jews are all sinners who have transgressed God's law, expressed for the Jews in the Mosaic code and for the Gentiles in the conscience. Because of this, nobody can be

---

85. Rom. 3:24 uses *dōrea* and Rom. 5:15–17 both *dōrea* and *dōrēma*, but these are synonyms.

86. As I hope I have shown above.

87. Note that 'do such things' (Rom. 1:32) is the same Greek phrase as 'do the same things' in Rom. 2:2.

88. It is perhaps significant that, almost immediately, Luke tells the story of the rich ruler, who said to Jesus, 'What must I *do* to inherit eternal life?' (Luke 18:28, italics mine).

declared righteous by observing the law (Rom. 3:20).[89] He then sets out the main principles of justification, that it is an act of God's grace, based on the efficacy of the blood of Christ, and secured by faith.

At this point he asks, 'Where, then, is boasting?' It is excluded. On what principle? On that of the law?[90] No, but on that of faith. 'For we maintain that a man is justified by faith apart from observing the law'[91] (Rom. 3:27–28). He then asserts that it is by faith that God justifies not only Jews but also Gentiles.

What, then, is the function of these two occurrences of the phrase 'works of the law' in Romans 3? At first sight, because Paul is here concerned to explore God's acceptance of both Jews and Gentiles, his use of this expression could harmonize with the New Perspective. It must, however, be read in a wider context, that of Romans 4:1–8, and when we do this, things look very different.

Here, commenting on the crucial case of Abraham, Paul writes about *works for which people are paid wages as an obligation* and he sets over against these God crediting righteousness without works. Faith is credited as righteousness to the person who does not work but trusts God who justifies the wicked. Here, surely, is Old Perspective theology and in this light the earlier passage looks different.

Piper is surely correct when he says, 'Romans 3:28 is most naturally interpreted in light of the parallel in Romans 4:6. "To justify" is parallel with "to credit righteousness" (4:6) and "apart from works of law" (3:28) is parallel with "apart from works" (4:6).'[92]

We might compare this with Romans 9:11, which refers to God's election of Jacob rather than Esau before either of them had done anything good or bad, and 11:5–6 where Paul shows clearly that by definition grace excludes works. Here we are very evidently in the realm of ethics, not simply religious boundary markers.

We would not expect Paul's use of the term to be markedly different in Galatians. Here it is of more frequent occurrence and it is of crucial importance for understanding Galatians 2:15 – 3:14, where Paul sets 'works of the law' over against faith. The number of references to faith in this passage is considerable.

---

89. i.e. 'by the works of the law'.

90. Not 'on that of observing the law', as in NIV.

91. i.e. 'apart from the works of the law'.

92. J. Piper, *The Future of Justification: A Response to N. T. Wright* (Nottingham: Inter-Varsity Press, 2008), p. 43.

He introduces the topic in these terms in Galatians 2:16, where the element of repetition serves to underline Paul's concern that he should be understood. Whatever 'works of the law' are here, Paul is very clear that it is not these but faith in Christ that effects justification and this not only for Gentiles but also for Jews.

Wright, commenting on Galatians 2:16 and asking what 'the works of the law' are here, says, 'The context is pretty clear. They are the "living like a Jew" of 2:14, the separation from "Gentile sinners" of 2:15. They are not, in other words, the moral "good works" which the Reformation tradition loves to hate.'[93] Is the context as clear as this though? This is doubtful, for two reasons.

First of all, can we be sure that Paul is dealing here simply with the immediate historical situation and not explaining the deeper reason why it is futile to 'force Gentiles to follow Jewish customs' (v. 14)? It is characteristic of Paul to take discussion of practical issues to a deeper theological level. We must surely allow for this possibility here.

Second, we should take the wider context, the teaching of the whole epistle, into account, particularly as the crucial phrase occurs a number of times in it. A key verse for it is Galatians 3:12 where Paul says, 'The law is not based on faith; on the contrary, "The man who does these things will live by them."' This is taken from Deuteronomy 27:26, which as we will see is from a section of that book which was apparently much in his mind in this part of Galatians. In dealing with Galatians 3:1–14, where the phrase occurs three times, Wright does not raise again the question of its meaning, presumably on the assumption that this was unnecessary because of his treatment of it in his comment on 2:16.[94]

Here Paul is thinking of the law in its comprehensiveness. It is difficult to avoid concluding that he is attacking the idea that justification can be by meritorious works. Such justification is seen to be impossible because of the comprehensive demands of the law. If this is a correct understanding of Galatians 3:12, it must surely affect our understanding of Galatians 2:16 also, as Paul can hardly be working with two different theologies within the space of a few verses.[95]

We should note too the very strong language Paul uses in Philippians 3:8 when he says that he considers everything, which clearly meant or at least included 'righteousness of my own that comes from the law' (v. 9), as

---

93. Wright, *Justification: God's Plan and Paul's Vision*, p. 96.

94. ibid. pp. 101–104.

95. See S. Chester, 'When the Old Was New: Reformation Perspectives on Galatians 2:16', *Expository Times*, vol. 119, no. 7, pp. 320–329, for helpful comments on how the Reformers interpreted this passage.

'rubbish' (i.e. excrement). The language is so strong that it is surely more appropriate if it is used of his self-righteousness than of his membership of a nation whom, even though so many of them rejected Jesus, he still loved dearly (cf. Rom. 9:1–5).

In Titus 3:4–7, a brief passage of great theological richness, Paul says that we are saved by grace apart from works and that we are justified by grace. This passage looks like a summary of his understanding of the gospel, and we note that now, at a late stage of his ministry, justification by grace and apart from works is still central to his theology.

Paul's references to boasting

Fallen human nature being what it is, pride in one's labour or in one's status often expresses itself in boasting. There are a number of passages related to this in Romans 1 – 5.

Gathercole's book is a major study of 'boasting', both in Jewish soteriology and in these chapters of the epistle. He says, 'The most controversial issue that divides scholars is this: *On what is Jewish confidence based – election or obedience?*' (his italics). The question is not only whether Jews were proud of their 'boundary markers' (to use Dunn's term), but whether they were also proud of their keeping of the law. The Rabbinic literature indicates that they were. Gathercole establishes this in the very full study of the Jewish sources which makes up the bulk of his book, and Romans 2 confirms this.

In that chapter, Paul addresses an imaginary interlocutor. Gathercole argues strongly that Paul's dialogue partner throughout the chapter is a non-Christian Jew and that he is a representative of the nation.[96] He shows considerable self-confidence, and he does so in the face of God's judgment. Gathercole says,

> It is not sufficient to say that the Jewish dialogue partner is criticized for overconfidence merely in national privilege: the confidence of the Jewish people in the covenant also presupposed an assurance of their own obedience to that covenant. It is that assurance of obedience, as the basis of final justification by God, which Paul criticizes at such length in 2:1–5; 2:21–24; and 3:10–20, which is why it makes sense to speak of the Jewish 'boast' in 2:17, 23 as including reference to confidence on the basis of obedience.[97]

---

96. Gathercole, *Where Is Boasting?*, pp. 197–201; cf. Dunn, *Romans 1 – 8* (Word: Milton Keynes, 1991), pp. 78–82.

97. Gathercole, ibid., p. 215.

Paul's teaching elsewhere supports this. His statement in Ephesians 2:8–10 that we are saved by faith, not works, 'so that no-one can boast', followed by an assertion that good works, originating in a creative work of God, *proceed from* salvation, harmonizes theologically with this, even though Paul does not use justification language here. We might compare Deuteronomy 9:4–6, which relates to God's gift of the land of Canaan to Israel and which sees it as God's gracious gift, which was quite independent of their works, for Moses declared these to be evil.

In fact, quite apart from the evidence Gathercole presents, we should recognize from our knowledge of fallen human nature that it would be very easy to move from boasting in possession of the law (i.e. religious racialism) to boasting in keeping the law. This might not be the case if the boast were simply in the covenant and not also in the law, for although covenants have requirements the chief feature of God's covenant with Israel is that it was a gift from him to them. It is true too that the law was often viewed as a blessing,[98] but it is of the essence of law that it is to be obeyed and this characteristic of it is prominent in the literature of early Judaism.

'Under a curse' – which curse?

Wrath, judgment, curse – do these terms have similar bearing in Paul's use of them? Certainly in Romans 1 – 3 wrath and judgment are cause and effect and neither is restricted to Gentiles or to Jews, nor to any specific sin or sins. Paul uses 'curse' only in Galatians 3:13, but this is important for our subject.

Has 'curse' a more specialized, more restricted sense? Does it relate quite specifically to the Deuteronomic curse pronounced against Israel which led to its exile? And if so, is the redemptive work of Christ in this passage related primarily to Israel and its restoration from exile, which then opens the way for Gentiles too to be incorporated in God's people? This is the view of Wright.[99]

Paul says, 'Christ redeemed us from the curse of the law by becoming a curse for us, for it is written: "Cursed is everyone who is hung on a tree"' (Gal. 3:13). Here he quotes Deuteronomy 21:23. Earlier (Gal. 3:10) he had quoted Deuteronomy 27:26 about the importance of *total* obedience to the law.[100]

---

98. e. g. see the psalmist's attitude in Ps. 119.

99. He expounds this in *Climax of the Covenant*; see also *Paul: In Fresh Perspective* (Minneapolis: Fortress, 2005), pp. 139–140.

100. Seifrid points out that Paul interprets this verse by adding the word 'all' from the immediate context in Deut. 28:15, 58 (M. A. Seifrid, *Christ our Righteousness*, Leicester: Apollos, 2000, p. 102).

It is important to note that both verses come from a section of Deuteronomy (chs 21 – 27) where the focus is almost entirely on the individual Israelite,[101] and that in Deuteronomy 27 the individual is in view throughout and is cursed for one sin after another. It is not until chapter 28 that the spotlight begins to fall on the nation as such and blessings and curses are pronounced on it, including the ultimate curse of exile from the land. Wright is therefore incorrect when he says, 'Deuteronomy 27 – 30 is all about exile and restoration, understood as covenant judgment and covenant renewal.'[102]

Moreover, in the light of this, the individual Israelite is most likely to be in view in Galatians 3:10–12, in such expressions as 'all who', 'everyone who' and 'no-one'. Certainly in verse 13 the emphatic position of the word 'us' clearly suggests a contrast with 'to the Gentiles' in verse 14,[103] but each of these terms, if interpreted in line with verses 10–12, may be understood distributively rather than collectively. It therefore seems unlikely that verses 13 and 14 refer to the nation as such and to its return from exile through the work of Jesus the Messiah.

It looks, therefore, as if the curse to which Paul refers is the curse of God against the individual's sin, which Christ bore as he hung on a tree, so experiencing the curse of God in our place. This ties up with 2 Corinthians 5:21, which uses different language ('made . . . to be sin for us' instead of 'becoming a curse for us') to make the same point, and which is not so easily related to the exile theme. Several writers have in fact pointed out that there is no evidence that Jews actually living in the land thought of themselves as still in exile.[104] Certainly we may agree that the verse is specifically about Israel (as a glance at the following verse immediately makes clear), but it is about Israelites distributively rather than the nation collectively.

In verses 6–9 Paul had argued that all, both Jews and Gentiles, who have faith in Christ are justified by God. In verse 12 he quotes his key text, 'The

---

101. He also quotes from this part of Deuteronomy in Gal. 3:10 (Deut. 27:26).

102. See his whole treatment of this in *Climax of the Covenant*, pp. 140–141.

103. See S. H. Levinsohn, *Discourse Features of NT Greek* (Dallas: SIL International, 2000), p. 285, for the significance of this.

104. See J. A. Dennis, *Jesus' Death and the Gathering of True Israel: The Johannine Appropriation of Restoration Theology in the Light of John 11:47–52* (Tübingen: Mohr Siebeck, 2006), pp. 80–81. See also L. T. Johnson, 'A Historiographical Response to Wright's Jesus', in C.C. Newman (ed.), *Jesus and the Restoration of Israel* (Carlisle: Paternoster, 1999), pp. 244–277, who comments on Wright's lack of precision in using the term 'exile'. Wright replies in the same volume.

righteous will live by faith', taken from Habakkuk 2:4. This too is about the individual Israelite.[105] Christ's bearing of the curse, therefore, is related to the sins of individuals.

Does all this matter? Yes, it does. It means that justification in this passage is about God declaring the individual sinner to be righteous because Christ had borne his or her sins. Certainly this results in believing Jews and Gentiles sharing together in the blessing of Abraham, but there is no suggestion that this is what justification actually means.

Justification as present and future

In one of his books, Wright has given a definition of justification. He calls it,

> God's declaration, from his position as judge of all the world, that someone is in the right, despite universal sin. This declaration will be made on the last day on the basis of an entire life (Romans 2:1–16), but is brought forward into the present on the basis of Jesus' achievement, because sin has been dealt with through his cross (Romans 3:21 – 4:25); the means of this present justification is simply faith. This means particularly that Jews and Gentiles alike are full members of the family promised by God to Abraham (Galatians 3; Romans 4).[106]

When Wright expounds justification in this way, this almost sounds like the Old Perspective, and at first reading he does not seem too far from Luther's position, but his double use of the word 'basis' here may give us cause for some concern. If 'on the basis of an entire life' simply refers to evidence, it would be better to *say* 'evidence' rather than 'basis', especially as the latter must then have a different sense from its use earlier in the same sentence.[107]

The whole principle of inaugurated eschatology is that through his work in his first advent Christ brings into present experience something which comes to fullest expression at his second. This has an application to unbelievers, for they are judged already by their present attitude to Christ (John 3:18),

---

105. 'Righteous' in the Hebrew is singular.

106. N. T. Wright, *Paul for Everyone: Galatians and Thessalonians* (London, SPCK, 2002), p. 169. He also writes in the same vein in *Paul: In Fresh Perspective*, p. 148.

107. Rom. 2:1–16, abstracted from its wider context, could be understood either of justification by works as meritorious or else as evidential, but in its wider context in Romans it can only be the latter, as the alternative would contradict Paul's justification teaching here quite radically.

and it applies in all sorts of ways to believers, who are already blessed with every spiritual blessing in Christ (Eph. 1:3) but who later will experience these blessings in fullest measure (1 Pet. 1:3–8).

Among these blessings is justification, which means that it is a present and not simply a future reality. There is no suggestion in Paul's writings that it is subject to degree; in fact the sense of the word, as the opposite of condemnation, hardly admits of degree. Nor is there any suggestion that it is only provisional, awaiting confirmation at the final judgment. That evidence of it is to be expected is quite a different matter.

In this connection, we must consider Romans 8, especially verses 1–4. Here Paul says that there is no condemnation to those who are in Christ Jesus, and that God sent Christ to be a sin-offering.[108] This sounds like a straightforward statement of forensic justification, but he then goes on to say, 'So he condemned sin in sinful man, in order that the righteous requirements of the law might be fully met in us [not 'for us'], who do not live according to the sinful nature but according to the Spirit.' Does this make justification at least partly contingent on our obedience?

The epistle to the Romans is perhaps the most logical of all Paul's letters in its arrangement. Everything is connected, but he sometimes does not turn aside from his current topic to handle something that logically and theologically arises out of it but which needs special treatment. Instead he completes the one and then addresses the other.

Studying Romans 8 shows that having dealt with condemnation for sin, then justification by grace and then with the relationship of sin and the law, he is now dealing with the work of the Holy Spirit in us that makes a life of practical godliness possible. It is most important that this should be seen as intimately linked to God's justifying verdict, and Paul indicates the link between them in his use of the preposition *hina* ('in order that') in verse 4. There can be no practical godliness unless we are justified, but it is also true that there is no authentic justification that does not result in practical godliness.

The plenitude of references to the Spirit in this chapter is in striking contrast with the absence of such references in chapters 5 – 7.[109] So, in the passage that opens chapter 8, Paul is saying that a purpose of justification is to transform us within, which he then goes on to demonstrate is due to the

---

108. Or 'for sin'. The translation difference does not affect the issue we are considering here.

109. With the exception of Rom. 5:5, which really anticipates 13:8–10.

presence of the Spirit in our hearts. Linking this with what he has already said in Romans 6:11–14, we see that the Spirit does not do this automatically but through our obedience. The perfect balance of Paul's doctrine is shown in Romans 8:13, 'If by the Spirit you put to death the misdeeds of the body, you will live.' Here, in the midst of Romans 8, is a key to the practical implementation of the teaching of Romans 6:11–14 as well as that of 8:4.

But is justification here *conditional* on our fully meeting 'the righteous requirements of the law'? This can hardly be his meaning in view of his use of the extremely demanding word *plerōthē* ('fully') here. There is no suggestion anywhere else in his epistles that God's justifying verdict is subject to that condition, and, if it were true, it would be most important to make it clear, not just once but over and over again.

That word is, in fact, a most helpful clue. In this epistle we need not only to follow the logic of the argument as it proceeds majestically through the epistle, but also to see the relevance of later sections to earlier. Here we must consider Romans 13:8–10, with its teaching that 'love is the fulfilment of the law', where 'fulfilment' renders *plerōma*, which is from the same Greek root as *plerōthē*. In verse 8, 'fulfilled' is *peplērōken*, again from the same root and where the perfect tense emphasizes that this is complete.

So, then, just as Romans 8:13 was a spiritual key to the practical implementation of 6:11–14, so 13:8–10 is the key to the implementation of 8:4. E. F. Harrison's comment on 13:8–10 is very helpful. He says,

> In saying that the one who loves has fulfilled the law, Paul presents a truth that parallels his statement in 8:4 about the righteous requirement of the law being fulfilled in those who live in accordance with the Spirit. The connecting link between these two passages is provided by Galatians 5:22, 23, where first place in the enumeration of the fruitage of the Spirit is given to love and the list is followed by the observation that against such fruit there is no law. So the Spirit produces in the believer a love to which the law can offer no objection, since love fulfils what the law requires, something the law itself cannot do.[110]

So, then, in 8:1–4, Paul is not introducing legalism by the back door, but rather is showing that he is no antinomian. The law is good (cf. 7:12), but God's marvellous plan and design is to put his love into our hearts by his Spirit so that

---

110. E. F. Harrison, 'Romans', in F. E. Gaebelein (ed.), *The Expositor's Bible Commentary* (Grand Rapids: Zondervan, 1976), p. 141.

we may be enabled to fulfil it. Such love does not justify us, but rather shows that we are justified. This means that the law is not abrogated but fulfilled, not because we become 'justified legalists', but because God's Spirit gives us love for God and therefore for his law, so fulfilling the law in us by taking it to a deeper level and writing it on our hearts, just as Jeremiah said he would (Jer. 31:31–34). This, then, is no renewal of legalism but a further marvel of the gospel.

In connection with this, we should note that Paul not only says that we are justified through Christ, that is through his work for us, but also in Christ (1 Cor. 1:30; cf. 2 Cor. 5:21, 'in him'). These are not rival truths but companion ones. To note this is to be delivered from the serious error of imagining that our justification is simply a kind of legal transfer which leaves no impression on the kind of people we are. To be justified through him shows that we are dependent on his work outside us, while to be justified in him shows that we need to be joined to him if that work is to become practically effective.

One further point: in Romans 5 Paul had written about some of the results of justification, and in the course of this he says, 'Since we have now been justified by his blood, how much more shall we be saved from God's wrath through him!' (Rom. 5:9). Could anything be clearer? Our justification by the blood of Christ is so decisive that it will not forsake us at the judgment. 'As now, so then!'

An appraisal of the New Perspective

It is always good to do new research on doctrines that are central to the Christian faith and we can be glad about the work done, even if some of the theological proposals made on the basis of it prove unacceptable.

Sanders has forced scholars to look carefully at the Jewish background to the New Testament
Good scholarship always goes back to primary documents. Sanders has let a breath of fresh air into studies of the Jewish background to Christianity by his independent study of the sources, in which he criticized some interpretations of Judaism that were long overdue for correction. He has forced his major critics to follow his example and, as we have seen, some of them have argued that his research was not extensive enough, so that some of his own conclusions are open to question.

This background is important because it was Paul's own pre-Christian background and also because its influence can be seen in the outlook of the Judaizers whose work caused him to write to the Galatians.

The emphasis on the gospel as good news about Christ is to be welcomed

This is perhaps the greatest virtue of the New Perspective, especially in Tom Wright's version of it, and his writings are full of profitable insights. For him the focus of the gospel is primarily on the victory and lordship of Christ, and the salvation of sinners is to be seen as the consequence of that victory. Christ is important as an end in himself and not just as a means to an end.

This is well summed up in the words of Thomas Kelly ('the Charles Wesley of Ireland'), whose hymns constantly strike this note:

> Look, ye saints, the sight is glorious, see the Man of sorrows now!
> From the fight returned victorious; every knee to Him must bow;
> Crown Him! Crown Him! Crown Him! Crown Him!
> Crowns become the Victor's brow.[111]

This is not only God-honouring but spiritually liberating, for it takes the focus of attention off ourselves and places it on Christ, yet even to say this is to think in terms of its benefits for us! We ought to focus on Christ, not simply because this is spiritually healthy but because such a focus of thought, faith, prayer and worship is exactly what he deserves.[112] Wright has also pointed out that Protestants have often tended to emphasize the teaching of Paul rather than the ministry of Jesus, who ought to be the centre of our attention, and therefore to major on the exposition of the epistles rather than the Gospels.[113] Wright's point may be taken, but this does not mean that we should regard the Gospels as of higher authority than the epistles, for all are equally inspired by the Holy Spirit.

A comment by Piper should also be remembered: 'One wonders how the death and resurrection of Jesus could be heard as good news if one had spent his life committing treason against the risen King. It seems as though one would have to be told how the death and resurrection of Christ actually

---

111. *Methodist Hymn Book*, no. 226, p. 87.

112. Sanders too says of Paul, 'The christological interpretation of the triumph of God ... is the central characteristic of his thought' (*Paul, the Law, and the Jewish People*, p. 5).

113. N. T. Wright, *Jesus and the Victory of God* (Minneapolis: Fortress, 1996), pp. 13–15.

saves sinners, if sinners are to hear them as good news and not as a death sentence.'[114]

Wright is correct, of course, in saying we can be too individualistic in our view of the Christian faith. It is not just about me, but is even more about Christ. The Bible's 'Big Story' concerns the conflict between God and Satan in which God in Christ is victorious. So it is personal but not individualistic. But a major consequence of this is the release of Satan's captives so that we are surely right to say that the good news is *both* that Christ has triumphed *and* that in so doing he has secured our salvation. After all, Paul's basic statement about the message he proclaimed to the Corinthians included the phrase 'for our sins' (1 Cor. 15:3).

There is a welcome emphasis on the union of justification and sanctification

Calvin in the *Institutes* writes carefully about this, indicating that we should distinguish and yet not separate the two. To confuse them is to move in the direction of the Council of Trent and its Counter-Reformation theology, while to separate them is to become antinomian. The God who in Christ justifies us is also the God who through the Spirit sanctifies us. Here the two great gospel imperatives of John 3, 'the Son of Man must be lifted up' (John 3:14) and 'you must be born again' (John 3:7), are united. Among critics of the New Perspective, Gathercole has taken seriously the fact that 'without holiness no-one shall see the Lord' (cf. 1 John).

These two great facts come together in the believer's union with Christ, which is the foundation of both.[115] There is no need for us to be over-occupied with the *ordo salutis*, in which the doctrines of grace are placed in their logical order. It may be well argued that union with Christ logically precedes justification, yet this is by no means to downgrade justification but simply to insist that it is never experienced outside vital union with the Christ who died for our sins and rose again for our justification.

The union of these two great doctrines, already present in the major Reformers, was further developed by the Puritans, whose teaching on this also affected John Wesley. We can be thankful that New Perspective writers are also reminding us of this.

---

114. Piper, *The Future of Justification*, p. 18.

115. S. Chester, 'When the Old Was New', has shown that the Reformers strongly connected justification by faith with faith-union with Christ in their handling of Gal. 2.

Its emphasis on the place of the church in the gospel and on its inclusive character is also to be welcomed

Evangelicals have often been weak on the doctrine of the church, neglecting the corporate dimensions of the gospel in general and of justification in particular. For instance, in our reading of the New Testament letters we almost invariably interpret the first and second persons plural distributively rather than collectively. This may be due to our individualistic understanding of justification, but it also tends to feed into it. Today it is not even expedient when so many in our society have a deep, unmet longing for acceptance into a social group.

Kim, one of its strongest critics, nevertheless agrees that the New Perspective school has led the upholders of the Old Perspective 'to appreciate better the doctrine's overall covenantal framework and its sociological or missiological implications'.[116] So we note that Paul not only sees the gospel as uniting Jew and Gentile, but also as breaking down other social barriers when in Galatians 3:28 he says, 'There is neither Jew nor Greek, slave nor free, male nor female, for you are all one in Christ Jesus.' In Colossians 3:11 he not only emphasizes the ending of the Jew/Greek division by referring also to 'circumcised or uncircumcised', but also adds 'barbarian' and 'Scythian'.

Sociologically this is explosive teaching and we in the contemporary church must submit to its searching judgment. We may *say* that there can be no second-class citizens in the church of Christ, but do we put this insight, based on the teaching of Scripture, fully into practice? Its implications for world mission too are patently obvious.

In questioning certain aspects of the New Perspective we do not need to reject its emphasis that works of the law like circumcision, sabbath observance and food laws constituted barriers between Jews and Gentiles, so long as we are clear that Paul was even more concerned to show that the law as a whole constituted a great barrier between sinners and God, because sinners must keep the law and yet because of their sins they cannot.

Its revised understanding of the Pauline doctrine is unconvincing and this is serious in relation to such an important doctrine with crucial gospel relevance

This has been the thrust of this chapter's argument. Craig Blomberg is surely right when he says that such Pauline passages as Romans 4:4–5, Galatians

---

116. Kim, *Paul and the New Perspective*, p. 295.

3:10–14 and Philippians 3:7–10 certainly seem to support the traditional Reformation rather than the New Perspective view.[117]

I believe that we should not be playing down the gospel's attack on legalism. This is the New Testament equivalent of the Old Testament's portrayal of the attack on mere ceremonialism by the prophets, who rejected sacrifice which was not accompanied by ethical evidence of repentance. This ceremonialism is close in significance to New Testament Pharisaism as normally understood.

Neither should we jettison justification conceived as a judicial verdict giving the believer full assurance of salvation from judgment. A book devoted entirely to the teaching of the Bible on the wrath and judgment of God might well run to several volumes. Paul was undoubtedly aware of this strong biblical emphasis in writing his epistle to the Romans and he lays a full and deep basis of this teaching before proceeding to an exposition of the gospel of Christ. The fact that Romans 1:18–32 immediately follows 1:16–17 probably indicates that in his mind wrath and grace were correlatives, so that in thinking of the one the Christian mind would turn naturally to think of the other. When we take full account of the fact that condemnation and justification are legal verdicts, we see how vital it is that both truths should be maintained and proclaimed.

Seifrid, having published a thorough study of the relevant Old Testament evidence,[118] says,

> Righteousness language in the Hebrew Scriptures (as in the Ancient Near East generally) has its basis in creational theology rather than in the framework of covenantal ideas. This assessment is especially relevant with respect to those passages that have to do with the administration of justice, and divine administration of justice in particular. It is these which serve as the background to Paul's announcement of the revelation of God's righteousness and his further statements on the justifying work of Christ.[119]

---

117. C. Blomberg, 'Critical Issues in New Testament Studies for Evangelicals Today', in P. E. Satterthwaite and D. F. Wright (eds.), *A Pathway into the Holy Scripture* (Grand Rapids: Eerdmans, 1994), p. 58.

118. M. A. Seifrid, 'Righteousness Language in the Old Testament and Early Judaism', in Carson, O'Brien and Seifrid, *Justification and Variegated Nomism*, vol. 1, pp. 415–442.

119. M. A. Seifrid, 'Paul's Use of Righteousness Language against its Hellenistic Background', in Carson, O'Brien and Seifrid, *Justification and Variegated Nomism*, vol. 2, p. 40.

Certainly there are some positive as well as negative features in the New Perspective, but can we not accept the positives (which do not, in any case, depend on the New Perspective) and reject the negatives (which are central features of it)?

Preaching the Pauline gospel of justification today

James Denney, a major Scottish New Testament scholar of a century ago, used to say that he had no interest whatever in a theology which could not be preached. No doubt that sentiment will be echoed by many readers of this book. If, then, our doctrine is biblical, how do we preach it? There are many barriers against it in today's society which we must face realistically.

There is a prejudice against Paul's writings
Many people view him as a misogynist and so tend to write him off. Even if two passages in his writings[120] are thought (wrongly, in my view) to show this, they represent only a tiny proportion of his large output. There is need for an apologetic here and also for pointing out that the doctrine is found seminally in our Lord's teaching, for instance in the parable of the Pharisee and the tax-collector (Luke 18:9–14).

Today there is a greater focus on biblical narrative than on biblical discourse
For many people, therefore, the Gospels are of greater interest than the epistles. Wright has pointed out, however, that there is narrative behind all the biblical material, and that Paul's theology arises out of and interprets this.

It has always been true that we need to give justification a background in the doctrine of God, and this has perhaps never been more necessary than today, but we must also give careful attention to the way we do it, showing how this teaching relates to the acts of God, the way the Big Story was written into human history by his great deeds of creation, judgment and grace. Especially we should show that it is grounded in the great events of the Gospel narratives. In other words, the God of our preaching should be presented as dynamic, not static, which is exactly the way Scripture presents him, without losing the Bible's emphasis on his reliability and stability.[121]

---

120. 1 Cor. 14:33–35; 1 Tim. 2:6–15.
121. See ch. 2.

Legal categories are unappealing

It is said that we should think of God in terms of personal, not legal, relationships. There is a widespread dislike of authority figures and they are certainly present in the courtroom. Not only so, but many people today are longing for acceptance and want to belong to a family. It is pointed out that the Christian gospel offers such a family relationship, and that this, rather than courtroom language, should be our emphasis in preaching.

God's relationship with us is multiform, but even in family terms we cannot escape legal categories. Through Christ God adopts us into his family, and adoption both in New Testament times and today has a legal dimension. Both justification and adoption are about a change of status. It may be said that adoption, like marriage, is nothing more than the securing of a piece of paper, but how important are those documents! Without them the very existence of the marriage or the adoption could be in doubt. The increasing demise of marriage in our society has induced a sense of insecurity into many relationships. The largely despised 'piece of paper' can give assurance when this is much needed.

Even if many in our society react against the idea of legal authority, our consciences bear witness to the fact that we are under law. It is not only the Bible that tells me I have transgressed God's law; it is my conscience too. It functions like a counsel for the prosecution. Only God's justifying verdict can silence its accusings.[122] Here is the link between justification and atonement. As we have seen in an earlier chapter, it is because Christ has taken my place and borne my punishment that I am justified, and it is this too that conveys assurance to my heart.

Preaching the gospel in terms of justification may be more difficult in some societies than in others, but all communities have laws of some sort. No society lets everybody do exactly as they like. If we are to preach effectively in any society, it is important for us to know in broad terms what kind of legal system obtains in that society.

Postmodern people do not think in terms of structures

This is true, and when such people think about relationships they think in informal terms. This is why the retreat from marriage, although preceding the advent of postmodernism, so harmonizes with it.

---

122. Although the epistle to the Hebrews does not expound the gospel in terms of justification, it too shows Christ's work meeting the demands of conscience (Heb. 9:9–14; 10:22).

Yet we all have an inbuilt need for structure. The child who runs to her parent from the dangerous or even the unfamiliar is acknowledging this. Guidelines in the family are really like family law. Note the word 'need' in the familiar saying, 'We need some ground-rules.' We are set adrift in a world that is partly exciting but partly threatening, and we look for a stability that imparts safety.[123] Finding disorientation we look for stability, whether or not we acknowledge or even realize it. Such stability and such safety are to be found in God's wonderful justifying verdict.

There is little awareness of God or sense of sin

This is certainly true in society after society and paradoxically it is particularly evident in what, with ever-increasing anachronism, we still call Christendom. That justification is the most wonderfully good news can only be true for those who are deeply aware of their spiritual need. What is most needed is a God-given revival in which a deep awareness of God and therefore of sin comes into a community, and for this we should earnestly pray.

Although we pray for revival, however, we cannot wait idly for it. If we believe in the power of the Word of God, we need both to proclaim it and to live with such an awareness of God and such a personal sensitivity to sin that this constitutes a powerful witness to the reality of these truths. Such proclamation should be done both faithfully and carefully, with due recognition that it cuts right across people's predispositions. We must avoid harshness, for the gospel must always be preached winsomely, but we cannot play down the fact of sin, nor fail to warn people of its eternal consequences.

We believe we must do something to secure our own salvation

This belief is extremely widespread and can be found in all cultures, all religions, including Christianity as commonly misunderstood. This is itself a product of sin, for our sin blinds us to the fact that everything we can offer God is soiled already by our sin. This too means that preaching the gospel as justification, to be effective, must lay a foundation in teaching not only about God but also about sin.

To find ourselves embraced by the grace of God is wonderfully liberating, and it is not surprising to find that the epistle to the Galatians, which majors on justification, has also been called 'the charter of Christian freedom', a title fully appropriate as its last two chapters in particular show so clearly.

---

123. For all its many inadequacies, the existentialist theology of a few decades ago emphasized this.

What, then, of repentance? The preaching of the gospel, both by Jesus himself and the apostles, involved a call to repentance and this is important. This should never, however, be presented as a legalistic list of prior require- ments before the gospel can be embraced, but rather as a call to a decisive change in the heart's attitude. This recognizes that to respond to God's call to trust in Christ for salvation and to determine to resist any change in my values and conduct are simply incompatible.

Faith and repentance, when both are genuine, are really the two sides of one changed attitude. As faith is a gift of God, so also is repentance (Acts 11:18), and just as true faith evidences itself in works, so does true repentance (Acts 26:20). It is the Holy Spirit's work in the sinner's heart that makes both faith and repentance not only possible but also real and true.

We wonder if we can trust God

Society is based on trust and yet paradoxically and sadly constantly erodes it. Many people feel they can trust nobody, and this kind of cynicism is becom- ing more and more widespread. Politicians, financiers and advertisers are all viewed with suspicion and words like 'sleaze' and 'spin' have become common verbal currency. Voting decisions in politics are often based on estimates of trust, whether of the candidate or the party, so that this kind of suspicion is probably a factor when there is a low turnout at election times. In times of financial crisis the word 'confidence' is constantly heard on news bulletins. It is perhaps in relation to marriage that trust has been most eroded and this is extremely serious as it threatens the family, the basic God-given building block in every society.

This widespread sense of distrust has as its counterpart a deep sense of need for somebody to trust. This relates to what we have already seen about the need for stability. Again this shows the need to place the good news of justification in a theological context. All the Bible's teaching about God's faithfulness is relevant to this. Here again we see the need for a teaching evan- gelism. At one time in Western society we could assume some rudimentary knowledge of Scripture and its teaching about God in many people, but today, here as well as elsewhere, we have to start virtually from scratch. Not only so, but we often have to combat those distortions of the truth which affect people's minds.

In view of all this, we should give much attention to our presentation of the message

A strange situation obtains today. Most of us have greater access to educa- tional aids than ever before. This is particularly true for those who use the

Internet. Yet the average person's attention span is much more limited than it used to be. If you doubt this, ask any teacher or television producer! We live in the age that invented the word 'soundbite'.

We have had to deal with some exegetical and theological niceties in this chapter due to the necessities of debate, both in Paul's day and in ours. But in actual fact a view of Paul's doctrine of justification that is highly complex denies its own validity, for this to Paul was central to the gospel and it had to be capable of clear and simple exposition.

In Acts 13:37–39 we find him at Pisidian Antioch preaching to Jews and 'Gentiles of the synagogue', and after relating the story of Jesus to the history of God's dealings with his people, he says, 'The one whom God raised from the dead did not see decay. Therefore, my brothers, I want you to know that through Jesus the forgiveness of sins is proclaimed to you. Through him everyone who believes is justified from everything you could not be justified from by the law of Moses.'

No doubt this is a summary of what he said, but we can see its basic simplicity, directness and appropriateness to the audience.

It is easy, especially for those who have recently completed a prolonged theological course, to preach jargon-ridden sermons that go right over people's heads. Simple, clear preaching often takes much preparation, but such preparation is vital. Clarity will be aided by good illustrations, but these must be fully appropriate. They need to be meaningful to the audience, but they must also be completely true to Paul's theology.

Dependence on the Holy Spirit is indispensable in all proclamation of God's Word

The importance of accurate exegesis and good biblical theology cannot be overstressed, but preaching is not simply the communication of ideas, no matter how true these are to the teaching of holy Scripture. All effective preaching involves constant dependence on the Holy Spirit. This is true both in the study and in the pulpit. His is the truth we are to proclaim, for he inspired the Bible writers and he is also the great Interpreter of Scripture. Most of all, he is the divine Advocate of Christ. The early preachers, as Acts shows us, were filled with the Spirit as they preached the Word. His empowering and at the same time humbling ministry is indispensable for us too.

5. ISSUES AFFECTING THE DOCTRINE OF SCRIPTURE

Because of its theme, this chapter relates to the concerns of biblical scholars as well as theologians. These two groups have different academic remits. No matter what issue is the subject of a theologian's book, the author's general theological stance can usually be discerned. This is because of the interlocking nature of the themes of theology. This is not always so, however, with works by biblical scholars, whose remit is often more concerned with understanding particular Bible books or passages than with larger theological issues, and who do not always feel the need to make clear whether or not they regard themselves as evangelicals. So when we are considering the work of biblical scholars we will concentrate more on principles than on the work of individual writers. The issue before us is whether, as we survey the contemporary theological scene, we can establish what theological and critical positions are compatible with evangelicalism and with a high doctrine of Scripture.

Now the importance of the Bible is evident to anybody who enters a Christian church or opens a Christian book. Its recognition as authoritative, no matter how that is perceived in detail, is a basic fact of Christianity. This is true even where significance is attached to some other authority such as the church, the creeds, reason or experience.

Evangelical Christians have always been characterized by the fact that to them Scripture's authority is unique and supreme. This is true no matter what form of words they use to structure their sense of this. When the Anglican

Church began ordaining women, some High Church Anglicans who were considering becoming Roman Catholics were unhappy about papal infallibility. At that time Cardinal Basil Hume commented that Catholic teaching must be accepted as a whole and should not be viewed as an *á la carte* but as a *table d'hôte* meal. Evangelicals hold a similar position, but in their case in relation to Scripture.

In terms of the purpose of this book, we need to enquire how Scripture has been viewed and employed by evangelicals in recent years. As long ago as 1981, W. J. Abraham observed, 'Contemporary Evangelical theology faces a crisis as regards its doctrine of inspiration.'[1] Whether the dramatic word 'crisis' was warranted may be debatable, but we should note that this was written before evangelical theologians and conservative scholars were faced with the challenge of postmodernism, which has introduced other issues for us.

The great importance of holy Scripture, especially in an age when heresies abound, becomes clear when we note how it is highlighted in some of the later books of the New Testament, books written at a time when heresies of various kinds were becoming active. Such passages occur in Paul's final letter (2 Tim. 3:10–17), in Peter's also (2 Pet. 1:16–21; 3:15–18), in 1 John 4:1–6,[2] and in Revelation 22:18–19. This phenomenon has not always received the attention it deserves.

What are the issues for us just now? They are of various kinds. For instance, in recent years some evangelicals have expressed reservations about the usefulness of 'inerrancy' as a theological concept,[3] while others have promoted positions on matters such as the authorship of biblical books which have normally been associated with liberals. Others are approaching the interpretation of Scripture in new ways, some of which raise serious questions, and some are tending to play down the importance of the discursive sections of Scripture (such as the epistles) in contrast to biblical narrative. So, for instance, in the debate about penal substitution, some writers appear to see more significance in the human opposition which led to the crucifixion, as seen in the Gospels, than to the theological meaning of the cross, which is set forth largely in the epistles. This is to be seen in the volumes by Chalke and Mann and by Green and Baker which occupied much of our attention in chapter 3.

---

1. W. J. Abraham, *The Divine Inspiration of Holy Scripture* (Oxford: Oxford University Press, 1981), p. 1.

2. Here 'we' in v. 6 clearly refers to the apostles, cf. 1:1–5.

3. See A. T. B. McGowan, *The Divine Spiration of Scripture: Challenging Evangelical Perspectives* (Nottingham: Inter-Varsity Press, 2007).

Issues concerning the authority of the Bible on the one hand and its interpretation on the other are distinct and yet related. This chapter deals with authority and the next with interpretation, but readers will soon become aware that the two cannot be kept completely apart. One important reason for this is that the *authority* of the New Testament covers its *interpretation* of the Old.

How is the Bible related to the church and to the academy? In the former it has a place of authority; in the latter it is studied as an important and fascinating literary corpus. The academy made much of the running during the late nineteenth and early twentieth centuries, the period when the historical-critical view of Scripture was often linked with a liberal theology. The great interest of the Bible is due very largely, however, to its special place in the church, the place it has been given by God. This means that we will not be uninterested in the way it has been viewed in the church down through the centuries. We must always remember, however, that the Bible is not the possession of the church in the sense that it can do with it what it will; rather, the church is under the authority of Scripture: a very different matter.

To address these issues helpfully, we will need first of all to consider the more traditional approach (or approaches) associated with evangelicalism, then note the cultural background in relation to which the work of evangelical scholars is being done today, then seek to assess the actual views that are being promoted, and finally suggest some practical conclusions.

The traditional evangelical doctrine of Scripture

In the past, the great majority of evangelicals have been in broad agreement on quite a number of matters related to the authority of the Bible.

The revelation of God

God reveals himself in two modes. The first is a general revelation which conveys the truth of his existence, supremacy and moral nature, a revelation made to all human beings, even though through sin there has been much suppression and distortion of this knowledge in their hearts.[4] The second is a special revelation, made in the history of Israel and culminating in Christ, through whom salvation is effected and offered. This special revelation is recorded in holy Scripture, which as the Word of God is itself divine revelation.

---

4. See especially Rom. 1:18–32.

The inspiration of the Bible

Inspiration is an activity of the Holy Spirit, who spoke through the prophets and apostles and who so operated in those who wrote the Scriptures that what they wrote was not simply human words (although it was that) but the Word of God. 'Inspiration', when applied to Scripture, means 'God-breathed',[5] indicating that it is the utterance of the Holy Spirit, the 'Breath' of God. It is important to differentiate this from its modern English use for a particular quality attributed to fine literature, music and art.[6] As applied to Scripture, it properly refers not to a mere heightening of the powers of the writer, nor simply to the imparting of ideas from God to the writer. It extends to the form in which those ideas are expressed.

We should note that the way in which the words were given varied greatly according to the literary genre concerned. To the prophets it was often through visions, for the historians through research, for the writers of epistles through prayerful consideration of the needs of the readers. The common factor, however, is that the end result was the words God intended, conveying the truth he intended. This means that the human characteristics of the authors were not bypassed but employed by the inspiring Spirit.

The UCCF basis, among others, uses the phrase 'as originally given' in reference to the inspired text. This is not a refuge for those embarrassed by or refusing to face the problems of textual corruption, but is simply a matter of logic. If it is the *Scriptures* whose words are the product of inspiration, as 2 Timothy 3:16 indicates, then in the nature of the case this can only apply to those words as they came from the pens of the writers, not from the work of copyists, otherwise we would have to assert the inspiration of the latter.

This does not mean that the copies we have are valueless, for responsible textual criticism gives strong grounds for believing that what we have now, by diligent comparison of manuscripts, can be relied on as very close to the autograph text, conveying its essential meaning.[7] This means that the text

---

5. 2 Tim. 3:16 NIV (Gk *theopneustos*). Bavinck, in his *Reformed Dogmatics*, vol. 1, *Prolegomena* (Grand Rapids: Baker Academic, 2003), p. 425, gives strong arguments for understanding it to mean 'God-breathed' here, not 'God-breathing', including the fact that it is supported by 2 Pet. 1:21.

6. McGowan (*The Divine Spiration of Scripture*, pp. 38–43) suggests that in relation to the Scriptures 'inspiration' should be replaced by 'spiration' as more accurately conveying the sense of the Greek.

7. It is disappointing that this argument from the logic of inspiration is not discussed in J. J. Brogan, 'Can I Have Your Autograph? Uses and Abuses in Formulating an

of Scripture as it has come down to us is the result of two divine activities, inspiration and providence.

The canon of Scripture

For Protestants, including evangelical Protestants, it is the books of the Palestinian Canon of the Old Testament, the books recognized as Scripture in the Holy Land in the time of Christ, plus the writings of the New Testament, recognized as Scripture by the patristic church, which constitute the Word of God and which are regarded as together normative and authoritative in all matters of faith and practice. It is important to note that their recognition is not the cause of their authority but the result of it. The authority of the Scriptures comes from and is conveyed to us by God the Holy Spirit.

Before moving further, we should note that acceptance of all the biblical books as canonical means that we should reject an improperly selective approach to the biblical data to support a theological or ethical position. Those who hold to annihilationism, for example, need to deal with Revelation 14:9–12, those who argue for the importance of a baptism in the Spirit subsequent to conversion with 1 Corinthians 12:13, and proponents of women's ordination with 1 Timothy 2:9–15.[8] It is not enough to say what the warning passages in the epistle to the Hebrews do not mean without at least asking what they do.[9]

We need to ask ourselves in the presence of God how seriously we are taking the supreme authority of his Word. It should always be a concern, for example, if decisions made at the business meetings of evangelical churches are made simply on the basis of expediency without full consideration of the biblical principles involved.

Evangelical Doctrine of Scripture', in V. Bacote, L. C. Miguelez and D. L. Okholm (eds.), *Evangelicals and Scripture* (Downers Grove: InterVarsity Press, 2004), pp. 93–111.

8. On p. 119 we noted a book on the atonement that failed even to mention the cry of dereliction.

9. My selection of these passages should not be taken as indicating a particular stance on any of these issues, especially as in some cases there are passages of equal importance that are quoted on the other side of the argument. I am simply contending for a principle, not for particular theological positions.

Differences of emphasis in apologetics

Systematic theology and apologetics are not identical, but they are often closely associated. In systematic theology the Christian church is addressing itself and its concerns. It is systematizing its teaching so that this may be used to instruct its members. In apologetics it addresses the world, the environment in which it does its work. The church's mission encounters resistance, some of which consists of objections to aspects of its message. These objections, although they arise normally from non-Christian sources, can also trouble church members. This means that although primarily apologetics is addressed to the unbelieving world, it also has a function for believers.

Evidentialists and presuppositionalists

Those who not only promote but defend the Christian faith and especially the inspiration and authority of Scripture from an evangelical perspective may be classified as either evidentialists or presuppositionalists. These two cumbersome words[10] express a distinction which can be simply and clearly explained.[11] They relate to the way Christian apologists interact with non-Christians and their ideas.

This may be somewhat unfamiliar territory for many readers of this book. It is, however, valuable to look at the issues raised, for they have important practical implications.

Evidentialists seek to find common ground with unbelievers. They believe there are laws of thought common to all, and so they argue for the reasonableness of the Christian faith. This is what most people think of as apologetics. It used to be called, quite appropriately, 'Christian evidences'. It involves examining the teachings and the phenomena of Scripture to show not only their internal consistency but also their consistency with what we find outside the Bible. There is interest, for example, in how the Bible relates to a number of other disciplines, such as science, history and archaeology. It necessitates much consideration of particular issues, and its work is never done. The 'Fact and Faith' films which were widely used some decades ago were popular-style products of this approach.

Presuppositionalists, on the other hand, hold that the apologist should not seek common ground with unbelievers but rather take a confrontational

---

10. There appear to be no less cumbersome alternatives.

11. There are some differences of outlook within each of the two schools, but these need not concern us here.

approach. They argue that the conclusions of non-Christians and Christians are bound to be incompatible because their assumptions are different. This is because the depravity of the fallen nature deeply affects the reasoning faculty, so that apart from the grace of God we cannot think God's thoughts after him. Through the gracious regenerative work of the Holy Spirit, however, the eyes of our hearts are opened to recognize and accept biblical truth and to repent not only of our wrong living but of our wrong thinking. Biblical truth then becomes the starting point of Christian reasoning.

There is, of course, an important difference between seeking common ground between ourselves and unbelievers, on the one hand,[12] and establishing a point of contact with them on the other.[13] The former means reasoning on the basis of unregenerate thinking, while the latter (as, for instance, in the case of the altar to an unknown God at Athens, Acts 17:23) is a means of provoking interest. Fallen humans are still aware of deity, but Paul, although starting from this altar, used it in order to underline what the Athenians did *not* know, before he then went on to declare to them the true God.

In the nineteenth and early twentieth centuries, the two approaches came to be associated particularly with Princeton Theological Seminary in the USA (evidentialism) and the Free University of Amsterdam (presuppositionalism). Charles Hodge and B. B. Warfield were major theologians at Princeton, and more recently Carl Henry represented their general outlook. The Amsterdam School of Reformed Theology was pioneered by Abraham Kuyper and included Herman Bavinck, Herman Dooyeweerd and notably, for his influence on the English-speaking world, Cornelius Van Til.[14]

The danger of misunderstanding and the need for balance
Both approaches have to be carefully handled. An evidentialist approach mishandled can give the impression that someone may be brought by reason alone to believe in the authority of Scripture and the truth of the Christian message and be converted to Christ. In fact conversion, although having an

---

12. At one time, in the London University BD examination, candidates were required to sit a paper entitled 'Philosophical Introduction to Theology'. Presuppositionalists dispute whether there can be any such introduction, because they reject the idea that natural theology with its theistic proofs is a necessary study before exposure to God's revelation in Scripture.

13. McGowan appears to identify them, *The Divine Spiration of Scripture*, p. 79.

14. McGowan gives a succinct summary of the outlook of Bavinck and Van Til, ibid., pp. 31–32.

important intellectual side, is always the reorientation of a person's whole life and only the Holy Spirit can effect this.

On the other hand, a mishandled presuppositionalist approach can also cause serious misunderstanding. This is because the word itself is potentially misleading. Based as it is on the verb 'to suppose', it can give the impression that the Christian's starting point is arbitrary, which is anything but true. It is not simply the necessary start to a chain of reasoning comparable perhaps to an axiom in geometry, but is based on a profound commitment of the whole being undergirded by the work of the Spirit. Nor is it purely subjective or mystical, for the Spirit elicits it through actual contact with Bible truth, and it is given an objective dimension by the fact, as we have seen, that the Bible teaches this view of itself.[15]

Clearly Christian apologists make use of reason, which raises an important question, particularly about the way the evidentialists engage with unbelievers. It is alleged that the great Princeton theologians were influenced philosophically by the rationalistic movement known as the Enlightenment, particularly by the Scottish Common Sense realism of Thomas Reid. Although they rejected the sceptical conclusions so often associated with the Enlightenment, it is said that they nevertheless followed its methodology, demonstrating its confidence in reason, viewing theology as a science and so making their outlook a Christian form of rationalism.

Certainly they worked in this milieu and they were concerned to defeat rationalism with its own weapons, meeting argument with argument, endeavouring to out-think the rationalists. It is almost inevitable therefore that their work should appear to have some Enlightenment colouring. Every evidentialist apologist faces this kind of possibility. It has its dangers, particularly that of an unconscious absorption of ideas from the outlook of those with whom the apologist contends, but the evidentialist holds that this method must be used if we are not to lose contact with non-Christians. So, for instance, verses taken from Paul's Areopagus speech (Acts 17:16–34) might give credence to the idea that he had succumbed either to Stoic or Epicurean thinking according to the verses chosen, but such a conclusion would be wrong. There is no doubt that the Princeton theologians believed in the importance of the Holy Spirit's regenerative work, although this did not for them rule out the value of presenting the evidence for Christianity to an unbeliever.

---

15. In a sense, of course, those who adopt this viewpoint are evidentialists too, but of a different sort, for they rely on the evidence of a Witness, the Holy Spirit, who does his work in the human heart.

We should not polarize these two approaches too much or regard them as incompatible, for they are actually complementary and are often little more than a difference of emphasis. Both can find support in Scripture and many theologians and Christian philosophers combine the two. Here is an example of compatibilism, a principle that can also be seen elsewhere in Scripture when two lines of teaching, which seem at first to be contradictory, are both clearly true.[16] D. C. Davis reminds us that 'Van Til considered his task as incorporating the best elements of both Amsterdam and old Princeton'.[17] What he was really opposed to was not evidentialism in itself but evidentialism divorced from true Christian presuppositions.[18]

The issue raised by this debate is not purely academic but highly practical and it affects not only the Christian apologist but the preacher of the gospel and also the ordinary Christian's witness in daily life. If we are to work effectively for the Lord we need to communicate Christian truth, truth based on Holy Scripture, but also engage in prayer for an internal work of the Spirit to be done in those to whom we communicate it. If we do this, we are following the example of the apostles, who with all diligence gave their 'attention to prayer and the ministry of the word' (Acts 6:4), and whose role in the declaration of the gospel and the establishment of the church on its basis was crucial.

The supreme evidence: the resurrection of Jesus

Although evidential apologetics is potentially a huge subject, for the Bible is a big book, it should have a special focus on Christ's resurrection, for it is this that is the rock-bottom guarantee of all we believe. This is because the resurrection validates both objective and subjective Christianity (1 Cor. 15:14, 17, 'our preaching ... your faith'). Without Christ's resurrection, the preacher has nothing to preach and the believer nothing to believe.

---

16. See also 65–66. Other important examples are the oneness and triunity of God, the union of two natures in Christ's person, divine predestination and human responsibility in the experience of God's grace. We may work to show compatibility in each case, but must ultimately confess the limitations of human wisdom and trust the perfect knowledge and wisdom of God, in whose mind alone all truth finds its ultimate coherence.

17. D. C. Davis, 'Inerrancy and Westminster Calvinism', in H. M. Conn (ed.), *Inerrancy and Hermeneutic: A Tradition, a Challenge, a Debate* (Grand Rapids: Baker, 1988), p. 43.

18. See G. L. Bahnsen, *Van Til's Apologetic Readings and Analysis* (Phillipsburg: Presbyterian and Reformed, 1998), pp. 634–648.

The Bible finds an important place for witness to God's truth. The apostles were specifically called to be witnesses and witnesses give evidence. They witnessed to all that Christ was and did and especially to his resurrection (Acts 1:3, 21–22), as their constant reference to this in their sermons recorded in Acts shows us. Paul lists those who saw the risen Christ and he saw himself too as a witness to this great fact and to this living Person (1 Cor. 15:3–11).

The resurrection is God's vindication of Christ's claims, validating all his teaching, including his teaching about the Old Testament, and also his appointment of the apostles through whom the authentic gospel was communicated, first in preaching and then in literary form. The death of Christ for our sins is the centre of the gospel, but the frequent link in the New Testament between the cross and the resurrection shows that God accepted the sacrifice of Jesus and also that he had reversed the negative verdict and sinful acts of those who put him to death.

There was a place also, of course, for an evidential approach to the life and teaching of Jesus, as we see in the introduction to Luke's Gospel (Luke 1:1–4). Luke had paid careful attention to what the witnesses to Christ had said. Emphasis on the fulfilment of Scripture in the Gospels too is clearly evidential. The transfiguration, in some ways an anticipation of the resurrection, was a confirmation of Peter's God-given understanding of Jesus as the Son of God (Matt. 16:16–17), and it also confirmed the testimony of the prophetic writings to him (2 Pet. 1:15–21).

All this reminds us that the resurrection is not important as a bare fact totally out of connection with anything else. What makes it important is that it is *his* resurrection, so that his coming as the fulfilment of Old Testament prophecy and his life, his teaching and his atoning death are intimately and necessarily related to it. It is the promised Christ, the Son of God – such a Person, such a Holy One, such a sublime Teacher, such an atoning Saviour – who is proclaimed by the witnessing apostles to be alive from the dead! It is in and through the inspired Word that the resurrection of Jesus is proclaimed to us.

So, then, the witness of the Old and New Testament writers to Jesus, in whom alone salvation is found, is confirmed by a direct act of God in raising Jesus from the dead. It is God's own testimony to the person and work of Jesus and so to the witness of many inspired writers to him. Here is evidentialism indeed! It is this that gives the resurrection its quite special place in Christian apologetics.

Other truths have their importance, and in some cases great importance, but we should not take up an unduly defensive stance. We do not believe in the truth of the Bible because we have solved all the problems, but we work patiently at the problems in the assured faith that the resurrection of Jesus has guaranteed everything. It is not that we have surrendered belief in the accuracy of what the Bible says, but simply that our faith is not dependent on minute demonstration.

This faith carries with it an inner assurance of fellowship with the living Christ (Gal. 2:20). To say that we are sure Jesus lives because we know his presence within our hearts and in our daily experience may seem unduly simplistic, but it is one half, the subjective half, of the Christian's assurance that he is alive.[19] We do not simply believe in the resurrection of Christ but in Christ risen, for true biblical faith always engages with a living Person. This inner witness is not simply to the authority of the Bible, but it is related to the apostolic testimony to the resurrection of Christ, for it is a joyful affirmation that he is alive (Rom. 10:8–13).

Somebody may object that there are many who accept the Bible's authority and even believe in the resurrection of Jesus as a fact who are unregenerate, whose belief is due perhaps to upbringing. But in this connection what does 'believing' really mean? It has never touched the heart.[20] To believe in the written Word while keeping remote from and in rebellion against Christ the living Word is not true faith in the authority of Scripture, for Scripture is the Word of the God against whom we are rebelling.

The indispensable presupposition: given in the Spirit's regeneration

Presuppositional apologetics focuses on the inner work of the Spirit and especially on his activity in bringing people to the new birth and so to a responsive attitude to the Bible and its claims.

John's first epistle seeks to sort out the real Christian from the spurious, and so it is concerned about professed faith that is inadequate for some reason. It is concerned too with the objective facts of the Christian revelation, as its opening verses clearly show, but John is also deeply interested in evidence of a different kind from that on which the evidentialists focus: evidence about the state of the heart. The epistle sets out three 'Tests of Life',[21] so

---

19. The other half is 'because the Word of God witnesses to his resurrection'.

20. Gordon H. Clark (*Faith and Saving Faith*, Jefferson: Trinity Foundation, 1983), overstresses the propositional and underplays the personal element in faith. His final sentences are, 'Faith, by definition, is assent to understood propositions. Not all cases of assent, even assent to Biblical propositions, is saving faith; but all saving faith is assent to one or more Biblical propositions' (p. 118).

21. Robert Law's book of this name, *The Tests of Life: A Study of the First Epistle of St John*, Kerr Lectures 1909 (Edinburgh: T. & T. Clark, 1909), expounds 1 John in these terms.

that the readers may know that they have eternal life (1 John 5:13). The first is keeping God's commandments (3:24), the second dwelling in love (4:10–21) and the third confessing that Jesus is the Son of God (4:15), which is clearly based on believing truth about him (2:22–24). This last obviously involves accepting the testimony of the Word of God.

The first two tests are moral, so this raises the question as to whether John viewed the third also in this way. We note that he says, 'no lie comes from the truth' (1 John 2:21), and that truth is something to be lived by (1:6). This suggests that such belief has moral qualities. It is only the godly heart that truly accepts the authority of God's Word and acts on it in confession (cf. Rom. 10:9), and, as John himself indicates, a godly heart, a heart that truly loves, is the product of new birth by the Holy Spirit (1 John 5:1–5). John also says that the Holy Spirit (1 John 2:20, 27, 'the anointing you received from him') bears witness to the truth and imparts real knowledge.

Luke writes of Lydia, whose heart the Lord opened, so that she attended to the words of Paul (Acts 16:14), so that it was regeneration that made true hearing possible. This may be a clue to the responses to the word of the gospel found elsewhere in Acts, a book dominated thematically by the work of the Holy Spirit. Paul in Ephesians writes of God giving the readers a spirit of wisdom and revelation in the knowledge of Christ (Eph. 1:17), which suggests a continuing work of the Spirit in relation to the truth about him.

This tunes in with Paul's joy that when the Thessalonians heard the gospel they accepted it not as the word of man but as the word of God which, he says, is at work in them (1 Thess. 2:13). And how was it at work? By causing them to turn to God from idols (1 Thess. 1:9) and to be transformed so that they loved each other (1 Thess. 4:9–10). The efficient cause of this radical conversion is shown in 1 Thessalonians 1:4, where Paul says, 'Our gospel came to you not simply with words, but also with power, with the Holy Spirit and with deep conviction.'

Exegetes may differ as to whether in Ephesians 2:8–10 Paul intends his readers to understand that he means salvation or faith or both when he says 'it is the gift of God', but the case for including faith is strong, because the epistle's penultimate verse says, 'Peace to the brothers, and love with faith from God the Father and the Lord Jesus Christ' (Eph. 6:23; cf. 2 Pet. 1:1). As a godly disposition of the heart, its origin must be from the work of the Holy Spirit. John Wesley, as well as Calvinists, firmly believed that faith is a gift of God.

Summary

So, then, the Bible is known as God's Word by the inner witness of the Spirit,[22] confirmed by Christ's teaching, which is finally validated by his resurrection from the dead, and this inner witness is to a book that reveals that crucified and living Christ to us for our faith. So it is through Scripture that the Holy Spirit assures us of the authority of Scripture. It was when Paul preached at Thessalonica in the power of the Spirit that the Thessalonians came to recognize his word to be God's Word (1 Thess. 1:5; 2:13–15).

The propositional element in Scripture

It is a familiar idea that in the Bible there are promises to believe, commands to obey and warnings to heed, but there are also truths to be accepted. The Bible is inspired literature, and literature, at least if it is non-fictional, normally contains propositions, affirmations which the authors intend their readers to accept as true. Now if the Bible is the Word of God, this means that the propositions come to us with divine authority.

The claim is not, of course, that everything in the Bible is both theological and propositional. It is recognized, for instance, that some of its propositions are ethical rather than theological, although the ethical rest on the theological. In fact both the ethics and the pastoral counsel contained in the New Testament epistles emerge out of the theology.[23]

What are the propositional elements? We may think, for example, of much of the teaching of Jesus recorded in the Gospels, and much given in the New Testament epistles. Other clear examples are to be found in the large corpus of the Old Testament prophetic literature; here through the prophets God makes statements about the past, the present and the future, evidently intended to be taken as true. In the book of Psalms there are, for example, the great statements about God in Psalm 145.

These examples are by no means exhaustive and an examination of the inspired literature as a whole shows that events in the past are of immense

---

22. McGowan helpfully spells out the implications of this, not only in terms of the Christian's recognition of Scripture as God's Word but also for its comprehension (*The Divine Spiration of Scripture*, pp. 43–48).

23. The most obvious example of this is to be found in the epistle to the Romans, where the exhortations, ethical in content and pastorally motivated, which form much of chs. 12 – 16 are grounded in the theology of chs. 1 – 11.

importance. So, the Old Testament writers look back to important events like the creation, the exodus, the giving of the law, the establishment of the Davidic kingdom and line, the exile and the return from exile, while the New Testament writings are solidly based on the life, death and resurrection of Jesus. All these events are understood theologically in the biblical documents themselves, so that the revelation is both historical and theological.

These propositional elements are foundational for the whole Bible, and it is in relation to them that the principle of inerrancy is particularly important. It is true that some of the biblical material, notably in the Psalms, is subjective in form. In the Psalter there are, however, historical/theological controls and the psalmists so often fall back on the great interpreted events of their nation's history when they are faced with problems, either personal or communal.[24] It can be shown too that Genesis 1 – 3 forms a theological base for Ecclesiastes and that Job had one in his understanding of the true God as both all-powerful and just, for these are non-negotiable convictions for him. How these truths were revealed to him we do not know, but they are perfectly consistent with the view of God seen elsewhere in the Old Testament.

Some evangelical writers are critical of what they call 'propositionalism'. For instance, K. J. Vanhoozer says, 'One can with some justification say of works like Charles Hodge's *Systematic Theology* what Ricoeur has said of Hegel's philosophy: "The greatest attempt and the greatest temptation." What is *tempting* in propositionalist theology is the idea that one can "master" divinity by learning the system of truths communicated through the language and literature of the Bible.'[25] It is clear, however, from the pages immediately following this comment, that he recognizes himself the importance of the propositional element in the Bible, so that his concern is about its misuse and the fact that some writers tend to turn other biblical material, such as symbols and metaphors, into propositional form.

We need, too, to emphasize that the Bible's propositions do not exist for their own sake. Like every other feature of Scripture, they address us in order to change us, for the purpose of Scripture is transformative. If the mind is truly persuaded by the Bible's propositional truths, this persuasion should become evident in its influence on our characters and conduct, as we will now see.

---

24. Ps. 77 is an outstanding example of this. What rebuilt the psalmist's faith after it had taken a battering because of his problem was the fact that he recalled the great deeds of God in the history of his people.

25. K. J. Vanhoozer, *The Drama of Doctrine: A Canonical-Linguistic Approach to Christian Theology* (Louisville: Westminster John Knox, 2005), p. 87.

The Word and the Spirit

As we have seen, the Bible is the Word of God because it is 'breathed out' by the Holy Spirit and the same Spirit also works within us to enable us to respond positively to the Word, for our hearts need to be softened towards God. It is the new birth that effects this. We can see this clearly if we look at different aspects of the Christian life.

So, when we consider *conversion*, it is evident that there can be no salvation without a Saviour, and salvation comes to us in practical terms when we know Christ in our inner being. This is not, however, a mystical experience but is mediated to us through biblical truth, whether this comes directly from the Scriptures or through preaching or reading or personal witness or in some other way.

We must not, however, give the impression that salvation is by the acceptance of a formula, which is anything but true. Personal salvation is by the Spirit of God working in the human heart but in connection with the hearing of the Word. 'Faith comes from hearing the message, and the message is heard through the word of Christ' (Rom. 10:17). Christ the incarnate Word meets us in personal encounter through the written Word, and it is the Spirit of Truth, of Grace and of Christ who so works in our hearts through that Word. Here, then, objective truth and subjective experience meet, with the former being used by the Holy Spirit to create the latter.

The Word and the Spirit are also involved together in *assurance*. Paul says, 'You also were included in Christ when you heard the word of truth, the gospel of your salvation. Having believed, you were marked in him with a seal, the promised Holy Spirit, who is a deposit guaranteeing our inheritance' (Eph. 1:13–14). Objective fact and inner assurance answer to each other.[26] So, then, assurance is not mystically conveyed but comes by actual contact with the Scriptures themselves, in the reading and hearing of them or in some exposition of their truth.[27]

Christian assurance embraces not only conviction of personal salvation, but carries with it also convictions about the Word through which salvation has come. In 2 Timothy 3:14, Timothy is told to continue in what he has learned and been assured of, and the learning was presumably, through the

---

26. 'Inner' or 'inward' are better terms than 'subjective' as the latter often implies self-origination or individualism.

27. The best kind of exposition occurs when the verbal message is accompanied and illustrated by contact with lives made Christlike by the Holy Spirit.

work of the Spirit, the cause of the assurance. He would have learned these things from Paul as an authoritative witness to God's truth.

It is through the Word and the Spirit, too, that *sanctification* takes place. The new birth is the first moment in inward sanctification, and in both the initial crisis and the consequent process there is a communication of Christ, for this is the purpose of all the means of grace. It is sadly possible to get to know the Scriptures better without knowing Christ better, but the reverse is never true. An examination of Ephesians 5:18 and Colossians 3:16 shows that they have remarkably similar contexts. For this reason it is surely significant that at the contextual point where in Ephesians Paul says, 'Be filled with the Spirit' (Eph. 5:18), in Colossians he says, 'Let the word of Christ dwell in you richly' (Col. 3:16), in both cases employing a continuous tense. It looks, then, as though the work of the Word and of the Spirit are two sides of the same coin. The Spirit constantly uses the Word in conforming us to Christ.

The God who works within us through his Word and Spirit in conversion, assurance and sanctification, is also at work in our *perseverance*. We read the Word, taking heed of its encouragements and its warnings, and as a result the Spirit of God preserves us as Christians and enables us to persevere in Christian discipleship.

This practical stress on the Holy Spirit's use of Scripture in every aspect of the Christian life was a major theme of the Puritans, as it was also of the early Methodists and the continental Pietists. This serves to remind us that, important as a high doctrine of Scripture and its verbal inspiration is, we should never forget that God gave the Bible as his means to his end, which is not simply orthodox thinking (which is not unimportant) but sanctified living.

In relation to all these divine activities the Spirit works through means that are objective and that are found in holy Scripture. Will this be true even of that great moment when Christians are glorified at the second advent? It seems so, because Paul tells the Thessalonians that 'the Lord himself will come down from heaven, with a loud command, with the voice of the archangel and with the trumpet call of God' (1 Thess. 4:16), and also that 'he who raised Christ from the dead will also give life to your mortal bodies through his Spirit, who lives in you' (Rom. 8:11). So from conversion to consummation the Word and the Spirit are effectively at work together.

Inerrancy and infallibility

These two words, although sometimes used as if they are exact synonyms, are not identical in meaning. Inerrancy means 'without error', while 'infallibility' means 'does not fail' and, when applied to Scripture, it means that it does not fail in its God-given purposes. So, then, inerrancy relates to what the Bible is and infallibility to what it does, or, to use more technical language, inerrancy is an ontological term and infallibility a functional one. All who hold to the inerrancy of Scripture maintain also its infallibility, but the reverse, although often true, is not invariably so.

The inerrantist view of biblical inspiration holds that because God is the Author of Scripture it must be without error, for God says only what is true. Not only does it matter that the Bible gives us a coherent view of God, of Christ and of salvation, it is said, but because it is the inspired Word of God it also matters that it tells the truth with respect to detail. For this reason, inerrantists often seek to show the accuracy of small details as well as large matters in the Scriptures.

Inerrantists may also use the term 'infallible' to describe their view of Scripture, and some of them even use it much more frequently than 'inerrant', but it is important for the reader of this book to note that because of the need to make a clear distinction between two positions, I will consistently employ 'infallibilist' to designate those who affirm the infallibility of Scripture without also asserting its inerrancy.[28] Those who are infallibilists in this sense believe and seek to demonstrate that the Bible does not fail in its stated purposes, set out particularly in 2 Timothy 3:14–17,[29] for it brings us to Christ and, convicting us of sin and correcting our crooked thinking, it teaches us God's truth and righteousness, so preparing us to serve him, but they are not prepared to assert its inerrancy.[30]

Andrew McGowan is an infallibilist in this sense. He does not believe 'inerrancy' and 'errancy' are useful concepts, because he believes they represent a false dichotomy, also because inerrancy is not a biblical word and because the Bible does not teach inerrancy.[31] He says, 'To speak of the Scriptures as inerrant or errant is to apply an inappropriate classification to them. We must simply accept the Scriptures as they are and trust that what they teach is for our good (and above all for our salvation) because they come from God.'[32]

---

28. T. Ward does the same in *Words of Life: Scripture as the Living and Active Word of God* (Nottingham: Inter-Varsity Press, 2009), p. 133.

29. cf. also Deut. 29:29; Isa. 55:8–11.

30. This is the position taken by McGowan, *The Divine Spiration of Scripture*, especially ch. 5.

31. ibid., especially ch. 5.

32. ibid., p. 125. In fairness to him, it should be noted that he rejects not only the concept of inerrancy but also that of errancy.

Infallibilists point out that inerrancy is not easy to define and certainly this has to be done with care.[33] There are also difficulties, however, not so much of definition as of extent, in infallibilism. So, for instance, all evangelicals recognize that a number of historical events are given great theological importance in the Bible, but how much historical accuracy is necessary to secure a sure basis for these theological truths? It is not easy for the infallibilist to say.

Infallibilists rightly emphasize that the Bible is human as well as divine in its authorship, but this is held in common by all evangelicals. The Greek verb *pherein* ('carry along', 2 Pet. 1:21) points to a divine/human relationship in which the Holy Spirit is the controlling Partner, while examination of the books of Scripture reveals much variety of genre, style and tone, clearly indicating that the individuality of the writers was not suppressed. Islam teaches that the Quran was dictated to Mohammed by the angel Gabriel, but there is no one means of revealing God's truth as far as the Bible is concerned, for it is evident that the inspiring Spirit used a number of different ways of communicating that truth both to and through the biblical writers.

The two authorships fit perfectly together and neither is reduced by the other. They are not mutually modifying but complementary. Bavinck, for instance, calling this an 'organic' view of inspiration, takes the fullest account of the personalities, gifts and experience of the human writers at the same time as he gives fullest emphasis to the work of the Spirit in securing through these means that what they wrote was both the word of man and the Word of God.[34]

McGowan enlists Bavinck in the ranks of the infallibilists,[35] but a study of his exposition of the doctrine of Scripture does not yield this conclusion. His emphasis on the human characteristics of the Bible is completely consistent with inerrantism, although not, of course, with a dictation theory of inspiration. He frequently admits to problems in Scripture and recognizes that some

---

33. As in the Chicago Statement on Biblical Inerrancy, the complete text of which can be found in N. L. Geisler and W. E. Nix, *A General Introduction to the Bible*, rev. ed. (Chicago: Moody, 1986), pp. 181–185. Conn (ed.), *Inerrancy and Hermeneutic*, a symposium from Westminster Theological Seminary, helpfully explores many issues related to this aspect of our subject.

34. The reader is encouraged to read Bavinck's most readable and helpful exposition of this, *Reformed Dogmatics*, vol. 1, *Prolegomena*, pp. 431–448.

35. In his comment in *The Divine Spiration of Scripture*, p. 158, n. 166, McGowan appears to take a reference to the guidance of the Holy Spirit to refer to Scripture, but it is much more likely to refer to the church, which is certainly not inerrant.

of these may never be solved, but this is perfectly consistent with belief that the truth of the whole will be vindicated in the end.[36]

Two questions must now be addressed. First of all, does the teaching of Scripture compel us to assert its inerrancy? Second, if it does, what prominence should this have in our doctrine of Scripture?

What is the basis of the inerrancy doctrine? This is a question of the same order as important questions about the Trinity and the Person of Christ. The patristic church discovered that the biblical evidence compelled it to go beyond a purely economic or functional view of the Trinity to an ontological one. This happened also in Christology, for the Chalcedonian formula, which may be summarized as 'two natures in one Person', although not stated in Scripture, is an inevitable inference from what the Bible teaches about Jesus. It is difficult to resist the conclusion that what the Bible teaches about God and his Word makes it necessary for us not only to make assertions about what the Bible does but also about what it is, in other words to go beyond functional infallibilism to ontological inerrantism.

The fact is that the doctrine of Scripture rests on the doctrine of God and especially on what he has revealed to us about his character. To use a simple illustration, we may think of a man attracted to a beautiful vase in a shop. He tells the manager he wishes to purchase it. The manager looks it over and then points out a minute flaw under the base of the vase, saying he intends to get another from the back of the shop. The would-be purchaser dismisses this, saying that the tiny flaw does not matter to him. 'Perhaps not,' says the manager, 'but it matters to me.'

Of course, the Bible is not God, but it is God's Word and as such is intimately related to what and who he says he is.[37] He is the God of truth and as such he cannot lie (Titus 1:2; Heb. 6:18). The perfection and truth of God's Word are asserted in Scripture,[38] the Spirit of inspiration promised by Christ to the apostles is called 'the Spirit of Truth',[39] and a major theme of Scripture is God's faithfulness,[40] a most important aspect of his character.

---

36. Ward goes into more detail on this than there is space for here, *Words of Life*, p. 140.

37. The relationship of God, the triune God, to Scripture is the main theme of Ward's book *Words of Life*.

38. e.g. in 2 Sam. 7:28; Pss 19:7; 119:142, 160; John 17:17.

39. John 15:26–27; 16:12–15 (cf. 1 John 4:6, where, in the light of its use in 1:3, 'we' appears to refer to the apostles).

40. See e.g. Isa. 49:7; Lam. 3:23; 1 Cor. 1:9; 2 Cor. 1:18.

Of course, all this is accepted by the infallibilist as well as the inerrantist, but we must ask what such biblical teaching implies. What is meant by the perfection of the Word of God? If it is God-breathed (2 Tim. 3:16), it proceeds from his very being and will surely bear the marks of that perfect being! This may be an inference, but is it not an inevitable one? Where God's uttered Word is concerned, any modification of its claim to be true would need to be demonstrated from the teaching of Scripture itself, and no such modification is ever suggested there.

So, then, for the inerrantist the Bible teaches us truth, it combats error, and so on, fulfilling all its God-intended functions, because it originates from the God of truth, which surely implies that it shares his ontological perfection.[41]

How prominent a place should we give inerrancy in our doctrine of Scripture? Timothy Ward, in a most helpful section of his book,[42] asserts and argues for biblical inerrancy but also warns us against such overemphasis on it that it is in danger of dominating our doctrine of Scripture. He says that stress on it should not be so excessive as to divert us from matters of great importance related to the functions of the Bible. That he has taken his own warning seriously is shown by the fact that he delays treatment of it to a fairly late stage of his book.

This seems right. We should remember that although theology and apologetics are closely related, they are not identical. It is appropriate for an apologist to highlight and argue in detail for the inerrancy of Scripture, but the theologian, although finding a definite place for this, will probably want to focus on the Bible's functions, for this is where for the believer 'the rubber meets the road'.

I regard inerrancy as true and therefore as theologically important, but infallibility as particularly important *in practical terms*. Like inerrancy, it rests on the doctrine of God, but it is much more verifiable in our experience here and now. Scripture does indeed bring us to Christ, it does teach us theological and ethical truth, in the process correcting our errors and rebuking our conduct,

---

41. The IVF (now the UCCF) was surely right when, in revising its doctrinal basis, it moved the article about Scripture from the first place to the third, after articles about God. Belief in God rests on general revelation (although misunderstanding of general revelation needs to be corrected from special revelation), while belief in Scripture as God's Word necessarily rests on who God is. See McGowan's comment on the proper theological order, *The Divine Spiration of Scripture*, pp. 28–31.

42. Ward, *Words of Life*, pp. 132–142.

it does equip us for Christian service, just as Paul says it does, it does all this unfailingly, and it does it because it is God-breathed.[43]

We will not want to avoid difficult questions, but we should not give the impression that all the Bible's difficulties can be solved, or even more that we have solved them all! This would be both arrogant and unrealistic. In asserting biblical inerrancy we are making a statement of faith in the conviction that, in the unfolding plan of God, these questions will be finally answered. In this respect it is somewhat like divine providence, which will always lack fully detailed justification until the final revelation of God's purposes, but which we accept by faith despite the problems we have with it.[44]

God will not only vindicate the inerrancy of his Word but, through what he effects in the consummation of all things, he will define it, which we do not find it easy to do. Just as he defined the prophecies of the Old Testament when Christ came the first time, so the accuracy of the whole will be vindicated when he comes again, for his return is the true omega point in God's revelation to his people. What V. S. Poythress says about the Old Testament fulfilment in the New is true of God's final fulfilling definition of his Word's inerrancy: 'What we know about him [God] includes his right to exceed our expectations.'[45]

We might ask: what is the proper place for the doctrine of Scripture in general works of systematic theology? I am inclined to think that the nature of Scripture should be handled under or immediately after the doctrine of God, for it is God's Word, and that its functions should be treated under 'the means of grace'. This would give equal weight to the concerns of the inerrantists and those shared by both inerrantists and infallibilists.

The differing mindsets of modernism and postmodernism

Modernism's broad concerns are with rationality and it is a view of things in which science rules and in which only what is scientifically verifiable or

---

43. 2 Tim. 3:14–17.

44. See S. Ferguson, 'How Does the Bible Look at Itself?', in Conn (ed.), *Inerrancy and Hermeneutic*, pp. 64–65. When God revealed himself to Job at the end of the book bearing his name, he did not answer all Job's questions, but simply reminded him of his power and his character. The answers could wait, but a renewed faith in God could not.

45. V. S. Poythress, 'What Does God Say through Human Authors?', in Conn (ed.), *Inerrancy and Hermeneutic*, p. 90.

at least falsifiable can be regarded as certain truth, as objective knowledge.[46] Postmodernism is a revolt against this, often somewhat inchoate, in which truth is viewed as subjective. There is a truth for you and a truth for me and they are not necessarily identical. Aesthetics and ethics are also affected by this outlook, so that extreme postmodernism says that we are completely free to follow our own path with no external constraints.

For modernism, if something is to be accepted as truth it should cohere with what is already known, and if it is concerned with past events it should be based on reliable documents and, where appropriate, be consistent with any assured findings of archaeology. Because the Bible is literature from the past, it is looked at from this point of view. The extent to which such an outlook may govern a whole theology may be seen in the work of Rudolf Bultmann, whose theology involved the wholesale 'demythologizing' of anything in the Bible that smacked of the supernatural.

It is true that many scientists now view the sciences as much more 'open' than used to be the case, but the older outlook is by no means dead, especially among those who have had little or no scientific training. History too has changed and historians are interested not only in the historical facts, but also in the interpretative perspective of the historian. Here too, however, many relatively unschooled in this subject are unaware of this, so that at the popular level modernism is still very influential, especially among older people.

The influence of Immanuel Kant on both modernism and postmodernism has been immense. The emphasis of modernism is on what is objective and accessible to the senses, while postmodernism stresses our subjectivity; Kant addressed the problem of bridging the objective and subjective realms. This and other epistemological questions have dominated philosophy ever since.

In Kant's view there is no way to a transcendent realm, to noumena, to things as they really are, by the empirical evidence we are aware of through sense-perception and which is the concern of the physical sciences. There is no way to absolute certainty by this, the metaphysical path. There is, however, an internal way, a moral way based on moral intuitions, which Kant called categorical imperatives. These imperatives are subjective in one sense, in that they are internal, they belong to the subject, to you and me, but they are objective in another sense in that they are not idiosyncratic but are universally recognized and so are of universal validity.

---

46. In 1923, J. G Machen noted that although science had made great progress, the arts and humanities had gone into decline (*Christianity and Liberalism*, Grand Rapids: Eerdmans, 1923, pp. 9–11). Has the situation improved since then?

Now modernism accepts Kant's view that apart from the ethical path we cannot know noumena or make any statements about a transcendent realm, about God, from anything in this world, the only world we know. Fully consistent modernism is positivist, which means that it concerns itself exclusively with phenomena and regards as true knowledge only what can be demonstrated scientifically. Scientific theories can only be validated if they give a satisfactory account of the evidence which falls within their domain. Particularly, as Karl Popper has argued, they need to be falsifiable.

This outlook is central to the modernism which dominated Western culture until well past the middle of the twentieth century and which still plays a major part in the thinking of many people today. If its positivism is rigorously applied, it is not favourable to the Christian faith, for it views Christianity's claim to revelation to be unacceptable, purporting as it does to describe the noumenal realm and to do so from phenomena, from events in history, especially the event of Jesus.

Following Kant, modernism was left simply with the ethical path to reality. Increasingly, however, as modernism ran its course, the objectivity of moral judgments was questioned and in postmodernism it is often abandoned altogether. Not only so, but there is a revolt against scientific positivism as well, so that subjectivism reigns in both the metaphysical and the moral realms. This is true in aesthetics also and beauty is said to be exclusively in the eye of the beholder and is never intrinsic to the painting, the sculpture, the building, the music, the poem.

In fact philosophers face a problem in epistemology, the branch of philosophy dealing with the nature of human knowing, which has some similarity to the issues we have already been considering in relation to evidentialism and presuppositonalism. We have seen that modernism, and the positivism associated with it, is concerned with evidence, but it has had to operate also with some presuppositions. It has to make a start somewhere.

Many of us have been exposed to this issue already when in our schooldays we moved from a presuppositionalist situation to an evidentialist one every time we moved from the mathematics classroom with its axiom-based reasoning to the science classroom, where evidence ruled all, although I doubt whether we realized this! In fact the physical sciences need mathematics and great physicists are often great mathematicians.[47]

In the twentieth century a number of important thinkers stressed the role of presuppositions. One whose thought was not *explicitly* Christian was

------

47. See T. F. Torrance, *The Christian Frame of Mind* (Edinburgh: Handsel, 2002), p. 21.

Michael Polanyi,[48] who influenced other influential thinkers such as Thomas Kuhn, Paul Ricoeur and Arthur Koestler. They all recognized the importance of the deep inner conviction or integrated set of convictions, the satisfying paradigm. T. F. Torrance, a major theologian greatly interested also in science, acknowledged a debt to Polanyi.[49] Kurt Gödel received an Einstein Award for showing that the premises of demonstration cannot be demonstrated, that every system of thought must rest on assumptions outside it.

Kuhn promoted the idea of the paradigm shift, which is rather like the shaking of a kaleidoscope and the production of a new pattern out of the elements of the old. Koestler has shown this happening in the history of scientific theory and also in the realms of the arts and humour.[50] One obvious example is the way Copernicus introduced a new theory out of the breakdown of the Ptolemaic cosmology.

These thinkers were preceded by the Gestalt psychology, which stressed the role of the perception of wholes and the approach to parts through wholes rather than vice versa. The more recent recognition by neurological scientists of the different functions of the two sides of the brain, which may be described in general terms as the analytical left and the synthesizing right, also seems significant.

All this may make us wonder if this kind of thinking is due to general revelation, so that the work of divine grace is reflected in and finds illustration in the human mental constitution. Through God's revelation in Scripture and the inner work of the Holy Spirit, the Christian experiences the profound paradigm shift the Bible calls conversion, and begins to see wholeness, unity and coherence in the facts of the universe because he or she sees all as the product of one Creator God, who is at the same time our gracious Saviour. The constant search of philosophy and science through all the centuries for a coherent view of things appears to be because we are made in the image of God.

This concern for coherence is also a search for beauty. There is both truth and beauty in our God's revelation of himself both in nature and in Scripture.

In recent times something like a paradigm shift has taken place for many people as they have moved from a modern to a postmodern mindset. This did

---

48. Polanyi's thought, which influenced both Kuhn and Koestler, is well presented and summarized in Drusilla Scott, *The Common Sense of Michael Polanyi* (Grand Rapids: Eerdmans, 1995).

49. As in his preface to Scott, ibid.

50. A. Koestler, *The Act of Creation* (London: Picador, 1977), and *The Sleepwalkers: A History of Man's Changing Vision of the Universe* (London: Penguin, 1986).

not happen overnight, and the ultimate origins of postmodernism are very early indeed. It may be found in much Eastern thought,[51] and its Western roots go back a long way, at least to the Sophists against whom Socrates argued, some of whom held that there are no objective moral principles but that all are in fact simply human conventions. In the arts there has been for over a century a more or less gradual move away from classical structures in the direction of individualism, even of irrationalism.[52]

The focus of attention has shifted from the object to the subject. R. G. Collingwood, for instance, stressed the role of the historian in seeing meaning in past events, so that history is more an art than a science. In literary theory the focus has moved from the intention of the author to the perception of the reader. In morality, for so many people, accepted norms have been discarded and everyone does his or her own thing.

Now if a paradigm shift is a reorientation, which it is, we may say that this apparent paradigm shift is really more like entry into a period of profound disorientation. As we shall see, the advent of postmodernism produces new questions for the believer in Christ and in the biblical revelation, and Christians should welcome these questions, for they give us new opportunities. Long-term disorientation is profoundly disturbing, and if a disorientated person longs for foundation, for structure, this must also be true for a society.

In Western society and increasingly elsewhere modernism and postmodernism are interacting. Postmodernism is very much alive, but modernism is by no means dead, and the two coexist in the minds of many people today. In their engagement with this mixed culture there have been alterations and adjustments in the outlook of some evangelical scholars. Have these been gains or losses, or perhaps some of each?

There are questions for the Bible believer arising from each of the two mindsets, and these we must briefly address.

Issues arising in a modern context

Without doubt, the situation today for evangelical theology and conservative scholarship is in many respects very different from what it was at the close of the Second World War. I recall, perhaps forty years ago, when evangelical scholarship

---

51. Zen Buddhism is an obvious example.

52. See H. Rookmaaker, *Modern Art and the Death of a Culture* (Leicester: Inter-Varsity Press, 1970).

was beginning to gather strength, being present when two men, both evangelicals, one a theologian and the other an Old Testament scholar, were discussing the views of another scholar. The theologian said, 'I regard him as a heretic,' while the other man commented, 'To me he is just another Old Testament scholar.' The second viewpoint is more common now than it was then.

In the first half of the twentieth century, evangelicalism passed through a period when many felt their backs were to the wall. Liberalism was in the ascendant and those who held a high view of Scripture were often regarded simply as obscurantists who refused to engage in serious scholarship. When I was a student (1947–51) there was very little good conservative scholarly literature available and it is perhaps not surprising that we tended to develop something of a siege mentality.[53]

We can be very grateful to those who made such a stand in the earlier years, even though occasionally there may have been resistance to new ideas mainly because they were new and therefore suspect. Clearly it was important that such ideas should not be accepted without very serious thought as to their implications, and at that stage resistance was perhaps inevitable. Today the atmosphere has changed quite radically. On some issues the lines are much less sharply drawn. Such an issue, for example, as the authorship of Isaiah 40 – 66 is discussed less stridently (on both sides) than it once was. Not only so, but there are some scholars who would be recognized by their peers as conservative who strongly dislike being labelled.

We cannot shut our ears to the questions being raised in the wider world of biblical scholarship. As J. R. Muether says, 'Evangelical scholars do not explore these matters in spite of their commitment to inerrancy; rather their high view of Scripture constrains them to pursue the difficult questions.'[54] It is taken for granted today that those who teach in evangelical colleges will engage in research, and research inevitably and quite properly affects the researcher. It would be interesting to consider the effect such research has had on those who have, for example, studied the Reformers or the Puritans and those who have been considering the works of more recent theologians who are not strictly evangelical but who have something positive to say. It is important that both groups of researchers should talk to and listen to each other.

---

53. The main institution doing scholarly work at a high level from an evangelical perspective before 1946 was Westminister Theological Seminary in the USA. See H. M. Conn, 'A Historical Prologue: Inerrancy, Hermeneutic, and Westminster', in Conn (ed.), *Inerrancy and Hermeneutic*, pp. 15–34.

54. 'Evangelicals and the Bible: A Bibliographic Postscript', in Conn (ed.), ibid., p. 261.

When I was first asked to review a book for a journal, I asked advice from an experienced reviewer. He told me that he always read a book through twice, first of all to learn everything he could from it and then to subject it to serious criticism. I believe we need, at least in principle, to follow that good advice in considering ideas that are new to us.

In looking now at some areas of debate, the main purpose is to suggest some principles for consideration. They represent my personal perspective and obviously are open to critical scrutiny. Any comment on specific issues, therefore, is simply to illustrate these principles, not by any means to explore the issues in any full way.

Authorship issues

Questions of authorship are important for the modernist mindset because they are concerned with origins. Nineteenth-century philosophers like evolutionists and Hegelians were very interested in development through history. Much that was written in the late nineteenth and early twentieth centuries about Old Testament authorship issues was deeply influenced by the theory of the evolution of religion. Works regarded as religiously superior were dated later, and so were sometimes denied to their stated authors. Scholars interested in the *Iliad* and *Odyssey* at that time tended to be sceptical about the existence of an historical Homer, and some carried over this scepticism to studies of the Pentateuch and Moses. The main (Graf-Wellhausen) critical theory viewed the Pentateuch as a composite work in which four documents from different times and with somewhat different theological outlooks were brought together late in the Old Testament period. Moses virtually disappeared from view.

The fact that modern thought has moved away to other philosophies has raised important questions about this type of criticism and therefore about authorship theories partly, at least, based on it. In some cases scholars are still looking for a more satisfactory theory. Among those writing most prolifically about the Pentateuch today there is no consensus.[55]

Nineteenth-century scholars with this general outlook dealt also with

---

55. See G. Wenham, 'Pondering the Pentateuch: The Search for a New Paradigm', in D. W. Baker and B. T. Arnold, *The Face of Old Testament Studies* (Grand Rapids: Baker, 2004), p. 119. This is still true. Moreover, scissors-and-paste theories of the use of literary sources, as in the case of the Pentateuch, are often regarded with scepticism by literary scholars working in other fields. C. S. Lewis poured scorn on the idea. Even though his special field was medieval literature, his view is worth noting (*Reflections on the Psalms*, London: Fontana, 1961, pp. 153–159).

other Old Testament literature. Sections of Isaiah, Micah and Zechariah were ascribed to other unknown prophets and the Davidic authorship of many psalms previously regarded as his and the Solomonic authorship of Proverbs were denied. Daniel was given a second century BC date.

Gospel scholars posited the existence of Q as a source employed by Matthew and Luke in addition to their use of Mark,[56] and sometimes also M and L as documents used by Matthew and Luke respectively.[57] The traditional attribution of the Johannine literature to John the apostle was widely disputed, at least 2 Peter and often both Petrine epistles were denied to Peter, and some of the Pauline epistles, notably the pastorals and Ephesians, but also sometimes Colossians and 2 Thessalonians, were denied to Paul. Particularly 2 Corinthians but also Romans were often regarded as composed of sections from several letters, although all normally by Paul. The idea that epistles like Ephesians, the Pastorals and 2 Peter were pseudepigraphic was widely canvassed.[58]

Other issues bearing on authorship have been discussed by scholars. It has been suggested that in the books that bear their names the oracles of some of the Old Testament prophets may have been put into order by an associate, or, in some of the New Testament epistles, the work of an associate may have influenced at least the style of the work.

What can we say about such views from a conservative perspective? Some critical views of this general type are held by evangelical writers. For instance, H. G. M. Williamson holds to the idea of 2 Isaiah, and A. J. Lincoln does not regard Ephesians as actually authored by Paul.[59] The Q hypothesis has been widely accepted. It has been argued that the differences between 1 and 2 Peter may be due to the fact that Peter was given help with his Greek style by Silas for the first letter, and possibly that somebody else was involved in the writing of the second.

In some cases, the pendulum has swung very considerably indeed. R. L. Schultz, writing about Isaiah, says,

---

56. The Two Document Hypothesis.

57. The Four Document Hypothesis.

58. N. T. Wright maintains it is high time for such issues to be revisited, and he considers such revisiting would lead to much more conservative conclusions (*Paul: In Fresh Perspective*, Minneapolis: Fortress, 2005, pp. 18–19).

59. H. G. M. Williamson, *The Book Called Isaiah: Deutero-Isaiah's Role in Composition and Redaction* (Oxford: Clarendon, 1994); A. J. Lincoln, *Ephesians* (Dallas: Word. 1990), pp. xxx–lxx.

Ironically, while critical scholars are moving in a more conservative direction, there is also a growing trend among evangelicals to expand the concept of Isaianic authorship and to embrace views regarding Isaiah that some critical scholars are discarding. To the extent that they hold to evangelical views of Scripture, these scholars are also expanding the boundaries of the doctrine of inspiration. At the same time, we can observe the shrinking role or even the 'disappearance' of Isaiah of Jerusalem.[60]

It is impossible in a book such as this to go into such matters in detail, but I believe there are important criteria we can establish from the perspective of a high doctrine of Scripture.

First, the God of the Bible is a God of truth, and so the biblical writers were always concerned with truth.

Second, the Bible books carry divine authority and it is their final canonical form that is authoritative for the church.

Third, in the absence of any indications to the contrary, we can assume the Bible writers followed the literary conventions of the day in so far as these were generally recognized to be valid and were not designed to deceive the reader. Some have suggested, for instance, that pseudepigraphy was a generally accepted practice, with no intention to deceive, but such a claim needs to be most carefully investigated and evaluated. The attitude within the early church's Christian subculture is more important in this regard than that found in the wider culture of the time, and there is no doubt that the patristic church was concerned about and subscribed to the authentic apostolicity of the New Testament books.[61]

Fourth, clear and explicit claims to authorship need to be taken seriously, and any involvement of others beside the named authors may normally be presumed to carry the imprimatur of those authors. If an exception to this is suggested, it is important to demonstrate how this is consistent with such explicit authorship claims.

Sometimes another person besides the named author may have had a part in the writing of a biblical book. The involvement of Tertius (Rom. 16:22) and Silas or Silvanus (1 Pet. 5:12) in the writing of two New Testament epistles is clearly stated, and at least in the case of Silas it may have extended beyond

---

60. R. L. Schultz, 'How Many Isaiahs Were There and What Does It Matter?', in Bacote, Miguelez and Okholm (eds.), *Evangelicals and Scripture*, pp. 154–155.

61. For a helpful brief discussion of pseudonimity, with special reference to 2 Peter, see E. A. Blum, '2 Peter', in F. E. Gaebelein (ed.), *Expositor's Bible Commentary*, vol. 12 (Grand Rapids: Zondervan, 1981), pp. 257–262.

merely acting as a scribe, because Peter says that he wrote 'with the help of Silas, whom I regard as a faithful brother', as if reassuring his readers and showing that everything in the epistle had his full approval.[62]

The use of somebody's name with a view to giving honour to that person, however, raises serious questions as to the authority of what is thus written. Obviously issues as to what was acceptable practice at the time are involved here, but deceit with a good motive is still deceit.

The inclusion of books in the New Testament canon that are not in the authorial sense apostolic appears to have been due to the fact that they are fully consistent with apostolic doctrine and were written by close associates of the apostles. An outstanding example is the Gospel of Mark, stated by the early Christian writer Papias to have been written by Mark on the basis of Peter's memories of the life of Jesus. Paul's reference to the church as founded on the apostles and prophets (Eph. 2:20), who are then referred to as now recipients of divine revelation (Eph. 3:5),[63] shows that the circle of those who received and communicated God's truth was wider than the apostles, with apostolic truth acting as the test of what claimed to be prophetic truth (1 Cor. 14:36–38).

Fifth, as this reference to Papias suggests, early traditions of authorship should not be lightly set aside. They are not, however, sacrosanct unless they are clearly supported by evidence from within Scripture itself.

Sixth, our belief in the deity of Jesus gives us strong theological and spiritual reasons for accepting his clear statements as to the authorship of Old Testament books. It is, of course, legitimate to ask whether in every case his references to books by the traditional authors' names are intended to be attestations of authorship or whether in some cases are simply an indication of a quote's location. We should note, however, that sometimes the validity of a point he is making undoubtedly depends on the authorship of the passage quoted, as, for instance, in Mark 12:35–37.

---

62. The basic sense of the preposition *dia* with the genitive case, rendered here in the NIV as 'with the help of', is 'through', but the reference to his faithfulness probably indicates that his role was more than that of an amanuensis. A somewhat parallel case could be the recognition that some paintings ascribed to a great artist may have been done in his studio and under his direction rather than by himself, or else a pupil or pupils may have been commissioned by him to complete what he began, with the responsibility nevertheless being that of the master.

63. The word 'now' shows clearly that the prophets referred to are New Testament, not Old Testament prophets.

Language issues

First, the historical books of both Testaments do not necessarily give us the *ipsissima verba*, the very words spoken by those whose speeches are recorded, but they do give us the *ipsissima vox*, the thoughts behind and expressed in the words.

In the Gospels, where the issue is obviously important, the actual words spoken are not generally used, for Jesus will normally have spoken in Aramaic,[64] and the Gospel writers reproduce this in Greek. No two languages are identical in their syntax or in the range of meanings covered by particular words, so that exact word-for-word correspondence frequently does not happen.

The expression 'kingdom of God' frequently occurs in the teaching of Jesus in three of the Gospels, but in Matthew's it occurs little[65] and is usually represented by 'kingdom of heaven'. We cannot be sure whether Jesus used 'kingdom of heaven', which was common among the Jews of his time, with three of the Gospel writers substituting 'kingdom of God' as more understandable for non-Jewish readers, or whether he used 'kingdom of God', with Matthew turning this into a form more acceptable to Jewish readers of his Gospel. The former is perhaps the more likely,[66] but it matters little, for 'heaven' as used here is simply the equivalent of 'God'. There is no change of essential meaning.

We find that sometimes accounts of what is obviously the same incident occur in more than one Gospel and the report of the sayings of Jesus or of others is not always precisely the same. At times, this could be because each account is true but incomplete, while at others it may be due to one or more techniques of abbreviation.

The Bible clearly teaches verbal inspiration, for both 1 Peter 1:21 and 2 Timothy 3:16 refer to 'Scripture', which is manifestly verbal. Why, though, do we value words? We may value them either for their beauty, as in our appreciation of poetry, or because of their meaning. They can be powerful, and modern linguistic theory places much stress on the varying effects of words, but to see them as valuable in themselves quite apart from their beauty or their

---

64. This is occasionally given and translated by Mark. Jesus may also have used Hebrew (with the religious leaders) and at times Greek, for many Galileans will have known some Greek because of the mixed ethnic and linguistic nature of Galilee and neighbouring areas.

65. Only in Matt. 12:28; 19:24; 21:31, 43.

66. After all, Jesus was himself a Jew.

meaning, for instance to treat them as spells, is superstitious or outright pagan. If the true meaning of somebody's utterance can be conveyed by other words, however, this surely raises no problem for a high doctrine of Scripture.

Second, writers of biblical narratives will often have abbreviated what was said. In Acts 2:40, Luke says, 'With many other words he warned them. . .' so that many of the sermons in Acts may have been abbreviated. This clear example suggests the possibility that if Luke did this in Acts, he may well have done the same in his Gospel, and so too may the other Gospel writers.

Abbreviation can, of course, be either by attenuation or by precis. The former preserves the *ipsissima verba*, the latter the *ipsissima vox*, which means that the thought of the utterance is truly, fully and accurately conveyed even though the actual words spoken are not employed. The latter term is sometimes used in a sense that falls short of this, but this is confusing and should be avoided. Authors of Old Testament historical books, too, may have given us summaries and paraphrases truly conveying the thought of those whose words are recorded.

Third, the use of the Septuagint translation of the Old Testament in the New Testament is what we might have anticipated, because this was the Greek translation known to the readers, and it is what we normally find was used.

Sometimes its wording departs somewhat from the Hebrew text, even in passages quoted in the New Testament. What matters here is that *the actual point at issue* faithfully represents the meaning of the Hebrew. So, to take a well-known instance, in the quotation of Psalm 8 in Hebrews 2,[67] the essential point is the inferior status of human beings, not whether they are lower than angels or God. Through Christ the lowly have been exalted.

Fourth, we would expect the recorded words of Jesus and other speakers to express their thought without addition or alteration.

Study of the Gospel of Mark shows the relevance of much of the teaching of Jesus in it to issues being faced by the church at Rome, while the same is true of the Gospel of Matthew in relation to a Jewish readership. Can we say that the Gospel writers adapted their reports of his teaching to fit the needs of their readers, or that this adaptation was done by early Christians with a charismatic gift?

E. E. Ellis says, 'Prophetic exposition and application of Scripture is one way in which the early Christian pneumatics exercise their ministry . . . The meaning of Scripture is not to be ascertained by "method" or by human wisdom, but through a charismatic exegesis that becomes a part of the divine

---

67. Here the Septuagint ('angels') differs from the Hebrew ('God').

revelation itself.'[68] This raises problems for a high view of biblical inspiration. It is the words 'that become a part of the divine revelation itself' which are the problem if it is the utterances of the prophets rather than those of Jesus which appear in the Bible text.

Of course, the early preachers will have applied the teaching of Jesus to situations in the churches, but we would not expect these applications, even if given under the inspiration of the Spirit, to be included in passages purporting to give the teaching of Jesus himself. If the teaching of Jesus is of special importance because it is basic to the whole New Testament revelation, it is important that it should be faithfully recorded. We note that in 1 Corinthians 7 Paul makes a clear distinction between commands of the Lord (i.e. the Lord Jesus) and judgments he gives under the inspiration of the Spirit, although of course both are authoritative.[69]

Religio-cultural issues

The Bible was not written in a religious or cultural vacuum and we must recognize this.

Clearly the Old Testament was written in an environment which was subject to many influences, with the dominant one changing from time to time. Because of this, it has been suggested that the religion of the Old Testament was influenced, sometimes in sequence, sometimes simultaneously, by the cultures and religions of the Egyptians, the Canaanites, the Assyrians, the Hittites, the Babylonians and the Persians, even the Greeks, and possibly others. Also it has been said that the faith of the New Testament or some of its leading concepts have been influenced by Rabbinic and/or Essene ideas, by Greco-Roman religion, by Hermeticism and the mystery cults, and even by emperor worship. Again, we ask what our attitude as evangelicals should be towards such theories.

First, not only the teaching of Jesus himself, but also the prophetic religion that preceded him and that he recognized as authentic and the gospel and theology of the apostles whom he commissioned should be accepted as true, because it all carries his personal validation.

Second, theories that cultural influences affected the form but not the content of the divinely given revelation are not unacceptable, for instance the view that the Old Testament covenants had a form reflecting the Hittite vassal

---

68. E. E. Ellis, *Prophecy and Hermeneutics in Early Christianity: New Testament Essays* (Tübingen: Mohr, 1978), p. xvi.

69. See vv. 10, 12, 40. Paul's reference to the Spirit in the last verse is clearly ironic.

treaties. The controlling feature in such cases, however, must be the divinely revealed content, not the cultural form.

Third, in Old Testament studies, to discover references to figures taken from pagan mythologies, such as Rahab, Leviathan and Baal, is no problem if these are used metaphorically, so that the assumption is not that the writer and readers believe such figures to be real, but simply that they may be used as metaphors because of their familiarity to the readers.

To ascribe to Yahweh what devotees of Baal claimed for Baal raises no problems either, for Yahweh had many roles (such as a Warrior-God) wrongly attributed to Baal. Genesis 1 shows knowledge of Babylonian astral religion, but this knowledge is used in order to attack it. How effective as a 'put-down' is the almost casual comment, 'He also made the stars' (v. 16)! Genesis 22 is particularly meaningful in a religious context where child sacrifice was widely practised. It was God's way of showing that he did not require it as well as using this background to set up a test of Abraham's faith and obedience.

Fourth, terms taken from non-Christian or heretical systems may be used in the service of the truth when they are filled with Christian content, which gives them a polemic function, showing that Christ fulfils and goes beyond any truth that the words signify. Paul, for instance, appears to have employed some of the terms used by the heretics at Colosse, such as 'fullness' and 'mystery', in combating their heresies.

Fifth, a distinction must be made between the revealed religion of Israel and its popular religion. By popular religion I mean not simply the worship of Baal and other deities, but even some aspects of popular Yahwism. The religion that was divinely revealed was one thing, but what was practised was often something different. This comes out clearly in Psalm 50, where many of the people were clearly treating Yahweh as if he were Baal.

Textual issues

Brevard Childs has promoted the idea that the scholar's main concern in dealing with Scripture should be with the final form, which is the canonical form of the text rather than with any intermediate stages on the way to that final form. This let a breath of fresh air into biblical and especially Old Testament studies.

This does not mean, of course, that there is no interest now in the processes by which this canonical form came into being. In fact, in some cases it is actually conservative writers who are showing the most interest in this. In relation to the book of Psalms, in particular, the final form is that of the ultimate redactor or redactors of the book, but each psalm has significance as an inspired literary entity as well as having its place in the overall message of the book.

Genre issues

Students of literature know the importance of considering literary genre in relation to each literary entity. The Bible is a collection of inspired literature with considerable variety of genre. Here there is history, law, wisdom, worship, reflection, prophecy, biography, epistle and apocalypse. Each book of the Bible conveys truth, but it does so in its own distinctive way.

Sometimes one genre occurs within the body of another. Exodus, for instance, which is a book of history, incorporates a considerable legal element and Acts, also a history book, records many speeches. So, then, in relation to a history book we have to ask whether the conduct of persons, even of godly persons, recorded in the book is always intended for emulation. Sometimes, of course, this behaviour is criticized either clearly or by implication by the book's author, but sometimes it is not and we need to bring general biblical principles of ethics to our assessment of the matter.

Questions have been raised as to whether fiction is ever used in the Bible in the service of truth. Careful consideration needs to be given to the implications of any such fictional identification, but some clear examples are Jotham's fable (Judg. 9:7–15), Isaiah's song of the vineyard (Isa. 5:1–7) and especially the parables of Jesus, even though some have wondered if the story of the rich man and Lazarus, for example, was intended to be a parable or whether, rather, it reflected an actual situation known to Jesus.

Today every discipline has its technical language and the well-educated person generally has some awareness of this when he or she encounters it. Very little of this language existed in biblical times. Even if it had, it is doubtful if it would have been much used, for the Bible is intended for all and the forms of language all understand are non-technical rather than technical. Not only so, but technical language develops and that of today may be outdated tomorrow.

Many modern concerns are not even in view in Scripture. Such issues as the relationship between time and space, the relative importance of particular rulers politically and economically, and so on, hardly come into view at all. Matters of great religious importance, too, such as the creation of the whole universe by the only God there is, the fall of the human race into sin, the particular effects of the influence of evil spirits on the minds and bodies of those afflicted by them, are not described in the technical language of cosmology, anthropology and psychiatry, but in popular language. In this realm, too, we need some guidelines, and the following may be suggested.

First, the language of the biblical writers should not be faulted if it is untechnical. A common illustration of this is that it is perfectly valid for the scientist to tell his wife that there is a beautiful sunrise today even though he knows, as a scientist, that the sun does not in fact rise.

Second, the identification of symbolic language needs to be carefully handled. The New Testament makes important theological use of the story of Adam and Eve, and without doubt it is important to maintain that they were real people and that their actions had profound theological significance.[70] Are the garden, trees and snake to be understood literally or symbolically? This is more debatable, and the best approach is probably an open one. It can be argued that the reference to the tree of life in Revelation is probably symbolic (Rev. 22:2), so that this raises the possibility that it is symbolic in Genesis.

We might expect the language of origins and of eschatology to share some symbolic features, for in the nature of the case neither is open to historical research. We are, however, talking here about possibilities, not certainties, and a symbol may start life in an objective fact accessible to sense-perception.

Third, identification of language as symbolic should not cause us to lower its importance, but rather to seek its meaning, to grasp the theological truth it is intended to convey, and by God's grace to make any adjustment to our thought or life that is required by it.

Issues of theology and history

Some studies of the historical material of the Bible have emphasized that their authors were theologically motivated. This poses no problems provided that this is not seen to involve distortion of the historical facts. Indeed, it is just what we might have expected.

The whole Bible is theological even if it is also historical. To say that 'Christ died' is to make an historical assertion; to say that 'Christ died for our sins' is to move on to a theological assertion. Evangelicals need to affirm that both are true. The four Gospel writers all had theological points to make, and their selection and arrangement of their material was determined by theological considerations, but this is perfectly consistent with fidelity to historical fact. The same is true of Samuel/Kings and Chronicles.

The supernatural factor

It is clear that the biblical writers believed in the supernatural intervention of God in human history, both in terms of miracles and of supernatural

---

70. See, for instance, the profound theological importance of Adam in Rom. 5:12–21.

prediction. This does not mean, of course, that we should see the supernatural where a completely natural explanation of the phenomena[71] is available and does full justice to the text. So, for instance, it has been suggested that God used natural means to bring about some of the plagues in Egypt. But the evidence must not be stretched in an endeavour to rid the stories of the supernatural at all costs.[72]

To accept the resurrection of Jesus and regeneration by the Holy Spirit is to accept the supernatural working of God, and so opens the door to both physical miracles and predictive prophecy. Moreover, to accept the resurrection and to experience regeneration are not just of the *bene esse* but they are of the *esse* of a Christian. This means that a true Christian believer is already conditioned to the supernatural.

Theological conviction and scholarly integrity – are they compatible?

As we have already noted, Christian theologians and biblical scholars are not identical, although their concerns overlap. Theologians are interested in concepts, and this is true whether they are biblical, historical, systematic or philosophical theologians. There is a concern with theological truth and with commitment to that truth. Biblical scholars are concerned with the text of Scripture, with its exegesis, with detail, and with many questions of introduction, such as authorship, date, intended readers, and so on. They are not always so interested in harmonization, although sometimes they are, as in dealing with various accounts of the same story in the Gospels.

Does the suggested establishment of guidelines which we have been concerned with mean the shackling of conservative scholars, so that there are no-go areas for them? By no means. A scholar or theologian must be completely free to pursue truth and in accordance with this to wrestle with phenomena which do not seem to fit a high view of the Bible. To suggest otherwise is to advocate evangelical brainwashing and to surrender our integrity.

Without doubt, scholarly pursuits do unearth problems and these should be frankly recognized and solutions sought. Sometimes the result may be a theory which appears to run counter to some theological principle. If this is so, it needs to be frankly recognized, and further light sought.

Suppose, then, the conservative scholar finds himself or herself driven to

71. An explanation which occurs within the normal God-given web of cause and effect.

72. For a recent study of miracles, see C. J. Collins, *The God of Miracles: An Exegetical Examination of God's Action in the World* (Leicester: Apollos, 2001).

embrace solutions to problems which seem to run counter to the integrity of the Bible, what then? For instance, should a scholar working in an evangelical college, who has signed the college's basis of faith or been employed on the clear understanding that the institution is committed to a conservative evangelical stance, resign her or his post in such circumstances? Possibly, but not necessarily, or so it seems to me.

If such situations occur, I believe we should distinguish between theories treated as provisional or tentative and, at the same time, recognized by the person embracing them to be unsatisfactory, and those that are accepted in full assurance and taught as such. The latter seem to me to require resignation in the interests of integrity, while the former may be regarded as possible stages on the way to truth.

What, then, of classroom teaching? The teacher should be sensitive to the needs of the students. Ideas you would canvass in a major way with a postgraduate PhD student to enlist his or her interest in seeking further light on the problem need to be handled particularly carefully and sensitively in the first-year undergraduate classroom. Evangelical theological teachers and conservative biblical scholars should recognize that as teachers they have some pastoral responsibility and must give an account to their Lord. If the fact that 'pastors and teachers' has only one definite article in Ephesians 4:12 means that in the Christian church every pastor has also some teaching role, it also suggests that all teachers should recognize that they have some pastoral responsibility.

Issues arising in a postmodern context

Here there is really only one issue, which takes various forms. It is the question as to whether in Scripture we have an objective divine revelation which calls for understanding, faith and obedience or whether, fascinating, stimulating and challenging as the Bible may be, we may make of it more or less what we will. In its extremest form, this is because not only is there no objective meaning in the Bible; there is no such meaning in anything. So, it is said, any idea of an objective approach to Scripture is naive.

For the evangelical Christian this is no small issue, and a great deal depends on our attitude to it.

The antecedents of postmodernism
We might go back as far as the Greek Sophists, but we will start with the nineteenth-century reactions against Hegelianism. Hegel's philosophy was in

some ways the antithesis of Kant's, for to him not only was the transcendent world open to us but all our knowledge, whether of philosophy, religion, the sciences or the humanities, was knowledge of the great Absolute Spirit, or rather, was that Spirit's ever-increasing knowledge of himself – which came to its consummation in Hegel's own philosophy!

The predictable reaction against this arrogant objectivism took several forms, including notably Marxism and existentialism. The former focused attention not on a transcendent world but on the here and now, the world of material things, while the latter turned away from the search for essences, the true nature of things considered abstractly, and focused on what they called 'existence', the situation of human beings as they face the uncertainties and anxieties of life in this world. Marxism is more in tune with modernism, with its interest in science and technology, and existentialism with postmodernism, in which science (with its child, technology) is often regarded as a bypath or even an enemy. The individualism of existentialism has certainly found a new home for itself in postmodernism.

The twentieth century saw an increasing emphasis on the importance of language and a proliferation of language theories. Those deeply engaged in linguistic studies often had significant other interests, to which they brought their linguistic insights, so that for them language theory had something of a philosophy's integrative role. Noam Chomsky, for instance, has been deeply concerned with biology, psychology and politics. This focus on language paved the way for postmodernism.

What really characterizes postmodernism, however, is that it is not so much a coherent philosophy as a widespread general mood. All the philosophies we have thus far alluded to in this chapter have their leading protagonists, but it is difficult to identify such in postmodernism. There is no major representative document that can be read, digested, analysed and (hopefully) refuted.[73]

Postmodernism and the authority and interpretation of Scripture

Postmodernism is interested in the relationship between authors, texts and readers, matters little considered under modernism, for modernism assumed that the main questions at issue in connection with Scripture were historical and, especially for earlier writers, history was regarded largely as an objective account of what happened. In modernism little attention was paid to the reader. In fact, the modernist approach has been characterized as one in which

---

73. The outlook of Jacques Derrida, the extremest form of postmodernism, is perhaps an exception to this. It is this that makes his thought important. See pp. 219–220.

'the meaning of the text is supposedly established for all time quite independ-ently of any reader'.[74]

This was true no matter the critical stance of the writers concerned. So, for instance, J. W. Jipp points out that the methodologies for New Testament study used by J. G. Machen (a major conservative writer) and his contem-porary Adolph Harnack (who has been described as 'the greatest liberal of them all') were remarkably alike. This is because they were both concerned with historical facts. 'What accounted for the major differences between the two was that Machen was open to the supernatural and Harnack was not.'[75] Both assumed that factual, historical issues were very important. This has all changed under the influence of postmodernism.

In considering issues arising in a modern context we noticed the emphasis on the final text of Bible books given by Brevard Childs. This puts him among the moderns rather than the postmoderns. Postmoderns have little inter-est in the intentions of writers. It is pointed out that even if writers are still alive, their memories of their original intentions in writing may not be sharp and clear and particularly they may be unaware of subtle or less than subtle changes in outlook affecting their interpretation of their own work.

One result of the postmodern approach is that for many it is no longer simple to make a clear distinction between discussions of the authority of the Bible, which confronts the reader with its call for faith and obedience, and its interpretation. For this reason, we will need to give much consideration in the next chapter to questions raised by the postmodern outlook, some of which bear on the Bible's authority.

The authority of the Son and the Holy Spirit

Is there a canon within the biblical canon? There is always danger in specially elevating certain books of Scripture and treating them as the key to the remain-der of the Bible. Some evangelicals have tended to do this with the epistle to the Romans. Important as this book is, it is wrong to do this, and moreover it is now more difficult to do so. This is because there are now a number of interpretative viewpoints concerning it, so that views as to its central purpose

---

74. C. Rowland and M. Corner, *Liberating Exegesis: The Challenge of Liberation Theology to Biblical Studies*, Biblical Foundations in Theology (London: SPCK, 1990), p. 67.

75. J. W. Jipp, 'The Quest for the Historical Machen', *Themelios* 30:3 (Summer 2005), p. 59.

and therefore the relative importance of its different parts have shifted from time to time. Are we to treat chapters 1 – 5, or 6 – 8, or 9 – 11, or 12 – 16 as the section giving perspective to the whole? Luther's relegation of James and Jude, Hebrews and Revelation to a lower status than the other biblical books, although understandable because of the enormous importance he attached to justification by faith as taught particularly in Galatians and Romans, has not found general favour in the church.

Some have treated the words of Jesus as of greater authority than those of the biblical writers. Now this is more understandable and yet it is mistaken.[76] His words will always be particularly precious for Christians simply because they are his, but it was Jesus himself who validated the authority of the Old Testament by the way he employed it and who set in motion the process which led to the New Testament by his appointment of the apostles and his enduement of them with the Holy Spirit as the Spirit of inspiration. We cannot set the words of the Second and Third Persons of the Trinity against each other.

We need to do some clear thinking here. To say that one set of teaching is the norm for others and to say that it is of higher authority than those others is not to say the same thing. To make a comparison, if for us the Father is the norm for what we understand by the word 'God', this does not mean that he is to be regarded as a higher authority than the Son and the Holy Spirit, for they are equal. As we compare what the Bible tells us about them with what it says about the Father, it is clear that they too are fully divine, so that we cannot set the Father's authority over against that of the Son or the Spirit.

So it is with the Scriptures. The two Testaments have two particularly important figures in terms of divine revelation and their teaching acts as norms.

The first is Moses. He was a prophet and true prophets are like him (Deut. 18:18), but he had a form of contact with Yahweh that was unique, as Deuteronomy 34:10–12 indicates. So, then, the teaching of the prophets can be tested by its conformity to that of Moses, making his a kind of canonical norm. The book of Deuteronomy is very important in this connection, and the oneness of prophetic and Deuteronomic theology is widely recognized.

The same is true although even more important in relation to Jesus. Not only can the teaching of the apostles be tested by his,[77] but because he is the

---

76. Bible versions that highlight the words of Jesus in some special way may foster this.

77. Incidentally, the validity of any present-day utterances professing to be prophecies can and need to be tested by the apostolic teaching (1 Cor. 14:36–38).

Son of God his imprimatur covers the Old Testament as well, thus reinforcing the 'Moses test'. So, then, the teaching of Jesus in the Gospels has performed a normative function for the New Testament and for the whole Bible, and of course that teaching was committed by him specifically to his apostles. Those books of the New Testament not strictly apostolic[78] were also based on apostolic teaching. It is worth remembering that the early patristic church referred to the Scriptures not as the Old and New Testaments but as 'the prophets and apostles'.

This therefore takes us to rock-bottom theologically, to a point below which we cannot (and indeed need not) go. Christians recognize the authority of Jesus and we know of no authority that can stand against his. It is his authority that validates the whole Bible and, because it has been validated as the work of the Holy Spirit, it is of equal authority with what he said. As Christians we need to be utterly committed to him and therefore to the Word of God and to the theological interpretation its writers give to the divinely initiated historical events on which their theology is founded.

Ministering the Word of God in a mixed culture

The coexistence of modernism and postmodernism

In the West, most congregations are mixed in age. There are people whose education and habits of mind, developed over many years, incline them strongly to modernism and against postmodernism. This is perhaps particularly the case in churches with a clear theological position and a strong expository ministry, where there has been a nurturing of the members on the objective truths of Scripture. It seems likely that the incursions of postmodernism are more to be found in full force outside the churches, although many younger people, both outside and inside the churches, are thoroughly postmodern. It has to be admitted that the level of Bible teaching in many churches is not adequate to combat the bad features of this. Also many Christians are more deeply affected by what they see on the television most nights of the week than by what they hear in church on a Sunday.

A situation of great challenge and opportunity

This means that in preaching and teaching the Bible today, the communicator must be aware of the complexity of the situation. I once knew the new

---

78. i.e. not actually authored by apostles.

principal of a college whose appointment coincided with the introduction of a completely new system of teaching. The old was being phased out at the very time that the new was being phased in. I was amazed at the way he was able to grasp both systems and see what steps had to be taken to move from the one to the other. This is the kind of skill a Christian preacher or teacher needs to have today in relation to the task of gospel communication, and to develop it takes both prayer and work.

The situation may be even more complex in some overseas situations, for in some cultures both modernism and postmodernism are now impinging on traditional forms of thinking, so that not two but three life-stances are in contact, in fact often in conflict, with each other.

This may seem very difficult, but it is for us the particular context in which we are to fulfil the Great Commission, and we can look to the Lord to guide us as we work within this situation.

We need more books to address, not just the challenge of postmodernism (there are plenty of these), but also that presented to us by the mixing of modernism and postmodernism in our society, in our churches and in many individual minds, and the added communication problems in some overseas cultures. This challenge should not depress us, but be seen as an exciting new opportunity to articulate the unchanging gospel of the crucified and risen Christ in ways that engage with the people of our day, and in which we can most assuredly seek the guidance of the Holy Spirit.

6. THE KEY TO CHRISTIAN DOCTRINE: PROPERLY INTERPRETING THE BIBLE

Theology does not stand still.

There have, of course, been times when the interested observer might have imagined it had reached a decisive omega point. So the great Reformation Confessions, which still have considerable influence today, may have seemed final to those who first read them. In the Roman Catholic tradition, the same may have seemed true of the decrees of the Council of Trent. In a completely different way, theology-watchers may have thought the 'Death of God' theology of the 1960s was really heralding not the climax but the total demise of theology. The loaded bookshelves of our theological libraries bear witness to the fact that this did not happen.[1]

One of my hopes in writing this book is that it will not only help readers to assess the particular theologies it deals with, but also prepare them to do the same with other theological positions, even those which have not yet come into view. This gives this chapter its distinctive character within the book. I hope it will underline how important it is to understand how Scripture should be interpreted in relation to present-day theological issues and their practical

---

1. The same happened in philosophy, for Hegel thought the onward march of thought had come to its consummation in his philosophy. How wrong he was!

outcomes. Nothing could be more important, provided, of course, that we act on what we learn.

This will take us into hermeneutics.

The nature of hermeneutics

Since the 1960s, hermeneutics, the study of the principles and methods of interpretation, has become a highly sophisticated and technical subject. Some books on it are so complex that the general Christian reader may well feel he or she is unlikely to cope with the subject at all, let alone master it. This complexity is chiefly because, at the level of academic scholarship, hermeneutics has to engage with the philosophy of language, an ever-growing and developing and to some extent splintering subject with its own technical vocabulary.[2] It is somewhat ironic that a study of the way we understand can itself be so difficult to understand!

It is not only the technical nature of the subject that has proved a problem. Readers with some acquaintance with the philosophy of language may have been turned off the subject because of the extreme scepticism of some of its more radical practitioners, just as evangelicals have so often been put off the historical-critical approach to the Bible by the extreme conclusions of so many critics.[3] In the philosophy of Jacques Derrida, in particular, all objectivity disappears and we are left with utterances and literature which cannot have any certain or fixed meaning for us or for anyone else. Not only so, but the way we read the text constantly changes because we are ourselves so subject to change. Moreover, we can never find the intention of the author and it would be of little help to us even if we could. Author, text, reader – in each of these realms all objectivity disappears and we find ourselves adrift in a sea of meaninglessness. It is a further irony that if Derrida is right we cannot even find his intention in his own works! Thankfully, such extreme scepticism is not by any means the only option.[4] It does mean, though, that evangelical

---

2. e.g. philosophers of language often discuss 'meaning' and discern a number of senses of the word. It is easy to get tied in logical knots when discussing the meaning of 'meaning', for any conclusion affects both uses of the word in this sentence and their relationship to each other.
3. We noted this in the previous chapter.
4. Interested readers should consult Kevin Vanhoozer, *Is There a Meaning in this Text? The Bible, the Reader, and the Morality of Literary Knowledge*, 2nd ed. (Grand Rapids: Zondervan, 2009), which is largely an answer to Derrida's outlook.

hermeneutics, if it relates to the philosophy of language, inevitably has an apologetic dimension to it.

Study of a subject is always easier when there is general agreement as to the meaning of its technical terms, yet there is not even complete agreement as to the word 'hermeneutics' itself.[5] Because I hope this volume will be of value to preachers, I am taking the widest and now the most common understanding of the scope of the subject, to include everything from exegesis to exposition, from text to sermon, from the preacher's study desk and prayer chamber to the mind and heart and will of the recipient.

In fact, biblical hermeneutics as so understood is simply the study of how we interpret and particularly how we ought to interpret the Bible to apply it to life in this present world, so that it aims to inform, to establish norms and to effect change. It is the bridge between Scripture and modern life and thought. It is therefore important for every Christian, and it is a relief to find that its central principles can be simply stated and that they have always been the basis of a proper handling of the Word of God.

This does not mean, however, that we can be simplistic in our use of these principles. Their implementation is not always easy and there is hard work to be done in seeking the relevance of Scripture to our contemporary life. The doctrine of the perspicuity of Scripture, its clarity, does not mean that every passage is clear but rather that the overall message, consisting of 'those things which are necessary to be known, believed, and observed, for salvation',[6] is clear. The need for diligent and prayerful study will always be real.

The mention of prayer may cause some readers to object that we may dispense with hermeneutics altogether because as Christians we are indwelt by the Holy Spirit, the great Interpreter of Scripture. The positive side of this comment is not only true but is of great importance. We should remember, however, that the Holy Spirit teaches us *within* Scripture how to interpret Scripture, particularly in the way the New Testament writers interpret the Old Testament. We can therefore see hermeneutical principles in operation that are the mind of the Spirit.

---

5. See R. L. Thomas, *Evangelical Hermeneutics: The New Versus the Old* (Grand Rapids: Kregel, 2002), pp. 20–37.

6. R. Shaw, *An Exposition of the Westminster Confession of Faith* (Fearn: Christian Focus, 1973), Article 1:7, p. 15. See the helpful exposition of this doctrine in T. Ward, *Words of Life: Scripture as the Living and Active Word of God* (Nottingham: Inter-Varsity Press, 2009), pp. 117–129.

Does this mean, as some have suggested, that the Holy Spirit is 'locked up in the pages of the Bible'? By no means. The Spirit *actively* employs what he has said in Scripture, showing it to be a living word. We still need to use the hermeneutical principles discernible in the Bible to interpret it for the people and situations of our day, including the conduct of our own lives. It is vitally important, however, always to remember that this must be in prayerful dependence on the Spirit, who is always to be seen as the One who both gave and interprets the Scriptures. The guidance of Scripture and a prayerful attitude – these are the hermeneutical essentials, and they are in any case basic to all healthy Christian life and growth.

We have in fact been applying hermeneutics throughout this book. Every discussion of the meaning of a biblical passage, every suggestion as to how this affects our theology and every indication of the influence of philosophy or general culture on theology or of the influence of theology on life has taken us into hermeneutics.

Before the book ends, I thought it might be useful to its readers to deal with these principles more explicitly and with the use of some examples so that they may apply them more effectively. When we encounter a new, stimulating brand of theology which may sound either exciting or troubling, we need some guidelines to enable us to discern both its strengths and weaknesses. This is because theology affects life, and it is our responsibility as Christians to live in the light of God's truth. If our hermeneutic is sound, our theology should be sound. How our lives are affected, of course, depends at the human level on our faith and obedience.

So, then, our concern in this chapter is to think through the implications of the basic hermeneutical principles in order to be more effective as interpreters of the Bible. A further aim, in terms of the purpose of this book, is to enable us to consider to what extent such principles are properly applied in contemporary theological systems. Good biblical and theological scholarship can help us in this, and a considerable and ever-increasing quantity of this is available today.

The purpose of biblical interpretation

In all study of literature, we need to note the purpose of it, whether this is clearly stated by the author or can be reasonably inferred from the literature's contents.

The purpose of Scripture is clearly stated in 2 Timothy 3:14–17, and it is the purpose of the *divine* author, for it is closely related to the inspiration of

Scripture, its status as the Word of God.[7] The purpose is practical, to lead us to Christ and to equip the Christian ('the man of God') 'thoroughly' for 'every good work'. In the pursuit of this goal, Scripture gives us both theological and ethical instruction and it does so both positively ('teaching . . . training in righteousness') and negatively ('rebuking, correcting').

Arguably the sequence of declared uses here follows the logic of Christian experience.

God's design is always that knowledge of his truth should result in wisdom, especially the saving wisdom that leads a person to trust in Christ. The Pharisees diligently studied the Scriptures but refused their testimony to Jesus and so did not experience eternal life (John 5:39–40). The reference here to the man of God could be to somebody with a teaching function in the church,[8] but in fact all Christians, those who have been made wise for salvation in Christ, are called to good works, and the production and growth of these requires the same biblical means as those required by the official teacher.

Scripture addresses our minds, teaching us truth about God, but it also rebukes our conduct, so that true conversion can never be simply intellectual, although it must have an intellectual side because we need to respond to the truth. So, then, initially (at least in the logic of the experience) the intellectual side has to be constructive and the moral deconstructive. Then we find that Scripture also corrects us as its truth encounters errors in our outlook, and it also gives us positive moral instruction. All this is with the ultimate aim of fitting us to work effectively for God (v. 17).

Treating the four expressions in verse 16 in this way should not be too inflexible, for often they become merged in actual experience. Some writers, especially H. H. Price and A. C. Thiselton, have stressed what they call the dispositional nature of belief, belief as commitment, not merely momentary.[9] This fits well with the recent interest in 'virtue ethics' which places the emphasis more on character than on the particular moral act. Billy Graham used to illustrate faith from a platform, making the point that faith in a platform finds its genuineness in actually standing on it, and this is true. Thiselton's point

---

7. This is true whether we should translate it 'All Scripture is God-breathed' or 'Every God-breathed Scripture', which simply recognizes that there are uninspired writings, but not, of course, in what we know as holy Scripture.

8. cf. Deut. 33:1; 1 Sam. 2:27.

9. See especially A. C. Thiselton, *The Hermeneutics of Doctrine* (Grand Rapids: Eerdmans, 2007), ch. 2, including his references to Price.

is the further one that commitment should be regarded as dispositional, not simply a momentary act. Having once stood, we continue to stand, with all the consequences that this standing involves. To use a phrase he often employs, we 'take our stand'.

If it is correct that true faith is also never merely mental, although it has a mental dimension, the same can be said of repentance. Faith and repentance are the two sides not only of a conversion experience, but of the continuing Christian life, and both have an intellectual and a volitional aspect to them. Belief is to lead to trust, and a change of mind (which is the root meaning of the Greek word *metanoia*, 'repentance') is to effect a change in our moral attitude, issuing in altered conduct. So, then, the emphasis on formation and transformation made by many writers on biblical hermeneutics is entirely appropriate, fitting the declared purposes of Scripture as indicated in 2 Timothy 3.[10]

How does this relate to hermeneutics? Most intimately, for it makes clear that a proper handling of Scripture must always have godly effectiveness as its goal.

This is made clear from a study of Paul's great doctrinal affirmations. Passages such as Philippians 2:6–11 and Colossians 1:15–20 are often abstracted from their contexts and considered in their own right, but we should never forget that their contexts are spiritual and moral.[11] The great argument of Romans 1 – 11 is followed by this kind of practical application. Doctrine never exists for its own sake in Paul's writings, but rather is a spur to deeper Christian commitment practically worked out in life.[12]

We should not, of course, so emphasize moral application that its roots in doctrinal truth are overlooked or even negated. This was what Ritschl and his followers in the late nineteenth and early twentieth centuries tended to do. Harnack, probably the most influential of them, so reduced the theological element in early Christianity and the teaching of Jesus himself as to say that

---

10. J. Goldingay dedicates *Models for Interpretation of Scripture* (Grand Rapids: Eerdmans, 1995) to the staff and students of a South African college who discussed with him the issues outlined in it and 'for whom interpretation of scripture is not only an examination subject but a matter of life and death' (dedication page). If this is God's Word, should we take it any less seriously?

11. The scholarly interest in these passages as possible early Christian hymns, valuable as this is, has sometimes obscured this, although it has often introduced a further context, that of the worship life of the early church.

12. See Thiselton, *The Hermeneutics of Doctrine*, ch. 1.

for Jesus the gospel could be summed up as the universal fatherhood of God, the universal brotherhood of man and the infinite value of every human soul.[13]

The main procedures of biblical hermeneutics

How do we go about the hermeneutical enterprise? In many respects, this may be illustrated from the field of English (and other) literature.

Take, for instance, Shylock's speech ('Hath not a Jew eyes?') in *The Merchant of Venice*. When the play was put on in Nazi Germany, Shylock was presented as repulsive and indescribably evil, and the speech was seen as from first to last a product of his craftiness or truculence and was spoken in a tone that suggested this. Today, however, when both production staff and audiences are concerned about anti-Semitism, he is often played sympathetically, with most of the speech coming across as a plea to be treated humanly. The sting in its tail, when the speaker speaks of revenge, may then be seen as prompted by the unmoved demeanour of Shylock's audience. The words are the same, for they are Shakespeare's, but the interpretation varies according to the appearance, demeanour, tone of voice and emphasis of the actor who plays Shylock. It is the cultural background of the interpreters and so what is brought to the text that makes the difference.

What, then, was the intention of Shakespeare and how may we discover this?[14] First of all, we look at the literary context, the whole play. We see that there is a certain ambivalence about its 'good' characters. Can we really view any one of them as a hero? Then we consider his other plays. Can we get some idea from this wider context? We investigate the historical background and discover that there was plenty of anti-Semitism in England in Shakespeare's day. This does not settle it, however, as a great writer sometimes moves against the general outlook of the day; it is one of the features of his or her greatness. Then we ask to what extent we are influenced in our attitude to the play by the form anti-Semitism took in Nazi Germany in the lifetime of some of us, and which therefore has become for us somewhat stereotypical. It is worth considering too whether the character of Fagin in

---

13. Adolf von Harnack, *What Is Christianity?*, ET, 5th ed. (London: Ernest Benn, 1958), pp. 54–59, 200–210.

14. I am simply illustrating principles of interpretation here, not proposing a particular interpretation of this play.

Dickens's *Oliver Twist*, at least before Dickens removed most of his references to him as 'the Jew', reinforces for us a negative interpretation of Shylock, or whether Sir Walter Scott's positive presentation of Isaac of York in *Ivanhoe* may have influenced us in the other direction. Finally, we need to consider our own attitude. What has the play done to us? Has it given us more sympathy with the Jewish members of our own community or the opposite, and will it alter our conduct at all?

Here, then, we have been taking a contextual approach to the play. Now without doubt we can sometimes be influenced in a right direction by the reading of good literature, but Scripture is in a different category altogether, for here not only is everything human but everything is divine, and to deal with it we need not just to study context, but to engage in contextual *theology*. At no stage can we forget that this is the Word of God. Because of this, so much depends on its right interpretation.

We may classify the necessary procedures of biblical hermeneutics in a fourfold way, with each of the four having two aspects. These are exegesis (including both literary and historical study), biblical theology (both major themes and the narrative structure), attention to presuppositions (both our own and those of others) and contemporary application (in both its theological and practical aspects).

It might seem a simple matter just to apply these principles in sequence every time we come to the Scriptures. It is not that simple, however, and this is because of what has been called the 'hermeneutical circle'. This is the idea that this pattern is not so much linear as circular and that we move along it in both directions, so that, for instance, not only does exegesis influence theology, but theology influences exegesis. We tend to interpret particular passages in the light of our general theological outlook and of course new light on such passages may also influence our theology.[15]

Some writers use the term 'hermeneutical spiral'[16] and, unlike the other, it suggests progress. In fact both terms conserve a truth, although not the same truth. It is perhaps best to use 'circle' when discussing the influence of one of the four factors on others but 'spiral' when noting progress. Using the two in

---

15. See the diagram and comments in G. R. Osborne, *The Hermeneutical Spiral: A Comprehensive Approach to Biblical Interpretation*, 2nd ed. (Downers Grove: InterVarsity Press, 2006), p. 356.

16. e.g. R. Lundin, A. C. Thiselton and C. Walhout, *The Responsibility of Hermeneutics* (Grand Rapids: Eerdmans, 1995), p. 25; and, of course, Osborne, *The Hermeneutical Spiral*.

this way is not contradictory, for 'circle' and 'spiral' are simply illustrations or models used to make the ideas more vivid and memorable.

Exegesis (or grammatico-historical interpretation)

Here the focus is on understanding the text in both its literary and historical contexts.

The literary aspect

This involves studying the text's vocabulary, grammar, syntax, structure and rhetoric within the book to which it belongs.[17] If the truth of God is conveyed in the words of Scripture, it is clearly important that we should know what these words, phrases and sentences meant to the writer and the first readers.

Context is all-important in literary interpretation of all kinds and therefore in biblical interpretation. After all, the division of the Bible into chapters and verses, while useful, was not the work of the authors themselves but of those who wanted to facilitate easier reference to particular passages, while each book comes to us from the Bible writers as a complete entity. This means that no interpretation of a passage which does not do justice to its place in the book as a whole can be adequate.

Modern philosophy of language has been helpful in underlining the different functions of language. Many Bible readers had some awareness of this prior to the advent of this kind of philosophy. It has long been a commonplace of biblical study at quite a basic level that the Bible contains statements about God, and promises, commands and warnings from him, so that the writers, and God through the writers, have a variety of ends in view in what is written. To use technical language, we are here encountering speech-acts, a term coined by J. L. Austin.

This expression is good because it shows the living quality of the Bible and the fact that it is given for practical ends. Scripture is meant to be transformative, not merely informative. Vanhoozer goes so far as to say, 'The great discovery of twentieth-century philosophy of language . . . is precisely the speech-act . . . We *do* something in speaking. To speak is not simply to utter

---

17. A most helpful analysis of the structure of the book of the Revelation (even though the author calls it 'a preliminary rather than a final outline') may be found in Osborne, *The Hermeneutical Spiral*, p. 45.

words, but to ask questions, issue commands, make statements, express feelings, request help, and so forth. Sometimes simply saying something makes it
so: "I pronounce you man and wife."[18] It also underlines, against Derrida, the
speaker or writer's intention.[19]

The most profound example of a speech-act or acts in the Old Testament
is to be found in Genesis 1, with its repeated 'God said . . . and it was so'.
John 1:14, 'the Word became flesh', goes even further, because John views
the incarnation as a divine utterance full of meaning and significance, with his
whole Gospel then showing us how dynamically active this Word was – and
is – climaxing in his death and resurrection.[20] John clearly does not intend us
to think that in Christ deed eclipsed word, for in his Gospel a large proportion
of the space is occupied by the words of Jesus; rather, here Deed and Word
embrace each other. It is not surprising that in the church's early centuries,
theologians placed much emphasis, at times even to the point of excess, on
what was called the Logos doctrine in thinking about the relationship between
the Father and the Son.

So, then, we need to consider not only the meanings of words, phrases,
sentences and larger literary units, but also their functions. For instance, to
interpret a promise as a warning or vice versa is to misunderstand the nature
of the speech-act concerned. An obvious example of this may be found in
Genesis 31:48–49, where the immediate context shows with crystal clarity that
what is often popularly treated as a promise is really a warning. A reference to
God's justice will have a different function in a message to recalcitrant sinners
from one addressed to godly people facing unjust oppression, and the reader
needs to take account of this. The function of a literary unit can usually be
discovered by studying its context in the larger unit which contains it.

Incidentally, not only is it essential for our theology to have a sound exegetical basis but also it is valuable, in our theological speaking or writing, to
include some actual exegesis and not simply take it for granted. To go back in
this way to the biblical roots of our theology and to do it reverently can often
impart devotional warmth to what we say, even when our main purpose is
not devotional, and it assures our hearers or readers that our concern is to be

---

18. K. J. Vanhoozer, *The Drama of Doctrine* (Louisville: Westminster John Knox, 2005),
    p. 63.

19. See Ward, *Words of Life*, pp. 57–62.

20. In Goethe's *Faust*, the central character tries to interpret the opening of John's
    Gospel and he toys seriously with the idea that *Logos* might be rendered 'Deed'
    (*Faust*, lines 1223–1237).

biblical. We should not only be biblical but be seen to be.[21] Why should not the heart be warmed while the mind is being informed and challenged?

One of the Bible's many wonders is the way its literary diversity ministers to its theological unity. The importance of identifying the literary genres is more and more being recognized today. We will briefly survey the main genres of Scripture and you are strongly advised to read further on the subject.[22]

Law and prophecy, psalm and proverb, Gospel and epistle, and also, of course, prose and poetry: here there is no wooden uniformity but such variety as to make Bible study an aesthetic as well as an intellectual and challenging experience. We are meant not only to understand and obey the Word but to love and rejoice in it. Psalm 119 shows that this was true for godly people in the Old Testament as well.

We should treat each literary genre with the respect its distinctiveness deserves, for it is the Holy Spirit who gave it this special character. N. T. Wright warns us against translating the Gospels into something like the epistles and then says that the lesser mistake, but still a mistake, would be to assimilate the epistles to the Gospels.[23] His rider is understandable, for there is something particularly fundamental about the historical material of the Bible, but we should remember that all is *equally* the Word of God and we need its inspired variety.

When reading the opening two chapters of Genesis, we should not expect technical scientific language, for this did not exist when the book was written. What we find is theological and historical language,[24] focusing on the work of the only God there is, and we are not surprised at reference to his creation of the heavenly bodies, for the Babylonians worshipped them, nor the linking of the entrance of sin into human life to temptation through a serpent, for the Egyptians worshipped this creature. The message is: 'There is only one God;

---

21. The volumes of H. Bavinck's *Reformed Dogmatics*, 4 vols. (Grand Rapids: Baker Academic, 2003–8) are a model in this respect.

22. See, e.g., G. D. Fee and D. Stuart, *How to Read the Bible for All its Worth: A Guide to Understanding the Bible*, 3rd ed. (Grand Rapids: Zondervan, 2003); Goldingay, *Models for Interpretation of Scripture,* is also very stimulating, although some of his views on critical issues are somewhat controversial.

23. N. T. Wright, 'How Can the Bible be Authoritative?', *Vox Evangelica* 21 (1991), p. 25.

24. 'Historical', of course, in the sense that it is an account of what happened in past time, but not in the sense that it was humanly documented, for at the creation there were as yet no humans to do this.

it is without question that he made it all and he is deeply concerned about the worship of false and evil beings.'

Genesis introduces us to historical narrative. We should not expect detailed political, social or military information, for this, and all the historical material of the Old Testament, is distinctively theological history with the purposes of God to the fore. It concentrates on a family first of all, then on the nation springing from that family, the people God was preparing so that through them – in Christ – he might bring blessing to the whole world. We will not expect all our historical questions to be addressed, let alone answered, and we find the usual literary features of historical narrative such as thematic development rather than strict temporal sequence.

The legal material was given to the chosen people, and, as we might antici-pate, its shape takes account of their historical, geographical and cultural cir-cumstances, which are different from ours, but we discover abiding principles in it, for the God of Israel, who is also the God and Father of our Lord Jesus Christ, does not change in his character or overall purposes. Here, as in all else, New Testament reflection on this material is a great help in interpreting and applying it.

The prophets addressed the people of their day in the name of the Lord, and, aware as they were of standing in the midst of God's historical engage-ment with his people, they interpreted the past and shone light on the future, all in the context of addressing the present state of the nation and its people. Their God was the God of the exodus and of Sinai, their gracious Redeemer and holy Law-Giver. They often used illustrative language taken from their history, geography and culture, including some standard forms of communi-cation such as the figure of the lawsuit in which God indicts his people, and a modest amount of technical language especially in relation to eschatology, such as 'in the last days'. It is important to learn this.

The term 'the poetic literature' is not altogether appropriate if restricted, as it often is, to Job, the Psalter, Proverbs, Ecclesiastes and Song of Songs, because there is much poetic language in the Prophets. Nevertheless, these five books do form a distinctive if a somewhat heterogeneous group. They are strongly reflective, and focus on the people's life with God in society. The Psalms express their worship and present their concerns to God in prayer; Proverbs deals with the practicalities of daily life in general terms, but also with many specific examples; the book of Job wrestles with the issue of the suffering of God's people in a world governed by an all-powerful and just God; while Ecclesiastes handles the problem of apparent meaninglessness in a fallen world but with frequent glances upward to God; Song of Songs extols pure sexual love, so vital for the development of a godly society. Each of these books needs to be understood on its own terms, and the Psalter in particular is almost like an encyclopedia of Old Testament genres, although always within a worship structure.

It is a great help in interpreting biblical poetry to study its characteristics. Parallelism or sense-rhythm is particularly important. In this, two or sometimes more consecutive lines have a special relationship. Either they express the same or a similar idea in two or more different ways, or else a contrast (as so frequently in the book of Proverbs), or they give some kind of development in which the thought expressed in the first line becomes the foundation for a further thought or thoughts. Translators of poetry into another language often find this exceptionally difficult if they want to convey something of the material's poetic form, but the sense-rhythm feature of Hebrew poetry makes this much easier. It is surely right to see the providence of God in this.

The New Testament Gospels are really the preaching of the good news of Jesus through accounts of his ministry. The historical interest is strong, but again these books do not answer many of our questions, for they are not biographies of the modern type. They are written to present Jesus, in all the attractiveness of his person, as Israel's Messiah and God's Son, and in all the costliness and effectiveness of his saving work, to move the readers by that attractiveness, that costliness and that effectiveness to trust and serve him. Each Gospel had its particular target readership and details were chosen from the common pool of facts and comments made which were appropriate for each.

Gospel scholars also speak of sub-genres, different kinds of stories. A broad sub-genre is the parable, although some scholars divide these into various types. It is worth paying special attention to the parabolic form, noting how many have a sting in the tail, making them 'Tales of the Unexpected', very powerful means of disturbing the complacent and those committed to the status quo.

Luke's Gospel is part one of a two-part work, in which themes from the ministry of Jesus recur in the story of the early church, showing that he continued to express his risen life and his purposes through his work in the church he established. This makes it a kind of link book between the Gospels and the epistles.

The epistles bear some marks of the literary conventions of the time, although also some distinctively Christian features such as the combination of 'grace' and 'peace' which occurs in the salutation of so many of them. They were written to deal with issues that were coming to the fore in various churches and were often peculiar to each of them. We should bear their occasional nature in mind, but also the fact that our local churches are part of the same universal church to which they also belonged. Even when the specific occasions were different from anything we face, as, for instance, the problems the readers of the epistle to the Hebrews were facing in moving from Judaism to Christianity, we will find abiding principles valid for us today.

The book of Revelation has a reputation for being the most difficult book in the Bible, but the reason for that difficulty is not always appreciated. It is not simply because the readers were faced with particular circumstances different from ours, as this is true of all the biblical books. It is not even simply because it is in a different genre (known as apocalyptic) from the other New Testament books, although this is true. It is chiefly for two reasons.

The first is that it assumes considerable knowledge of the rest of the Bible, especially the Old Testament, which holds the key to most of its symbolic language. It will not have been easy even for its original readers to understand at its first reading, although they would have advantages we do not possess. Perhaps the writer was even hinting, through his many Old Testament allusions, that the readers should study the Old Testament more, not just for understanding his symbolism, but also to fortify them for the coming persecution. Whatever we face, this is true for us too.

The second reason is that it does not yield its riches to superficial study. Richard Bauckham says, 'Close attention to literary composition opens up a remarkable density of meaning in the text, which has been so crafted as to be capable of yielding its full meaning only to repeated reading and appropriate study.'[25] This is so true.

Genre needs to be taken seriously, but we should not become so preoccupied with it that we disregard the important differences between writings that are in the same genre. Even two almost identical items in Scripture are never totally so. For instance, Psalms 14 and 53 are not quite the same and even if they were each would take on a slightly different significance because 14 is in Book 1 of the Psalter and 53 in Book 2 and the five books of Psalms have some distinctive features within the Psalter as a whole. Even if the same story occurs in two Gospels in similar contexts, it is important to consider each within the overall context and in the light of the distinctive purposes of the Gospel in which it is found.

The historical aspect
This also embraces such matters as geography and culture, and involves handling the biblical text in a way faithful to its background, taking into account

---

25. R. Bauckham, *The Climax of Prophecy: Studies in the Book of the Revelation* (Edinburgh: T. & T. Clark, 1993), p. x. I have here given disproportionate comment on the Apocalypse because of its acknowledged difficulty for the interpreter.

how it relates to the culture of its age and place, in other words seeking to enter its world. If the grammatical aspect of exegesis needs disciplined study, so does the historical, but it also profits by the use of a disciplined historical imagination. It was said of a fine teacher of classical history that he 'took you by the scruff of the neck and thrust you into ancient Rome'. The interpreter needs a good knowledge of the historical, geographical and cultural world of the Bible, so that he or she can enable others to live in it imaginatively too, before they can imaginatively apply truth given in that context to life-situations today. The word 'disciplined' is important, of course, for we must accept the discipline of the facts.

It may be objected that this means the ordinary Bible reader needs the kind of expertise only a specialist can be expected to have. If true, this would be a serious objection. There is plenty of helpful historical material available today but it was not always so, and the Bible was meant to be understood in every period of the church's life. What the objection ignores, though, is the extent to which the Bible provides its own background. It is appropriate that in the arrangement of their books both Testaments begin with so much history. Understanding of the Psalms and the prophetic books is greatly enriched by diligent study of the Old Testament's historical material. How meaningful would the epistles be if we had no Gospels, no Acts of the Apostles?

We can learn much more from this historical material than is usually recognized. Take, for instance, the books of Samuel. Go through them. See how rich is the panorama of human life there, with about a hundred different individuals, some named and others unnamed. Note indications of their domestic life, their proverbial expressions, their society's etiquette, their ways of showing their emotions. Live in their world, and then see if that helps your understanding when you read the book of Psalms. In the Acts of the Apostles, note the way preachers began their sermons, using the appropriate forms of address, such as 'Men of Israel' or 'Rulers and elders of the people'. We can learn not only from their forthrightness but also from their courtesy.

To advocate this approach is by no means to minimize the value of literary and historical scholarship, but it is good to recall that understanding the major truths of God's Word, although enriched by good scholarship, is not dependent on it.

Before considering biblical theology, it is important to affirm that we should let the text speak its distinctive message to us first of all. This gives freshness and is often extremely challenging. So, for example, the warning passages in the epistle to the Hebrews need to be seen first of all in their contexts before we go on to consider them in the light of wider biblical themes. This may prove challenging, but we need to accept this challenge, otherwise we may not be listening to the Word of God but to our own theological inclinations.

Biblical theology

Christians believe that the Bible, although consisting of sixty-six books, can also be rightly described as one book. It is a literary corpus in which one book anticipates another or quotes another or interprets another, or takes another for granted. There are themes that run through it and these are developed, sometimes lineally, sometimes contrapuntally, sometimes in obvious harmony, sometimes in creative tension, all contributing to the great message of the whole.[26] The study of such themes in biblical theology is closely related to exegesis, although it involves considering the historical development not only of words but of ideas. Here James Barr's *Semantics of Biblical Language*[27] did service to the world of biblical and theological scholarship when he insisted that ideas are often found when the words and phrases we most associate with them are absent. After all, theology is about ideas, biblical ideas but ideas nevertheless, although they are better called 'truths' because they are not just the products of human thinking but emanate from the mind of God.

The nature of biblical theology has been much discussed. Is it a descriptive or a normative discipline? Certainly it has a descriptive and historical dimension, for the biblical theologian is interested in how words, phrases and ideas developed over the centuries of biblical history. It is not, however, only descriptive if we believe the Bible to be the Word of God. It forms a permanently normative basis for the continuing theological task because its principles are valid in every generation of the church's life, even though we need also to consider how they apply today.

It enriches understanding of a particular passage to set it in the context provided by biblical theology, so adding a theological to the literary and historical contexts. To see that a word, a phrase, a theme is not isolated but contributes to the overall message of Scripture is to see its value, and value is closely connected to meaning. This is why such works as the *New Dictionary of Biblical Theology*[28] can be so helpful at this stage in the hermeneutical process.

---

26. Somewhat in the way a great symphony is constructed.

27. J. Barr, *Semantics of Biblical Language* (Oxford: Oxford University Press, 1961).

28. T. D. Alexander and B. Rosner (eds.), *New Dictionary of Biblical Theology* (Leicester: Inter-Varsity Press, 2000).

Seeing a particular passage in the light of biblical theology is recognition that the literary context, although starting with the particular Bible book in which the passage occurs, actually extends to the whole Bible. For evangelical Christians, of course, both the part and the whole are the work of the inspiring Spirit.

Discussions of the nature of biblical theology have highlighted two contrasting and yet complementary approaches, which we will consider in turn. It will help us in seeing their significance to note that in some ways, biblical theology is the first stage of historical theology. Like historical theology, its subject matter has a time line and we survey its movement from one historical period to another. Unlike historical theology, however, it has normative significance, because it is about the theology of the Word of God. In both approaches both the history and the theology are important, but in the first the theology is the more dominant partner, while in the second it is the history. A balanced biblical theology requires that we treat the two approaches as complementary.

The thematic structure of biblical theology

Leading biblical themes
In seeking to identify these, material related to each is gathered together, with recognition that these themes develop historically until each reaches its final form when it is seen in the light of Christ. It is a distinctive feature of biblical theology that this be done without the imposition of some structure from systematic theology. The Bible is to dictate the thematic structure by the use of its own terms.

The value of this is fairly obvious, although it is not without its difficulties, for it is not always easy to see biblical ideas without viewing them through the spectacles of the particular theology we have inherited from others. As an example, we might consider the word 'sanctification'. Christians often regard it as exclusively related to the work of the Holy Spirit in transforming our inner life, while in the New Testament it is often used also of God's initial gracious act in setting us apart for Christ, which brings it rather closer to justification.[29]

The search for a central theme
In any literature it is important if possible to identify its central theme as this gives perspective to the whole work. It is a serious hermeneutical error

---

29. For a survey of the theme in Scripture, see D. G. Peterson, 'Holiness', in ibid., pp. 544–550.

to interpret it through secondary ideas. Among New Testament theologians there is wide agreement that the kerygma, the proclaimed gospel, establishes the theological centre in Christ and his death and resurrection. This kerygma is to be found in the sermons in the Acts of the Apostles, but its roots are in the teaching of Jesus and its influence can be seen, as a kind of theological substructure, in many and varied contexts in the New Testament. Even though there are some differences of emphasis, there is always a common core.[30] The Old Testament is much more diverse in its literature and covers many centuries, so it is no surprise to find various views as to its central theological theme.

Old Testament theologians have often attempted to identify this.[31] Some important and influential examples are the covenant, communion, the kingdom of God, the promise of God and deliverance. A good case can be made out for each, and none is without its merits, but two features of these attempts need to be noted.

The first is that in each case the theme identified is one that appears in every biblical theology. So, then, Walther Eichrodt suggested covenant as the theological centre of the Old Testament and of course it is still there in the New Testament's teaching about the new covenant in Christ. Any work on biblical theology which does not treat it as important is gravely deficient, and the same is true of the other themes suggested as the central one.

The second feature is that each of them is really about God, so that some have suggested that the central theme is simply God or God in his dealings with his people, while others have said this is so obvious as to be hardly worth saying. All the themes identified can be shown to prepare the way theologically for the coming of Christ, in whose Person and Work they find their personal point of unity.

In fact, the very concept of a Bible as distinct from two separate Testaments takes its rise from the way our Lord opened the Scriptures of the Old Testament, interpreting them in terms of himself, for, of course, the New Testament is the inspired literary deposit of the revelation in Christ. This means that however we interpret the Bible theologically we must understand

---

30. See C. H. Dodd, *Apostolic Preaching and its Developments* (London: Hodder and Stoughton, 1936).

31. See D. L. Baker, *Two Testaments, One Bible: The Theological Relationship between the Old and New Testaments*, 3rd ed. (Nottingham: Inter-Varsity Press, 2010); and B. C. Ollenburger (ed.), *Old Testament Theology: Flowering and Future*, vol. 1 (Winona Lake: Eisenbrauns, 2004) for full surveys of these attempts.

it in terms of Christ. All the themes suggested as central by Old Testament theologians are taken up ultimately in the New Testament and the revelation of God in Christ's Person and Work.

The Old Testament is often seen as a book of promise, the New as a book of fulfilment. This, although broadly true, is an inadequate way to express their relationship. There is fulfilment as well as promise in the Old Testament, notably in the way Genesis 12 – 50 finds a measure of fulfilment later on, and promise as well as fulfilment in the New, for Christ is to come again. So, then, at every stage God shows how utterly true and reliable he is, and the second advent will assuredly establish this beyond doubt and in the fullest way possible.

One issue connected with this search for a central theme, which may at first seem troubling but which on further investigation is highly illuminating, is that Old Testament theologians have often found it difficult to integrate the Wisdom literature[32] thematically with the rest of the Old Testament. It is important, of course, to attempt this, as otherwise we will operate with a canon within the canon.[33]

It is not simply that there is very little reference to the great events of Israel's history, but it is the somewhat discordant note some of this literature introduces. As we have seen, the book of Job, for instance, raises the question of apparently innocent suffering in a world ruled by a good and all-powerful God, while much of Ecclesiastes seems to some readers to have an almost cynical tone. Some psalms raise all kinds of questions about God's strange providence. It is worth saying, of course, that this theme also occurs elsewhere in the Old Testament, in the books of Jeremiah and Lamentations, for instance.

It is here that writers like Terrien, Brueggemann and Goldingay have an important point to make because of their emphasis on creative tension.[34] Terrien identifies a theology of the Glory (in Judah) and a theology of the Name (in the Northern Kingdom). Goldingay notes that the Old Testament has a theology of creation and a theology of redemption. Perhaps Brueggemann's approach is at once more troubling but also potentially most helpful, even though we may not always find ourselves in agreement with him. He writes not only of Israel's Core Testimony but also of its 'Counter-

---

32. Chiefly Job, Proverbs and Ecclesiastes, with some psalms.

33. We might note, for instance, that there is a creation theology in these books, just as there is in many other parts of the Old Testament.

34. See the Bibliography for their works. We may make a comparison with systematic theology, in which we need to hold together the unity and the threefoldness of God, the deity and humanity of Christ, and also divine sovereignty and human responsibility.

Testimony'.[35] There is affirmation of God's good purposes for Israel, but also deep questioning of this, a questioning that just will not go away.

Now tension is the very stuff of great literature. Without conflict there can be virtually no literature, whether this be the external tension of the 'eternal triangle' seen in so many love stories, or the internal tension in which a person is mentally or emotionally divided.

This is characteristic of great literature because such literature is realistic and, whether we like it or not, conflict is a characteristic of life.

No literature exists that is more realistic than the Bible. The external tension is there in the biblical story, beginning with the intervention of Satan in Genesis 3 and climaxing in his utter defeat and judgment in Revelation 20. But most of us find that external tension is often easier to deal with than internal, and that the most difficult traumas arise for us from our own minds and hearts.

Here we must be so careful how we express ourselves, but in the Old Testament, in the great overarching metaphor in which God's acts and even his feelings are presented as if they are human ones,[36] we see this tension, not within the writers but within God himself, in the agonizing and profoundly moving words of Hosea 11:8–9. The New Testament goes further, much further, for the tension is there at the cross, in all its starkness, in all its awfulness, in the cry that rent the sky, 'My God, my God, why have you forsaken me?' (Matt. 27:46; Mark 15:34) Here, treading on the holiest of all holy ground, we may say that at the cross we see the internal tension of divine holiness and love,[37] agonizingly presented, with full expression given to both, and there resolved by God himself for the salvation of humankind.

The historical structure of biblical theology, the biblical metanarrative

The nature of a metanarrative
This term[38] refers to a comprehensive account of what we know or an overarching story that includes many smaller stories, giving overall structure. So

---

35. W. Brueggemann, *Theology of the Old Testament: Testimony, Dispute, Advocacy* (Minneapolis: Fortress, 1997), pp. 117–313, 317–403.

36. See pp. 40–52.

37. The penal substitutionary doctrine of the atonement shows us that the tension caused by human sin was real, but that its resolution by God was never in doubt.

38. This term was first used by J. F. Lyotard, *Introduction: The Postmodern Condition: A Report on Knowledge* (Minneapolis: University of Minnesota Press, 1979), pp. xxiv–xxv. He called it 'incredulity towards metanarratives'. It is now employed more widely than he used it.

the theory of evolution is a metanarrative and so is any general history which sees one motif embracing all that has happened, such as the class war as in Communism or the progress and triumph of a master race as in National Socialism.

There is today a widespread rejection of metanarratives, for several reasons.

First of all, there is a feeling that they restrict freedom, especially intellectual freedom. A metanarrative necessarily affects the interpretation of the smaller stories it embraces. This may even develop into an ideology, which is really only a set of ideas considered as a whole, but for some writers the term has become pejorative, with the sense of an oppressive intellectual scheme. The two extreme political ideologies of the twentieth century, Fascism and Communism, both have metanarratives and are ideologies in this sense. It is perhaps significant that Hitler was fond of the music of Wagner, whose music dramas used a metanarrative, most notably in the *Ring Cycle*.

Then there is the undoubted fact that some major metanarratives have proved mistaken, leading to widespread disillusionment. The downfall of Communism in Bulgaria led to many suicides among older people who had believed in and lived for Marxist ideals for forty-five years, and who now saw that their own life stories had been without positive meaning because the Big Story had been totally discredited.

Then there is the postmodern revolt against structures as such, even scientific structures. It has certainly affected the arts, in which irrationalism has been an increasing factor for a hundred years or so. Where are the great dramas or the great symphonies today? There are very few. This is because both these art forms involve order, structure, movement towards a goal.

In fact the very idea of a general goal or purpose in things is often suspect. As long ago as 1935, the historian H. A. L. Fisher said he could discern no plot in history. He said, 'I can see only one emergency following upon another as wave follows upon wave . . . only one safe rule for the historian: that he should recognize in the development of human destinies the play of the contingent and the unforeseen.'[39] As in Samuel Beckett's play of that name, we may be 'waiting for Godot', but Godot never arrives. Much modern music, since Debussy, fails to stop on the home tone, the note normally marking a decisive end in the music of the past.

Yet at the same time there is a felt need for a metanarrative. What is life all about? Is there a larger purpose? Beethoven's Fifth Symphony is still popular

---

39. H. A. L. Fisher, *A History of Europe*, vol. 1, *From the Earliest Times to 1713* (London: Fontana, 1960).

in today's concert halls. In it Fate knocks at the door at the opening of the first movement, and the audience experiences satisfaction as its threat is overcome in the triumphant final movement. Does this not reflect an abiding psychological need?

We do need structure. We start life in the womb, in a secure environment, and we feel the need for a structure within which to live. This is true mentally as well as physically. Christians believe it is true spiritually as well. In Scripture God has graciously given us this structure.

The biblical metanarrative and its character

Biblical theologians recognize the importance of the metanarrative, the Big Story, the great historical narrative running through the Bible which is logically prior to its theology,[40] and that the theology is grounded in the Big Story. Even if they identify the Bible's main theme as salvation, or covenant, or promise, they recognize that the metanarrative gives it historical structure. Gerhard Von Rad did not attempt to find a theological centre for the Old Testament, which he saw as having insuperable difficulties, but instead, recognizing that 'in principle, Israel's faith is grounded in a theology of history',[41] he emphasized the metanarrative, even though he did not actually employ that word.

What, then, is this metanarrative? It is the true story of God's dealings with a people, the people of Israel, and through them ultimately with the whole world through Christ. In the Old Testament part of this story, the exodus and the gift of the land of Canaan find special emphasis. Certainly there is also some stress on the exile and the return to the land from Babylon, but these rest for their significance on the earlier events in which Israel became a free people in its own land.

For New Testament theology this metanarrative, with its redemption and inheritance themes, finds its climax in Christ crucified and risen and the story of the church he founded. Jesus himself, followed by the New Testament writers, indicated that the whole of it should be interpreted in terms of himself (Luke 24:27, 44).

The biblical metanarrative is starkly realistic. Death is not only embraced

---

40. But not necessarily chronologically. Of course, as the sequence of word and act in Gen. 1 shows, ultimately it is the Word that is prior, for the acts of God are the product of his eternal mind and heart and so often they are anticipated by his promises (cf. Amos 3:7).

41. G. Von Rad, *Old Testament Theology*, vol. 1, *The Theology of Israel's Historical Traditions*, tr. D. M. G. Stalker (Edinburgh and London: Oliver and Boyd, 1962), p. 105.

(and how fully it is embraced!) but overcome, in the cross and resurrection of Christ. This is sure and decisive. Here is a metanarrative that is not triumphalist like, for example, those of Fascism and Communism, and yet it ends in triumph.

We need to understand the small stories of the Bible in the light of the Big Story. Not only so, but the earlier events of the Big Story must be understood in the light of its climax. Even Aristotle recognized that it is the end that should interpret the path that leads to that end, so that it is the oak tree that is the ultimate interpretation of the acorn. So Goldingay says, 'Any concern with political and social liberation that does not recognize spiritual liberation as the more fundamental human problem has failed to take account of the development of the story of Israel after the exodus via the exile to Christ's coming and his work of atonement.'[42]

In the story various human figures have important theological significance, and this is highlighted in many New Testament passages. This can be seen, for instance, in the following: Adam (Rom. 5:12–21), Abraham (Matt. 1:1; Rom. 4; Gal. 3), Moses (Luke 9:28–36; Rom. 5:12–21; Heb. 3:1–6), Joshua (Heb. 4:8), David (Matt. 1:1), Elijah (Luke 9:28–36), and those who went into exile and those who returned from it (Matt. 1:11–12, 17). All these can be seen, either explicitly or implicitly, in their relationship to Jesus, in whom either by comparison or contrast and sometimes both, they find their significance. We see here that the creation and the fall, the call of Abraham, the exodus and the giving of the law, the entry to the land, the contest with Baal-worship, the exile and return, were important moments in the story.

The biblical metanarrative as an interpreted and proclaimed narrative
This story, as told in the Bible, is an interpreted one, and that is why, because the interpretation was given by God, we can describe it as a theology and a normative one at that. Historians today rightly regard the idea of a bare historical fact as somewhat naive, as every fact is an interpreted fact, taking its place in relation to other interpreted facts. As Christians we may reverently recognize that even for God they are interpreted, for it is he who gives them meaning. The word of creation was a meaningful as well as a powerful one, the product of eternal Thought,[43] and so also is the inspired word of the Old Testament historian and his New Testament counterpart.

---

42. Goldingay, *Models for Interpretation of Scripture*, p. 70.

43. The Greek term *logos*, although as used by John is appropriately rendered 'Word', also meant 'reason', for instance in Greek philosophy. This would make John's

Not only is the biblical metanarrative an interpreted story; it is kerygmatic, for it is a proclaimed story. We find this in its earlier forms in the utterances of the prophets and the psalmists, and its final form in the preaching of the apostles. Greek drama had a narrator and narrators appear in the biblical drama of doctrine. Here again, Von Rad and G. E. Wright's emphasis on proclamation is helpful, for the drama was not only enacted, but its nature as divine revelation-through-action was made clear by the narrators, who were agents of the one divine Narrator, for this is *God's* Word. In the biblical drama the role of the narrator, the writer, is vital, for he not only records but interprets and he does both by divine inspiration.

In the New Testament there are times when some major Old Testament elements of the metanarrative are narrated and then the cross and resurrection are proclaimed as their climax, notably in two sermons in the Acts of the Apostles (Acts 7:2–53; 13:16–41). This built on the sense of anticipation that was evident among the pious community in Israel when Jesus was born (Luke 2:25, 38; 23:51). They were the people of the future, the people of the promise, and they found that future and the fulfilment of that promise in Jesus.

This metanarrative is also reflected in the great creeds of the church, for the clear revelation of the deity of the three holy Persons was given in historical sequence, although of course each is eternally divine in the unity of the triune Godhead. So, then, for the creeds the story provides a structure for the theology.

Most Christians, if they know the creeds at all, know them chiefly in the context of services of worship, and this is highly appropriate, for the biblical metanarrative, in its various forms, is really a proclamation, a confession of faith, and a communal one at that. It is rooted in the corporate life and worship of God's people. This again shows the union between truth and life and, moreover, it does so in communal terms.

The dramatic model of Christian doctrine

It is not surprising that some writers are promoting the idea of doctrine as drama, as this is a vivid way of telling a story.[44] Language from drama used illustratively occurs in the writings of Paul.[45] If we view the book of Job as a

---

Prologue of immediate interest to many with no contact with the biblical revelation.

44. See especially Vanhoozer, *The Drama of Doctrine*.

45. See Thiselton, *The Hermeneutics of Doctrine*, pp. 69–70, with special reference to 1 Cor. 4:9.

kind of drama, the action occurs on two planes, at the back of the stage in the encounters of God and Satan, and at the front in the interchanges of Job, his friends and Elihu. John 7 and 8, where the religious leaders are at the back and Jesus and his followers at the front, is another example, although here there is some coming and going between the two planes of the action. The visions of Daniel and of the Apocalypse are like the scenes of a drama.

Can we say, though, that there is a dramatic dimension to biblical *doctrine*? In a sense we can, because it is firmly based on the history, and although God revealed himself in the whole of that history, there were special 'dramatic' moments in it. Because biblical doctrine is really the interpretation of the biblical story, this means that doctrine is a developing feature in Scripture.

But, some may ask, did this story and the revelation of God associated with it come to a full stop when Jesus came? If he is the final Revelation of God, surely this must be so! No, for the language of revelation, of manifestation, of unveiling, is used of both comings. The second coming means, not that there will be further revelation *beyond* him, but further revelation *of* him, so that God's great disclosure of himself and his purposes in Jesus will be fully exegeted and expounded. The last act of the drama has started, but we still await its final scene when the meaning of the whole will be plain to see.

What, then, in dramatic terms, is the present age? Is it the Interval, a time when we may simply reflect on what has already happened and anticipate the final act? It is here that the concept of inaugurated eschatology is so helpful. This is a better term than realized eschatology, for this has sometimes been used to play down the importance of the second advent, or even to deny it altogether. Inaugurated eschatology means that in Jesus the eschaton, the final act in the drama, has already begun. Christians are now in the age of the Messiah. This means that the divinely staged drama is participatory, not merely spectator drama. By God's grace, we are in the story. Primarily it is about him, but it is about us too.

The status of the biblical metanarrative

How important is it? It is difficult to exaggerate its importance. It is not a mere model that may be dispensed with.[46] The 'hermeneutical circle', 'the hermeneutical spiral' – use them or dispense with them according to their

---

46. In a fascinating article, based on an equally fascinating experiment with a group of young people, Fergus Macdonald suggests that a way into the biblical metanarrative for many today could be through the psalms ('Do the Psalms Speak Today?', *Scottish Bulletin of Evangelical Theology* 28:2, Autumn 2008, pp. 170–186).

level of usefulness. Drama, symphony – these are useful models but they are not indispensable. Metanarrative – this belongs to the 'given', for it is there all the time, as the indispensable background to everything in Scripture, holding it all together and moving constantly forward to its goal.

All this means that biblical theology is not static but dynamic, for at each historical stage and in each divine act revelation was given until the supreme blaze of divine light came in Jesus Christ. This did not involve unlearning the past, but it did mean that there was constant theological enrichment. This did not necessarily make people of later generations more godly than earlier, but it does mean that their understanding of God and his purposes could be fuller.

For evangelicals, the biblical interpretation of the metanarrative, as of Scripture as a whole, is sacrosanct and we are never at liberty to dispense with it, but it is not necessarily exhaustive. There may be other levels of significance beyond those actually spelled out, but we always need biblical grounds for going beyond what is explicit. In this connection, we should heed the words of Goldingay: he says that the biblical stories bring to life the events on which the faith is based, and then he comments,

> Disagreements about the present relevance of some stories (e.g. the use of Exodus in liberation theology or the use in charismatic renewal circles of stories from the gospels and Acts about healing or raising the dead) are sometimes disagreements about whether these stories relate solely 'events on which the faith is based' or also offer paradigms of how God may act now or of how we should act now.[47]

This means, surely, that we need to see if there is more explicit teaching in Scripture on these matters.

A word of caution is in place here. Although in the Bible the story-form in general and the metanarrative are very important, this should never lead us to play down other biblical genres, as some are in danger of doing. We are committed to the whole Bible as God's Word and no fascination with one form of it should overshadow the remainder.

Two complementary approaches

Major themes, biblical metanarrative – these should not be set against each other, but should be seen to be complementary, for this book is all about God, the God of the covenant, the promise, the kingdom, who reveals himself to be all this and more in the context of the story of his great acts.

---

47. Goldingay, *Models for Interpretation of Scripture*, p. 61.

If you want another model, one that fits this two-sidedness of biblical theology, consider the crossword puzzle. Some of these are devised in such a way that every square has two functions, one in relation to the clues across and the other the clues down. In biblical theology the clues across are the great themes and the clues down the great events of the metanarrative, and no square functions for only one word.

The relevance of biblical theology to hermeneutics

It is clear that no passage should be interpreted out of its full biblical context. We need, too, to observe the emphases of the Bible, making sure that the interpretation takes full note of them. Everything must be understood both in its historical setting and also in terms of Christ, the glorious consummation of God's revelation.

So, for example, we will seek to understand the Mosaic law not only in its own context, but also in the light of the gospel of Christ, and to ask in what sense it finds its fulfilment in him. We will recognize that Israel's God-given institutions, such as the tabernacle, the temple, the priesthood and sacrifices, also find a fulfilment in Christ of such a nature that all their typological significance is gathered up in his work. We will also see that all prophecy finds its focus in him and in his two comings. In viewing the psalms in the light of the New Testament, we will recognize him to be both the perfect Object of worship and the perfect Worshipper. We will rejoicingly see that the God-given principles of kingly rule, exercised so imperfectly by even the best of the Old Testament kings, are fulfilled perfectly in Christ, to whose kingdom we already belong and for whose perfect coming rule we earnestly long.

How, then, do we relate exegesis and biblical theology? The greater the exegete's grasp of biblical theology is, the better his or her exegesis will be, and the better the exegesis, the more it will confirm or challenge our understanding of biblical theology.

In seeking for an adequate biblical theology, we are not looking simply for a theological structure that appeals to us, as this would be a gross mishandling of Scripture, but rather one that reflects the theology of the biblical writers themselves, for there can be no doubt that they had one. G. R. Osborne, alluding to New Testament theology and its relationship to exegesis, says this: 'A biblical author's statements apply a larger doctrine to a particular issue in a specific church setting and stress whatever aspect of the larger teaching applies to that situation.'[48]

---

48. Osborne, *The Hermeneutical Spiral*, p. 29.

There should be both openness and caution. We will not easily adjust in some major way our understanding of the whole, but neither will we refuse to accept the criticism of our view of biblical theology that comes from a particular text. D. A. Carson says, 'We will not go far astray if we approach the Bible with a humble mind and then resolve to focus on central truths. Gradually we will build up our exegetical skills by evenhanded study and a reverent, prayerful determination to become like the workman "who correctly handles the word of truth" (1 Tim. 2:15, NIV).'[49]

Meaning and significance

Before moving on we should briefly consider a matter on which two schools of thought exist, with major scholars on either side, and which is perhaps best handled here because it emerges in the context of discussions of biblical theology.

Sometimes two terms, normally treated as synonyms, come to have differentiated uses within a particular discipline in order to make a distinction which is important within that discipline. This is true for 'meaning' and 'significance' in the study of hermeneutics.

One side, defining 'meaning' as the sense intended by the author and 'significance' as the implications of that meaning for other people and in other situations, asserts that every biblical passage has only one meaning, that intended by its author, although it may have further significance. The other side maintains that a Bible passage may have more than one meaning, especially if the Bible itself uses it in more than one way. These two points of view we may perhaps designate the 'One Meaning' and the *Sensus Plenior* schools.

The 'One Meaning' school see great dangers in the other position. They cite numerous instances when all kinds of fanciful ideas have been discerned in straightforward biblical passages and these have been promoted as the deeper meanings of the passages concerned. On the other hand, the *Sensus Plenior* school show that Scripture itself contains many examples of a further or deeper sense, for instance in the way the New Testament writers see Old Testament events, offices and institutions as typifying Christ, the great Antitype.

A high doctrine of Scripture is helpful when we address this issue, for this means that all Scripture is both fully human and fully divine. It seems best to recognize that the human writers had one intended meaning in what they wrote,[50] and that this meaning was always true and foundational for the

---

49. D. A. Carson, *Exegetical Fallacies* (Grand Rapids: Baker, 1984), p. 144.

50. Even if on comparatively rare occasions their *intention* was to be ambiguous.

divine Author, but that his intention was sometimes that there should be fuller meaning beyond this. For the divine Author, meaning always started from the intended sense of the inspired human author, and this should never be denied, but it often proceeded further. This is particularly the case in relation to the interpretation of the Old Testament in the New. Even here, though, it is important to insist that the New Testament interpretations are not arbitrary, but are normally based on the principle of analogy, and therefore on the doctrine of God, because they are evidence of God's consistency.

What, then, of the warnings of the 'One Meaning' school? They should be heeded, for the dangers to which they point are real. We are on safe ground, however, if we accept *sensus plenior* only in the places where we find its evident use in the Bible itself. So typological interpretation should only be employed when there is clear warrant for it in the New Testament. We know then that this is part of God's meaning, not simply that of a fallible interpreter. This is why I have dealt with the matter at this point instead of under the later heading of 'contemporary application'.

What of passages where the thought is so dense or complex that further study constantly reveals further meanings? This does not depart from the principle of the one meaning so long as all the meanings discerned are part of the surface text. So, for instance, Ephesians 1:3–14 is such a rich passage that it seems almost inexhaustible. If a Bible student realizes, at some stage of investigation, that 'in Christ' is a key concept in the passage, uniting its many features, this is of course related to the surface text. The same applies to the book of the Revelation. Bauckham says, 'The meaning concealed in the text by the literary technique . . . is no different from, but reinforces the message that lies on the surface of the book.'[51] This is very different from interpretations which purport to find deeper meanings *below* the surface of the text and which have no more authority than the imagination of the interpreter. The Apocalypse has been more subject to this misuse than any other book of the Bible.

This does not mean, of course, that a passage's *significance* is restricted to the way the biblical writers draw it out. If that were so, there could be no expository preaching, for this applies the text to the present-day hearer, who is not the person to whom the text was first addressed. It does mean, though, that we need to take very seriously any indications in Scripture as to the way it should be handled, and, as we shall see, the principle of analogy applies to contemporary application too.

---

51. Bauckham, *The Climax of Prophecy*, p. 2.

Critical awareness of the influence of pre-understandings on theology

It is in their focus on this that recent books on our subject differ so much from older ones, for they reflect a general trend which, as so often happens, has both strengths and weaknesses. Older books focused on the text, setting out principles for its interpretation. They also showed interest in the biblical authors, in their differences of style and the various purposes they had in view. There was little attention paid to the reader, however, except to encourage seriousness of purpose, openness to deeper understanding of truth and readiness to respond.

Now things are very different. The process of reading is thoroughly investigated with a special concern about what the reader brings to the text, variously referred to as assumptions or presuppositions or pre-understandings.

The approach of the Amsterdam school can help us here, for that school is interested not only in the assumptions about the Bible made by a Christian because of the new birth, but also in those of the non-Christian. For the Amsterdam theologian, attention to presuppositions is of great importance in relation to all points of view. The value of this in a postmodern milieu is obvious.

None of us comes to Scripture without some prior assumptions and these reflect our background.

Philosophy has played a large part in the history of theology and changes in the prevailing type of theology have often been due to shifts in philosophy. Now major philosophies often have their own attractiveness, especially if they have a Big Story of their own and purport to give a comprehensive account of our experience of the world. Moreover, they often affect general culture, influencing many who have never even heard of them, becoming such a part of their mental structures as to be taken completely for granted just as if they were implanted at birth.

As we have already seen,[52] there is a place for philosophical tools in communicating biblical truth, but a non-Christian philosophy must never provide controlling concepts. It is the Bible, not philosophy, which should make the running. It is therefore vital, in encountering a theological system, to critique it in such a way that alien influences are seen for what they are. I have tried to do this in other chapters in this book.

We must now distinguish different types of pre-understandings.

---

52. See pp. 23–24.

Modernist pre-understandings

From an evangelical standpoint, modernism has one undoubted strength, the recognition that there is such a thing as objective truth. In a television programme many years ago, Marghanita Laski, a well-known British agnostic, was debating a point with a Christian minister, when she suddenly stopped and exclaimed, 'I can see now why we are getting nowhere. It is because I still believe in objective truth and you don't!' Already, several decades ago, the seeds of postmodernism were being sown, and in the minister rather than the agnostic!

It does, however, have a markedly negative feature: its anti-supernaturalism. This was applied to the Scriptures by the rationalists of the Enlightenment, and it found its way into the church. The extent of its influence varied considerably, but it was particularly evident in the way commentaries in the liberal tradition treated miracles. They often never even mentioned the possibility of a supernatural interpretation, so that the reader was left to decide between two or three different rationalistic explanations.

The ultimate in this, at least as far as the New Testament is concerned, was to be seen in the work of Rudolf Bultmann. He proposed that the whole New Testament should be 'demythologized',[53] and yet, for him, this did not spell the end of the Christian faith. To him the gospel was found in its essence in Romans 6, which he interpreted in terms of Heidegger's existentialism. Heidegger taught that a person may move from what he called inauthentic to authentic existence when she or he embraces beforehand the fact of death. This Bultmann saw in Romans 6, so that the call to identification with Christ in his death and resurrection is what the gospel call is. The fatal flaw in this, however, is the fact that although Christ's death was real, for Bultmann his resurrection was mythological. 'Death and resurrection' became little more than a formula for existential living, and in this life only, for with no resurrection of Jesus there is no life beyond.

Are evangelical commentators subject to this kind of rationalism? This is hardly likely, for to them a Christian, virtually by definition, is a person who accepts the supernatural, believing in the resurrection of Jesus and experiencing the supernatural work of the Holy Spirit in his or her heart. There may be a nod in the direction of this negative outlook, however, if a less plausible natural explanation of an event is suggested instead of an evidently supernatural one.[54] This then becomes an unacceptable concession.

---

53. See H.-W. Bartsch (ed.), *Kerygma and Myth: A Theological Debate* (London: SPCK, 1972).

54. Of course, we should remember that there is an economy of miracles in some parts of the Bible, and it is not good exegesis to suggest a supernatural explanation

Postmodernist pre-understandings

As we have already noted, a major feature of postmodernism is its association with developments in the philosophy of language. This has given increasing recognition to the subjective factor in interpretation, sometimes with negative and at others with positive implications for biblical interpretation.

The literary movement known as New Criticism, flourishing in the middle of the twentieth century, before the advent of postmodernism, emphasized the importance of reading texts simply as self-contained literary entities, without considering their background, implications for conduct, or anything else. The text was everything and its context, whether literary, historical, cultural or contemporary, nothing. This is, of course, at the farthest remove from the postmodern approach. The pendulum of literary criticism has certainly swung from one extreme to the other. If this was to be applied to biblical hermeneutics, it would be reduced to exegesis, and then only to the strictly literary as distinct from the historical aspects of it.

The advent of structuralism seemed to be a move towards a greater openness in literary interpretation. It owes much to the views of Noam Chomsky, who held that there are particular structures common to all human minds, forming a kind of hidden text of 'deep structures' lying beneath the actual words.[55] Interesting as this idea is, it has dangers, because the interpreter may over-psychologize the authors of the literature and read into the text what is not really there, while possibly taking little account of the surface text, which is in fact the Word of God. The deep structure theory can become an interpretative straitjacket.

Then came reader-response criticism, pioneered by Stanley Fish and others. Less extreme than Derrida's deconstruction, it nevertheless focuses on the reader's role in understanding the text. In a sense, it is said, readers create a text, for, in the engagement between the text and the reader, the reader has the initiative, perhaps trying out various approaches. There is obviously some truth in this, although, of course, even to say this is to recognize some objective truth-criteria. If we honour the text as God's Word, we need to respond to its truth, allowing it, or the Spirit of God through it, to have the dominant role.

---

for something evidently natural, something that belongs to the normal God-given web of cause and effect.

55. This has some kinship with the idea that there are really only ten stories in literature (or twelve or twenty, according to different calculations), because particular stories are always variations on basic themes.

A phrase increasingly used today is the hermeneutics of suspicion. Paul Ricoeur identified Marx, Nietzsche and Freud as the three masters of suspicion. Each brought a suspicion to speech and texts, especially religious speech and texts, to show these are often not what they appear on the surface. Marx saw religion as 'opium for the people', to keep them politically and socially subdued; Nietzsche, because of his philosophy of the will to power, saw religion as a refuge for the weak and therefore despised it; Freud viewed it as a form of projection: we feel the need of a father figure, so we invent one – God.

So, these thinkers say, we should exercise deep suspicion in considering interpretations of religion in general and so of the Bible. Interpretations which keep the poor docile by giving them comfort or which insist on male dominance in the church or which frown on certain forms of sexual expression are all suspect. Are these things really in the text or are they brought to it by the reader? This assumes that the minds of Christians have presuppositions deeper than the teaching of Scripture itself and with a more profound effect on our interpretations.

What, then, about our own approach to the biblical documents? It is time we turned to consider evangelical presuppositions.

Evangelical pre-understandings

It is no weakness, but rather a strength, to recognize elements of truth in an outlook we reject. The masters of suspicion have done us a service in making us aware that our interpretations may be biased. In fact Scripture itself contains implicit warnings as to this.[56] Self-criticism is important and we need humility in our approach to Scripture. We will consider first of all the role of the Christian reader, then the role of the church, and finally that of the Holy Spirit.

The role of the Christian reader

In our study of literature, including Scripture, we do not start with a blank sheet. This applies to the non-Christian, to the new Christian and also to the mature Christian. Because all human beings have an innate awareness of God, we are all theologians of sorts. In fact, even the demons have a theology (Jas 2:19)! We sit at the feet of Christ and we need both to be willing to put aside our own preconceptions and at the same time to realize we will never do this completely. They are not always easy to discern. They come from our cultural,

---

56. e.g. in 2 Pet. 3:15–16.

political and religious backgrounds, and some of them go back to the days of our youth. We need deeper awareness of them and complete openness to Scripture.

Derrida's extreme position makes us think hard about our assumed (or even vaunted) objectivity in our approach to the Bible. It is so easy to be far more influenced by our upbringing, by the tradition of our church or even by certain historical positions on doctrine than we may imagine.[57] We also need to be aware that the shape of our Christian experience can influence our interpretation of Scripture. It is helpful when the two coincide, but if they do not we may interpret Scripture in terms of a form of piety which is really alien to it.

Strange as it may seem, there are times when the biblical language used in the church may actually militate against accurate understanding of Scripture. It is, for example, all too easy for us to make a mistake in our understanding of such terms as 'minister', 'elder', 'deacon', 'evangelist', in their use in the New Testament. We may assume that our own experience of the way these terms are used today reflects accurately the meaning they have in the New Testament, when it may not. J. B. Lightfoot's excursus on the Christian ministry in his commentary on Philippians is a model in this respect, for even though he was himself a bishop he showed convincingly that the terms *episkopos* ('bishop') and *presbyteros* ('elder') apply to the very same people in the New Testament.[58] Here, then, is where exegesis and biblical theology are of practical value.

Don Carson writes, 'Religious knowledge is close to impossible if we fail to recognize our own assumptions, questions, interests, and biases, but if we recognize them and, in dialogue with the text, seek to make allowances for them, we will be better able to avoid confusing our own world-views with those of the biblical writers.'[59] This is where the 'hermeneutic of suspicion' can be of such real value, helping to free us from what are sometimes deeply un-Christian ideas to enable us to hear the Word of God afresh. Certainly it can be applied in an extremely sceptical way, as we have already noted, but it should never be out of our minds; we need constantly to recognize that we so often come to Scripture with personal agendas and with vested interests, and that these need to be exposed so that we can see them clearly and, by the grace of God, forsake them.

---

57. Although, as we will see, there is a place for the church in biblical interpretation.

58. J. B. Lightfoot, *Saint Paul's Epistle to the Philippians* (New York: Macmillan, 1900), pp. 181–269.

59. Carson, *Exegetical Fallacies*, pp. 106–107.

It is a feature of the Word of God that it confronts and challenges many of our assumptions, and sensitive Christian believers who seek to be responsive to the Spirit through the Word will accept such challenges and adjust their thinking and their lives accordingly. It has to be admitted that it is possible to hold on to a mistaken or inappropriate interpretation because we do not want to admit we have made a mistake or even because the true meaning is more demanding of us than the one we hold dear. So we need to be constantly self-critical in the light that comes to us from Scripture.

Thiselton says, 'A responsible hermeneutics will do something to prevent a shallow skimming from the text of the preformed viewpoints of the interpreter, now deceptively and dangerously clothed in the vestments of the authority of the text.' He then says that in this way hermeneutics can be reduced to 'a purely defensive device for maintaining the status quo of the interpretive procedures of a religious community'.[60]

Christians can find in the Bible doctrines and exhortations they do not want to believe or act upon. Accepting such is therefore a matter of obedience. The helpful term, 'a hermeneutic of obedience', is being used today in studies of the Anabaptist approach to Scripture,[61] which although at times somewhat literalistic, was mainly concerned to take Scripture seriously and to follow meticulously its calls to action, ethical, social and political.

If we follow the hermeneutic of obedience along with that of suspicion, we will turn the latter on ourselves, especially if we find ourselves interpreting Scripture in a way that makes obedience unnecessary. We should bear both kinds of hermeneutic in mind in our approach. To be under the control of the Holy Spirit is to become suspicious of ourselves but also very concerned to please God by our understanding, faith and obedience.[62]

This gives hermeneutics a moral quality. The purpose of Scripture is transformative, to change us into the image of Christ, and this strongly ethical dimension is always the final point in the hermeneutical circle when we start in that circle with exegesis.

In fact the Bible is a highly deconstructive book, the most deconstructive

---

60. In Lundin, Thiselton and Walhout, *The Responsibility of Hermeneutics*, p. 80.

61. See the treatment of Anabaptist hermeneutics in M. Stuart, *Biblical Interpretation in the Anabaptist Tradition* (Kitchener: Pandora, 2000).

62. Jacques Ellul has some helpful, if rather sharply worded, comments on this whole issue, related to the way Liberation theologians handle Scripture, yet in a way that is of wider relevance, in *Jesus and Marx: From Gospel to Ideology* (Grand Rapids: Eerdmans, 1988), pp. 76–84.

ever written. As 2 Timothy 3:16 shows ('rebuking, correcting'), a major purpose of it is to put us right by undermining our confidence in ourselves, in both our actions and our ideas. Stephen Williams, writing about Genesis 3, says that it is 'brimful of deconstructive purpose . . . It purports to expose all who would expose the narrative as themselves propelled by religious instinct, innately, characteristically, universally and compulsively a desire to dispose of God. And it does so far more directly and far less subtly than any deconstructive operations we presume to bring to bear on it.'[63]

Sometimes, however, for some writers, the hermeneutic of suspicion goes deeper still and relates not simply to the reader's interpretation of the biblical text but to the biblical writers themselves and their approach to the facts of the faith. The biblical writers interpret history, the story of God's dealings with Israel and that of Jesus Christ and his church. Were they activated by the motives the masters of suspicion think they discern in the Christian approach to the Bible?

We need to see how totally unacceptable this proposal is. It would mean that the very instrument of divine deconstruction would itself now be subject to deconstruction. Ultimately such an approach would destroy the whole Christian faith, and Christian assurance, resting on Christ, the Christ of the Bible, in fullest and gladdest confidence, cries out against it. So too does Christian obedience, for it recognizes it not only as unbelief but as opening the door to the ultimate in disobedience.

One further matter: some have said that Christians must go along with postmodernism's view that texts should be regarded as completely open and not closed in meaning. Yet if we do this, it opens the possibility that in the name of hermeneutics we may distort the gospel. Especially valuable here is the work of Umberto Eco, who held that although texts are often open to many meanings, they are not open to all meanings.[64] The text exercises a measure of control.

Biblical passages, set in their contexts, do have objective meaning. We are not at liberty to interpret Scripture in any way we like. We need to sit humbly before the Word of God, ready to be rebuked, corrected and instructed, in the confidence that the Holy Spirit will more and more open that Word to us, or rather will more and more open us to the Word.

---

63. S. Williams, *Revelation and Reconciliation* (Cambridge: Cambridge University Press, 1995), p. 106.

64. U. Eco, *A Theory of Semiotics* (Bloomington: Indiana University Press, 1976).

The role of the church

Evangelicals are used to the idea that it is Scripture and not tradition which is to be the supreme authority in all matters of faith and practice, and this is true and important. Scripture must always be the final arbiter. This does not mean, however, that there is no role for the church in interpretation.

There is increasing interest in this among evangelicals today and work is being done on the creeds and confessions and on the *regula fidei*, the rule of faith.[65] Even denominations which do not normally employ any of the historic creeds or confessions often have a common declaration of principle or principles furnishing a theological basis for their particular group.

It is worth remembering that most of the New Testament epistles were written not to individuals but to churches, that the same is true of the book of the Revelation, and is probably true also of some of the Gospels. Even the pastoral epistles, addressed to Timothy and Titus, were written to them because of their work in local churches.

We all read Scripture in the light of our context, and an important part of that context for most Christians is the culture and tradition of their church. This means that we will not lightly put aside the way the Bible has been understood in the history of the church and the way it is being handled and applied by our church today, if this is being done on a Bible-believing basis.

It is true that evangelical Christians are not in full theological agreement with each other, but it is easy to exaggerate our differences, for there is a considerable measure of doctrinal concord. Evangelical societies of various kinds usually have little difficulty in putting together a doctrinal basis which will find assent among all evangelical believers. To work for an extended period in an evangelical theological college which is interdenominational is to see this with crystal clarity, and in fact to be deeply moved by it.

Does this good measure of doctrinal unity tell us something about Scripture itself? Yes, it does. In important ways it demonstrates the triumph of the Word of God over human thinking. This is because Bible readers who are Christians often find themselves sharing insights not in tune with their natural inclinations. None of us likes the Bible's teaching about sin and judgment (until the Spirit of God radically changes our attitudes), yet Christians share convictions about these because they find them in Scripture. A truly Christian approach agrees

---

65. We note, for example, that the symposium, V. Bacote, L. C. Miguelez and D. L. Okholm (eds.), *Evangelicals and Scripture* (Downers Grove: InterVarsity Press, 2004) is subtitled *Tradition, Authority and Hermeneutics*, although the tradition referred to is largely evangelical tradition.

with God even when every human inclination is against that agreement.[66] This is true of what the Bible teaches about the sin and judgment not only of the non-Christian but also of the Christian. We accept the Bible's teaching even when it is most unflattering and undermines our pride. This is the best form of deconstruction, and it clearly has a communal as well as an individual dimension.

Is there no place today for new understanding of Scripture? Certainly there is, for the Bible is a book of riches untold and it would be presumptuous for us to think that all its truth has been already distilled. The Reformers thought of reformation, not so much as an event but as a continual process, but they were rightly concerned about extreme forms of individualism in the handling of Scripture, and such extremes did not die with their generation. Even so, it is important that the Bible in the pulpit or on the lectern should always be open, in principle if not physically, so that the church may experience that constant reformation by the Word of God.

The role of the Holy Spirit and the indispensable pre-understanding

Good hermeneutics is based at every point on the doctrine of God, on the fact that he speaks in Scripture, that we need to listen with care to what he says, that we should test all other voices by his voice, and that he is consistent, so that the principles of his action and revelation that can be seen throughout Scripture remain true for us today.

Whenever we open the Bible, we read it in the light of ideas of God and his purposes which we possess already. In theory our understanding should become more and more accurate and our theology more and more reflective of the truth of Scripture, but it has to be admitted that this does not always happen and, moreover, that the process is never complete. It is not only our sanctification that is always imperfect; it is also our understanding of the Bible. All of us retain some elements of unregenerate thinking.

So, then, must the whole idea of an objective approach to Scripture be abandoned? By no means, for it should always be there as an ideal, even though we recognize we will never attain total objectivity any more than we will ever achieve total likeness to Christ. The Holy Spirit works within us both to interpret Scripture to us and to make us like Christ, and undue scepticism is really a denial of the reality of his work. Paul is very clear that sin has affected human understanding of the things of God, but also that the Holy Spirit works within the Christian to give us understanding of God's truth (1 Cor. 2:6–16). He even says 'we have the mind of Christ'.

---

66. cf. the truly solemnizing 'Hallelujah' of the saints in Rev. 19:3.

This is why an essential prerequisite for understanding Scripture is a true Christian humility which recognizes the continual need not only for positive teaching but also for being put right where we are wrong. As we have seen, Paul alludes to these two factors in 2 Timothy 3:14–17, where he refers to 'rebuke' and 'correction' as well as 'teaching' and 'training in righteousness'. Perhaps the most serious criticism of a rationalistic approach to Scripture is that it is not easy to unite rationalism and humility.

For evangelical Christians, the authority of Scripture is basic. As we have seen, this is because conviction as to this is actually given in regeneration as well as being found in the Bible's own view of its nature and authority. The Spirit's witness in the book and his witness in the heart speak with one voice. This means that one presupposition should rule all our handling of Scripture: this is the Word of God.

One of the great blessings of this, from a hermeneutical point of view, is that our outlook can be constantly under the correction of God through his Word as the Spirit applies that Word to our thought and life, for this correction has a loving purpose, to take us further towards God's great goal for us, which is likeness to Christ. Humble willingness for correction, even to late in life, is no optional extra.

Here, then, is the proper evangelical pre-understanding, and it is not of human creation. As we saw in the previous chapter, this is not merely subjective or arbitrary. It is due to the internal testimony of the Holy Spirit. This, in fact, is internal in two ways, the one normally intended by the expression which means the testimony of the Spirit within the heart of the Christian, but the other the Spirit's testimony within the Bible itself, which teaches that it is the Word of God. When the Holy Spirit, whose inspiration gave the Word, works in the heart of the Christian believer, the Spirit initiates a response, so that the reader's response is undergirded by divine grace.

We must not, of course, forget that we are not always properly attuned to the Spirit. There needs to be constant response to his instruction, so that we 'keep in step with the Spirit' (Gal. 5:25). It is therefore time we considered the application of Scripture today.

Contemporary application and the use of analogy

This is the final hermeneutical stage. We ask how the passage relates to contemporary issues, and how it can become transformative for the individual and the church. Without this, Scripture may still be of literary interest and historical value, but we are at best ignoring and at worst denying its special status as the eternal Word of God. Goldingay has well said, 'Arguably any true biblical interpretation must eventually take the form of preaching,'[67] and Osborne, 'It is my contention that the final goal of hermeneutics is not systematic theology but the sermon.'[68]

R. L. Thomas argues that it is important to distinguish hermeneutics from application. This is due to his restriction of the term to exegesis and his rightful concern to insist on an objective meaning for the text of Scripture.[69] We may, however, still insist on this even if, with most contemporary writers on the subject, we do employ the term to embrace more than exegesis.

Here the principle of analogy is of great importance. To what extent are there parallels with today's world and with the particular situations faced by the interpreter and those to whom he or she is ministering? This is no arbitrary principle, for it is one employed by the New Testament writers in their own approach to the Old.[70] They assumed, and, following their example, we may assume, that God does not change and that, despite a multitude of cultural changes over the centuries and from country to country, human beings have not altered fundamentally. This is why, for instance, a divine rebuke through a prophet to the people of his day for their formalism could be applied by Jesus to the legalists of his day, for the attitudes of the two groups had so much in common (Matt. 15:8–9). It is this that makes the Bible so relevant to every generation of God's people.

In dealing with the story-content of the Bible, Goldingay stresses the role of imagination, in which we are first drawn into the story and the concerns of its first audience and then relate it to our own concerns.[71] Here, then, imagination and analogy go hand in hand, for analogy feeds on imagination, even though in time its imaginative basis may be forgotten.

Now application has two related aspects, the theological and the practical. These are distinguishable, but they should never be separated. We are to look at both the theological and the practical issues of our day in the light of Scripture. Moreover, because in Scripture there is always a theological basis for ethical precepts, the same must be true as we seek to relate Scripture to the issues of today.

---

67. Goldingay, *Models for Interpretation of Scripture*, p. 8.

68. Osborne, *The Hermeneutical Spiral*, p. 29.

69. Thomas, *Evangelical Hermeneutics*, pp. 171–180.

70. Typology, for instance, is used extensively in the New Testament and it is based on analogy, reflecting as it does the consistency of God.

71. Goldingay, *Models for Interpretation of Scripture*, pp. 36–39.

Theological application

If we are dealing with issues of truth, we will need to relate Bible teaching to the theological questions that are raised today.[72] A number of these are not directly addressed in Scripture. In every case, however, we will discover, as the Reformers did in their day, that there are biblical principles that bear on them.

In this there is a place for the study of historical theology. This is because we can see in it how Christians of the past have dealt with such issues and we can learn both positively and negatively from them. For the Christian this is a major use of the past. We will not be hidebound by tradition, but neither will we ignore it. Rather we will seek to learn from it and to assess it in the light of Scripture.

Practical application

The importance of this requires no arguing. Deuteronomy 29:29 lays down the important principle that for the Old Testament believer the purpose of the law was not just understanding but action ('that we may follow all the words of this law'). This is confirmed for all that is rightly called Scripture in 2 Timothy 3:16–17. This means that theology does not exist for its own sake. It should never be abstracted from life.

In the New Testament, theology is the basis of ethical judgments and exhortations. This is patently clear in the epistle to the Romans, where the theological exposition of chapters 1 – 11 is followed by the ethical exhortations in chapters 12 – 16, with 12:1–2 as the bridge between them. It was because of their apprehension of his teaching on the mercies of God that Paul exhorted the Roman Christians to present themselves to God and to be transformed in their minds and characters. It is, however, true in other cases where it is less obvious.

Practical application goes beyond ethics, although it is never unrelated to it. It applies, for example, to matters of church life. It must relate to the real issues of our time and place, but decisions should not be taken on purely pragmatic grounds.

As an example, we might take the application to church life of principles taken from business or management studies. At one time university courses on such matters were non-existent; now they are not only available but are increasingly popular. Without doubt they can be of value in church life,

---

72. Because of the overlapping concerns of theology and philosophy, philosophical ideas that are influencing theology also need to be discerned and assessed.

but there are dangers. Church leaders may be chosen on the basis of their management skills rather than their gifts of spiritual leadership. Wisdom and expediency are by no means identical. Always Bible teaching must take priority, establishing principles and norms for church action. The Bible should have as central a place in the church business meeting as it has in the pulpit.

It is sometimes said that this is a particular danger for North American churches because of the influence of pragmatic philosophy there, but it is by no means confined to them. It is right to say that the truth has practical consequences and outcomes, but not that truth may actually be defined in terms of these consequences. 'Does it work?' is not the same question as 'Is it true?' even if some think it is.

We have already noted how interrelated exegesis and biblical theology are. Now we must see the close interconnectedness of presuppositions and application. There is movement in both directions in the hermeneutical circle, and this comes to have considerable theological importance at this stage. This is because, although it is logical to consider our presuppositions before we seek to apply the theology of the passage to present-day life, our own and others, this is not how it normally happens in experience.

This is because darkness hides while light exposes. It is so often only in the light of God's truth that we see how wrong our thinking and our living are. Many preachers have found that to preach the gospel of the cross biblically is more effective in making the listeners smartingly aware of their sin than to preach very specifically about sin itself, although there is certainly a place for the latter. In harmony with this, although we may see repentance as logically prior to faith, it is so often when we turn our eyes on Christ in faith that we turn in abhorrence from our sins.

Osborne, who makes a helpful distinction between presuppositions, which may be positive,[73] and prejudices, which are always negative, goes on to say, 'The interpreter must not only address the text, but allow the text to address him or her (the hermeneutical circle). In exegesis, our presuppositions/preunderstanding must be modified and reshaped by the text. The text must have priority over the interpreter.'[74]

The challenge of the text to both our own understanding and our own attitudes and consequent actions must both precede and accompany our ministry to others. There should never be a situation in which we simply abstract

---

73. An example of this could be that what we are reading is the Word of God.

74. Osborne, *The Hermeneutical Spiral*, p. 517.

it from our own personal lives and preach it to others. Truth is for living, and it is not just for your life but for mine.

A fourfold appraisal of a theological viewpoint

The main purpose of this book is to appraise particular theological positions. How can hermeneutics help us as we seek to do this? What we have seen already in this chapter suggests we should apply four tests.

First of all, we should look at the way key biblical passages are interpreted. Every text is important, of course, but there are often passages which assume some special importance for a theological viewpoint. Are they handled properly, or have they been interpreted in a way that does less than justice to their contexts? Sometimes contextual patterns, our own or those we have learned from others, if they become ingrained in our minds, may hinder the freshness which should always characterize our approach to the biblical text. Many years ago, after prolonged study of the epistle to the Romans, I constructed an outline of the book. I used this for a long time in a number of different teaching situations. I realized later that it had come to hinder me from taking fresh approaches to the text.

Closely related to exegesis is a critical estimate of the author's biblical theology. Has he or she kept the grand story of Scripture and its interpretation by the biblical writers in view? What about the great themes that arise out of that story? An individual passage may appear to be rightly understood in terms of its immediate context and yet this interpretation may become open to doubt when set in the context of the wider story or the general theme.

These first two tests obviously impinge on each other, as the way we understand an important passage can affect our interpretation of the whole Bible and vice versa.

Then we consider the influence of non-biblical ideas. These are not always declared; in fact at times the writers concerned may be unaware of their influence. We all absorb a great deal from the environment of ideas in which we do our thinking. In making an appraisal we need to take account of the fact that it is not only the prejudices of others that come into play, but our own, leading either to approval or disapproval of the thought of the writer concerned.

Finally, we must look at the way the theology is applied to contemporary issues, both theological and practical. Is the application natural or is it forced? How do the courses of action suggested fit with the ethical precepts and standards found in the Bible? In what way or ways, when they are taken seriously, do they effect transformation in the thought and life of the readers?

Thiselton says (approvingly), 'It is almost commonplace nowadays for those who write on biblical hermeneutics to stress the formative and transformative impact of biblical texts,' and he goes on to say that this is true of Christian doctrine too.[75]

These tests need not necessarily be applied consecutively nor in a pedantic manner. What matters is that they should all be borne in mind as of fundamental importance in considering a theological position.

We must remember, of course, that this testing should not be applied only to the theology of others, but also to our own. J. I. Packer has well said,

> If [the interpreter's] exegetical procedure is challenged, he defends it from his hermeneutic; if his hermeneutic is challenged, he defends it from his doctrine of biblical authority; if his doctrine of biblical authority is challenged, he defends it from biblical texts by exegesis, synthesis and application. At no point does he decline to accept challenges to his present view of things, but at every point he meets them by renewed theological exegesis of relevant passages in the light of the questions that have been asked.[76]

A specific example

A famous and widely influential example of an interpretation which fails to take adequate account of context occurs in the work of Rudolf Bultmann. In 2 Corinthians 5:16, as rendered in the NIV, Paul says, 'So from now on we regard no-one from a worldly point of view. Though we once regarded Christ in this way, we do so no longer.' The phrase 'from a worldly point of view' is rendered more literally in the English Standard Version as 'according to the flesh'. Does this phrase modify the verb 'regard' or qualify the noun 'Christ'? Bultmann took it that it was the latter and he concluded from this verse that Paul was not interested in the earthly life of Jesus. This is, however, quite alien to the context, which the NIV rendering takes fully into account. F. F. Bruce, quoting Bultmann and commenting on his interpretation, says that 'the interpretation of the text can only be read out of the text if it is first read into it'.[77]

---

75. Thiselton, *The Hermeneutics of Doctrine*, p. 81.
76. J. I. Packer, 'Infallible Scripture and the Role of Hermeneutics', in D. A. Carson and J. D. Woodbridge (eds.), *Scripture and Truth* (Grand Rapids: Baker, 1992), p. 349.
77. F. F. Bruce, 'Jesus and Paul', *Theological Students' Bulletin* 46 (Autumn, 1966), p. 22.

But should not attention to biblical theology, with its emphasis on history, have raised doubts about this interpretation in Bultmann's mind? A truly biblical theology has to take very seriously the teaching of both Testaments, and a superficial reading of some of Bultmann's works might give the impression that he had little time for the Old Testament, but, as D. L. Baker has shown in his balanced summary of his view, this is not true.[78] Bultmann did recognize both continuity and discontinuity between the Testaments, nevertheless he held that although in the Old Testament God's revelation came through his acts in history, now God's act in Christ has brought God's people into a new era in which the actual fact of Christ is very important but its historical details are not. In fact he showed himself to be a thoroughgoing reductionist in his attitude to the narratives in the Gospels.

Clearly there are some important presuppositions operating here, and they come from the influence on Bultmann both of rationalism and of Martin Heidegger's existentialist philosophy, which emphasized the importance of moving from what he called 'inauthentic' existence to 'authentic' through a life-changing decision. Bultmann gave this a Christian flavour. For him, as we mentioned earlier, Christian commitment was to a life-pattern of crucifixion and resurrection with Christ, the classic expression of which is in Romans 6.

This might sound orthodox enough, until we find that his rationalism led him to conclude that although the crucifixion was real (the only event in the Gospels which Bultmann regarded as certain to have happened), the resurrection was mythical, as were the incarnation, the virgin birth, the miracles, the transfiguration, references to angels and demons and so on, in fact everything in the Gospels with a supernatural flavour.[79] Here the historical content of the Christian faith is reduced to one event and its true theological content evaporates into mythology and is replaced by existentialist philosophy. This outlook is not only not evangelical (which Bultmann never claimed to be in the sense of this book), but it is hard to describe it as Christian at all.

What, then, are the theological and practical consequences of this interpretation of 2 Corinthians 5:16? It means that we can give no theological significance to the life of Jesus except for the bare fact that he was crucified. If so,

---

78. Baker, *Two Testaments, One Bible*, pp. 63–78.

79. See P. E. Hughes, *Scripture and Myth: An Examination of Rudolf Bultmann's Plea for Demythologization* (London: Tyndale Press, 1956). I was present when Philip Hughes gave the public lecture which formed the basis of this monograph, and remember the gasp from the audience after he had read out Bultmann's long list (which was even longer than the selection noted above) of so-called Gospel 'myths'.

then how can prayerful meditation on what the Gospels tell us of him be of real Christian value when its factual basis has gone?

In all this we can see that philosophy has taken over from both the narrower and the wider biblical contexts as the main means of interpreting this text. There can be no doubt that a proper hermeneutical method is vitally important if we are to retain the authentic biblical gospel.

In conclusion

Two things should be said, one arising from the human characteristics of Scripture, and the other from the fact that it is the Word of God.

First, in hermeneutics context is everything. We need to recognize the literary, the historical and the theological contexts of the writers, and also the cultures of the contemporary social and ecclesiastical worlds in which we do our own work today,[80] not forgetting the context of our own life and thought.

Second, good hermeneutics is based at every point on the doctrine of God, on the fact that he speaks in Scripture, that we need to listen with care to what he says, that we should test all other voices by his voice, and that he is consistent, so that the principles of his action and revelation that can be seen throughout Scripture remain true for us today.

To speak or write of 'contextual theology'[81] is to handle a very large concept indeed, in fact an all-embracing one, for 'contextual' reminds us of the human factor and 'theology' of the divine, both factors all-embracing, because the Bible is fully a human book and fully a divine one, and in it the message of God comes to us in and through human language. It is this that gives importance to the theme of the present book, because nothing can be more important, for ourselves and for those we influence, than that we should rightly understand and faithfully obey the Word of God.

Please join with me in asking the Lord to enable us by his Spirit to do just that.

---

80. These are the 'two horizons' of hermeneutics, a phrase originating with Hans-Georg Gadamer, whose great interest was in the 'fusion of horizons'. These two phrases have become influential in biblical hermeneutics through the writings of A. C. Thiselton.

81. It is a pity that 'contextualize' tends now to be used more in connection with what the text means than with what it meant. I am using it in the wider rather than the narrower sense.

7. WHITHER EVANGELICALISM?

I hope this volume will be of help to many readers with a serious interest in Christian theology, but the matters with which it deals should be of special concern to ministers and theological students. These are actual or potential leaders whose highly responsible calling and privilege involves the preaching and teaching of the Word of God. They may appreciate some suggested guidelines as they continue to survey and to participate in the theological scene in the churches.

We should continue to stress that Christianity is based on the biblical gospel

Personal Christian conduct and Christian social involvement are important, indeed indispensable, and they should never be divorced. Some Christians tend to emphasize what has been called 'the moral agenda' of the church, placing their emphasis on the Ten Commandments and on Christian personal morality generally. Others, while not discounting this, stress instead 'the social agenda', and are concerned about social, political and environmental issues. Moral agenda Christians tend to be to the right of centre politically, while social agenda Christians tend to be to the left, although there are many exceptions to this generalization. Just as the prescriptions of the

Old Testament law and the social concerns of the Old Testament prophets should not be treated as if they were in conflict, so we should not polarize these two agendas.

What is common to both groups is their concern with practical issues, and for this reason some readers may wonder whether this book is putting the emphasis in the right place. Surely, they may say, the real issues for our churches are practical ones. Our needy world so badly needs to see the love of Christ in action, both in evangelism and social service and also in any aware-ness people may have of what goes on in our churches, and this is far more important than whether we are accurate in our theology.

This kind of argument can be very persuasive and it is important to take it with due seriousness. Our theology may be impeccable, but if the people of our town or village know that our church is a hotbed of gossip, that many of its members do not get on with each other, and that we have no interest in the problems of the society in which we live, who will give our gospel a hearing?

Such entirely appropriate concerns should not, however, blind us to the fact that there could be no church at all without the gospel, that the whole basis of the Christian life, both individual and corporate, is the Christian message, and that the authenticity of this depends on its conformity to Scripture. Lose this, and personal conduct and social involvement will eventually be based on little more than humanitarianism using Christian language.

A somewhat strange passage in Paul's writings shows with crystal clarity the great importance he attached to the Christian message. In Philippians 1:15–18 he makes reference to some who preach Christ with low motives, and then says, 'The important thing is that in every way, whether from false motives or true, Christ is preached. And because of this I rejoice.' This is very striking, not simply as a testimony to Paul's graciousness, but as a clear indication that to him the gospel as the message of God was of supreme importance. It can be no less so for us.

It is important also to say, however, that it is very doubtful if small differ-ences of doctrine dealing with side issues should stop us from cooperating in the work of the Lord. Having worked for many years in an evangelical Bible college setting, I have seen how rarely any such differences have caused prob-lems either in cooperative teaching situations or in the practical work students have done in cooperation with local churches. It is the big issues, affecting the nature of the gospel itself, that are crucial.

We should apply a gospel test to both theological and practical issues

Not all the issues facing us today are explicitly theological, for some are ethical, although the ethical issues are normally theologically based. For instance, ethical questions about sexuality, abortion and marriage take their rise from the Christian doctrine of humanity. We should get into the habit of relating everything to the gospel, seeing how it affects and is affected by the gospel.

We can see evidence that the apostle Paul did this. In 1 Corinthians he deals with a number of questions that were current in the Corinthian church, some theological and others practical. It is worth going through this epistle and seeing how each of these issues relates to the gospel.

The most obvious example is the one that dominates chapter 15. Here Paul is addressing the question of the resurrection of the dead, which apparently some were denying. He says,

> For what I received I passed on to you as of first importance: that Christ died for our sins according to the Scriptures, that he was buried, that he was raised on the third day according to the Scriptures . . . If there is no resurrection of the dead, then not even Christ has been raised. And if Christ has not been raised, our preaching is useless and so is your faith . . . And if Christ has not been raised, your faith is futile; you are still in your sins. Then those who have fallen asleep in Christ are lost.
> (1 Cor. 15:3–4, 13–14, 17–18)

Here Paul employs impeccable theological logic. All logical argument must have its starting point, and Paul's is the gospel.

In 1 Corinthians 6:12–20 he is dealing with sexual immorality. His treatment of it is related throughout to the union Christians have with Christ, and he ends by saying, 'You are not your own; you were bought at a price. Therefore honour God with your body' (vv. 19–20). Note the logical word 'therefore' which ties the ethical precept to the gospel.

These are simply two particularly clear examples, but this is a general feature of the letter. It is worth reflecting on the following passages: 1 Corinthians 1:22–25; 2:1–5; 3:10–11; 5:6–8; 6:9–11; 7:23; 8:11–13; 9:12, 16–23; 10:14–17; 11:23–26 and 12:3. To consider these passages, which all make reference to aspects of the gospel, to relate them to the contexts in which they appear and to the issues Paul is addressing in them, shows clearly that in each case the gospel is crucially relevant.

Lest we overlook it, it is worth pointing out that he also deals in this epistle with party spirit, devoting four whole chapters to it (1 – 4), but even here (as the references in the previous paragraph show), he never loses sight of the gospel. So, then, let us keep working and praying for a spirit of unity in the churches to which we belong, but let us also keep constantly in view the need to be true to the message God has given us to proclaim. As our Lord said about another matter, 'You should have practised the latter, without neglecting the former' (Matt. 23:23).

We may sometimes find ourselves in debate with non-Christians on some theological or practical matters, or with those who profess Christ but whose theology is not evangelical. When, however, there are issues among evangelical Christians there is always the gospel court of appeal. All the main issues we have been facing in this book are current among evangelicals, and their importance is due to the fact that they all relate to the gospel, for the gospel starts with the God who in his grace has provided it (ch. 2), it centres in the Christ whose atoning death has secured it (ch. 3), it promises a new justified status with God through faith which the Holy Spirit induces (ch. 4), and the assurance of all this comes through the Word of God in holy Scripture (ch. 5), which needs to be properly interpreted (ch. 6).

This means that we all need to give much deeper thought to the gospel and its many-sided implications. To hear the gospel presented faithfully, clearly and winsomely and in the power of the Holy Spirit should always be a joy to Christians, and it should always stimulate our minds as well as warming our hearts. It is indeed a simple message which can be presented so clearly and so attractively in the power of the Spirit that a child can understand it and embrace it, but it also has profound depths that the deepest Christian thinker will never exhaust.

It also means that we will recognize secondary issues to be secondary, minor issues to be minor. As Christians totally committed to the gospel we need each other and we should 'make every effort to keep the unity of the Spirit through the bond of peace' (Eph. 4:3). Not only so, but the unity of Christians whose central concern is the biblical gospel is an important part of our witness to the world. Romans 14 – 15 show Paul at his most conciliatory. The man whose passionate concern for the preservation of the authentic gospel burned so strongly in his epistle to the Galatians could here say to two groups who were critical of each other, 'Accept one another, then, just as Christ accepted you, in order to bring praise to God' (Rom. 15:7).

Even here, though, it is the gospel that is the test, not this time for its discriminating but for its uniting power. Paul saw clearly that the issue that was in danger of producing division in the church at Rome did not affect the gospel (even though some in the two parties may have thought it did) and therefore it should be resolved in a spirit of love. No doubt we can all think of situations in our churches, either past or present, which come into this category and which were or are therefore a call to a deeper love which springs from a deeper discipleship rather than a divisive spirit which may even lead to actual division.

We should be both alert and open

We need to be theologically vigilant and yet at the same time we should not cultivate closed minds. It is very tempting, but unwise, on finding something apparently unscriptural in a book by a particular writer, to dismiss his or her writings comprehensively. Experience shows that a writer may make a variety of theological contributions, some of which may be of positive value while others may be more doubtful.[1]

We may take as an example the writings of C. H. Dodd, who did not profess to be an evangelical in the sense in which that word is being used in this book. In his work *The Apostolic Preaching and its Developments*,[2] he showed very helpfully that the one gospel message or kerygma is the theologically uniting element in all the New Testament literature, although what he wrote on its developments raises some questions. His work *According to the Scriptures*[3] is helpful too, for in it he showed that when the New Testament writers quoted the Old Testament they intended their readers to understand the quoted passages in their Old Testament contexts. He says also that they clearly learned this approach from Jesus himself. On the other hand, his view that the wrath of God is the operation of an impersonal principle and his rejection of the propitiatory significance of the work of Christ are unacceptable,[4] and if we take them on board we lose vital elements in the gospel. We may find the same ambivalence in the writings of a few current writers who, unlike Dodd, are regarded as evangelicals.

To contract out of academic debate in theology or biblical scholarship is certainly not the way. Experience shows that obscurantism may stifle doubts

---

1. Much, of course, depends on the spiritual and theological maturity of the reader, and those who are young in the faith or new to theological reading are encouraged to get advice from a much more experienced friend.

2. C. H. Dodd, *The Apostolic Preaching and its Developments, Three Lectures with an Eschatology and History* (London: Harper and Row, 1964).

3. C. H. Dodd, *According to the Scriptures: The Substructure of New Testament Theology* (London: Nisbet, 1957).

4. See pp. 108–109.

for a while, but they have a way of exacting considerable vengeance later. Not only so, but we have been told to contend for the faith once for all entrusted to the saints (Jude 3). Moreover, there is much we can learn from dialogue with others, provided (and this is vitally important) we are sufficiently perceptive, and true Christian perceptiveness is the product of the Holy Spirit's work in us in response to the inspired truth of the Word of God.

We should learn lessons from the present that will stand us in good stead for the future, and it is to be hoped that this book will have value from this point of view. We need to discern the signs of the times, to be reading our Bibles and estimating trends in general culture, in philosophy and most of all in theology, in the light of Scripture. We need to pray for evangelical theologians who are wrestling with today's issues.

We should learn from the history of theology, particularly nineteenth- and twentieth-century theology, that if a philosophy with theological implications becomes influential we are bound sooner or later to see some effects on theology, and then, through the preaching of those affected by the latest trends in theology, on the life of the churches. The philosopher's study, the theologian's classroom, the preacher's pulpit, the church member's mind, heart and conduct – that is so often the order.

What should we be watching just now?

We ought to be particularly concerned with the following elements.

Developments in philosophy

Philosophy has occupied our attention frequently in the course of this volume, and its importance for our subject is difficult to exaggerate. A theological course designed to prepare Christians for service in today's world but which involves no engagement with philosophy is seriously deficient. The word 'engagement' is important, for we need to engage in apologetics, and so to go beyond historical description of philosophical movements to confront the challenges that come to us and to our theology from contemporary philosophies. When this is done at a sufficient level of maturity it can be most helpful, strengthening faith.

This is where theological course construction takes on a pastoral dimension. Many years ago Glasgow University, even though it was a secular teaching institution, would not enrol younger first-year students in classes in moral philosophy, because they were not reckoned mature enough to cope with it. The early part of a theology course should be strongly positive, with particular emphasis on the contents of Scripture and on the great doctrines of the Christian faith. This is particularly important today when the theological input many students get in their churches, including many evangelical churches, is often so thin, so weak in biblical substance.

This does not mean that students should be subjected to a kind of evangelical brainwashing. The questions are to be faced realistically, but this needs to be done at the right time and in the right way. To launch students into engagement with philosophy at too early a stage can produce theological casualties, but never to embark on this at all is likewise unhelpful. To see that the Christian faith can stand all that is cast at it by leading influential thinkers is not only very encouraging, but an important aspect of preparation for the Lord's service.

Students should be introduced to the Christian world view, the great biblical metanarrative, as the theological structure in which they can view everything. As C. S. Lewis, himself no mean apologist, once marvellously said, 'I believe in Christianity as I believe that the sun has risen, not only because I see it but because by it I see everything else.'[5]

Developments particularly in the philosophy of language

We recognize the authority of a particular literature, the sixty-six books of the Bible, and so anything which touches the approach to and interpretation of language and literature must concern us.

For nearly two centuries now it is epistemology, theory of knowledge, which has occupied centre stage in philosophy and this centrality shows no signs of diminishing. More recently there has been a still more specialized focus on the philosophy of language, which is, of course, a very important aspect of epistemology. There may be other ways of knowing besides the use of words, for instance through the imagination, but the importance of verbal understanding and verbal communication needs no arguing. Some of the approaches advocated by these philosophers have been helpful, as in the case of speech-act theory, while others have been the opposite. We need discernment.

Developments in postmodernism

As we have seen, especially in relation to the doctrine of Scripture, both modernism and postmodernism have considerable implications for theology. We

---

5. In a 1944 address reprinted in a collection of his essays, C. S. Lewis, *The Weight of Glory* (Grand Rapids: Zondervan, 2001), p. 140.

will be interested to see if the movement away from modernism to postmodernism becomes even more general than it already is, or if there is some reaction against it. Is it a passing phase, or will it go on for many decades? What effects will it have on the educational world? Can people live in the long term with a largely unstructured view of things? Do not our minds demand that we structure knowledge and experience?

Many people today, especially younger people, find themselves drawn to postmodernism and yet they still make use, even increasing use, of the technology which has been produced as a result of modern science. We want more and more of it – faster planes, speedier broadband, more effective medicine, and so on. How inconsistent can we be, to what extent can we live with such a disjunction between theory and practice, before we come to a stop and start to take stock of the situation?

Unstated presuppositions in both philosophy and theology

Without doubt attention to presuppositions is the first principle of valid criticism. Failure to note such is often what distinguishes a poor from a good book review. We may laugh when we hear yet again the hackneyed example, 'When did you stop beating your wife?' but wrong presuppositions are no laughing matter when they occur in theology.

When we are estimating the value of our personal libraries, we recognize that we need to weigh the books in terms of their content rather than simply count them. Yet there are popular, even comparatively trivial books that some of us will need to read. Those with particular pastoral responsibilities should be aware of books that are proving Christian best-sellers and should read them with attention to their presuppositions so as to enable them to guide others. Some years ago I read an appallingly bad book by an evangelical writer. Its faults were so glaring that I could not believe it would have much influence. I was wrong.

Our own presuppositions about Christ and the Bible will be attacked, perhaps even ridiculed, but we should admit them, stand by them and defend them and if we have teaching responsibilities encourage those we teach to do the same. As we have already noted, reasoning must always have a starting point, and our Christian beliefs are not irrational but involve reasoning from a distinctively Christian starting point.

Trends in the general culture of our time

We have already noted that trends in philosophy often affect general culture and influence the thinking of people who have never heard of the philosophers concerned. We need also to remember, though, that our culture is subject to many non-philosophical influences, at least influences that are not explicitly philosophical. These include political propaganda, high-pressure advertising, newspapers and television.

Of course, every human culture is a mixed phenomenon. Just as total depravity does not mean that every human is as bad as he or she can be, but rather that every part of human nature has been marred by sin, so the effects of sin on the environment in which human beings live is by no means total. God still has his witness both in the human heart and in the external world. Much Reformed theology has promoted the doctrine of common grace, the idea that God's Spirit is at work in human culture to conserve some truth amongst the error, some beauty in the midst of ugliness, some morality alongside wickedness. This is not saving grace, which comes only through the gospel, but it ensures that there is a difference between our present society and hell.

There are also negative influences. Can the music we listen to have a theological effect? Yes, it can, and not only in the lyrics of popular songs. To listen constantly, for instance, to music that is grindingly discordant or largely formless can communicate to us a feeling that we live in a world which is totally discordant and formless, when in fact God has given both form and harmony to his universe.

Trends in Christian worship

Styles of worship vary considerably today. Some churches are more traditional, others more contemporary, while still others seek to blend the two. Worship is, of course, directed to God, and it is much more important that it should glorify God than that it should appeal to the worshippers. Nevertheless, if the minds and hearts of the worshippers are to be fully engaged in it (and worship should always be an engagement of our whole being), it needs to be meaningful to the worshippers themselves. No doubt there will be wide agreement as to this principle even if there is disagreement as to its implementation.

It is a mistake to consider only the music. This is not unimportant, but the words are all-important, because the words of hymns and worship songs have theological significance. This means that in our churches the sermon is not the only means by which teaching is conveyed. We teach by the way our services are conducted and by the hymns or Christian songs our congregations are taught to sing.

Many of these, both the older hymns and many of the modern Christian songs, are full of good Christian truth, but this is not true of them all. We should remember particularly that the older ones have been passed through the sieve of history, with the poorer ones becoming gradually excluded, whereas this has yet to happen to the modern ones. It has to be said that some are almost totally devoid of true Christian content and others tend to distort the balance of Scripture. Songs which emphasize the exaltation of Christ are very popular today, but many of them rarely mention that the Christ who is exalted is also the one who was crucified. The supreme worship book of the New Testament is the book of the Revelation and the exalted Christ is there characterized over and over again as 'the Lamb', a constant reminder of his sacrifice for our sins.

A worship leader is as much in need of theological instruction as the preacher, although obviously not in so much detail, and a primary task of the pastor should be to see that such instruction is given. The consequences of failure to do this can be serious, even in some cases potentially disastrous.

Then we should be concerned about possible low-key prosperity theology. It is not only good but highly desirable that there should be prayer for the sick in our churches, but if it takes too big a place it may give the impression that the health of the body is as important as the health of the soul. It is a matter of proportion. It is good, too, to encourage Christians to believe we can trust the providence of God for the supply of our needs, but we should beware of anything which promotes the idea that a main concern of God is our comfort, especially if it overshadows the call of Christ to deny ourselves, to take up our cross and to follow him. To sideline both the atoning cross of Jesus and the discipleship cross of the Christian is very serious.

There can also be an overemphasis on the charismatic gifts. We can be thankful for every gift Christ has graciously given through the Holy Spirit to his church, but, as 1 Corinthians makes clear to us, some can be overemphasized. This can draw too much attention to those exercising the gifts, diverting attention from Christ himself. F. D. Bruner points out the importance of reading each of the two Corinthian epistles in the light of the other.[6] The focus on the gifts in part of the first letter should be balanced by the focus in the concluding chapters of the second on the Christian's weakness. To exalt the gifts at the expense of the weakness is to give the impression that the work of the Spirit in equipping us for service is more important than his sanctifying work. It can even lead to moral shipwreck.

Churches have good reason to be grateful to God when the Holy Spirit gives some of their members deeper insight into God's truth and its practical implication, but it is possible for a stress on contemporary prophecy to

---

6. F. D. Bruner, *The Doctrine of the Holy Spirit: The Pentecostal Experience and the New Testament Witness* (Grand Rapids: Eerdmans, 1970), pp. 285–319.

overshadow Scripture itself, suggesting particularly to young Christians not simply that such prophecy is equal to Scripture in status, but that it is superior to it as a means of grace with practical application to today's church.[7]

It is not legalism nor ritualism to make a point of ensuring that there is always a reading from Scripture in every service in our churches, but simply the honouring of God's truth. If the Bible is not only read publicly, but this reading is also done superbly, with due attention to clarity and to proper points of emphasis, and in a prayerful spirit, in other words after adequate preparation, this carries its own message about the importance of God's Word.[8] The psalmist says, 'You have exalted above all things your name and your word' (Ps. 138:2). If God has done that, should we do any less?

If these various elements of concern occur together frequently in our worship, we are in danger of moving eventually towards something that is little more than Christianized humanism. Something rather like the hermeneutical circle can take place so that unsatisfactory practice induces unsatisfactory theology, which then makes the practice still more unsatisfactory, and so on. The end of all this inevitably is the loss of the gospel itself.

The special importance of Christology

We have been thinking about the gospel and so inevitably have been referring frequently to 'it', but there is nothing impersonal about the Christian message. From start to finish it is about personal relations between the amazingly gracious God and us, the needy sinners who have rebelled against him. Paul said, 'For to me, to live is Christ and to die is gain' (Phil. 1:21), and this, not because he was looking forward simply to 'heaven', for such expectation can degenerate into idle speculation, but because he would 'be with Christ, which is better by far' (Phil. 1:24).

---

7. I have not dealt with the charismatic movement in this book. My own view is that some aspects of it are to be welcomed while others are a cause for concern. It is clearly a mixed phenomenon which has passed through a number of phases. It would be quite impossible to do justice to it in such a volume as this.

8. The preacher would also be wise to weigh up prayerfully the pros and cons of displaying the reading on a screen. This can be good for those members of the congregation who rarely open a Bible, but we need to find ways of encouraging the personal use of the Bible, and following the passage by reading it in my own Bible may be helpful to this end.

Not only so, but the Christ of the gospel is no vague, ethereal figure but Someone about whom God has revealed a very great deal, a real Person who lived and died and rose again in the real world, in an earlier period in the history of the same world as we live in day by day. The gospel is not a set of truths, even timeless truths, which can exist without historical foundation. It is solidly based on biblical history and, of course, supremely on the revelation of God in the history of a particular Man, the God-Man Jesus Christ. Who he was and is forms the touchstone of authentic Christianity.

The classic statement of Christology is the fifth-century Definition of Chalcedon, which builds on but goes further than the Nicene Creed, for it deals not only with the deity and humanity of Jesus but also with the union of his two natures in his one Person. In this he is confessed as 'one and the same Christ, Son, Lord, Only-begotten, made known in two natures, without confusion, without change, without division, without separation; the difference of the natures being by no means removed because of the union, but the property of each nature being preserved and coalescing in one *prosopon* and one *hypostasis*'.[9]

The Chalcedonian formula sometimes provokes negative reactions, which is somewhat understandable if this is because of its abstract nature. Abstractions are unavoidable, but it is right to insist that they must not replace the concrete Reality: the Son of God, the Last Adam, our wonderful Saviour and Lord. Their function is, however, to secure, not to obscure, the great biblical truths concerning him.

There have also, however, been some reactions against the Greek terms employed in this historic definition. Yes, they reflect the issues of their day, and yes, we would do well to seek for present-day equivalents of them. But if we do find such they must conserve the biblical truths just as adequately as the Greek ones did. The ancient formulae may not be sacrosanct (although we would be foolish to dispense with them altogether), but the biblical truths are. Fully divine, fully human, yet one indivisible Person – these truths are not negotiable.

At present and probably in the foreseeable future, the most likely source from which biblical Christology could be undermined is to be found in our multifaith society. We have to face it that the devotion to their religion of some of our non-Christian neighbours may put us to shame. But this should

---

9. Quoted in J. N. D. Kelly, *Early Christian Doctrines*, 2nd ed. (London: Adam and Charles Black, 1960), p. 340. The two transliterated Greek words both translate into English as 'person'.

challenge our own devotion, not divert it. I have tried elsewhere to suggest some guidelines in this respect.[10]

There are some truths that belong to the circumference of our faith, others that are more central to it,[11] but at its very heart is Christ himself, who has embraced us with his marvellous grace, whom we love, in whom we trust, whose service is our great privilege and our perfect freedom, to whom we give our worship and who will receive that worship to all eternity.

We should note, though, that there is an important sense in which Christian truth is indivisible.

It is possible for us to move away from scriptural truth in other theological areas and in so doing to promote ideas which will eventually touch the Person of our Lord. For example, any ecclesiology which unduly exalts particular offices in the church may threaten in practice the lordship of Christ because he is the Head of the church, and any misconception of the nature of human beings will affect our view of him, because of his true and perfect humanity.

Lord, keep us true to you, and by your Spirit enable us to bear a vital and consistent testimony to you in every circumstance as the day of your glorious coming draws ever nearer!

---

10. In *The Christ of the Bible and of the Christian Faith* (Fearn: Christian Focus Publications, 1998), pp. 261–276.

11. In this book we have been largely concerned with the latter.

BIBLIOGRAPHIES

Chapter 1

ANDERSON, J., *Paradox in Christian Theology: An Analysis of its Presence, Character and Epistemic Status* (Carlisle: Paternoster, 2007).

BARCLAY, O., *Developing a Christian Mind* (Leicester: Inter-Varsity Press, 1984).

—, *Evangelicalism in Britain 1935–1995: A Personal Sketch* (Leicester: Inter-Varsity Press, 1997).

BARR, J., *The Semantics of Biblical Language* (Oxford: Oxford University Press, 1961).

BEBBINGTON, D. W., *Evangelicalism in Modern Britain: A History from the 1730s to the 1980s* (London: Unwin Hyman, 1989).

COLLINS, C. J., *The God of Miracles: An Exegetical Examination of God's Action in the World* (Leicester: Apollos, 2001).

DOOYEWEERD, H., *A New Critique of Theoretical Thought*, 4 vols. (Lampeter: Edwin Mellen, 1997).

GÄRTNER, B., *The Areopagus Speech and Natural Revelation*, tr. C. H. King (Lund: Gleerup, 1955).

HOOK, S. (ed.), *Religious Experience and Truth* (New York: New York University Press, 1961).

HORN, B., *Ultimate Realities: Finding the Heart of Evangelical Belief*, 2nd ed. (Leicester: Inter-Varsity Press, 1999).

IRENAEUS, *Against Heresies*, in *The Ante-Nicene Fathers*, vol. 1 (Grand Rapids: Eerdmans, 1973), pp. 309–567.

McGrath, A., *A Passion for Truth: The Intellectual Coherence of Evangelicalism* (Leicester: Apollos, 1996).

Marshall, I. H., *Beyond the Bible: Moving from Scripture to Theology* (Grand Rapids: Baker, 2004).

Olson, R. E., 'Postconservative Evangelical Theology and the Theological Pilgrimage of Clark Pinnock', in S. E. Porter and A. R. Cross (eds.), *Semper Reformandum: Essays in Honour of Clark H. Pinnock* (Carlisle: Paternoster, 2003), pp. 16–37.

Packer, J. I., *Knowing God*, 2nd ed. (London: Hodder and Stoughton, 1993).

Weinandy, T. G., *Does God Suffer?* (Edinburgh: T. & T. Clark, 2000).

Wells, D. F., *The Courage to Be Protestant: Truth, Marketers and Emergents in the Postmodern World* (Nottingham: Inter-Varsity Press, 2008).

Chapter 2

Augustine, 'On the Holy Trinity', in *The Nicene and Post-Nicene Fathers*, vol. 3 (Edinburgh: T. & T. Clark, 1974), pp. 125–133.

Basinger, D. and R. Basinger, 'Theodicy: A Comparative Analysis', in S. E. Porter and A. R. Cross, *Semper Reformandum: Essays in Honour of Clark H. Pinnock* (Carlisle: Paternoster, 2003), pp. 144–159.

Berkouwer, G. C., *Sin* (Grand Rapids: Eerdmans, 1971).

Bloch, E., *Atheism in Christianity: The Religion of the Exodus and the Kingdom* (New York: Herder and Herder, 1972).

Book of Common Prayer (Oxford: Oxford University Press, n.d.).

Boyd, G. A., *God of the Possible* (Grand Rapids: Baker, 2000).

Bright, J., *Covenant and Promise: The Future in the Preaching of the Pre-Exilic Prophets* (London: SCM, 1977).

Brueggemann, W., *Theology of the Old Testament: Testimony, Dispute, Advocacy* (Minneapolis: Fortress, 1997).

Caneday, A. B., 'Veiled Glory: God's Self-Revelation in Human Likeness – a Biblical Theology of God's Anthropomorphic Self-Disclosure', in Piper et al. (eds.), *Beyond the Bounds: Open Theism and the Undermining of Biblical Christianity* (Wheaton: Crossway, 2003), pp. 149–199.

Carson, D. A., *The Gagging of God: Christianity Confronts Pluralism* (Leicester: Apollos, 1996).

—, 'The Gospel of Matthew', in F. E. Gaebelein (ed.), *Expositor's Bible Commentary*, vol. 8 (Grand Rapids: Zondervan, 1984), pp. 3–599.

Clines, D. J. A., 'Humanity as the Image of God', *On the Way to the Postmodern, Old Testament Essays 1967–1998*, vol. 2, *JSOT* Supp. 292 (Sheffield: Sheffield Academic, 1998), pp. 447–497.

EDWARDS, J., *Freedom of the Will* (New York: Cosimo Classics, 2007).

FAIRBAIRN, A. M., *The Place of Christ in Christian Theology*, 2nd ed. (London: Hodder and Stoughton, 1893).

FRAME, J. W., *No Other God: A Response to Open Theism* (Phillipsburg: Presbyterian and Reformed, 2001).

FRETHEIM, T. E., *The Suffering of God: An Old Testament Perspective* (Philadelphia: Fortress, 1984).

FULLER, R., 'The Rabbis and the Claims of Openness Advocates', in Piper et al. (eds.), *Beyond the Bounds: Open Theism and the Undermining of Biblical Christianity* (Wheaton: Crossway, 2003), pp. 23–41.

GROGAN, G. W., *Praise, Prayer and Prophecy: A Theology of the Book of Psalms* (Fearn: Christian Focus, 2001).

HARNACK, A. von, *History of Dogma*, 7 vols. (1894–9), tr. N. Buchanan (Whitefish: Kessinger, 2008).

HASKER, W., 'A Philosophical Perspective', in Pinnock et al., *The Openness of God: A Biblical Challenge to the Traditional Understanding of God* (Downers Grove: InterVarsity Press, 1994), pp. 126–154.

HATCH, E., *The Influence of Greek Ideas and Usages on the Christian Church*, Hibbert Lectures 1988 (London: Williams and Norgate, 1991).

HODGE, A. A., *The Confession of Faith: A Handbook on Christian Doctrine Expounding the Westminster Confession* (Edinburgh: Banner of Truth, 1958).

HODGSON, L., *The Doctrine of the Trinity*, Croall Lectures 1942–3 (New York: Charles Scribner and Sons, 1944).

—, *The Doctrine of the Atonement*, Hale Lectures 1950 (London: Nisbet, 1951).

HORTON, M. S., 'Hellenistic or Hebrew? Open Theism and Reformed Theological Method', in Piper et al. (eds.), *Beyond the Bounds: Open Theism and the Undermining of Biblical Christianity* (Wheaton: Crossway, 2003), pp. 201–235.

LEWIS, H. D., *Philosophy of Religion* (London: English Universities Press, 1965).

MCFAGUE, S., *Models of God: Theology for an Ecological, Nuclear Age* (Philadelphia: Fortress, 1987).

MACLEOD, D., *Behold your God* (Fearn: Christian Focus, 1990).

MAYS, J. L., *The Lord Reigns: A Theological Handbook of the Psalms* (Louisville: Westminster John Knox, 1994).

Methodist Hymn Book (London: Methodist Conference, 1933).

MOBERLY, R. W., *The Old Testament of the Old Testament: Patriarchal Narratives and Moses Yahwism*, Overtures to Biblical Theology (Minneapolis: Fortress, 1992).

MOLTMANN, J., *The Crucified God: The Cross of Christ as the Foundation and Criticism of Christian Theology*, tr. J. Bowden (London: SCM, 1974).

—, *The Trinity and the Kingdom of God*, tr. M. Kohl (London: SCM, 1981).

MOZLEY, J. K., *The Impassibility of God* (Cambridge: Cambridge University Press, 1926).

PACKER, J. I., *Knowing God*, 2nd ed. (London: Hodder and Stoughton, 1993).

PINNOCK, C. H., *Most Moved Mover: A Theology of God's Openness* (Carlisle: Paternoster, 2001).

—, 'Systematic Theology', in Pinnock et al., *The Openness of God: A Biblical Challenge to the Traditional Understanding of God* (Downers Grove: InterVarsity Press, 1994), pp. 101–125.

—, (ed.), *The Grace of God and the Will of Man* (Minneapolis: Bethany House, 1995).

PINNOCK, C. H., R. RICE, J. SANDERS, W. HASKER and D. BASINGER, *The Openness of God: A Biblical Challenge to the Traditional Understanding of God* (Downers Grove: InterVarsity Press, 1994).

PIPER, J., J. TAYLOR and P. K. HELSKETH (eds.), *Beyond the Bounds: Open Theism and the Undermining of Biblical Christianity* (Wheaton: Crossway, 2003).

RICE, R., 'Biblical Support for a New Perspective', in Pinnock et al., *The Openness of God: A Biblical Challenge to the Traditional Understanding of God* (Downers Grove: InterVarsity Press, 1994), pp. 11–58.

SAILHAMER, J. H., 'Genesis', in F. E. Gaebelein (ed.), *Expositor's Bible Commentary*, vol. 2 (Grand Rapids: Zondervan, 1990), pp. 1–283.

SANDERS, J., *God who Risks: A Theology of Providence* (Downers Grove: InterVarsity Press, 1998).

—, 'Historical Considerations', in Pinnock et al., *The Openness of God: A Biblical Challenge to the Traditional Understanding of God* (Downers Grove: InterVarsity Press, 1994), pp. 59–100.

—, in S. E. Porter and A. R. Cross (eds.), *Semper Reformandum: Essays in Honour of Clark H. Pinnock* (Carlisle: Paternoster, 2003).

SHAW, R., *An Exposition of the Westminster Confession of Faith* (Fearn: Christian Focus, 1973).

TALBOT, M. R., 'True Freedom: The Liberty that Scripture Portrays as Worth Having', in Piper et al., *Beyond the Bounds: Open Theism and the Undermining of Biblical Christianity* (Wheaton: Crossway, 2003), pp. 77–109.

TEMPLE, W., *Christus Veritas: An Essay* (London: Macmillan, 1924).

VAN TIL, C., *An Introduction to Systematic Theology* (Nutley: Presbyterian and Reformed, 1976).

WARE, B. A., *God's Lesser Glory: A Critique of Open Theism* (Leicester: Apollos, 2000).

—, 'An Evangelical Reformulation of the Doctrine of the Immutability of God', *Journal of the Evangelical Theological Society* 29 (1986), pp. 431–446.

WEINANDY, T. G., *Does God Suffer?* (Edinburgh: T. & T. Clark, 2000).

WRIGHT, N., *The Radical Evangelical: Seeking a Place to Stand* (London: SPCK, 1996).

Chapter 3

ANSELM of Canterbury, *Cur Deus Homo?* (London: David Nutt, 1903).

AUGUSTINE, 'Against Faustus', in *Nicene and Post-Nicene Fathers*, vol. 14 (Grand Rapids: Eerdmans, 1974).

AULÈN, G., *Christus Victor: An Historical Study of the Three Main Types of the Idea of the Atonement*, tr. A. G. Hebert (London: Macmillan, 1931).

BARRETT, W., 'Heidegger and Modern Existentialism', in B. Magee (ed.), *Men of Ideas: Some Creators of Contemporary Philosophy* (London: BBC, 1978), pp. 92–95.

BAXTER, C., 'The Cursed Beloved: A Reconsideration of Penal Substitution', in J. Goldingay (ed.), *Atonement Today: A Symposium at St John's College, Nottingham* (London: SPCK, 1995), pp. 54–72.

BEBBINGTON, D. W., *Evangelicalism in Modern Britain: A History from the 1730s to the 1980s* (London: Unwin Hyman, 1989).

BECKWITH, R. T. and M. J. SELMAN (eds.), *Sacrifice in the Bible* (Exeter, Paternoster, 1995).

BLOCHER, H., '*Agnus Victor*: The Atonement as Victory and Vicarious Punishment', in J. G. Stackhouse (ed.), *What Does It Mean To Be Saved? Broadening Evangelical Horizons of Salvation* (Grand Rapids: Baker Academic, 2002), pp. 67–91.

BOYD, G. A., *God at War: The Bible and Spiritual Conflict* (Downers Grove: InterVarsity Press, 1997).

CALVIN, J., *Institutes of the Christian Religion*, tr. F. L. Battles, 2 vols. (Philadelphia: Westminster, 1960).

CARSON, D. A., *Becoming Conversant with the Emerging Church* (Grand Rapids: Zondervan, 2005).

CHALKE, S. and A. MANN, *The Lost Message of Jesus* (Grand Rapids: Zondervan, 2003).

CHRYSOSTOM, J., *Homilies on Second Corinthians*, in *Nicene and Post-Nicene Fathers*, sect. I, vol. 12 (Grand Rapids: Eerdmans, 1969).

CLARK, D., 'Why Did Christ Have to Die?', *New England Reformed Journal* 1 (1996), pp. 35–36.

DENNEY, J., *The Death of Christ: Its Place and Interpretation in the New Testament*, ed. R. V. G. Tasker (Eugene: Wipf and Stock, 2008).

DODD, C. H., *The Epistle of Paul to the Romans* (London: Hodder and Stoughton, 1932).

GOLDINGAY, J., *God's Prophet, God's Servant: A Study of Jeremiah and Isaiah 40 – 55*, rev. ed. (Toronto: Clements, 2002).

—, 'Your Iniquities Have Made Separation between You and Your God', in J. Goldingay (ed.), *Atonement Today: A Symposium at St John's College, Nottingham* (London: SPCK, 1995), pp. 39–53.

GREEN, J. B. and M. D. BAKER, *Recovering the Scandal of the Cross* (Downers Grove: InterVarsity Press, 2000).

GUILLEBAUD, H. E., *Why the Cross?* (London: IVF, 1946).

GUNTON, C. E., *The Actuality of Atonement: A Study of Metaphor, Rationality and the Christian Tradition* (Edinburgh: T. & T. Clark, 1988).

HENGEL, M., *The Atonement: The Origins of the Doctrine in the New Testament*, tr. J. Bowden (London: SCM, 1981).

HODGSON, L., *The Doctrine of the Trinity*, Croall Lectures 1942–3 (New York: Charles Scribner and Sons, 1944).

—, *The Doctrine of the Atonement*, Hale Lectures 1950 (London: Nisbet, 1951).

JEFFERY, S., M. OVEY and A. SACH, *Pierced for our Transgressions: Rediscovering the Glory of Penal Substitution* (Nottingham: Inter-Varsity Press, 2007).

LETHAM, R., *The Work of Christ* (Downers Grove: InterVarsity Press; Leicester: Inter-Varsity Press, 1993).

LEWIS, C. S., 'The Humanitarian Theory of Punishment', in P. E. Hughes (ed.), *Churchmen Speak* (Marcham Manor, 1966).

LUCAS, E. C., 'Sacrifice in the Prophets', in R. T. Beckwith and M. J. Selman (eds.), *Sacrifice in the Bible* (Carlisle: Paternoster, 1995), pp. 59–74.

LUTHER, M., *St Paul's Epistle to the Galatians* (London: James Clarke, 1953).

McLAREN, B. D., *The Story We Find Ourselves In: Further Adventures of a New Kind of Christian* (San Francisco: Wiley, 2003).

MacLAREN, D., *Mission Implausible* (Carlisle: Paternoster, 2004).

MANN, A., *Atonement for a 'Sinless' Society: Engaging with an Emerging Culture* (Milton Keynes: Paternoster, 2005).

Methodist Hymn Book (London: Methodist Conference, 1933).

MILGROM, J., 'Atonement in the OT', *Interpreter's Dictionary of the Bible*, supp. vol. 3A (Nashville: Abingdon, 1976).

MOLTMANN, J. (ed.), *How I Have Changed: Reflections on Thirty Years of Theology* (London: SCM, 1997).

MORRIS, L., *The Apostolic Preaching of the Cross* (London: Tyndale, 1953).

—, *The Cross in the New Testament* (Exeter: Paternoster, 1965).

—, *The Atonement: Its Meaning and Significance* (Leicester: Inter-Varsity Press, 1983).

MOZLEY, J. K., *The Doctrine of the Atonement* (London: Duckworth, 1937).

OVEY, M., 'The Son Incarnate in a Hostile World', in D. Peterson (ed.), *The Word Became Flesh: Evangelicals and the Incarnation. Papers from the Sixth Oak Hill College Annual School of Theology* (Carlisle: Paternoster, 2003).

PETERSON D., 'Atonement in the Old Testament', in D. Peterson (ed.), *Where Wrath and Mercy Meet: Proclaiming the Atonement Today* (Carlisle: Paternoster, 2001), pp. 1–25.

—, 'Atonement in the New Testament', in D. Peterson (ed.), *Where Wrath and Mercy Meet: Proclaiming the Atonement Today* (Carlisle: Paternoster, 2001), pp. 26–67.

PINNOCK, C. and D. BROWN, *Theological Crossfire: An Evangelical/Liberal Dialogue* (Grand Rapids: Zondervan, 1990).

SHAW, I. J. and B. H. EDWARDS, *The Divine Substitute: The Atonement in the Bible and History* (Leominister: Day One, 2006).

SKINNER, J., *Prophecy and Religion* (London: Cambridge University Press, 1936).

SMAIL, T., *Once and for All: A Confession of the Cross* (London: Darton, Longman and Todd, 1998).

—, 'Can One Man Die for the People?', in J. Goldingay (ed.), *Atonement Today: A Symposium at St John's College, Nottingham* (London: SPCK, 1995), pp. 73–92.

SPURGEON, C. H., *All of Grace* (Fort Worth: R. D. McCormack, 2001).

STOTT, J. R. W., *The Cross of Christ* (Leicester: Inter-Varsity Press, 1986).

TAYLOR, V., *Jesus and His Sacrifice: A Study of the Passion Sayings in the Gospels* (London, Macmillan, 1929).

—, *The Atonement in New Testament Teaching*, 2nd ed. (London: Epworth, 1946).

—, *Forgiveness and Reconciliation*, 2nd ed. (London, Macmillan, 1946).

THISELTON, A. C., *The Two Horizons: New Testament Hermeneutics and Philosophical Description* (Grand Rapids: Eerdmans; Exeter: Paternoster, 1980).

—, *New Horizons in Hermeneutics: The Theory and Practice of Transforming Biblical Reading* (Grand Rapids: Zondervan; Carlisle: Paternoster, 1992).

TIDBALL, D., *The Message of the Cross: Wisdom Unsearchable, Love Inexhaustible* (Leicester: Inter-Varsity Press, 2001).

TILLICH, P., *Systematic Theology*, 3 vols. (Chicago: University of Chicago Press, 1951–63).

TRAVIS, S. H., 'Christ as Bearer of Divine Judgement in Paul's Thought about the Atonement', in J. Goldingay (ed.), *Atonement Today: A Symposium at St John's College, Nottingham* (London: SPCK, 1995), pp. 21–38.

VANHOOZER, K. J., *Biblical Narrative in the Philosophy of Paul Ricoeur: A Study in Hermeneutics and Theology* (Cambridge, Cambridge University Press, 1990).

WELLS, P., 'A Free Lunch at the End of the Universe?', *Themelios* 29:1 (Autumn, 2003), pp. 38–51.

WENHAM, G. J., *The Book of Leviticus*, NICOT (Grand Rapids: Eerdmans, 1979).

WESLEY, J., *Explanatory Notes upon the New Testament* (London: Epworth, 1976).

WESTERHOLM, S., *Perspectives Old and New on Paul: The 'Lutheran' Paul and his Critics* (Grand Rapids: Eerdmans, 2004).

WILLIAMS, S., *Revelation and Reconciliation: A Window on Modernity* (Cambridge: Cambridge University Press, 1995).

Chapter 4

BLOCHER, H., 'Justification of the Ungodly (*Sola Fide*): Theological Reflections', in D. A. Carson, P. T. O'Brien and M. A. Seifrid, *Justification and Variegated Nomism: Vol. 2. The Paradoxes of Paul* (Grand Rapids: Baker Academic, 2004), pp. 465–500.

BLOMBERG, C., 'Critical Issues in New Testament Studies for Evangelicals Today', in P. E. Satterthwaite and D. F. Wright (eds.), *A Pathway into the Holy Scripture* (Grand Rapids: Eerdmans, 1994), pp. 51–79.

BULTMANN, R., *Theology of the New Testament: Historical Developments and Contemporary Challenges*, tr. K. Grobel, vol. 1 (New York: Charles Scribner and Sons, 1951).

BURKE, T. J., *Adopted into God's Family: Exploring a Pauline Metaphor* (Leicester: Apollos, 2006).

CARSON, D. A., P. T. O'BRIEN and M. A. SEIFRID, *Justification and Variegated Nomism, Vol. 1: The Complexities of Second Temple Judaism; Vol. 2: The Paradoxes of Paul* (Grand Rapids: Baker Academic, 2001, 2004).

CHESTER, S., 'When the Old Was New: Reformation Perspectives on Galatians 2:16', *Expository Times*, vol. 119, no. 7, pp. 320–329.

CHESTER, T., 'Justification, Ecclesiology and the New Perspective', *Themelios* 30:2 (Winter 2005), pp. 5–20.

COOK, P. E. G. and G. HARRISON (eds.), *Christian Hymns* (Bridgend: Evangelical Movement of Wales, 1977).

COTTRET, B., *Calvin: A Biography* (Edinburgh: T. & T. Clark, 2000).

DAS, A. A., *Paul, the Law and the Covenant* (Peabody: Hendrickson, 2001).

DENNIS, J. A., *Jesus' Death and the Gathering of True Israel: The Johannine Appropriation of Restoration Theology in the Light of John 11:47–52* (Tübingen: Mohr Siebeck, 2006).

DUNN, J. D. G., *Jesus, Paul and the Law: Studies in Mark and Galatians* (London: SPCK, 1990).

—, *Romans 1 – 8* (Milton Keynes: Word, 1991).

—, *The Epistle to the Galatians* (Peabody: Hendrickson Publishers, 1993).

—, *The Theology of Paul the Apostle* (Grand Rapids: Eerdmans, 1998).

GATHERCOLE, S. J., *Where Is Boasting? Early Jewish Soteriology and Paul's Response in Romans 1 – 5* (Grand Rapids: Eerdmans, 2002).

—, 'The Doctrine of Justification in Paul and Beyond: Some Proposals', in B. L. McCormack (ed.), *Justification in Perspective: Historical Developments and Contemporary Challenges* (Grand Rapids: Baker, 2006), pp. 219–241.

HARRISON, E. F., 'Romans', in F. E. Gaebelein (ed.), *The Expositor's Bible Commentary* (Grand Rapids: Zondervan, 1976), pp. 1–171.

JOHNSON, L. T., 'A Historiographical Response to Wright's Jesus', in C. C. Newman (ed.), *Jesus and the Restoration of Israel: A Critical Assessment of N. T. Wright's Jesus and the Victory of God* (Carlisle: Paternoster, 1999).

KIM, S., *The Origin of Paul's Gospel* (Tübingen: J. C. B. Mohr, 1981).

—, *Paul and the New Perspective: Second Thoughts on the Origin of Paul's Gospel* (Grand Rapids: Eerdmans, 2002).

KRUSE, C. G., *Paul, the Law and Justification* (Leicester: Apollos, 1996).

KÜMMEL, W. G., *Römer 7 und das Bild des Menschen in Neuen Testament* (Munich: C. Kaiser, 1974).

LEVINSOHN, S. H., *Discourse Features of NT Greek: A Coursebook on the Information Structure of New Testament Greek*, 2nd ed. (Dallas: SIL International, 2000).

Methodist Hymn Book (London: Methodist Conference, 1933).

MOO, D., *The Epistle to the Romans*, NICNT (Grand Rapids: Eerdmans, 1996).

MORRIS, L., *The Atonement: Its Meaning and Significance* (Leicester: Inter-Varsity Press, 1983).

MUNCK, J., *Paul and the Salvation of Mankind* (Atlanta: John Knox, 1959).

MURRAY, G., *Five Stages of Greek Religion* (London: Watts, 1935).

NEUSNER, J., *Rabbinic Judaism: Structure and System* (Minneapolis: Fortress, 1995).

PACKER, J. I., *Knowing God*, 2nd ed. (London: Hodder and Stoughton, 1993).

PIPER, J., *The Future of Justification: A Response to N. T. Wright* (Nottingham: Inter-Varsity Press, 2008).

RITSCHL, A., *The Christian Doctrine of Justification and Reconciliation*, H. R. Mackintosh and A. B. Macaulay (eds.) (Edinburgh: T. & T. Clark, 1900).

SANDERS, E. P., *Paul and Palestinian Judaism: A Comparison of Patterns of Religion* (London: SCM, 1977).

—, *Paul, the Law, and the Jewish People* (Philadelphia: Fortress, 1983).

SCHREINER, T. R., *The Law and its Fulfilment: A Pauline Theology of Law* (Grand Rapids: Baker, 1993).

SEIFRID, M. A., *Christ our Righteousness: Paul's Theology of Justification* (Leicester: Apollos, 2000).

—, 'Paul's Use of Righteousness Language against its Hellenistic Background', in Carson, O'Brien and Seifrid, *Justification and Variegated Nomism*, vol. 2, pp. 39–74.

—, 'Righteousness Language in the Old Testament and Early Judaism', in Carson, O'Brien and Seifrid, *Justification and Variegated Nomism*, vol. 1, pp. 415–442.

SPRINKLE, P. M., 'The Old Perspective on the New Perspective: A Review of some "Pre-Sanders" Thinkers', *Themelios* 30:2 (Winter 2005), pp. 21–31.

STENDAHL, K., 'The Apostle Paul and the Introspective Conscience of the West', reprinted in K. Stendahl, *Paul among Jews and Gentiles and Other Essays* (Philadelphia: Fortress, 1976).

TAYLOR, S. S., 'Faith, Faithfulness', in T. D. Alexander and B. S. Rosner (eds.), *New Dictionary of Biblical Theology* (Leicester: Inter-Varsity Press, 2000), pp. 487–493.

THIELMAN, F., *Paul and the Law: A Contextual Approach* (Downers Grove: InterVarsity Press, 1994).

WEBER, F., *Jüdische Theologie auf Grund des Talmud und verwandter Schriften* (Leipzig: Dörffling und Franke, 1897).

WELLS, D. F. (ed.), *By Faith Alone: Answering the Challenge to the Doctrine of Justification* (Grand Rapids: Crossway, 2007).

WESTERHOLM, S., *Israel's Law and the Church's Faith: Paul and his Recent Interpreters* (Grand Rapids: Eerdmans, 1988).

—, *Perspectives Old and New on Paul: The 'Lutheran' Paul and his Critics* (Grand Rapids: Eerdmans, 2004).

WRIGHT, D. F., 'Justification in Augustine', in B. L. McCormick (ed.), *Justification in Perspective: Historical Developments and Contemporary Challenges* (Grand Rapids: Baker Academic, 2006), pp. 55–72.

WRIGHT, N. T., *The Climax of the Covenant: Christ and the Law in Pauline Theology* (Edinburgh: T. & T. Clark, 1991).

—, *Jesus and the Victory of God*, Christian Origins and the Question of God, vol. 2 (Minneapolis: Fortress, 1996).

—, *What Saint Paul Really Said: Was Paul of Tarsus the Real Founder of Christianity?* (Grand Rapids: Eerdmans, 1997).

—, *Paul for Everyone: Galatians and Thessalonians* (London, SPCK, 2002).

—, *Paul: In Fresh Perspective* (Minneapolis: Fortress, 2005).

—, *Justification: God's Plan and Paul's Vision* (London: SPCK, 2009).

—, 'The Paul of History and the Apostle of Faith', *Tyndale Bulletin* 29 (1978), pp. 61–78.

YARBROUGH, R. W., 'Paul and Salvation History', in D. A. Carson, P. T. O'Brien and M. A. Seifrid, *Justification and Variegated Nomism: Vol. 2. The Paradoxes of Paul* (Grand Rapids: Baker Academic, 2004), pp. 297–342.

Chapter 5

ABRAHAM, W. J., *The Divine Inspiration of Holy Scripture* (Oxford: Oxford University Press, 1981).

BAHNSEN, G. L., *Van Til's Apologetic: Readings and Analysis* (Phillipsburg: Presbyterian and Reformed, 1998).

BAVINCK, H., *Reformed Dogmatics*, vol. 1, *Prolegomena* (Grand Rapids: Baker Academic, 2003).

BLUM, E. A., '2 Peter', in F. E. Gaebelein (ed.), *Expositor's Bible Commentary*, vol. 12 (Grand Rapids: Zondervan, 1981), pp. 257–289.

BROGAN, J. J., 'Can I Have Your Autograph? Uses and Abuses in Formulating an Evangelical Doctrine of Scripture', in V. Bacote, L. C. Miguelez and D. L. Okholm (eds.), *Evangelicals and Scripture* (Downers Grove: InterVarsity Press, 2004), pp. 93–111.

CLARK, G., *Faith and Saving Faith* (Jefferson: Trinity Foundation, 1983).

COLLINS, C. J., *The God of Miracles: An Exegetical Examination of God's Action in the World* (Leicester: Inter-Varsity Press, 2001).

CONN, H. M. (ed.), *Inerrancy and Hermeneutic: A Tradition, a Challenge, a Debate* (Grand Rapids: Baker, 1988).

—, 'A Historical Prologue: Inerrancy, Hermeneutic, and Westminster', in H. M. Conn (ed.), *Inerrancy and Hermeneutic: A Tradition, a Challenge, a Debate* (Grand Rapids: Baker, 1988), pp. 15–34.

DAVIS, D. C., 'Inerrancy and Westminister Calvinism', in H. M. Conn (ed.), *Inerrancy and Hermeneutic: A Tradition, a Challenge, a Debate* (Grand Rapids: Baker, 1988), pp. 35–46.

ELLIS, E. E., *Prophecy and Hermeneutics in Early Christianity: New Testament Essays* (Tübingen: Mohr, 1978).

FERGUSON, S., 'How Does the Bible Look at Itself?', in H. M. Conn (ed.) *Inerrancy and Hermeneutic: A Tradition, a Challenge, a Debate* (Grand Rapids: Baker, 1988), pp. 64–76.

GEISLER, N. L. and W. E. NIX, *General Introduction to the Bible*, rev. ed. (Chicago: Moody, 1986), pp. 181–185.

JIPP, J. W., 'The Quest for the Historical Machen', *Themelios* 30:3 (Summer 2005), pp. 59–68.

KOESTLER, A., *The Act of Creation* (London: Picador, 1977).

—, *The Sleepwalkers: A History of Man's Changing Vision of the Universe* (London: Penguin, 1986).

LAW, R., *The Tests of Life: A Study of the First Epistle of St John*, Kerr Lectures 1909 (Edinburgh: T. & T. Clark, 1909).

LEWIS, C. S., *Reflections on the Psalms* (London: Fontana, 1961).

LINCOLN, A. J., *Ephesians*, Word Biblical Commentary (Dallas: Word, 1990).

MACHEN, J. G., *Christianity and Liberalism* (Grand Rapids: Eerdmans, 1923).

McGOWAN, A. T. B., *The Divine Spiration of Scripture: Challenging Evangelical Perspectives* (Nottingham: Inter-Varsity Press, 2007).

POYTHRESS, V. S., 'What Does God Say through Human Authors?', in H. M. Conn (ed.), *Inerrancy and Hermeneutic: A Tradition, a Challenge, a Debate* (Grand Rapids: Baker, 1988), pp. 81–99.

ROGERS, J. B. and D. K. McKIM, *The Authority and Interpretation of the Bible: An Historical Approach* (New York: Harper and Row, 1979).

ROOKMAAKER, H., *Modern Art and the Death of a Culture* (Leicester: Inter-Varsity Press, 1970).

ROWLAND, C. and M. CORNER, *Liberating Exegesis: The Challenge of Liberation Theology to Biblical Studies*, Biblical Foundations in Theology (London: SPCK, 1990).

SCHULTZ, R. L., 'How Many Isaiahs Were There and What Does It Matter?', in V. Bacote, L. C. Miguelez and D. L. Okholm (eds.), *Evangelicals and Scripture* (Downers Grove, InterVarsity Press, 2004), pp. 154–155.

SCOTT, D., *The Common Sense of Michael Polanyi* (Grand Rapids: Eerdmans, 1995).

TORRANCE, T. F., *The Christian Frame of Mind* (Edinburgh: Handsel, 2002).

—, 'Preface' to D. Scott, *The Common Sense of Michael Polanyi* (Grand Rapids: Eerdmans, 1995).

VANHOOZER, K. J., *The Drama of Doctrine: A Canonical-Linguistic Approach to Christian Theology* (Louisville: Westminster John Knox, 2005).

WARD, T., *Words of Life: Scripture as the Living and Active Word of God* (Nottingham: Inter-Varsity Press, 2009).

WENHAM, G., 'Pondering the Past: The Search for a New Paradigm', in D. W. Baker and B. T. Arnold, *The Face of Old Testament Studies: A Survey of Contemporary Approaches* (Grand Rapids: Baker, 2004), pp. 116–144.

WILLIAMSON, H. G. M., *The Book Called Isaiah: Deutero-Isaiah's Role in Composition and Redaction* (Oxford: Oxford University Press, 1994).

WRIGHT, N. T., *Paul: In Fresh Perspective* (Minneapolis: Fortress, 2005).

Chapter 6

ALEXANDER, T. D. and B. ROSNER (eds.), *New Dictionary of Biblical Theology* (Leicester: Inter-Varsity Press, 2000).

BACOTE, V., L. C. MIGUELEZ and D. L. OKHOLM (eds.), *Evangelicals and Scripture: Tradition, Authority and Hermeneutics* (Downers Grove: InterVarsity Press, 2004).

BAKER, D. L., *Two Testaments, One Bible: The Theological Relationship between the Old and New Testaments*, 3rd ed. (Nottingham: Inter-Varsity Press, 2010).

BARR, J., *The Semantics of Biblical Language* (Oxford: Oxford University Press, 1961).

BAVINCK, H., *Reformed Dogmatics*, 4 vols. (Grand Rapids: Baker, 2003–8).

BARTSCH, H.-W. (ed.), *Kerygma and Myth: A Theological Debate* (London: SPCK, 1972).

BAUCKHAM, R., *The Climax of Prophecy: Studies in the Book of the Revelation* (Edinburgh: T. & T. Clark, 1993).

BRUCE, F. F., 'Jesus and Paul', *Theological Students' Bulletin* 46 (Autumn, 1966), pp. 21–26.

BRUEGGEMANN, W., *Theology of the Old Testament: Testimony, Dispute, Advocacy* (Minneapolis: Fortress, 1997).

CARSON, D. A., *Exegetical Fallacies* (Grand Rapids: Baker, 1984).

DODD, C. H., *Apostolic Preaching and its Developments* (London: Hodder and Stoughton, 1936).

ECO, U., *A Theory of Semiotics* (Bloomington: Indiana University Press, 1976).

ELLUL, J., *Jesus and Marx: From Gospel to Ideology* (Grand Rapids: Eerdmans, 1988).

FEE, G. D. and D. STUART, *How to Read the Bible for All its Worth: A Guide to Understanding the Bible*, 3rd ed. (Grand Rapids: Zondervan, 2003).

FISHER, H. A. L., *A History of Europe*, vol. 1, *From the Earliest Times to 1713* (London: Fontana, 1960).

GOLDINGAY, J., *Models for Interpretation of Scripture* (Grand Rapids: Eerdmans, 1995).

GOLDSWORTHY, G. D., *Gospel-Centred Hermeneutics: Biblical Theological Foundations and Principles* (Nottingham: Inter-Varsity Press, 2006).

GOTTWALD, N. K. and R. A. HORSLEY (eds.), *The Bible and Liberation: Political and Social Hermeneutics* (Maryknoll: Orbis, 1993).

HARNACK, A. von, *What Is Christianity?*, ET, 5th ed. (London: Ernest Benn, 1958).

HUGHES, P. E., *Scripture and Myth: An Examination of Rudolf Bultmann's Plea for Demythologization* (London: Tyndale Press, 1956).

LEWIS, C. S., *The Weight of Glory* (Grand Rapids: Zondervan, 2001), pp. 116–140.

LIGHTFOOT, J. B., *Saint Paul's Epistle to the Philippians* (New York: Macmillan, 1900).

LUNDIN, R., A. C. THISELTON and C. WALHOUT, *The Responsibility of Hermeneutics* (Grand Rapids: Eerdmans, 1985).

LYOTARD, J. F., *Introduction: The Postmodern Condition: A Report on Knowledge* (Minneapolis: University of Minnesota Press, 1979).

MACDONALD, F., 'Do the Psalms Speak Today?', *Scottish Bulletin of Evangelical Theology* 28:2 (Autumn 2008), pp. 170–186.

MARSHALL, I. H., *Beyond the Bible: Moving from Scripture to Theology* (Grand Rapids: Baker, 2004).

OLLENBURGER, B. C. (ed.), *Old Testament Theology: Flowering and Future*, vol. 1 (Winona Lake: Eisenbrauns, 2004).

ORR, J., *Revelation and Inspiration* (London: Duckworth, 1909).

OSBORNE, G. R., *The Hermeneutical Spiral: A Comprehensive Approach to Biblical Interpretation*, 2nd ed. (Downers Grove: InterVarsity Press, 2006).

PACKER, J. I., 'Infallible Scripture and the Role of Hermeneutics', in D. A. Carson and J. D. Woodbridge (eds.), *Scripture and Truth* (Grand Rapids: Baker, 1992).

PETERSON, D. G., 'Holiness', in T. D. Alexander and B. S. Rosner (eds.), *The New Dictionary of Biblical Theology* (Leicester: Inter-Varsity Press, 2000), pp. 544–550.

SHAW, R., *An Exposition of the Westminster Confession of Faith* (Fearn: Christian Focus, 1973).

STUART, M., *Biblical Interpretation in the Anabaptist Tradition* (Kitchener: Pandora, 2000).

THISELTON, A. C., *The Hermeneutics of Doctrine* (Grand Rapids: Eerdmans, 2007).

THOMAS, R. L., *Evangelical Hermeneutics: The New Versus the Old* (Grand Rapids: Kregel, 2002).

VANHOOZER, K. J., *The Drama of Doctrine: A Canonical-Linguistic Approach to Christian Theology* (Louisville: Westminster John Knox, 2005).

—, *Is There a Meaning in this Text? The Bible, the Reader, and the Morality of Literary Knowledge*, 2nd ed. (Grand Rapids: Zondervan, 2009).

VIRKLER, H. A., *Hermeneutics: Principles and Processes of Biblical Interpretation* (Grand Rapids: Baker, 2004).

VON RAD, G., *Old Testament Theology*, vol. 1, *The Theology of Israel's Historical Traditions*, tr. D. M. G. Stalker (Edinburgh and London: Oliver and Boyd, 1962).

WARD, T., *Words of Life: Scripture as the Living and Active Word of God* (Nottingham: Inter-Varsity Press, 2009).

WELLS, W., *Improvisation: The Drama of Christian Ethics* (London: SPCK, 2004).

WILLIAMS, S., *Revelation and Reconciliation* (Cambridge: Cambridge University Press, 1995).

WRIGHT, N. T., 'How Can the Bible Be Authoritative?', *Vox Evangelica* 21 (1991), pp. 7–32.

Chapter 7

BRUNER, F. D., *The Doctrine of the Holy Spirit: The Pentecostal Experience and the New Testament Witness* (Grand Rapids: Eerdmans, 1970).

DODD, C. H., *According to the Scriptures: The Substructure of New Testament Theology* (London: Nisbet, 1957).

DODD, C. H., *The Apostolic Preaching and its Developments, Three Lectures with an Eschatology and History* (London: Harper and Row, 1964).

GROGAN, G. W., *The Christ of the Bible and of the Christian Faith* (Fearn: Christian Focus Publications, 1998).

KELLY, J. N. D., *Early Christian Doctrines*, 2nd ed. (London: Adam and Charles Black, 1960).

LEWIS, C. S., *The Weight of Glory* (Grand Rapids: Zondervan, 2001).

INDEX OF SCRIPTURE REFERENCES

INDEX OF NAMES